RAFIKI

RAFIKI

Letters to Omar

Joseph C. Shenk

To order additional copies of this book, contact:
Xlibris Corporation
1-888-795-4274
www.Xlibris.com
Orders@Xlibris.com

42291

CONTENTS

Swahili translations

Banda	hut/open-sided shed
Bati	corrugated iron metal sheet
Bepare	capitalists
Bwana	sir
Chai	tea
Chapati	round flat unleavened bread
Choo	toilet
Chuma	strong or dependable person, metal
Dawa	medicine
Dona	whole-grain maize flour
Duka	small shop
Fundi	expert
Hodi	"Hello" (said at the door to someone's home)
Jembe	hoe
Jimbo	district
Kabalia	bluebloods, landowners, overlords
Kabisa	totally
Kijiji	village
Komiti Kuu	overall committee
Kongoni	hartebeest
Kumbe	(interjection) "behold!"
Ku-nyampa	make a stinker/fart
Mandazi	doughnut
Matatu	public service van
Mjumbe	delegate/political representative
Mtemi	chief
Mwalimu	teacher
Mzee	term of respect, "elder"
Mzungu/Wazungu	white person/people
N'gombe	cow
Nyayo	footsteps
Panga	machete
Piki	motorcycle
Pori	bush/wilderness

Rafiki	friend
Roho	spirit. Also used to refer to a Renault R4
Saba-Saba	"seven-seven," Tanzanian national holiday celebrated on July 7
Safari	journey
Shamba	garden/farm
Shifta	(Amharic origin) bandit
Simbe	husked maize flour
Sukuma wiki	collard greens
Tuomba/Twaomba	"Let's pray"
Ugali	staple food of stiff maize meal porridge
Uhuru	freedom
Ujamaa	family ties/socialism
Wasi-wasi	second thoughts
Zimika	to be put out/extinguished
Hakuna nyapala, wote ni wafanyakazi	"There is no boss, all are workers."
Hakukosa kuniheshimu na kuthamini maneno yangu	"He doesn't fail to give me respect and values my words."

Preface

For nearly twenty years (1963-1981), Joe Shenk and I wrote letters to each other. Those were the days before computers and their subsequent emails; thus, our letters were pounded out on typewriters-not even electric-but equipped with a bell and a sling back carriage. Or handwritten. Long letters about life: the balance between professional work and domestic chores, the confessional longing for greater faith, the candid acknowledgement of comfortable routine religiosity, and the admission of being irritated with one's colleagues.

Joe followed a calling from Christ and His Church: teaching math and science at a boys' secondary school, being principal of a theological college, then representing Mennonite ventures in East Africa. During his years at the Nairobi post Joe was absorbed in negotiating the tricky terrain between a North American Mennonite mission agency and the newly-independent Tanzania and Kenya Mennonite Churches. His letters to me withered away under psychic exhaustion.

I worked at Mennonite Central Committee, Akron, Pennsylvania, for three years. Later, one of the two years that I taught journalism at the Africa Literature Centre, Mindolo Ecumenical Centre, Kitwe, Zambia, Joe was in grad school at Temple University, Philadelphia. Finally, I taught writing and literature at Eastern Mennonite University, Harrisonburg, Virginia.

One day Joe wrote to tell me that my university had accepted him to become its new campus pastor. And so he came home and our correspondence turned to conversations. Later, he went silent.

In 1986 Joe became lead pastor at my church. From the pulpit I heard regularly fine sermons, chiefly narrative, biblical and contemporaneous. The years passed, and in January 2003, Joe with Edith returned to his beloved Tanzania Mennonite Church. One morning he went out for his routine jog near Bukiroba. Joe was struck by a lorry and died a week later in a Nairobi hospital.

These lengthy excerpts from his 238 letters to me over the years are a tribute to a friendship, which I want to make available to his children and grandchildren, and to a few friends. Great chunks have been omitted to protect the living and the guilty. Also, all references to my life have been eliminated. These letters are to reflect solely the inimitable Joseph C. Shenk, the Joe of his young second-generation missionary years: his musings on being a husband, a father of four daughters, a teacher in a theological college, a student of the African psyche, a confidant of the first African Mennonite Bishop in Tanzania. Here, too, we read of Joe's delight in motorcycle safaris and his joy of being in village Africa. Wrote all this to one good friend-I a most fortunate recipient of his confidence and grace.

I am keenly aware that the full dimensions of a person are not manifested in correspondence with only one person. Also, may no one take offense at anything Joe wrote. He did not know that one day others would read his letters to his *rafiki*. If the reader is angered, blame Joe's editor. If the reader is blessed, give thanks that once there was a good man who believed in a friendship worthy of letters.

Omar Eby
October 2006

Musoma Alliance Secondary School

Musoma

January 1963-August 1965

1963

January 23, 1963

Boy, what a place! (Musoma Alliance Secondary School, a boys' boarding school, Forms I to IV, equivalent to American high school grades 9th to 12th.)

Edie's staying out at Kisaka (a rural village), with Daddy, Mother, and 14-year-old brother Danny. The students came yesterday and today. I'm baching it in a house with one good insect sprayer for company. Right now there are thousands of mosquitoes outside the screen.

I couldn't stand the loneliness anymore, so I just decided to run away to Kisaka for a day. After exhausting all *piki* (motorcycle) leads, I ran across Uncle John's (Leatherman) 500 cc monster; he let me borrow it. The thing weighs around 500 pounds, twice as heavy as Daddy's old cycle. I cut the motor at the top of the Kisaka hill and coasted down to the garage where Daddy was working at the power saw. It took him a while to figure out who this *mzungu* was. Then we went down to the house and surprised dear Edie. That was one of the happiest 24-hours I've ever spent. Over too soon and had to tackle the job of getting back to Musoma.

School starts for real tomorrow. This being in charge of one of the dorms takes up tremendous gobs of time. Additionally, I'm responsible for one class, Form III, and the dining and kitchen arrangements.

It's been quite a drill so far. How to get next to these boys. It seems so much as though we staff are at one end of a rope and the boys at the other.

February 23, 1963

We are happy and glad to be here and at no time would have rather returned to the States, but there are adjustments and we write with the intention of giving a realistic picture of what it looks like to us on this side of the briny deep. The first struggling beginnings of a higher education system in any country will look shabby against American sophisticated background.

One of the rewards of this type of situation is that there is a greater degree of prestige attached to the position of teacher because here the teacher much more than in the States makes the student. In the States you have the teacher illuminating the text and little more. Here you have the text illuminating the teacher. There it is a transfer of knowledge from book to student, while here, it is much more a transfer of knowledge from teacher's mind to student's mind. This also carries with it a tremendous responsibility as the good student may do very poorly if guided by a poor teacher. It is because here your main resource is the teacher, while at home the teacher almost becomes the operator of an assembly line.

We were over at Bukiroba (headquarters for the Tanganyika Mennonite Church) for the dedication of the Mennonite Theological College. The plant isn't awfully big but what is there is truly impressive. There are two new houses for the faculty. Jacobs' (the principal) house is a lovely little mansion. It could sit comfortably beside any president's house in the states. The rest of the plant is distinguished by a large ultra modern chapel that acts as focal point. Don (Jacobs) calls it "the church tangible." It is impressive and exquisitely beautiful in its simplicity. It has a huge cross over the entrance and another huge cross (both of concrete) over the pulpit. There were people from every corner of the church. All but four of the missionaries were present. President Nyerere was invited, but unable to attend. He sent a special representative. There were very many speeches by all kinds of dignitaries. All the students from the girls' school were there, each in a differently colored uniform. The middle school from back on the hill sent its Standard Five band to play before and after the service. They really added bang and rhythm to the festivities that followed the service where *chai* followed freely and everyone munched on store-bought buns, which had been given a liberal flowing of thoroughly sticky icing. The teachers were decked out in the appropriate robe to suit their training. Poor Uncle John just wore a plain black vest under his coat. Phoebe had a coal black robe with a black hat and a black tassel. Aunt Dorothy and Uncle George wore black gowns with crimson capes, black hats with yellow tassels, and Don was decked out in black with royal purple for his cape. Uncle George looked like Martin Luther as he flowed through the crowds giving benevolent nods to everyone. The purpose for all the academic regalia was to give concrete evidence to the fact that at least some of the faculty were well-trained people. Part of "the church tangible" again.

The other day I went to Musoma and ordered four pairs of shorts. It is amazing how cool these things are. From now on it's shorts in the classroom!

March 13, 1963

There's really something interesting about a student who can race through the hardest geometry theorem and see through the theories of physics and yet goes all to pieces when he, for the first time, sharpens his pencil with a mechanical sharpener. Or the Form IV chap who exclaims excitedly as he looks into a cheap four-inch telescope that the pictures are indeed true, that there are mountains on the moon, and then wonders if the moon would look the same from a telescope in London. Then there's the class that just couldn't believe it when I told them that I paid back the money borrowed from my own grandmother and paid six percent interest. They are fun, lots of fun, and especially so since it is so very easy to really shock them.

The other day Anglican Bishop Stanway, largely responsible for the start of this school, spent a day with us. We'd planned for him for over a month. Every effort bent to give him the best possible impression of our school. He was to arrive on a Wednesday, so Monday and Tuesday were spent in feverish last minute attempts to get the school worked up to a level of immaculate perfection. Several boys were put to whitewashing the stones which line the drives and walkways. Somehow someone gave them a sack of cleansers, similar to Bon-Ami. They had an awful time getting the stuff white enough. When finished and the error weighed out it was found that our stones contained over seven pounds of cleanser! Unfortunately, a torrential rain fell at night the Bishop was here. The next day the stones were kitchen clean bare. One wonders if the Bishop noticed.

March 25, 1963

This past Sunday it was my turn to take my dorm to town to church. I walked in and back with my fellows and found it a very rewarding experience. As we get to know the boys personally we find that we are becoming much more attached to this place. You find that if you meet the fellows in the right way that they are friendly and responsive, practically all the time. I have recently taken to riding a bike to town when we need things and find this also a most rewarding experience. The other day I nearly got fined 50 shillings for riding my bike in the market place. Fortunately, the man who apprehended me saw my penitence and innocence and forgave me. We have just about come to the conclusion that the transportation problem for us is to be solved by getting a bicycle. It takes only ten more minutes to get to Musoma by bike than it does by motorcycle or car.

I've been doing some thinking about starting in new places. We started in about seven or eight new things since we've been married. It seems somehow that each start has its really low spots at first but after a time the happy and rewarding things eclipse the difficulties. At first you have the sense of your life being wasted and you may be frustrated at how little with which you are involved. Surprisingly, within a matter of days you will be involved with precious little other than your school. You suddenly realize how much you were dependent on contacts outside of school for your social life. Your going and coming suddenly stops and the landscape simply doesn't change anymore. But after you've been here awhile and become adjusted to it then you wonder what it was that you didn't like at first. Now I've just been sharing how I felt about living out here. At first I felt that certainly this is but a stepping stone to something new in the States. But now I have begun to love it and feel comfortable and at home.

April 25, 1963

Several Saturdays ago President Nyerere went by. We had been notified weeks in advance of his motorcade passing our campus. The headmaster had a huge sign made saying WELCOME. Our boys were to stand ten paces apart on both sides of the road. This made for a very long string of flag-waving boys in khaki shorts, white shirts, and blue shoulder tabs. We waited a very long time in the hot sun. The road was dry and dusty, as it hadn't rained for a week. Finally, the herald drove past with someone advertising through a megaphone that the father of the nation was on the road and would soon be here. We waited longer before he came around the bend in the road in a passenger car with a hard top, preceded by a police van. There was quite a caravan—46 cars, trucks, and buses. A little old motorcycle carrying two men brought up the rear. You can imagine what dust must have been stirred by a train of 40 some closely-spaced vehicles. The people in the buses and trucks at the back end of the line were brown with caked dust. Even their hair was brown. After the dust subsided one student excitedly asked me if it is just like that in New York. A good number of the students didn't even recognize their president.

Last Saturday we went to Musoma to the wedding of Perusi Muganda. She married a Makerere University student. She wore a white gown with a long train carried by two little girls in white and one bigger girl also in white. The Musoma Mennonite church was decorated with red flowers. Every windowsill contained a soft drink bottle filled with red blooms. The bride herself carried roses. The church was packed and there was special singing by a group from our school (The next night quite a number of boys talked about dreaming of weddings!) Pastor Ezekiel, the bride's father, preached a powerful sermon on marital fidelity and purity. It was very frank and clear cut. There were two bands to render music afterwards, one from our school and a Catholic outfit resplendent in high hats and plumes. Afterwards, everyone who wanted to came and gave the bride a gift. Some were symbolic: a broom, a dish, a hoe, a bed, a cooking pot. Speeches all around. Then the wedding party left in one car, one bus, and one lorry for the groom's home out in Zanaki land for further celebrations.

June 3, 1963

About two weeks ago Edie and I made a motorcycle trip to Bukiroba, leaving the school around eight, with Joyce already in bed. Since the road was being repaired because of the lake inundation, a detour had been hacked out of the fields. It had rained heavily and Mark's (Brubaker) *piki* light didn't shine straight ahead, so we had quite a time finding our way through the mud holes. Finally, we got stuck, so Edie got off and walked ahead while I tried to drive alone. Then I got hung up with front and back wheels in the mud. After a considerable amount of grunting and sliding around we got out and were on our way. We had coffee at Jacobs,and talked until their generator quit. The *piki* lights wouldn't go on at all, so Don got out his *piki* and we covered Mark's with a tarp. We said our belated good-byes and took off. It began to drizzle, and the *piki* wasn't driving well, so at the bottom of the first hill I stopped and checked the tires, only to find that the back tire was nearly flat. So I turned the cycle around and put Edie on the seat and showed her how to accelerate and brake and sent her up the hill while I ran behind. At Jacobs we pumped the tire and left again. This time, passing the Morembe School lane a wild cat ran out in front of us and I clipped it. When we got to the detour we didn't take it and managed to get through the water without stalling. We got home by 11:30 p.m. and Joyce never knew we were gone. How's that for a date?

October 1, 1963

Maynard (Kurtz) and I have decided to pool our resources and purchase a motor scooter that our wives can drive to town. We've decided to get a new one and share the expenses.

A new bird guidebook to East African birds just came off the press. It has plates of something like 400 birds, 180 in color. It's set up like the Peterson guides in the States. I'm excited about it and have already invested Shs 46/= to purchase it.

I seldom cry on the outside, but I did cry inside, reading your descriptions of autumn in the States right now. I was so hungry for spring this past spring that I even wrote to friends in the States and explained to them what their spring was like! Maybe next year we will be able to enjoy a full year of North American seasons again. We could be home around Christmas 1964.

The government doesn't seem nearly so anxious to swallow us as what it had appeared to be, some time back. So our secondary school fulfills Bukiroba's function. Bukiroba sort of looks to me like a big pile of parasites living off the religion from North America (I never said that before, not even to myself. Please keep it most strictly confidential. It's just that we are sold on the validity of our school here and as yet we haven't been sold on the theological scheme.)

I should say just a bit about the clubbing, jailing, and expelling that went on here (Musoma Alliance Secondary School) about two weeks ago. Jealous classmates clubbed a school prefect one night after prep. The two boys directly responsible for the deed were locked up in the police station. In the morning the charge was suspended and the boys expelled. If government puts pressure on the headmaster to re-admit them, he'll simply revive the charges and have them jailed instead. All this happened in Form III of which I am class-master! This term four boys have been expelled from school, three of them from my dormitory, two of them from my class!

November 18, 1963

Last Sunday afternoon we began our bird watching society: Don (Jacobs), Maynard (Kurtz), Mark (Brubaker) and I. Plans are for us to meet every Sunday afternoon at four at Jacobs' place for tea and then to go somewhere to see birds. We saw quite a few down at what used to be the lake garden, but we didn't keep track of the number. Next week we hope to further perfect our trade. I'm so happy that this has finally started as it does give us all quite an outlet and right now Jacobs is still here to coach us a bit.

1964

March 25, 1964

I'm happy to say that the Headmaster considers Maynard and me to be his most trusted staff members. This might not be true, and I certainly would not want him to hear that I had said it. But by what Jacobs lets drop sometimes and by what the HM himself says, we can at least be reasonably sure that we are at least in a measure appreciated. I still remember how baffled the HM was the Sunday I preached my first sermon in articulate, proper English. An Australian, and he fears our American English. He is very proud of the high record of passes, our school second in Tanzania. He attributes it to his Form IV English, which is certainly, to a measure at least, correct.

On the other hand, just in case you come out here to teach, you should know that Headmaster Shellard is a dictator. He runs the show, and if you make it a point of rubbing him, then nothing you do will click because he will boycott it at every turn. I think we Mennonite teachers owe much to our mission board which emphasizes adjustability and patience. In my narrow experience it seems that the Mennonites have gone farther than most, in being able to make something of a situation and fit into it smoothly. The HM is particularly afraid of missionaries from Australia and New Zealand, as he has notions of not being able to keep them in their place. He's particularly wary of over-enthusiastic persons and people who have a clear-cut idea of what they are going to do at the school.

June 25, 1964

The farewells for Bishop Stauffer (Mennonite) have finally ceased after close to six months of activities. The last great blow was up at Shirati this past weekend. Just to give you a bit of an idea. People started arriving Friday afternoon and evening, on three lorries and a bus. All the guests were assigned places to sleep and eat. Tents were set up all over the place. Bishop Stauffer came on Saturday morning. At around 10:00, the doings were officially opened by having the Bishops march about a mile onto the Shirati grounds, preceded by a motorcycle and a school band, flanked by spectators, and trailed by dignitaries such as myself! At the church, all order broke down as people jammed the entrances. A theological college student grabbed me and hustled me off to a secret door; thus, we got good seats. There was a short opening after which we all followed Bishop Stauffer outside for the unveiling of a corner stone for Elam (Bishop Stauffer) and then into a huge *banda* (thatch-roofed pole construction) so Stauffer could make appropriate remarks over a loud-speaker. That was Saturday morning.

Saturday afternoon consisted of one very long service, 2:00 to 5:15 in the *banda*. This was the Tanganyika Mennonite Church Youth League show. They ran it well, with numerous speeches, special singing, gift giving, and picture taking. They even produced the first African chief with whom Bishop Stauffer negotiated to secure the land when he first got to Shirati. Tea and buns followed all of this "for one and all." You had to pay ten cents to get into the evening meeting, which was like one grand social with different chapters of TMCYL participating. The most striking feature to me was a rapid-fire, perfect rendition of Revelations 14, 15, and 16 in Swahili. As it was loud-speakered, I left around 9:30 and enjoyed the remainder of the show from the doctor's living room.

The Sunday morning service had about 1600 people present. There was a great deal of shouting to people to sit down, come in, quit pushing, clap louder, give your seat to someone more important, etc., but the tone was excellent. The service consisted of six congregational songs, ten special music numbers by choirs, three half-hour sermons in translations, three speeches, a lengthy gift-giving ceremony with expressions of thanks from four VIPs, and a closing prayer by George Smoker that wasn't exactly short—plus all the moderating. This was followed by Holy Communion in which about 450 participated. We got around to having dinner at about 2:15. The trucks began to roll out right after Sunday dinner.

The farewell had a new tone of dynamism, particularly among the youth, that I hadn't yet seen. The secretary of the TMCYL is a prince in every sense of the word, as are all the officers, except two, one a clown, the other a silly girl. It was new to see a full-scale production which had no European operators in evidence, except for the electricians. I enjoyed the weekend fully, happy to have been able to attend.

August 25, 1964

The Headmaster took me into the Musoma bus terminal early Friday morning so I could catch the seven o'clock bus to Mwanza. The trip takes over six hours, and by that time you've missed the dinner hour and you're hot and tired and have a headache. I spent most of Friday afternoon walking around Mwanza trying to figure out the lay of the place. Having come at least mildly acquainted, I began to make my 400 pounds of purchases of chairs, toilet paper, brushes, brooms, mattresses, pillows, *duka* supplies, etc., etc.

Saturday morning I got four teeth filled for free by a very capable African dental surgeon. Saturday afternoon I finished the purchases and got all the stuff ferried over to the bus depot in preparation for the 6:30 a.m. loading the next morning. I got up at 5:30 to walk the two miles from the guesthouse to the bus terminal. Fortunately a friendly Somali gave me a lift in his car, so I got there at six and had to wait a half-hour in the dark. The Somali said that one time in Arusha two American women pulled him out of the mud, so he ever after goes out of his way to help Americans. I assured him that I would now help Somalis in return for his kindness. After another grueling 6 hours, I was able to stumble through the front door of my house. Tomorrow the schoolboys return.

September 24, 1964

As far as we're concerned, the most important event this month was the arrival of little Dianne Louise. Labor started for Edith in her sleep. At about 11:30 the waters broke and she was flooded out of her bed. Real labor started with a big BANG up at the hospital (Shirati) at 2:30 a.m. In twenty minutes the baby was born. Dr. Eshleman (Lester) says this was the first birth in ages that was not attended by an African. "No time to call anyone!" Nurse Cora was with Edie the whole time. Nurse Lois managed to arrive in time to administer a bit of gas for the final push. Little Dianne was taken to the nurses' house in the basket on Lois' bicycle And Edith was back in her own bed by 4:30 a.m.! Joyce slept through the whole event.

I, of course, was down here at Musoma Alliance. The HM gave me permission to take the day off. So I drove up to Shirati on Daddy's *piki*. Edith was quite surprised to see me walk into her room. We had a very nice time together for several hours before it was time for me to get back to school. Hershey (Leaman, hospital administrator) said my trips into Shirati and back were something of records, having done the fifty miles in one and a half-hours.

Dianne is a wee mite. Less hair than Joyce at birth, but it is black. Her noise is more pronounced; her fingers and toes, long and lithe. She is skinny compared to her fat sister. Her neck is long. It seems that she'll take after Edie's side of the family.

October 23, 1964

Tom (name changed) arrived from his school to see Jacobs, bringing with him sad news. Last year he apparently asked the night watchman to find him a girl for the night. That led to Jacobs making a trip out to his school, and Tom's apparently sincere conversion. In the light of that it was decided he should remain at his assignment. But now he's been involved in homosexual activities with his schoolboys, for sometime apparently. I suppose he'll go home this time. But the whole thing raises in my mind all kinds of questions of why. Is it that he was never converted? Can't some non-converted people help how they act? Is he mentally ill? Why did he ever come to Africa in the first place? What is his view of himself? How much of what we are and do is determined by the environment provided for us by our parents, brothers, sisters, friends, etc., when we are too small to determine our own course. How many of us are no more sincere in our devotion to Christ than Tom appears to be, but who don't get into his difficulty, and so aren't exposed? Maybe I should have come to Africa single and sought for the answers to those questions. The Headmaster doubts if ten per cent of our students are sincere in their following Christ. I wonder if the percent is any higher among any other church group. Most people live in relatively stable situations and so they never experience the opportunity to have their sincerity tested.

November 2, 1964

Yes, we do, occasionally, have time to ourselves. But here's what fills up the day. This term I'm teaching Form IV geography, Form III biology, some advanced maths, all three of which are quite new to me and require a good bit of prep time. Then, too, we now have two babies about the place and we have just fired our cook for petty theft. Also, there're still those bathroom cupboard doors to paint, the sandbox to finish, the cementing of the rocks around the place is still not finished, the motor scooter is awaiting its long overdue servicing, and there are countless things to be done around the school. Like this evening I spent time weighing out ninety pounds of sugar into three and two pound lots for the school store, for which Edie is responsible.

However, in addition to reading, I get great relaxation from watering my trees and watching them grow. But even this doesn't happen as often as it used to. Here is today: Awake at two when Dianne yelled; Edie got up to feed her. Awake again at seven. Got up. Got Joyce up and re-diapered her; cleaned up two cat puddles; dressed and shaved; heated water for coffee; sat in on our bed with the family to drink the coffee; then off to school; spend some time at my desk going over what I shall say in Geography class; off to chapel; slip back to the school kitchen to straighten up some trouble among the cooks; got into a great stew with the head cook over how head he is; I go to class and find it canceled for the day due to Form IV tests; bump into the head cook who wants to take the matter to the HM; go down to the house and search for assistant for Edie with neighbor's help; back and teach one period, have staff tea at the HM's house; have double biology period for which I am unprepared, so spend the periods working on biology projects; spend last free period before lunch working on complicated geography map I'm trying to mimeograph; go home for lunch, rest, go off to prepare for afternoon physics lab; have lab; go to town with Edith and others for school supplies; offload the stuff; come down to the house to work on long overdue correspondence; complete weighing out sugar; come home and type until supper; supper; give Joyce a bath; Edith puts her to bed, and I sit down to write to you; in a few minutes two to four staff members will be here to see a film as a birthday celebration for someone's wife; coffee; all go home after lights out; feed Dianne; to bed at 11:30; 2:30 Dianne cries; 7:00 awake; get Joyce up and re-diaper her; make coffee; drink it on the edge of the bed . . . . Ad infinitum.

Really, it's not so bad. Edith just remarked that it would be much worse at home in the States.

November 22, 1964

Can you remember back to when you were twenty and just bursting with energy? Back then when you did everything with a passion? I wonder how long that kind of push lasts with most people. For my part, I have found it being slowly eroded away. Our last holiday at Kilimanjaro and Nairobi was such a time of boundlessness, but since Dianne has come, I've been almost continually unenthusiastic. I still planted some thirty trees yesterday, with the help of school lads. But I had to push myself. You feel this coming into everything—your love, your devotions, your preps of lessons, your duties about the school. It takes pushing and you see more spots of shoddy work. Anyway, I like to blame some of it on my teaching in fields that I'm not well versed in, such as Form IV Geography and Form III Biology. I find that all my extra energies have gone into preparation for these classes and the others have just simply slipped. It means, too, that noon rests are a thing of the past. But holiday is soon here; I'm looking forward to some refreshment.

Here in Tanzania we're going about wondering about the recent nation-wide anti-American demonstrations that have taken part during the past week with the kick off in that National Stadium last Sunday afternoon. The President made a lengthy speech, some two hours, about the confiscation by the Minister for Defense of a number of documents uncovering a plot by Portugal, South Africa and the United States to overthrow the Tanzanian government. The US ambassador shouted, "forgery" at once, but has since shut up and we've heard positively nothing from anywhere outside the country. Some of the captured documents were printed in the newspapers. They were written in French and translated into English. If they're authentic they seem to deal with the Congo communist infiltration and the camps set up by the

OAU around Dar for the purpose of training men to make things unpleasant for the Portuguese in Mozambique and the English in Rhodesia. In any case, the fire seems concentrated on the US, and the populace is understandably alarmed. Imagine the great big bully US trying to overthrow Nyerere's government. The country is still courteous, but it is again very wary of slights. The demonstrations were peaceful; no property was damaged. (Incidentally, could you take my young brother aside and explain to him that we don't live in Tanganyika Territory, not even Tanganyika. That we live in a place called TANZANIA!)

1965

February 4, 1965

It has suddenly developed within the space of a half hour this afternoon that we will be coming home for training in New York Biblical Seminary and New York University, during this coming academic year, in preparation for coming back out here and being Principal of the theological college at Bukiroba. This is traumatic, positively devastating in its long range implications.

February 21, 1965

We now plan to leave here on August 13, two days after the end of second term of school. Spend three days in Somalia with David and family; two days in London, a week in Pellston, Michigan with Edith's folks; then to Lancaster. It's thought that my family will live with me in New York City. Still have no idea about how much we shall be involved in weekend preaching in Lancaster. Jacobs thinks it's a good way to make a little money. But he also assured me that I should be prepared to read "twelve hours a day!"

February 23, 1965

In spite of all the dreadful things the newspapers say about US foreign policy, we feel practically none of it directly in the school or in town. People seem to be able to think of us as people and not as Americans. However, it is impossible for us to see how the US can continue its blind policies toward the African states. The US can never expect to be an influence for good as long as she persists in trying to direct the political affairs of these nations. And particularly as long as the Western press takes such a "down-the-nose" attitude. I keep thinking that the US will repent like a good Christian. But then I have to remind myself that in the world, repentance is always wrong and so we see continually the situation deteriorate. It seems that the US is bent on a course of systematically driving the Africans away.

May 26, 1965

My yen to write to my kin has quite evaporated. I guess it is that everything here is in a groove that isn't exciting. We grind out our days in the monotony of the regular routine in the abrasive cross-roads of West, East, and Africa, of white and black, of rich and poor, of Christian, Muslim and traditional, of knowledge and ignorance, of mission and church, of Swahili and English. So what is there to write about? Everything is much too complicated to explain. But before I get off it I must say that I am increasingly convinced that the short-term worker here does precious little to bridge the gaps. They come young and confident and they think they know but after a few years they begin to understand that they haven't got very far or even far at all and so they go home and the school must get used to yet another short-termer. But the ones that come can teach physics, biology, English, and math. And this is all that is concerned. You get milked and used and discarded. And you, of course, fight back with logic, intelligence, and heat, but who cares for logic; ignorant and downtrodden man cares only for how he feels. And maybe feelings are closer to truth than facts.

The outcome of a row with Musoma College at a football match in town last evening was that two of our boys got hit by rocks, one right over his eyes. The situation arose when their coach—a green American Catholic brother, came up here after we had complained about numbers of players on their team being not at all connected with their school. He suggested that we both drop all teachers and extraneous players. We had two teachers on our team, but the Headmaster agreed. The first game with them after the agreement was last night and they had a man on from the town council. The Headmaster was irritated and accosted the American brother to demand if he was going to stick to the bargain or not. Words flew then, and at the end of the game. We were leading 3-1 right up to the end when they got two, tying the score. It seems, however, that the ref didn't blow the whistle in time, so their third goal was won on overtime. Consequently their boys threw rocks and sand at our boys. Our headmaster reported to the police. Now we await developments.

June 6, 1965

We're still fighting with the Musoma College boys. I told you about the stone throwing at the close of a tied game. We had to replay that game and tied again. Now the rules are that anyone may play on a team provided he doesn't play on two teams and that he has been living in town at least a fortnight. The third game tied again at 2-2, so a seven-minute overtime was called and we won 4-2. Consequently there were rocks again, principally at our Headmaster's car. So we have hit a new low of angry thrust and counter thrust at football. We shall have to cooperate in testing at the end of the month and shall compete in sports at Saba-Saba (Tanzania's Independence Day) celebrations on July 7, so I suppose shall continue having fun.

June 17, 1965

The other evening we went over to our enemy, the College, in order to speak to one of their married teachers about a Mock Cambridge Exam which our schools were to concoct in concert. Sloan is attached to the one and only lady on the entire Catholic campus. So took along Edith. We stuck the girls in bed and scootered over at 8:30. Found them viewing a film in a room heavy with the smells produced by too may people in too small a place, with the odor of beer. Sloan didn't like my version of the test, so we spent considerable time going over everything. Their coffee was strong. We were home by 12:20 midnight. The kids hadn't detected our absence. But the coffee kept me awake until close to two. Sleep wasn't deep for the rest of the night. (Really do you spell it "deap" or "deep"? I think it must be the latter, but Edie isn't in the staff room and I'm embarrassed to ask my African friend again how to spell the English!)

June 19, 1965

If I had the time to write, I might tell you about:

— Our fifth wedding anniversary and the chocolate-chip ice cream we made to celebrate the occasions, and the huge pieces of angel food cake Edie served with it, and the delicious coffee I made.

— The stray dog Henry and I killed this evening. It had fallen into Henry's trash pit and couldn't get out, this having happened previously. I much worried about its spirit coming back to remind me of the dastardly deed I committed in striking it. Africans don't kill dogs on account of this spiritual deal.

— I should be able to make your hearts weep with nostalgia should I have time to tell of the great clouds of grit which drift over us from the main road these days; dust is in a constant state of turmoil agitated by the racing buses and grinding lorries.

— The hazy, smoke-filled skies in the winter evenings, the crisp, cool nights with the blazing stars, the breezy mornings, and the stifling stillness of the dehydrating afternoons.

— Our great swarm of half-grown cockroaches, which we are patiently waiting to mature at which time, we can harvest them for the biology lab.

— The smoke producer which I have burning behind Edie's chair. It's supposed to scare away the mosquitoes. I got it this evening from one of the African staff members and Edie keeps telling me about the delicious aroma of African campfires which she smells drifting towards her through the open window!

— The perfectly lovely office building which is to be opened officially at Bukiroba next Saturday, complete with terraced lawns and shaded walkways.

— Edie shaking in bed this morning. I woke her to find out whatever was the matter and found she was shaking our cook's wife who is messing around in the kitchen for some two weeks now while her husband's arm gets better.

— The day I fixed up the scooter for the next year and decided to have a spin around the place with the muffler off. By the way people talked it must have been rather noisy.

— But we just don't have time to write about any of that! (This quick dash took a good 20 minutes out of our jam-packed schedule.)

June 24, 1965

I must bring you up-to-date on the fight between the College boys and us. After the last stone-throwing incidents, our HM fired off sharp letters to the Regional Education Officer and sent copies to the HM of the College and to the police. He clearly felt it to be a black-and-white case, and he left no doubt about whom he thought was black and who was white. Last week he got a three-page letter from the REO which painted the picture white and very, very black, with the tables turned. The letter was a violent attack not only on our HM but also our school. What eats at our HM is that the REO is Catholic (as is the College), and he naturally assumes that the REO is gunning for him, who is Anglican.

July 13, 1965

We're going to be living (while studying) in New York City, leave the muggings, knifings, and killings with the Lord. The New York University catalogue arrived and I've had a look through. Here's what I plan to study. World Religions, Philosophical Theology, Philosophy of the Christian Religion, Sociology of Underdeveloped Areas, Social Anthropology, Acculturation, Geography and World Politics, Eastern Hemisphere Problems, Economic Geography of Africa, etc. 17 hours per semester; finished in June.

About our weekends. I confess that after being out of the limelight for three years, my love of the stage strongly tempts me to load up on preaching appointments in the Lancaster area. Lancaster doesn't really know Edie and me. Therefore, as full-time Tanzania missionaries, I owe it to the church to let them have a look at us. It's not very difficult to be a traveling speaker. The new is always exciting. And my sin is that I really do like it. And I feel that I have something to say. I also have a deep sense of a call from the church. You have failed to recognize in me the strutting missionary lying freely about conditions and exploits abroad. I will always appreciate your loving knocks, which help me to get things into perspective and lose a bit of the Elmer Gantry-ness that's in all of us. Having said all that, our present plans lean towards getting down from New York to the Lancaster churches twice a month.

August 8, 1965

We are churning our way through the clouds somewhere above Kenya, on our way to Somalia, to see brother David and his family. I'm quite disappointed that we can't see anything below, as such studies generally aid my knowledge of geography. In about another hour we shall be in your beloved Somalia. I know that I shall never be able to begin to feel the attraction you developed for that place.

Thinking about costs of again living in the States I think in terms of $250 per month being barely enough. Further, it has continually been pounded into me that our allowance at home is kept terribly low—"because we are expected to get money gifts."

From out here in Africa, it looks as though the mission board has ideas to use me as shadows of Elam Stauffer and Clyde Shenk, which we really are not! Am I vain to suggest that we should get around in order to help project a newer image of missionaries? I get the feeling sometimes that one gets right after one came out here and people make a conscious effort to make you understand that after all you are still wet behind the ears and horribly naïve and good only when silent and unseen. I admit it all, but we have an urgent need, which can't wait until I get dry. (Just saw the Tana River below!) Don't I sound like a grumpy, maladjusted, useless missionary getting all fired up for his furlough?

We're landing in your beloved Mogadiscio, Somalia!

Mennonite Theological College of East Africa

Nyabange/Bukiroba I

August 1967-July 1971

1967

August 28, 1967

I told Annie, when I got back here to Musoma, that we saw you off on the plane and that the last we saw of you was a little red light and a little white blinking way up in the sky. Hope you had a good trip, and that you were warmly welcomed at Tel Aviv.

I left Nairobi in a gentle drizzle which developed into fog and heavy rain. Twelve miles out of Nairobi I ran out of gas, but fortunately was able to use a bit from the spare tank, by laying the machine (cycle) on its side. Some Africans told me that the next station was just a short distance up the road, so I filled up and went happily on my way. Shortly thereafter, however, the machine began to sputter badly, whenever I opened the throttle a bit. This was because the mechanics had torn the rubber connection between the air cleaner and the carburetor. This eventually developed into a hunk of rubber blocking the airflow to the carb. So, I stopped at the base of the escarpment and bought some tape with which I fixed the thing properly. Shortly after getting through Nakuru I noticed that the fixture holding the headlamp was beginning to get loose. Fortunately, it held until I got to Kericho, but by that time it was about to fall off. There I bought two bolts and fixed that up properly. It was in Nakuru that I noticed that the motorcycle was using about twice the amount of oil that it used on the way to Nairobi. This I found alarming, as they had just overhauled the motor again.

Also, shortly after leaving Nairobi the horn quit working. After getting home I found that a connection had come apart. I am suspicious that the mechanics did the damage when they took the seat off. Maybe it was just my imagination, but it did seem that the shock absorbers were worse on the way back. I think it was just that I was tired and not enjoying the motorcycle trip as much as I had enjoyed it going up. After getting home, I managed to find a total of nine things that the mechanics did wrong in working on the cycle. I guess I shall be mean enough to write to Ali about it, just to let him know that his guys aren't quite up to snuff.

September 4, 1967

This past weekend we all went up to Shirati Hospital. All Saturday morning I followed Dr. Weaver around the operating theater. The first case was a C-section under local anesthetic due to the low condition of the woman.

The placenta was grown fast to the entire uterus surface, which meant that he had to do a hysterectomy. During the operation her breathing stopped, so they had to do the breathing for her. She came through it wonderfully and in a week doc said she can go home. The next operation was to take a little growth out of a woman's ankle. The third was to remove a swollen—probably due to cancer—testicle from an old man. He got a spinal block, which paralyzed him from the waist down. The next was a woman who had bleeding from the vagina and was thought to be four or five months pregnant. Doc thought it was an abdominal pregnancy.

Tomorrow school starts here at the theological college. We have a new staff member. He feels that an institution such as ours should have three salaries and three houses attached to it. He of course wants one of those three salaries and one of those houses. I was talking to him about it and made the ill-advised comment that he should not compare himself with the missionaries but with his fellow African teachers. Anyway, it ended with him stomping out of the house in a cursing rage, threatening to burn down the whole station. I went after him later in the evening and found him pouring out the whole thing to the pastor. That gave me an opportunity to apologize for antagonizing him. By the next day things seemed pretty well back on the mend. To my surprise, around noon the Bishop's wife came to see me. She had heard that we had had a fight, and she came to see what she could do to restore the peace. I really appreciated it, as I knew that she had already talked to the staff person. We need good mothers like her to keep us hot-blooded young men from tearing each other to shreds. We are back to excellent relations again, as far as I can see. Incidentally, you're the only person I told this to. There is nothing like being able to repent for clearing the air on these things.

September 14, 1967

I have finally waxed sufficiently bold to open a five-day refresher course under the pastor of this *Jimbo* (District). We are doing it without being specifically ordered to do so by *Komiti Kuu* (overall committee). It is a trial balloon, just to see if we can be free to work out this sort of thing with the *Jimbo* pastors, if they want help for their church leaders. Anyway we as a staff sat with the pastor and outlined what would be taught and who would teach when and what. Everything seemed in order for the Tuesday morning opening of the refresher course. Then, this morning, the Thursday before the Tuesday, Mr. Orondo informed me that he did not feel free to take his eighth period contribution to the course. (He only has ten periods a week in the college). I was floored, but remembering the scene in our living room over salary I refrained from appearing distressed. It turned out that he does not yet consider himself a member of the staff and that he is only helping to fill the gap left by Smoker, but he does not feel free to do any sort of plus service. I thanked him for being so kind as to help with the courses and left it at that. But I am still in a quandary for a fill in as Smoker is building from dawn to dusk and other hopefuls will be in *Komiti Kuu* during three of these fives days that the course runs.

An older student told me this morning that students started laughing at him again and he wanted to have it out with them. I asked him if I should see the culprits individually or if he would like to see them with me. He said that he preferred that we have the matter out in class with everyone. There, this afternoon, I opened the word for the class and we spent an hour charging and counter-charging. Eventually we prayed about it but it really isn't a closed affair. Trouble is—he would like everyone to fear and obey him, as though he were their grandfather and everyone just jolly well won't do that.

I dropped into the office to work for an hour. Behold a distraught woman came in. I welcomed her and offered her a chair, but she started demanding money. I told her that I hadn't a cent in the office, so she began demanding pencils or paper. These I told her were school property and not mine to give away. Thereupon she began to curse me violently, drawing circles on the floor and generally consigning me and all my kind to the works of hell. By this time there was a huge pile of local school kids both inside and outside the office. I had to admit that I was quite at a loss as to what to do with her. So, I returned to the typewriter and after a few more minutes of cursing, she retired to outside the window for cursing. Later I found that she threw dirt into my parents' house, just as they were inviting the headmaster from the boys' secondary school inside. She cursed everyone who didn't produce a shilling on the spot. I happened to be at our house when she got there later in the evening. And although I gave her two shillings, she consigned Edith to barrenness and all of us to eternal fire for not giving her a new blanket. To top it off she unhitched her blanket and did a little parade for the benefit of the domestic science women who had come up to visit Edith. In the end it was a bit pathetic, but at first I admit that I was not a little shaken at being so thoroughly castigated. I hate castigations.

Just this evening I got to thinking how really nice and lovely it is here at the theological college.

September 17, 1967

We cry about not wanting overseas money, and apparently even the bishop was quoted to that effect, but at the same time there is so little being done to make the college self-sufficient. Anyway, it smacked to me of trouble when I heard it, so I wasn't awfully surprised to hear that someone wanted a "discussion." The point is that there is a TMC church back there near the Roman Catholic Church that we saw when I took you through the bush. An African there is giving his time free of charge to not only build a church but also a two-room school with office which can double as a church. The structure is identical in materials with the one George is building, only a good bit bigger. But these things my dad doesn't know. Earlier this year I visited a shack with Pastor Jonah where there was only a square yard of thatch on the roof; this evening I saw the same thing, now a lovely little mud brick building with a tin roof. Pastor Jonah built it himself—free of charge. Only yesterday the whole theological college student body walked over to Nyamitwebiri and worked like slaves until after two in the afternoon, gathering the bricks to the site of the church. So it goes . . . .

September 27, 1967

The crops are harvested, the grain threshed, the granaries are full. It has been over two months since the last of the life-giving rains, the barren dry winds blow incessantly, the parched grass curls further under the merciless sun and burns to ash in the occasional grass fire, the roads have turned to ribbons of dust. During these months the thousands of peasant farmers who are the Tanzania Mennonite Church have a break from work in the fields. It is the time for building houses, re-thatching old ones, and visiting. And this is the time of the year when the various TMC districts hold their annual three-day inspirational conferences.

TMC is divided into districts very much like the Lancaster Conference bishop districts. Each district is headed by an ordained pastor who has up to twenty or twenty-five small congregations under him. Every year most of the districts have an inspirational conference, called "mission," which last from Friday morning through Sunday noon. Guest speakers are invited, each of the congregations within the district send representatives, some of the congregations send trios and quartets for special music, and the local primary school choir polishes up their best numbers. Offerings are taken, a couple of fat cows are purchased, plenty of flour (white cassava and maize and red millet), rice, tea and sugar.

A few weeks ago I had the privilege of attending the conference of the Kisaka district. The hub station of the district where the pastor lives lies eight miles beyond the last bus stop in an area which was open wild animal country just ten years ago. Today pioneer farmers are rapidly filling the once empty land; you no longer hear lions at night; there is a Missionary Aviation Fellowship air strip, a small dispensary and maternity ward, a beautiful red-brick church, a primary school, and whiffs of prosperity-through-hard-work in the air.

The pastor's some fifteen congregations lie up to thirty rugged cross-country miles from the main station. These he tries to visit regularly by bicycle or motorcycle. The baptized membership of the district has doubled in the last three years from some 250 to nearly 500, which reflects the commitment of Pastor Mato to his task of evangelism and nurture.

Pastor Mato, with his wife and family, moved a hundred miles from their home district to take up this frontier assignment. Although they are far from supplies and transportation is difficult, they have a testimony of joy and peace in our Lord.

This "mission" was typical in many ways. The theme of the messages was, "Behold the Lamb of God that takes away the sins of the world." There were morning and afternoon sessions on Friday and Saturday. In the evenings after supper we guests had prayers and good fellowship in the pastor's spacious living room. Sunday morning was the cap-sheaf meeting with two sermons, special music ranging from a penetrating, minor key number sung by a trio of grandmothers to the rousing rhythms of the local school choir. The highlight of the service was at the close when each congregation present brought its special offering. Although these missions consist of about forty to fifty per cent school children, I have seen offerings of up to a dollar per person.

After the service we had another meal served in the grand style of a thanksgiving banquet. Then there were good-byes and slowly the mass of people at the station began to leak away into the bush. A Land-Rover, a motorcycle, a couple of bicycles, and lots of feet took us back to our homes to share with those the good things we had enjoyed.

October 2, 1967

I went out to Mugango with one of the theological students. Our objective was to try to clean up Bishop Ray Wenger's grave a bit for the annual conference there this coming weekend. I had quite an ambitious program outlined and *kumbe* this man came in a white shirt, polished Sunday shoes, etc. I put another shirt into the bucket of stuff we were taking along. We took lime from Musoma for whitewashing and all else that we thought we'd need, except food and hoes. Hoes we got at Mugango, but we worked from ten to three-thirty in one of the hottest days I've ever been out in, and we got nothing but water from the local people. The reason we didn't get started before ten was that Daddy had taken my cycle to Migori for the weekend and I had borrowed Maynard's motor scooter that didn't travel very fast. Further, we went to greet the pastor and his wife before starting work. He was not at home but we chatted a bit with his wife and a church leader, who was doing the same. They gave us some sugar cane to chew. Behold, after I had spit out the last husk I found that there was a big open space in place of my left incisor.

We first hoed the whole thing, including the entrance road. The place must have been used as a latrine by the adjacent village because there were feces even right on top of the grave. I complained about this to the head of the village. He agreed that it was a shameful thing to defecate on a grave. After hoeing everything we gathered rocks from the hill, rocks as big as we could carry. We sweated at putting these into the ground in a big rectangle all around the grave. We then made an entrance road with rocks as well. This accomplished, we whitewashed everything and went home. We stopped at the village shops for *mandazies* and tea. Then hit the road, getting home a bit before eight.

October 9, 1967

The theological college is closed for Friday so students can attend the "mission" at Mugango. I helped George Smoker put the roof on the church at that place you called Twin Breasts. He had everything cut and a good bit of it together out behind his house. We had to load it up, haul it over to that church, and put it on. By the time it was so dark that I could no longer see the nails, we were within an hour of finishing the wood structure. We got home at eight, just in time for Edie to get off to Musoma Secondary to see the film, "Serengeti Shall Not Die." I got the kids to bed and was myself asleep by the time she returned. By seven the next morning George and I were on our way back to the church for a half-day of work. Today, after lunch, I went back and helped finish the roofing job. Got back in time to take some students to help go for firewood for the school. Back by dusk with a huge load. Will wait until tomorrow to offload.

As for the school, it appears that Orondo has been creating a lot of noise among the students, to the effect that Shirati Hospital is making some fat cats in the US nice and rich. Nevin, the hospital director, told me that they had a lot of static after the Shirati "mission" the other weekend, when Orondo and party were there. To clear up some misconceptions myself I've been using my class on the nature and mission of the church to discuss the topic, "The Church Has Finance." The incredible fact is that many of these theological students can't seem to conceive of philanthropy. It just can't be believed that the church, the bookshop and the hospital haven't been designed as money-making schemes for anyone. I find that this finance thing is very touchy, and I nearly got burnt several times. Finance is so foreign to the students that they can't conceive that the church leaders understand where the missionaries and their allowances fit into the scheme of things.

October 15, 1967

There is so much that one feels and yet so little that one—I at least—can express. Often I wish I could paint or sing—or even cry. These being beyond my grasp, I just get headaches. You know that one can get headaches as much from exultation as from depression. I remember the first such that I ever had. I was down in Majita when I was just a ten-year-old boy. It was a conference and by some stroke of good fortune, I was allowed to accompany the few missionaries that went. Daddy pitched his little pup tent for me and for three days we ate *ugali*, took baths in the lake and went to meetings. I remember Mahlon Hess praising the Lord—conversation directed to me, squashed in the front seat of some ancient Ford—that my dad had taught him how to double-clutch, and that he now did it automatically. I remember one of Stauffer's messages on how Jesus left his heavenly glory, made himself like men, died, rose again, and is given a Name. I remember that one evening we walked down to the lake for a bath and that on the way Daddy peeled a grapefruit, which he shared with me. I bathed with my underpants on and that when I got out of the lake and took them off I threw them back into the water's edge to soak while I dressed and that Dad ordered me to retrieve them for he thought it not proper to throw clothes into the lake and that I was mortally embarrassed to retrieve them, white bare butt flashing. But what I remember the most is the fellowship on the last night of the meeting. There were testimonies and singing and a very high level of emotion flowing through the crowd gathered in the bough-covered *banda* with light from pressure lamps. I went off to bed at an appropriate time for young children. But sleep would not come and as I lay listening to the spirited bursts of singing, my little package of emotional potential filled that tiny cubical of canvas and blankets with an intensity that had, within an hour, reduced my consciousness to the blaze of fire filling my cranium. "Beware of letting things get out of hand," I was warned. But things still do, sometimes today.

Saturday Edie and I had the time of our lives. We drove down to Mwanza to pick up a grain hammer mill with its diesel engine. We took along a nurse needing transport. We left about 5:30 a.m., letting the children to get themselves up; apparently everything went off okay with them. We got to Mwanza at 8:30 and by noon we were through our business. You may have heard that Mwanza is about the hottest town in Africa right now. Parliament is meeting there, as is the annual TANU conference. So the town was full of police and by what people and the newspapers say, it is also full of wheels. Second Vice President came into town while we were there, but we didn't see him. Today, Obote, Kaunda, and Kenyatta were to arrive. Mobutu and others couldn't come. President Nyerere himself got there last Monday. He'd been visiting his home at Butiama and started walking to Kiabakari in support of the Arusha Declaration. The walk continued for days and eventually he wound up in Mwanza, nearly 140 miles away. It was quite a thing. The Arusha Declaration—"Education for Self-Reliance."

I finished reading van der Post's "Venture into the Interior." It was great, and like a missionary, I have been looking for someone else to whom I can give the book to read. It would be great to discuss with you some of his theories and to see them working out in one's experiences. I like what he has to say about little moves that put you into a matrix of events which must be lived through before one can again be free of the situation. Some of these things last longer than a mountain climb. Among his descriptions I found his account of the plane trip into Africa most fascinating. Annie has no doubt told you how we flew from Cairo to Kasumi in a French four-motor prop plane back in 1948. Post's description fits so very vividly into what I remember of the experience as a child.

Edith says that she doesn't mind our writing to each other, just as long as she gets to read the letters. I told her that Annie was no doubt just as jealous of our exclusivity as she is. But as I can write better when writing to a person rather to people, please ask Annie to bear with us. Further, I think I write best when writing to you, brother!

October 22, 1967

Hess had the devotional meditation over at Musoma Alliance He spoke on failure. This came right on the heels of a weekend of "mission" here at Bukiroba, which left me feeling like a success and not a failure. I chaired the two Saturday meetings. We had an African pastor and his wife for house guests. A number of favorable comments were made over the pulpit about the garden "Joseph Shenk" has a heart for down at the lake. I'd gone along to collect firewood with the college men and earned favorable comments from a few. Ndengi apologized in class for getting mad about a test grade that he got. Orondo came for a half-hour and left quite mellowed. So, as Hess spoke about failure, I couldn't help but think that failure is bad but it must be so very much worse not to fail. If I stop failing, then the alternative is to become one of those horrid creatures that won't give up his post because none can do it better than he, that seeks the lime-light on all occasions because none is so clever as he; that stops putting his ear to the ground because none could send signals of value to him; that preaches in terms of "you" rather "we" because none is so righteous as he. We hear the lies of people until we suddenly come to believe them and from that day onwards we cease to fail. Oh, we fail in little things, but all due to misunderstandings, nothing basically out of whack. It seems that this is the disease that eventually gets all of us to a greater or lesser extent. Certainly it is worse than failure itself.

One of the interesting illustrations told in one of the weekend mission sermons was as follows: The Rev. Muganda, when he was just a boy turning into a man, found the young wife of his cousin to be very attractive. So he committed fornication with her. He took her into his grandmother's house for the act. His grandmother was a native doctor, and it was also taboo in his tribe for someone to have intercourse in his grandmother's house. The grandmother was away when the act was committed but when she came home again and drank water in her house, she became very sick. Investigation was made as to why she was sick, and it was found that a taboo had been violated and it appeared that the young man was the offender. So he was called and told to confess. He refused to confess, feigning innocence. They then told him to not bother with confessing but to just go and take dirt from the bodies of both of them who had committed this act. The dirt was duly brought and was mixed into a concoction which the grandmother then drank. "At once she became well! It is amazing—the ways of Satan!" My missionary colleague was scandalized *kabisa*!

President Nyerere has been saying some terrific things in Mwanza these days. "Leaders cannot do anything for the people. We can only provide the necessary information, guidance, and organization for the people to build their own country for themselves. Leaders of Tanzania should not be making promises; we cannot fulfill them for others. We should not be complaining; complaints help no one. We should know the facts of Tanzania's situation, understand them, and give guidance to the people in the light of them."

October 29, 1967

Dr. Dick Weaver, surgeon at Shirati Hospital, asked me if we Shenks would like to go along with his family out to Seronera, on the Serengeti, for a few nights of camping. We agreed and tried to make plans to stay at the motel there. You can bring your own food and the rates are not so high, as they are for regular visitors. Unfortunately, they were booked solid, so we couldn't get in. We decided to go camping instead and made bookings for this. Ruth, the doctor's wife, wasn't exactly happy about camping, but figured that there wasn't any other way, if we want to go.

We used Daddy's Toyota jeep. Got an early start so by ten we were already in the park. We went in by the corridor. Just as soon as we got inside the gate we began to see animals. We stopped to have a bit of tea about a mile in, and right there we began seeing buffalo in the thickets off to one side. A little later we came on to three huge rhino. They didn't charge us or anything like the ones that Omar and Anna Kathryn saw in Ngorongoro Crater; we got some good pictures anyway. That corridor route is almost ninety miles long and the whole way was full of game. The first twenty miles I drove through mud and we had to be careful not to stick, but the rest is good gravel road. We saw buffalo, eland, rhino, wildebeest, gnu, zebra, ostrich, fox, hyena, impala, Thompson gazelle, wild pig, giraffe, elephant, water buck, and later, reed buck, hartebeest, Grants gazelle, and rabbits. It was ninety miles of pure delight. Halfway to Seronera Camp we stopped on the slope of a lovely little green hill under a spreading thorn tree for our packed lunch. The pigs must have been in their bearing season because all the pairs had a cute little shaver running along ahead of the couple. The largest pig family had five little ones. The wildebeest had also just dropped their calves, and we saw scores of their young. It had begun to rain, so the plains were a brilliant fresh green. None of the animals we saw seemed to be migrating yet. They were spread out everywhere over the hillsides and among the freshly budding bush. The corridor doesn't have any spreading expanses of plains, as there are beyond Seronera. Rather, here one finds bush country with little idyllic valleys and glens with an occasional rolling pasture. It makes surprises because you never know what you'll see beyond the next bend in the road. The animals have the trees eaten off up to about four or five feet so that you can look through the trees for quite long distances, until the multitude of trunks finally obscure one's sight.

When we got to Seronera, we were given a map and told how to get to our campsite. About three miles from Seronera, the campsites were staggered in such a way that none was nearer than a mile from another. This was sort of a surprise to us, to be way out in the *pori* so far from any other places that all we could see was ourselves, a road, a toilet shack, a sign telling us to sleep inside tents, with tent flaps down, with a light outside—and lots of *kongoni*, *topi*, and Tommies. The grass had been mowed under a number of big thorn trees. We chose two big ones as our shelter and set to work at once to get the tents up. Night wasn't too far off, and we had a lot to do. First we put up the kitchen tent so that the women could get cracking on supper. Then we worked on the tent the Weavers brought, but none of us were familiar with it. We worked a long time without being able to figure out how it was to go up. We finally left it and worked on Daddy Shenk's tent which also took quite a while to figure out. But in the end, our combined genius—six degrees among the lot of us—conquered and we got all the tents up. It was interesting to us that with all of God's wild Africa to set up camp in we two families chose to camp in a very tight little circle. By nightfall the ladies had supper ready—a good meal and soon we're ready for bed. We put a small kerosene lantern outside in the courtyard and slept peacefully until morning.

Dick said the next morning that they'd heard lions early in the morning, but we hadn't heard anything. We had a leisurely breakfast and then set out to see what we could see. Amazingly, just before we left campsite, I picked up the truck keys from my suitcase where I had put them for the night, but for a minute later they had completely disappeared. We looked everywhere but could not find them. Fortunately, Daddy, with his characteristic foresight, had given Dick a second set of keys, so we used them and went off for the rest of the morning. We scouted everywhere, but didn't see a thing of consequence. Finally went back to camp for dinner and a rest.

That evening we tried again to see game and finally spotted a couple of cars congregated in a spot close to where we had been told there were some cheetah in the morning. We drove over and sure enough there was a sinewy "leopard dog" stretched out on the lee side of a little anthill. Playing around her, their long hair whipped by the stiff breeze, were two little cubs. It was the most delightful thing, and we watched them for some time. We then looked again for leopard but were unsuccessful. About dusk we again wend our back to camp.

That evening, supper was late and the lions started roaring early. First, we could hear them at what seemed to be a distance of two or three miles. Then we heard them at twice that distance and again at half that distance. We sort of thought that the two nearer roarings were the same group and that they were moving toward us. Dick got out his tape recorder in the hope that he could get a bit of recording. All he got though from the nearest roars was the fizzing of our pressure lantern. Edith had felt earlier that it would be nice to sort of have a bit of time around the campfire that night. So we all went leisurely about our evening preparations for bed. The children got baths, out on the tailgate of the jeep. I took a sponge bath out in front of the car. We, of course, got the supper things cleared away. It was after eight before we got around to telling the children their evening Bible stories and eating toasted marshmallows. We sat around the fire and the children listened, but not happily. By this time the nearer lions had stopped roaring. We figured that they had gone off to join the farther ones. Just the same, the children were happy to be able to get inside the tents. After we had them in bed, Edith and I called Dick and Ruth out for some more chat around the fire.

We had the pressure lantern going and a nice little fire; we sat and talked until nearly ten. By this time the nearer lions had started roaring again and indeed they were very close. We decided to read a passage from the Bible, pray, and go to bed. I read something, and Dick and I got to discussing it, but Ruth, who could by now hardly sit still anymore, begged us to get on with it. So Dick led us in prayer. Just in the middle of his prayer, something made me jump around. I don't know what it was—possibly a snap of a twig or the pad of a foot or even just a breath or the sense of some presence. In any case, there slinking through the light cast by the pressure lantern was a huge female lion. She was moving along from behind our sleeping tents to the kitchen tent.

I immediately gasped in a hoarse, dry whisper that there was a lion and grabbed the pressure lantern, so as to keep her in the light. Ruth dived for their tent, but both Dick and Edith got a good look at the brute as she slipped behind the kitchen tent and then out on the other side. The kitchen tent flap was still open, and suddenly I thought of a lion in our breakfast things, so I pulled the flap shut. Then I pulled the box on which the lantern sat over into the center of our campsite, so that everything would be well illuminated. I pumped the thing up hurriedly, so that it would burn for a while. Then we were all inside our zippered tent flaps and whispering frightenedly to each other. We called on Dick to finish his prayer; he said a loud, "Amen." The pressure lantern cast shafts of light out between the tents, but we couldn't see anything of the lion through the mosquito netting in the tent windows. So we went to bed.

In a little while, however, the two old boys whom we had heard roaring not too far away, started to come closer and closer. First, they took up a station about fifty feet to the right rear of our tent and then the same distance to the left rear. It was tremendous, I tell you. We would lie there and listen to the faint noises. Joyce was breathing heavily, so we couldn't hear everything. There would be a slight cough, then a rustle, then a snap of a twig, and permeating the whole was the heavy weight of great power, sensed more than felt. Then there would be a few unmistakable coughs, and we knew they were about to roar again. The one would start and his companion would join in. The director must have had a slipped vocal cord because he had a peculiar high pitched, horse-like shaft of sound mixed into the billows of beastly power that would engulf us. He would begin, and after he had about two great bursts of thundering decibels rolling across the plains and echoing through the valleys, his companion would join in and away we would go in a transport of sound until the last grunt died away and the waiting and listening started all over again for us. I tell you it was tremendous. It was even majestic, if the source of such terror may be majestic. The whole canvas walls of the tent would vibrate to the sound. The whole area quaked. And that's not fancy language either. I assure you that the tent did physically vibrate like the head of a drum. But then the waiting was almost worse than the roaring. I am sure that the female was still prowling around our campsite. I expected at any moment to see the tent walls pushed here and there by an inquisitive nose. Each of us had a lantern inside our tent. Dick had a little axe; I had a *panga*. Ha! Ha!

Poor Ruth was the most scared. She was sure the lions were right up beside our tents. She was also very afraid that the children would wake up and become hysterical, causing the lions to . . . . It was a good thing that we had the children's potty and the Weavers had an old tin can. Actually, the male lions never came closer, at least in their roaring moments, than fifty feet. They further kept to the shadows thrown by the kitchen tent and the big tree beside it. I could, however, shine our flashlight on to the spot from which the thundering came, but they averted their eyes and were in some grass. The flashlight was a bit dim, so I didn't actually see the lions. We should have shouted to the Weavers to assure them of the position of the lions. It was all Ruth could do to keep from going hysterical and she vowed never to sleep there again should she live through the night. Next to Ruth, I was the most scared. Both Edith and Dick seemed to take it sort of in stride. Dick got some good recordings of the roaring although some of his takes are blunted from excess volume. Finally, at about two in the morning the lions shifted to the back right of our tent. Suddenly, the feeling of a powerful presence left. We dozed fitfully until morning. Early the next morning we were running around in our pajamas looking for tracks and wondering at such oddities as the fact that the pressure lantern had burned until sunrise.

We had arranged to have a guide take us around that morning, so we put off the decision about packing up that day or not, and decided to wait to see what all we could see that we hadn't seen yet during the morning's guided tour. We finished up breakfast quickly and set off. About a half mile from the camp I suddenly noticed something shining in one of the ruts of the road and stopped to see what it was. Sure enough, a good omen, the lost keys sparkling in the morning light. I must have put them on the car somewhere the day before.

Our guide almost at once found two lovely female lions for us, possibly one of them was the brute of the night before. It is amazing how different it is to meet a lion when you are in a car in broad daylight, than it is too meet one in the dead of night, far from anyone and without any protection. In a few minutes we came on a whole pride—a cocky dad, moms, and lots of kids lazing in a thicket. We then went in search of a leopard, which had been seen the day before. Leopard is the hardest to find and our guide told us that often he can't find them. We drove for ten or more miles up a riverbed, which slowly petered out, into an occasional thorn tree in heavy grass. Suddenly the guide called our attention to a thorn tree to our left. There a leopard was picking its way down the trunk. The guide told me to drive quickly into the tall grass so as to stop the leopard. Apparently this one was used to cars because he seemed scarcely to take any notice of us. He did stop, though for some time in the lowest crotch of the tree, and then dropped silently to the ground. We could drive a bit behind and to the side of him. He moved low, slow, and silently through the thick grass and finally climbed another tree. He went up near the top and stretched himself out on a limb and went to sleep. Of all the animals we saw none was so beautiful as the leopard. The lions have scratches and scars; they are smelly and they have a kind of parasitic fly crawling around their tummies; they sleep on their backs with their legs up in the air in a most disgraceful manner. The cheetah was lovely, but she looked a bit too much like a dog—a sort of gray hound, long and lank. But that leopard, relaxing in the bough of a brilliantly green thorn tree, the bright morning sun playing little patches of brilliance over his gold, black, and white coat of smooth velvet was simply breath-taking. He had no imperfections; he was graceful in every movement; he had magnificent dignity in his refusal to even look at us. With reluctance, we finally left him and went in search of more smelly old lions.

We soon found them—a black-maned old codger with his mate—lying under another thorn tree. Nestled by the side of the old boy was half the head of a zebra, which they had apparently killed and eaten the night before.

Then we came on another large group of females, some thirteen, basking in the sun. One old bitch in particular was on her back in the most frightful manner. One would never see a leopard acting that way.

Since that was about all there was to see, we returned to camp for dinner. Somehow, it didn't seem good to us then to pull up stakes and go home, so we decided to build a big fire that night and stick it out. Later in the evening we went hunting again but found nothing significant. Interestingly, it had rained on a number of sides of us, but we didn't get a drop. We were grateful for this, as it meant that our tents would be dry for folding the next morning.

Dick and I got a tow rope and got to pulling and hauling branches from dead trees into camp for a truly big fire. We got two huge tree trunks pulled out of the ground and laid them like a big X a little way in front of our tents and lit a fire in the X. We had fire to burn, as the saying goes. That night we went to bed early, but we heard nothing. At nine and at ten, Dick and I stirred up the fires and pumped the pressure lamp. By about four I got awake again and found that the pressure lamp had gone out and the fires were about dead. I got out and stirred up the big fire and went back to bed. Again, just around morning we heard a bit of very distant roaring, but that was all.

We packed up and by nine we were on our way out of Serengeti. Again we had the lovely drive out the corridor. This time we managed to pick out three lions, one female, blind in one eye, and two proud young princes, all at widely scattered places. The young males would not let us get close to them. They ran with dignity and majesty, keeping us to a certain distance. On the trip out the tsetse flies were terrible. Every time the car slowed to less than twenty miles per hour the place would become aswarm with the biting insects. At one place we saw seven hyenas all in a row, wallowing in a water diversion ditch. We again saw lots of buffalo—a hundred I would say. The three rhinos were just a couple of miles from where we saw them on the way in. The twenty miles of mud flat were muddier than ever and at one place we nearly got stuck. The trick was to get going fast and to keep going. In numbers of places I am sure that if we had stopped we would have never got going again. We amused the children by singing, to the tune of "Charlie went over the mountain," that "Ruthie went to the *pori*." The kids got a big bang out of it.

After we were home and could get a good night's sleep, I realized how keyed up I had been. We had looked for a few days of relaxation and refreshment. What we got was a lot of excitement and just a little scaring.

November 8, 1967

This evening the missionaries are sort of all despondent again. A nurse on furlough has written telling of the current attitudes of TMC students overseas. The letter is to be circulated here among us. Although I haven't seen it yet, it seems that there is a lot of hate missionaries, hate church leaders, assurance of occupancy of the big houses here on the station as soon as they get back from America, assurance of a hand on the helm to straighten out things, etc., etc., and we are all sort of closing ranks against the common foe. Oh dear, is it really necessary to advertise these grim facts? Wouldn't we all be better off without the knowledge that there are certain people who hate us? Why must we write letters about that?

Today the Bishop had chapel for us and then spent two periods answering questions from the college men. He is to speak to us again tomorrow morning for two periods. I tell you, this man does not lose his composure under attack. He has a tremendous grasp on the essentials. Granted, he gets fuzzy on the details sometimes, but no one will trick him as to how the forest lies. He does not get his foot in his mouth. After the morning session Orondo remarked to me, "That man is very wise. I didn't know that he was so wise." This from a young Turk.

I have one last scandal which you must promise to keep under your hat. Should you reveal this, you could ruin us. A commercial movie was shown in the chapel to the Mennonite Theological College men. It was open to the public for the sum of ten cents per adult, five cents per child. What was shown? "Mary Poppins"! At tea the next morning there was great distress expressed from our oldest single missionary woman on the indecency displayed by the heterosexual dancing so blatantly featured in the film. The planner for showing the movie, a married woman, resignedly decided that probably we shouldn't use our projection for such things. Tut, tut!

November 23, 1967

The other week in class we were talking about "freedom and power," "predestination and foreknowledge" and the role of "fate in the Christian experience." If I can clear the fuzz from my head, I said something like this—

If God gives power to his creatures and then adds freedom as a special gift to the human creature, then He must allow that person to act as he chooses. God can't allow people to act as they choose and at the same time operate on any sort of fate basis. This does not mean that God doesn't have a plan or purpose. He does have a plan for all situations, all the way from the rise and fall of kingdoms to the rise and fall of sparrows. Certainly He acts toward the end that man may be redeemed. But what God purposes is not fated. It is subjected to the whim of man whose job it is to bring the thing to pass. Man must certainly continually jimmy the works, causing God to re-route His army in order to attain His ultimate objective. And certainly God in His super knowing, super ableness, and super loving must be able to bring out of the jimmied situation something of blessing to those who being His children are attuned to the new battle formation.

December 1, 1967

I think I've been learning something. I went to see the church treasurer and then the Bishop, to see how much of that Shs 4,000/=, which I had left over I could get out of the kitty before the books close.

The Bishop couldn't understand my finances with complexities about eleven and thirteen month years, about an exact itemization of what had to be spent yet from this year's budget, etc. Then I got into the business about refresher courses and we just passed each other the whole way along. He got to thinking that I was dead set against refresher courses for the old men and wanted only the theological college for the young men. He is scared of the young men and doesn't want to spend any money on them. I felt that he was being unreasonable in wanting us to jimmy our terms to fit the whims of the elders. Further, I was convinced that he didn't understand half of what I was trying to get at. Anyway, I finally quit and went home. But I felt terrible.

What I saw very clearly was that (1) if we are going to try to make our plant work double time it will take some pretty sophisticated tinkering with schedules, and I'll need to be given the freedom to work things out on a take-it-or-leave-it basis, and (2) the Bishop certainly didn't have enough confidence in me to give me a green light. Now what does this mean?

Does it mean that in order to achieve confidence one must drop his own identity? So long as I haven't denounced the youth and at the same time haven't made capitulatory overtures to the elders, I am in neither camp and so can't be trusted by either. And here is where the East African Revival Fellowship bit comes in. Maybe the way here is to identify fully with a certain group and, at least visibly, drop the whole concept of individual independence, which is so dear to us westerners. It is certainly anathema here to hold a strong position which is at variance to that of the group.

So I lived with that over the weekend and then this morning I went up to see the Bishop again. I told him that it was not right of me to explain something to him which I had thought about for a long time and which he didn't fully understand, then to push him into commitments about it. He told me, and this surprised me, that he did fully understand what it was that I was after. He knew that I was after just the youth and had no care for the older men and that this was quite at variance to what he was after. This, of course, wasn't in the least true, but in retrospect I can see how he may have come to read me that way. Anyway, I apologized for having pushed him, not for the youth part. He said that if my confession was sincere he would be happy to forgive me, but that he was familiar with missionaries who come begging forgiveness so that when they are forgiven and the other's guard is down they can go right ahead with what they had intended all along. He said that after I had gone home the other day, he said to himself, "The old missionaries are loudmouth pushies and behold, here their children do it, too!"

What happens is that from our knowledge of how things work, we sometimes see things which we feel to be most urgent and so we push for action. He from his background doesn't see anything except the white man pushing him to do something about which he sees no relevance at all. Then the missionary feels sorry about pushing and comes to apologize. The African thinks he is apologizing for the action, something about which the missionary hasn't the least intention of back-peddling on, and expects that the missionary will stop pursuing that particular course of action.

This then comes back to say that basically one has a right to speak by virtue of his age. Certainly the right to dissent comes only through age. Certainly the right to push a program comes only through superior age. The role of the youth is to fit as a tool into the program, or lack of it, of those older than he. If, by some miracle, the youth is asked to give counsel, it is by a miracle of trust for the moment and it is something about which the youth dare never deceive himself. The voice of youth when raised in dissent can be none other than the voice of the traitor. The voice of the youth which isn't raised at all must most certainly be subject to suspicion.

It's been hard for me to write this, brother, because it has cut pretty deeply into who I am, but I feel better having forced myself to say it aloud. Thanks for listening.

Remember that you once wrote about your living room furniture? It is the sort of thing which I spoke about on our way home from Kisaka in the jeep that last time. You can't get scared watery by lions, and I assume that you did envy us our trip to Serengeti? You can't slosh around in boots on a dim rainy night, hunting for hippos. You can't advise a Bishop on refresher courses, not that I can! You can't take trips to Mwanza. You can't sway dizzily from the top of a pile of furniture while you clean your office lampshades. So, when you get to feeling jealous, just snuggle a little farther down into the softness of your easy chair and enjoy it a bit more—for me. Enjoy the stimulation of a competitive, hard-working community at MCC, where the problem is keeping up rather than dragging others after—for me. Enjoy the artistic taste in the colors of your home, in the selection of really nice works of art, in the feel of your new car on the by-pass—for me. And when I get jealous then I shall lie in bed and enjoy the patter of rain on the *bati* roof—for you. Enjoy the riotous springing of life at the onset of the rains—for you. Enjoy the brilliance of the flamboyant, the flash of the tropical sunbirds, the wildness of this vast country, the mountains with their piled up boulders—for you. Enjoy the luxury of being able to drop out when I need to—for you. Okay?

We are working hard to get our college's acre of peanuts into the ground before we leave for the Christmas holidays. We are also hard at work down at the lake, expanding the garden there. I hope to have the new fence put in before going away. The sort of conflict one runs into on this thing is whether or not it is good stewardship for a man with an MA to put himself on the end of a *jembe* instead of on the end of a pen. Let me assure you that this digging with a hoe is about as hard work as making hay. There is a tremendous amount of energy expended for just a few cents worth of produce once it is all said and done. I ran across part of my answer later.

This morning the pastor and I strolled up to the Bishop's house after breakfast to give him good morning. We found a couple of other young men there and we stayed and talked for about an hour. In the course of the conversation we got to talking about the *shamba* of peanuts that the college was putting in and there was a great argument on how much it costs for oxen to plow one acre and how many acres can be plowed in a day. The conversation turned to the Domestic Science School plot of ground which until how is still just as it was because it is recess and there are no girls to get it and dig it up.

The Bishop said something like this: The young people in America ask me why Mrs. Wenger is going to Africa. Isn't she an old woman? they asked. Surely she can't work; why didn't you call for a young person? Now I see that truly she is just an old woman. All these rains and her entire plot still lies untouched. I see now that indeed she is an old woman. All this was said pleasantly and without bitterness; it was just the bald statement of an interesting fact.

The pastor felt just a bit uneasy about such an evaluation of overseas fraternal workers so he suggested that maybe the Bishop should suggest to her that she could get oxen to plow it up for her. "No," the Bishop said, "If I suggest something to her which she has not already got in her mind to do, she will just find arguments against it. Now maybe one of her own kind, like Joe here, could approach her about it and get her to have it dug up, but I can't." There ended the conversation. I did approach her this afternoon and the machinery is already in motion to have it dug up. After it is dug up is anybody's guess on what shall then be done with it.

What I learned is that we are primarily here to produce and to produce for the good of the African community which has called us. It makes us bitter sometimes when we see ourselves producing so very much more than our hosts, but they don't look at it that way. We must say like Jesus taught us, that we are unprofitable and unworthy servants. But there is a second thing here. I saw also that much of what we produce in this community is not evident to the community. I could have spent last week in the office finishing the science booklet, but all the community would have seen was my sitting on a chair. Instead, they saw me sweating under a huge basin of tomatoes perched on my head which I brought up from the college garden. They saw me sweating in the peanut *shamba* swinging a *jembe* alongside my students and the school cook. They saw me in muddy boots peddling tomatoes from door to door. Most of those who saw me gave me advice on how it was really to be done and what still needed doing. They also started saying things to me that they hadn't yet said. You find yourself discussing how much your back aches, how your finger and arms quickly become stiff after resting during a little rain squall, how it is that Joe keeps going during his cold when other Europeans would lie in bed, why Joe's children are so disrespectful of their father in terms of African culture, why Joe got to work so late this morning, etc., etc.!

I am coming to see that he who would be of service in the higher echelons of power must also be of service in the matter of hoeing. There is a measure of confidence developed that is hard to come by otherwise.

December 9, 1967

The other day I came into the house and heard a female voice in Swahili crooning in the kitchen. "My but you have lovely buttocks, lovely buttocks, my what lovely, lovely buttocks you have." I wondered what kind of show this was, and if someone was getting Esta (our house servant) prepared for marriage. So, I went about my business but arranged to slip into the kitchen just to see who was there. To my surprise there was huge Nyabweki (Aunt Miriam and Miss Yoder's cook) sitting on Dianne's rickety stool. Bouncing on her knees, facing me, was my daughter, Joyce!

The other day when I was greeting an elderly lady, I accidentally let fly a little gas, which made just a very small squeak. The old woman immediately laid her hand on my arm and with a sly grin in her eyes asked, "Did you make a stinker, pastor? Was that a stinker that you made? Wasn't that you?" When I admitted that indeed I had made a stinker (called *ku-nyampa*, in Swahili), she said, "That's the way to take care of them. If you hold them in (all said with appropriate gestures) then they just go back inside and get lost and then they go growly, growly, growly. So the best way to take care of them is to let them fly, let them fly! Yes, that's the best way to take care of them." We shook hands again, and I assured her that certainly that was the only possible way to deal with the problem. Rather red-faced I hurried off for the house as she continued her slow way up the hill.

I'm afraid that sometimes you will get the idea that I write to you my personal diary and that what I'm really doing is writing a diary and not really writing to you. Anyway, get that idea out of your head. I'm sorry if my letters sound diary-ish. What I really want to do is write to you. But sometimes the spirit is cold or dull and the words become a wooden chronicle. At other times the spirit blazes in warmth and brilliance and then I write a bit more like it is that I really want to write to you. Why do I write to you? Because you are the first that has ever listened to what I write.

The Bishop and I are as father and son these days. He has given me the green light on (1) a three-week refresher course for pastors, deacons and elders, (2) A refresher course for Meso's district, and (3) the purchase of fourteen bunk beds to accommodate the students attending the courses. He makes me feel so good that I get a headache!

We're on the lake boat, finally on our way, the first leg of our Christmas holidays. And I forgot my passport—again.

1968

January 4, 1968

Item: When we got home from vacation, the first news awaiting us was that Orondo has been fired as teacher here at the college. Actually it is sort of a gentleman's agreement that whereas Orondo is most admirably suited to farming and in-as-far as he is not particularly adept at teaching, the church feels that he could more fruitfully serve in the capacity of manager of the farm the youth have just started, rather than as tutor of theology. Apparently everyone including Orondo, is highly pleased with this new arrangement.

Item: Shake in with Bill Snyder (Omar's boss at MCC, Akron, PA). In the few jobs which I have been privileged to undertake and the situations I have worked in, I have sort of come to believe that what is going on is superficial until one has shaken-in to the point where one is aware of the places where his personality is going to touch his surroundings. I am sure that it is needless for me to make so trite an observation for you. But it was none-the-less interesting for me to see how you are beginning to find your borders in relation to those others with whom you are working. You threw in a comment about being like me, in that you think that both of us are "usually too eager to please others." The other month I sat in on a lecture at the Catholic complex in Musoma on Christian Psychology. About the only thing I remember was that the professor made the point that psychologists are beginning to see that the man who is super-conscientious and the man who has no moral scruples whatsoever are twins—simply opposite sides of the same coin. Doesn't one who knows that he is too eager to ingratiate himself to others find his balance by trying to hard to define himself in relation to his associates? Sometimes when I feel terribly guilty about making my opinion felt or making my will mold others, then I tell myself that I must learn to be callused to these guilt feelings so that I do grow into a "man and not a mouse," to use Jack Shellard's phraseology. Anyway, thanks for all the inside finagling at MCC. One last thing on the above is that it seems to me that after a while one begins to know what it is that he wants others to know—speaking in terms of teaching or information services. At first one does not know what others know and what they don't know, nor what they feel strongly about what they don't. After finding out how they are in relation to how you are, you then can begin to rub them effectively—that is, effectively in terms of what you think and feel and have strong opinions on.

Item: Your failure to maintain bargain. It seems to me that somewhere in the dim distant past we agreed that I was to keep you abreast of what is going on from this end of the eye glass and you were to keep me abreast of what is going on at your end of the eye glass. The other day I got a letter from my big brother I suddenly realized just how much you have been letting me down. Omar, I admire you and love you, and I am most grateful for the time you take to write and the stimulus you have been to my development. Please take me seriously.

Item: Today I worked on the *piki* for half the day and got it to tip-top shape again. It now has on shock absorbers for a 350cc cycle (mine is a 250cc). This means that we can now go anywhere with loads on the back and we won't have any trouble hitting bottom. The only trouble is that you aren't here to ride along on the back.

Item: Christmas. Thank you very much for your generous Shs 70/= (US $10) Christmas gift. Let's say that we spent it for the most pleasurable part of our holiday. On the way to Mombasa we stopped at an inn at the halfway point of Mtito Ndei. The four of us (one spouse, two children) got a delicious dinner for Shs 36/=. It was fun to splurge and Edith particularly enjoyed it. The entrance fee to the game park was Shs 22/=. (Incidentally, the Kenyans have now followed Tanzania's lead and have put up their rates for game parks for non-Kenya residents. We were in the park on Dec. 31, so we still got the old rates. The next day the price is Shs 60/=! Also, it now costs Shs 55/= for two people to drive in at Nakuru to see the flamingos. Aren't you glad that we did it that cold morning, just about a year ago?) One afternoon while in Nairobi, I took the girls to see "The Sound of Music," which cost Shs 10/=. There was just the cutest bright little girl at one of the cold, dusky railway stops, who was selling onions. She was so vivacious that I gave her 50 cents. The rest of the change we spent on ice cream while in Nairobi. Thanks again for the gift.

January 7, 1968

You'll remember the trouble Edith had about a year ago, and the little baby we lost. This year her condition was just about like last year. To our great dismay she began to lose blood, again at Nakuru on our way up to Nairobi. It looked as though she was going to have a miscarriage. Fortunately, things weren't too bad and we got to Nairobi, where she went to bed. She stayed there for a whole week, which for her was quite a bad way to start off our vacation. But her condition cleared up and the doctor gave his okay for her to go on to Mombasa. We had planned to go by bus, but we didn't mention that to the doctor; instead we told him that we would go by car. Elizabeth Hostetter let us rent her *Roho*, and we had a grand, wonderful time going down to the coast.

The place we stayed in Mombasa was about twenty miles south of the ferry, a place called Mizpah, where there are three houses for rent. The houses were simply a number of walls enclosing cement floors with a big roof thrown over the works. The place is about two miles from the Two Fishes where you stayed last August. The ocean is just out in front of our door. In the evenings there was always a breeze, so we never suffered from the heat. We quickly all turned a nice roasted brown. Especially the girls, who got a beautiful tan.

Sometimes at night we went out to the water to see the crabs. There were just hundreds and hundreds of big white ones all along the water's edge. The first night Dianne saw them floating along the wave-washed sand like leaves scuttling before an autumn wind, she went a bit crazy and rushed screaming after them. Unfortunately she stood on one and then she indeed went a bit crazy. The poor crab was most offended and a bit broken up, so we had to dispatch him. At night you could also see a lot of hermit crabs ponderously dragging their houses after them, so very much in contrast to the floating crusts of white that swayed and darted here and there under our spot of flashlight.

For Christmas we got a few greens from one of the many evergreens around the place. We hung some from a spot in the ceiling, which made it look sort of like a tree. We fixed up one corner of the cabin, under the hanging bough, with candles and pinecones and gifts. We ate with candlelight Christmas evening and most of the evenings after that until we left for home. Edith got some fiberglass trays with beautiful pictures on them, so if she is ever sick in bed again she can have nice trays for her meals. I got a new belt. The girls each got Koala bears. The Koala is a bear in Australia that eats gum tree leaves. These toy bears are made out of genuine kangaroo and wallaby skins. The girls also gave me a yellow balloon and a toy car! I blew up the balloon for the trip home but it floated out a window and burst before we could get it! We tried to teach the girls what Christmas is about and why we give gifts to each other. I hope that next year we can stay home for Christmas.

En route back to Nairobi, an elephant happened to cross the road about twenty feet in front of the car. I stopped the car and turned off the motor. Then a second elephant's grazing path was squarely obstructed by our car. He caught on to what we were about so he moved up the road to where his companion had crossed. But fear got the better of him half way across the road. He shook himself all over and made fierce trumpeting noises, flapped his ears, shook his trunk, and sort of pranced sideways, and then lumbered off to safety on the other side of the road. I don't know how he felt, but it made little trickles of shivers race around my heart and up and down my spine. I'm afraid that I even lost my cool as well because I quickly turned the motor on and prepared to back away as fast as I could. Later I discovered that a Peugeot was parked right behind us, enjoying the little fracas.

When you pray for us at TMC (Tanzania Mennonite Church) keep in mind that we are having rising tensions between the young men just back from training in the States and the old men who control the church. The old men are eager to have the youth work for them, but they are not interested in having the youth make off with their authority. Right now, the old men, which incidentally are the "in" group some of which aren't much older than me, as compared to the "out" group, some of which are older than me, are a bit afraid of the youth and we have to walk carefully to retain or rebuild their confidence. It's my hope that this refresher course for pastors will be an opportunity for me to build some bridges, by God's grace. I'm sure that some of the pastors consider it a good opportunity to get a good look at me, this youngster!

January 10, 1968

This story is too good not to share. Miss Yoder declared war on an old turtle which got into her garden three times in six months, each time leaving a hole in the fence.

It was a Sunday noon that she found the turtle for the third time in her garden. He was a big boy, as these turtles go, being over a foot long and about eight inches high. Having decided to execute him, Miss Yoder now had to devise a way to do so. She thought this over and finally decided to kill by boiling. So she went into her kitchen and heated a kettle of water to boiling, which she took out to the garden and proceeded to pour into him through the cracks between his legs. Unfortunately she got the wrong end, and so after warming his tail she turned him over and warmed his brain. All this did no good, but she had anticipated this and had brought a bottle of kerosene which she then poured into his head end. This too didn't seem to kill him.

Having survived the ordeal by water and kerosene, the turtle was next subjected to ordeal by the sword. Miss Yoder had a new sharp *panga* which she proceeded to try to ram into him from both front and behind, even to the extent of trying to pound the *panga* into both ends, but all to no avail. Having been conquered to put him to the sword, she decided to lay him on his back and wait for him to stick out his head. But he apparently didn't feel inclined to do on Sunday. As I have got the story, he lay on his back all Sunday afternoon, Sunday night, all day Monday, Monday night, all day Tuesday. It was on Tuesday that it seemed that he might have got sufficiently adjusted to the idea of dying as to put out his neck far enough to get a good hold on it while his head was cut off. Miss Yoder called Faraja for the operation. They planned their strategy very carefully. When the head would get out the full way, straining in typical turtle fashion to get turned over on its feet, then Faraja was to pinch the head down with an old *panga*, after which he was to saw through the neck with his new sharp *panga*. Poor Faraja muffed his chance, as he took one violent swing at the head before it even got properly extended. All he did was cut a gash in the shell, which Miss Yoder wanted to keep. Of course, after that close call, Mr. Turtle wasn't going to stick out his head for the rest of the day. Miss Yoder asked Faraja to come back that evening because she thought Mr. Turtle would have his head out at night.

Faraja forgot to come Tuesday night. By mid-morning on Wednesday the turtle was sort of far-gone and he had his head lolling out as far as it would go. Miss Yoder was then able to pin the head out of the shell with her old *panga* while she severed the neck with her new *panga*. She said that it didn't cut too hard, except for the enormous windpipe.

Miss Yoder next put about four inches of water in her washing tub and put both turtle and head into the tub so that the flies could not get at him until she got to consult biology teacher Ernie at the secondary school on how best to get the turtle out of his house so that she could use the shell for a souvenir to send to one of her brothers-in-law. It was at this point that I saw the poor beast, and Aunt Miriam assured me that he was to be boiled for soup for supper. Miss Yoder by this time was considering him an old friend and she explained all that had come to pass between them. It reminded me of a time in college when they had some turtles in the biology lab and one of their heads somehow got up into the dormitory. Remember Johnny Fisher? Anyway, the turtle head got into his bed and it drove him almost insane because he felt that it looked like a cut off penis. It also reminded me of the time I ate some gold fish in college, which everyone thought was nuts, and I couldn't figure out what wrong. Miss Yoder seemed to feel nothing wrong with relating the whole affair to anyone who would listen.

January 16, 1968

A note from the executive committee: A number of recent weddings have taken place when the bride was in a state of beginning to become "heavy," it has been decided that hereafter no pastor is to marry anyone who does not have a signed, filled-out form from a doctor who has examined both parties to determine that there is no "heaviness" or sickness present. The Bishop and secretary are to sit down and make out the forms, but until the forms are ready for distribution to the pastors, the examinations are to take place anyway. (Search me what happens if "heaviness" is found to be present.)

This all reminds me when dear old Brother Shertzer at Millersville (PA) church would begin crying over the pulpit about pajamas or bandanas or something, and we'd all sit up to see how bad it would be this time!

The whole business makes me tired, partly because I know that I can't do anything about anything. The youth are forever in huddles, and I forever avoid them. The old men are forever in huddles, and they avoid me. I personally feel that both have some amazing blind spots, but I'm tired of touching them because of the blind rage that it produces. Certainly blind rage does no good, so why touch the blind spots? It reminds me of what happened when some *Newsweek* writer said something in his paper to the effect that the US might as well take over the administration of South Vietnam, since all the money and know-how comes from the US anyway. A Saigon paper remarked, "What right do these Vietnamese have to expect full sovereignty, while depending on US support?" One Saigon paper ran a poem accusing the American writer of every known vice, concluding with, "You S.O.B., a curse on you and your father and your mother and all your family and all your ancestors!"

Blind spots aside, it is increasingly clear to me that in the Bantu world, the youth is honored for his strength, and the elder is honored for his wisdom. If you have got that thought firmly in your brain then you will know how the cookie will crumble in TMC affairs. Any youth who presumes to spout wisdom instead of strength—physical strength to dig *shambas* and to walk to youth meetings—is going to be in great, great trouble with the elders. The youth's wisdom is exceeded only by the wisdom of the Old Men. Let the young men of the church beware of trying to peddle wisdom!

January 18, 1968

This evening I had offered to take the Old Men down to see the college garden. I thought we would walk, but they complained of carrying their great tummies all that way. So I got Dad's jeep and sure enough thirteen of them, plus the Bishop, plus me, got into it. I made the terrible mistake of driving out the bottom lane near the print shop. When I got back, Mr. Shenk asked, "Did you go out the bottom lane?" "Yes." "I would never go out the bottom lane with a load like that." Anyway, I felt about 16 years old. The Old Men had some wisdom for me down at the garden, including the fact that the sweet potatoes needed weeding, the carrots needed a shelter, the tomatoes didn't need watering, the cabbages had died (only some of them!), and the fence still wasn't good enough to keep out cattle and goats, and there was great emphasis on the fact that 30 new banana shoots are all at the wrong end of the garden. They must be uprooted and planted where the sweet potatoes are, and the sweet potatoes are to be planted where the bananas are. Spraying isn't necessary in dry weather. (I learned this: if the Old Men can't advise the young on how to farm, it indicates that their wisdom isn't worth much!)

January 21, 1968

They say that masculine hormones run the strongest in the morning, which is what gives man his great morning energy to get out of bed and do things. Sometimes my hormones seem not to flow at all for days at a time, but for the last couples of days, they seem to be flowing only in the evenings. Like tonight; I want to do something, but haven't anything to do except read serious books and somehow I don't feel like reading serious books just now. Incidentally, I have started reading that little Bonhoeffer book (*Life Together*) which you sent. I've found it rather hard going, partly because it is a translation and partly because I was reading it after the 11:00 p.m. BBC broadcast. You mentioned his chapter on "Confession" and I did find it more interesting than some other chapters. I'll report further when I've read the book properly.

The bitterness I expressed throughout my last letter and even in the previous one was an isolated bitterness felt by one person in the gut where he lives. I am sure the Bishop has no idea at all how deeply he affects me. He feels no bitterness towards me and frankly I feel none towards him, except in occasional dull low spots. If you will tolerate another quote from Jacobs, one of the TAP teachers told me that Jacobs said of student discipline that the important thing in Bantu culture is to not let the relationship deteriorate. The fundamental position from which we interact with these people must be one of friendly relationship tempered by our position in the pecking order. The Bishop is my father and I am his son. This is a fundamental relationship, which must never be violated. If I try to push him around, then I am no longer his son, and the situation falls apart. This is what happened some months ago. He as my father can ask of me almost anything, and I must quickly rearrange my personal situation to fit into his requests. He can then ask me to close school on the spur of the moment, and I have no option but to do so. His is to ask me to do for him and in this he acknowledges my relationship of son to him. Mine is to do for him above the call of duty, and in this acknowledge his relationship of father to me.

So when I write of my set backs by the Bishop, they are not matters of relationships and so are really superficial. What particularly drained the blood from my face this last week when we were talking together was that I could see that he thought I was going ahead with plans which he had expressly forbade earlier and had warned me that missionaries ask forgiveness but try to get their plans through anyway. After twenty minutes of talk, however, he came to see that I in no way shape or form was about to violate what he had told me not to do (i.e., run three-month Bible School courses for young people). Since our recent problem had nothing to do with our fundamental relationship, it was and is for all practical purposes superficial.

The Westerner or even the young educated African suffers from this sort of thing because he sees that program is not moving ahead, that for the lack of vision, we are not moving ahead. This is what frustrates, not that the Bishop got mad at someone or something. I have never seen him angry. I know that my immediate, firm decision to scratch the short course, as soon as I fully realized that he was not with me, strengthened greatly the position of son to him which I was beginning to feel. He immediately trusted me about twenty per cent more and almost at once tried to give me as much green light as he could, without going totally back on his word about not having anything to do with it. In essence, he said that he would not stand in my way in any attempts which I may have to help the pastors. My continued refusal to have anything to do with something which did not enjoy the church's full and solid backing made him feel even better, and we seem much closer ever since. If he realized how deeply I felt about it, I don't know. He did say that maybe I have eyes to see something which he didn't!

So then, my frustration is not one of relationships with my employers. If I have read the signs rightly there is a growing depth of respect and confidence on both sides. It is rather that I see that new ideas take hold slowly and intricately coordinated situations are hard to understand. Igira told me the other day that the African mind cannot comprehend categories more complicated than "full" and "half." He said that a quarter, half, or four-fifths—all are "half" to the uneducated African mind. This means that Paul Kraybill will be faced with perpetual frustration as he tries to implement new projects here. I could see in Dar es Salaam last February, when the Mission Board had that meeting there, that Paul was seeing bright new opportunities opening up for them to take initiative in new projects through the placement on each field of a man who would represent the Board's interests.

Two incidences lead me to suspect the ability of the present hierarchy to cope. One was when we were at Alliance Secondary and the town pastor was breathing down our necks to pay our tithe to him. I came over here to see Meso, then the treasurer, about it. I wanted to know how we could give without swamping any particular church's budget. He said that we must wait until Jacobs came back from some trip. When Jacobs came back I approached him about it in Meso's presence. Jacobs at once carried the issue away and said that they would figure out something. They never did, but the significant thing for me was that Jacobs acted as though Meso, the treasurer, did not exist, during our discussion. I was surprised but suspected it was because through long experience Jacobs had come to know that the matter was too complicated for Meso and so he made no pretense at trying to get his ideas. The other situation was when I tried to get the electricity payments on a non-racial basis right after we moved here to the college. I told Jacobs about my attempts and the scale of rates I had drawn up as a suggestion. He laughed and said that it was okay. "If you can get them to understand it." He didn't say it cynically, like Shellard would. It was merely an expression of fact as he had come to know it. At once I thought, "Well, if they can't understand that, then pray tell what can they understand?"

The Christmas party was on this wise: Before leaving for Mombasa, we personally shelled out Shs 30/= to buy a goat for a feast for the students who remained during holidays. But the students would not consider having the party in our absence. Finally decided on the evening of January 6.

That morning the goat was brought from the village where he was being fed. He was a beautiful shiny black specimen with an appropriately sized goatee. He smelled as any self-respecting young gentleman goat should smell. He was a gentleman to the end and took everything very well, giving vent to frightened squeals only upon feeling the knife. Nobody wanted to slit his throat. But finally Clifford stepped forward.

Each family had been assigned four pounds of rice which was to be cooked at the pastor's house. Each of the African families was to bring three mounds of *ugali*. We were to bring ten pounds of wheat flour to be turned into *mandazies*. Jackson was to bring tea; Zebedayo the milk. We went together on getting the sugar.

It was decided to cook the meat in two pots, one for "outside meat" which was any muscle meat, the red meat, the testicles and penis. There was a great argument about the penis, with Jackson declaring that none of the women would eat the meat if they knew that it had been included; Clifford assured him that he had often cooked it with the rest of the meat and his wife only laughed. So, in it went. Clifford also wanted badly to cook the head with the "outside meat." He declared that the only way to make a good pot of meat was to cut off the lower jaw, split the skull (throw away the brains) so that it lay open between the eyes.

The "inside meat" was to go in the other pot. This included the kidney, the heart, the lungs, the pancreas, the liver, and all the intestines and assorted stomachs. The intestines were emptied by drawing them between closed fingers. They were then washed on the outside and braided into long braids. The rest of the stomach was scraped and washed and cut into little pieces.

Towards evening we carried chairs and tables down to the pastor's house. (His full name is The Reverend Nashon Nyamwino Mashaga Nyambalya!) We fixed them so that the adults could sit at two tables while all the children sat at a third. Everything moved smoothly. The total number present was around thirty-five. We ate *ugali* and meat and then we ate rice and meat and then we drank tea and ate *mandazies* until everyone one was full. Then there were some songs and scripture. But then it was dusk and a full moon was rising in a clear sky out back of Bugoshi. By way of firsts, I think this was the first time this station had a pot luck meal conceived and executed interracially. All previous interracial doings here have been affairs in which the church paid for the spread and everyone of any account was simply invited to eat.

February 6, 1968

On Monday night there was a riot at Alliance Secondary. The hubbub started in the mess hall just at supper time and the Headmaster with the East German teacher went down to see what was up. It had to do with food. The boys wanted *simbe* flour in their *ugali* instead of *dona*. (*Simbe* is husked maize, while *dona* is whole-grain maize.) Students got to standing on tables and pandemonium broke out. The Headmaster decided to get out of there and hurried back to his house with cries of, "Kill the Headmaster; he's a tight-fisted Scrooge!" He got his wife and son into their car and took off for town.

The students then turned off the lights of the faculty houses, leaving their own lights on, and they started howling toward staff houses. Mrs. Hess, telling about it three days later, said it sounded like animals. Maynard's house was a bit off the beaten track and he went over to the staff room, or at least started to, when rocks began to whiz past his head. So he beat a hasty trot back to his house. There were loud cries for admittance at the HM's house and when the boys discovered that he wasn't home, they pitched rocks through windows and tore down his banana and pawpaw trees. They pitched rocks through the roof of the library and did other damage, mounting to some Shs 400/=, which included spilling two bags of peanuts and flour all over the ground.

Finally, at about 9:30 police Land-Rovers came careening onto campus and there was a roll call, at which 25 boys were missing. The police took ten boys to the paddy for the night. Three of these were little first-year students, which shows how well the selection was made. Later three students were expelled, one of which was Boniface, whose father arrived on campus at noon on Tuesday, before the boy was even out of jail, to plead for his son. It continued impossible to teach, due to the uproar in the classes, for two more days. Finally, *simbe* flour was substituted for *dona*. It's reported that on Tuesday some students came around to the HM's house with camera to photograph the damage they'd done. Mrs. Lukindo chased them off with shouts of "Animals!"

My parents went to Mwanza on Monday. Down there they found one of my theological college students advocating clitorectomy in his district which caused the leaders to look askance upon him. He assured my mother that he was coming back to school, but he hasn't shown up; I heard from someone else that he has work in Mwanza. I truly don't expect to either hear from or see him.

Last week we elected a vice-captain for the school, as the former has gone back to teaching and the security which that gives him. We had to discuss for nearly a half-hour whether or not we wanted a vice-captain. Finally it was agreed. The obvious choice was named, but the class continues nominating until four names stood on the chalkboard, ready to do battle. Among the four was Mete. The school captain nominated him by saying, "As it appears that this work is not very demanding, I nominate . . . ." It was a slur on Mete, as everyone knows that he is great in talking about work but he is just absent when the actual work needs to be done. But the fantastic thing is that Mete got four votes on the first ballot. We had to re-vote because the total came to one more vote than we had voters. On the second vote, Mete still got two votes. Dear chap was a different young man for a few days. He suddenly started speaking with authority. All around him, confidence, poise, and self-assurance swirled like a cloud. The students in private joked, amazed at the vote Mete polled. We had many a chuckle over it.

Is the church here being inspired by examples coming out of Dar? Actually, I don't think that President Nyerere is trying to run the country on consensus. He's a sort of Jacobs, smart enough to keep a jump ahead of things. Nyerere is calling the punches and setting the pace, but he is doing it in a way which makes the whole country feel that they are part of it. Even so, the present church leadership does not have a sufficient grasp of the new day in the nation to take effective leadership. This is the whole trouble with the bishop and me. If I get creative, I get into water over his head. His alternative to brushing me off is to let me run part of the show. To do this is to cease being independent and so is not really possible. You cannot brother between two people who don't have a common grasp of what is going on. You're making me say things that don't sound nice. But to say them anyway, it is that if the bishop and I brother then in some things I will lead. For him to allow me to lead means that he has absolute confidence in me because he must let me do some things which he doesn't understand. With the world the way it is and people the way they are, I can't see that the bishop will ever have anywhere near complete trust in me.

What does Christ have to say to our being brothers? I have come more and more to see this thing as not so much being brothers as being forgivers. We live in a perpetual state of being forgiven and of in return, forgiving. To be a brother does not mean that each has his say. Rather, it means that each forgives the other for not being what he should be. I forgive the bishop for intruding into my domain as principal and for not being a good father to me. He in turn forgives me for being hesitant in some cases in following the role of obedient son. He forgives me for not visiting him every day. He forgives me for being impatient with the older leadership. They forgive me for not knowing all the sacred cows that have brought us to this place. And so, we live as brothers, forgiving 70 times 7. To forgive and to be forgiven seems to me to be the essence of brotherhood.

Today as I sat in my office I suddenly noticed a strange young woman walking across the campus. She was really an eye-stopper, in a stunning bright green dress, and a European. I had to sigh, in that I am married and so could not dash off to see just who she was and from where she had come. Imagine my surprise when I found her pouring tea at tea-time. It was none other than my wife in a borrowed maternity shift!

February 13, 1968

Last night at about one o'clock, Edith woke up and thought she had heard a gunshot blast. In a few minutes a husky whisper was calling "*hodi*." It was Robart; he reported that Nyarere, the church treasurer, had been attacked in his house, that he was being forced to open the church safe. This is how the story pieces itself together.

At about one, men tried to stave in Nyarere's front door, just as they'd done about a month ago. He grabbed his shotgun loaded with six shells. They couldn't get the door to stave in—Daddy had repaired it—so they ran around the house to the back door. And just as Nyarere was opening a window to get a crack at their legs, they burst in on him. A scuffle followed in which they got his gun away from him as well as his flashlight. He claims that they battled for a half-hour in the house. I doubt if it was that long, as there were three or four against one. But blood in most of the rooms testifies to the fact that he did put up quite a resistance. He got his head cracked open, which required stitches.

Eventually they subdued him and offered him the alternative between being murdered or opening the safe. He agreed to open the safe, so they tied a rope to one arm and with their shotgun in his ribs, marched him up to the church offices. By this time the whole station was getting awake, but the robbers fired warning shots in the direction of anyone who tried to come near. The surprising thing was that through it all there was no yelling, which seems almost inexcusable. The first to discover what was up should have yelled, but Robart says that he was afraid that they'd kill Nyarere if people began to shout. Indeed, that quite likely would have happened. George, got into his car and drove down to Nyarere's house, but when he got there he found that they had all left. When Daddy got up he got in his car and drove down past the dining hall and out the drive to the print shop. I was up by then, and could hear men shouting to shoot Daddy as he drove by them. Mother was standing in her doorway, shouting to me to turn on the station lights, little knowing the thieves were shouting for Daddy to be shot and that the office was already full of thieves. I stood behind the tree and saw the men start up from the office past the garage past Dorothy in her voluminous nightgown standing on her porch shining her flashlight at them. They called for her to be shot too, but nothing happened. I was relieved to hear Nyarere's near hysterical, high-pitched jabbering—knew that everyone was safe.

We then went to town, and the police came out and wouldn't go near the office until I cranked up the generator for light. Samuel doctored Nyarere and Mother made him coffee. By five it was pouring rain and it was time for us to go to bed again. Nyarere was in hospital today and got checked over. He got his head sewed up and got his muscles pronounced "torn," but there were no broken bones and apparently no internal injuries.

The thieves took between five and six thousand shillings, one signed check, along with two checkbooks. They missed another two thousand!

Today was pronounced a day of quiet and we all acted sort of like someone had been killed, except that we were all very grateful. Students were sent to the various church districts to notify all the church pastors of the event.

March 4, 1968

Here at the college we introduce theology by taking a year to examine the Bantu traditional religions. After we've understood their theology, we then try to mate this to Christian theology. At least we try to use the Bantu concepts as points for showing similarities and irreconcilables. It seems to me that most of the students and many other Christians feel that their revelation in Bantu faith was something that filtered to them from Adam and the first prophets. They say, "We have had all of Moses. It's the Savior about whom we've not heard." The mainline Protestants do not try to wrest scripture to fit into African forms. At least I haven't seen Mennonites doing this consciously. But the Roman Catholics have had a history, at least in some places of trying to Christianize just as much as they can. RC bishops got into trouble on this score in South Africa a century ago and in China two or three centuries ago. The RCs of course can quite easily Christianize the idea of ancestor worship, which is the heart of Bantu religion. Some Anglican churches in southern Tanzania have tried to Christianize the traditional circumcision ceremony in an attempt to make it a sort of confirmation into the church.

The things which I find hardest to get across here in the college are (1) the concept of free choice, and (2) the divinity of Christ. It is practically impossible for a Bantu not to take a fatalistic view of God and his dealings with man. It is both a Bantu concept and it is furthermore thoroughly Muslim. A bus runs off the road and several people get killed. This was certainly the direct hand of God, something impossible to have been avoided. A Bantu is sure that Judas was forced by God to betray Jesus, and he is also sure that Peter was forced by Jesus to deny him. I also find that when you get beyond pious platitudes, my students have grave doubts about Jesus having been God. They think that he was God's son, but he was fully man. He was a perfect man, to be sure, but he was not God. We have had such a thorough discussion of that subject that this evening the school captain asked me to ask you how you would answer one who does not think that Jesus was God. (He came in while I was reading your letter. He was stunned at its length, and I told him that we discuss theological issues. He wanted me at once to present the problem before you, and I promised him that I would. How would you answer your most trustworthy student if he had doubts about Jesus being God?!)

Let me pose one of my theological questions about the church. Our various questions certainly are colored by where we live and by who we are. My question has to do with church-building in a pagan society.

May it not be that the concept of the liberty and freedom one has in Christ through faith in what he did on Calvary is rather a sophisticated concept which finds true meaning only in a situation where the law is a potent force in the religious community? I am asking if the freedom one has in Christ does indeed have much to say to a person who knows nothing of religious disciplines. Can you build a church by preaching salvation?

It seems that the missionaries were so overwhelmed with the sense of freedom, which they discovered in Christ, that this became the heart of their message. In fact, that was about all that got preached. It even became the core of the Bible School instruction. Leatherman especially had nothing anymore to do with structures. But can you build a church this way? It seems to me that if you do, then your church will fade into the bush and emerge again from the bush pretty much as the wind of popular feeling seems to be at any particular time blowing. Certainly at no time will you have a strong structure. To have a strong structure, I think that you must have all ages represented and whole family units represented. Further, you must have large numbers making up sizable chunks of the local population. If you don't have people, you can't support your leaders, and the whole thing remains a foreign affair. Further, if you don't have people, then it is very hard to bring to bear the sanctions necessary for Christian conduct to be maintained.

Maybe then the Catholics have a point, when they work toward absorbing a sizable chunk of the population by any means and then working to slowly make these people more Christian. Maybe what the church should be concerned about is simply building a structure in which faith may be found. They could then leave God to the business of saving those whom He would. I am sure that the revival fellowship would collapse in short order if there were no denominational structures to give it support.

Right now TMC is in the poor position of fading back into the bush faster than we can baptize new members. Our pastors are preaching that we have had enough of religion. We don't need Mennonitism or Islam or Catholicism. What we need is to be saved. We are not saved by works but by FAITH. Therefore, we have a generation of youth who feel that all they need is faith. It comes as a sort of shock to them when you ask them what faith is. They don't even think that you need to believe anything to have faith.

Should we not have set about establishing a list of things that we must do in order to be "saved" or at least to gain merit? Every Christian gains merit by buying a Bible. He gains merit by faithful attendance on Sunday. He does not work on Sunday. He gains through Bible memorizing. He gains great merit through giving. Etc. We should have preached what Christians must do to find favor in God's eye rather than what he should not do. It is noteworthy that the Israelite's introduction to God was the harsh discipline they experienced under Moses. It was only in the light of this harsh discipline that the message of grace could have any meaning. Even Isaiah already had some beautiful passages relating to God's love and grace. Jesus is, of course, the fulfillment of man's longing for grace, and for a reconciliation to God wrought through a resting faith and not through a striving action. The question comes back to ask: can Jesus be understood by people who have never had the discipline of the law?

These people have had the discipline of the law but it was the tribal law. Maybe the Christian church could have built on the message of freedom in Christ from the tribal law, and if they would have discussed this with the tribal elders for years—having firstly thoroughly understood the African law—then maybe it would have been possible for them to have led their people into the new found freedom in Christ. But to base our message of freedom to them on something that WE have experienced from OUR background seems to be trying to do something that they won't understand.

Now no one likes to be a Moses and me one of the least, but I am just thinking that if freedom could not be preached through the eyes of the tribal religion then just possibly we should have been Moseses, cracked the old religion, molded the tribe into Christian forms, and then preached salvation by faith.

I have done some more thinking on this during my long motorcycle ride to Nairobi and back, and I must admit that all Christian thinking goes against what I've said. I still ask if the eggheads would make good church builders or not.

March 29, 1968

I'm reading Michener's *Hawaii*. I find him to be full of wind, and therefore not at all pungent like Van der Post, for example. He covers tremendous ground and puts in all the imaginable occurrences. His structures when read out of context are awfully flat. But he does tell a good story and gives a superficial picture of how it was and is. His characters are not very well developed, with the exception of his missionary, and it is for the sake of this missionary that I would like you to read the book. Michener is able to change tone with this man so that at times he is the very picture of the benighted, egotistical, foppish, ethnocentric, civilized missionary in his stinking woolen underwear. At other times he is a prince whose character is true blue, who by the dint of his blind convictions is able to change a whole people's way of life. I don't know if Michener is doing it consciously or not, but in effect, he is saying that you cannot evangelize with "nice" people. It seems to be the awfullest people who in the end leave the greatest legacy. I think we need missionaries with the message of reconciliation and brotherhood in their hearts, but I am increasingly suspicious that they do not build churches.

I overheard this conversation. Missionary: "Kishamuli, forgive me, please, for having become angry with you over the matter of the truck. It was not right for me to become sharp about it." Kishimuli: "I forgive you for becoming sharp with me about the truck. I, too, felt like being sharp with you when you were angry with me, but I remembered who God is and so I thought that I'd better just keep quiet." Missionary: "Thank you; it was not good of me to become angry." Kishamuli: "I forgive you because when I remembered who God is I just kept my mouth shut."

Another one: Female missionary: "I have to repent very much for having become terribly angry with my sister over something yesterday. I have repented and asked her forgiveness and the Lord has given me complete freedom and liberty over the matter." Ludia: "I have forgiven my sister. When she became angry with me I felt like becoming angry too, but then I remember that this is just the nature of my sister to get angry like this, so I should not take it too much to heart." An amazing thing I have seen in Africans is that they seldom refuse a confession. They usually admit that the confessor truly needs to confess, and they may make it even more than the confessor even intended making it but then in spite of all this they will forgive one.

You asked what I said when I preached about Joseph being forgotten by Pharaoh. I started with the idea that an African's concept of life after death is strongly tied up with how he is remembered. The living can kill him simply by forgetting him and no longer giving him offerings. He doesn't actually die, but his effectiveness ceases. The dead will, therefore, become angry with those who forget to bring offerings and prayers to his grave. It is through these that he remains strong. A man while living will do all in his power to ensure that he is remembered for the longest possible time after he has died because in this way he can keep on living even after death. He must leave behind sons because these are they who do the sacrifices. He should be rich and have a lot of wives.

What I tried to do was to take this traditional African worldview and put into it Christian meaning. I thought that in Joseph I saw a perfect picture of the deceased Bantu patriarch. Joseph had influence and power and after he died this power continued to hover protectively over the Hebrew people just as the Bantu grandfather hovers over those of his family who continue to remember him. After Joseph was forgotten then we find that that protection his memory provided has disappeared. Therefore, the verse that reads: "There arose in Egypt a Pharaoh who knew not Joseph."

So people want to be remembered and in so wanting they devise laws to try to ensure that they will be remembered. The Bantu makes his laws and he then produces a curse as a binder for this law. The old man before death will call together his sons and tell them his dying wishes and this will be sealed with the promise of cursing if they fail to carry out his directives. What he is doing appears selfish because it is directed towards himself, but in it there is a primitive wisdom that even today is still the wisest of wisdom. He in effect tells the young men that their lives will have meaning only within the context of their obedience to him. Let them waver from that obedience and his curse awaits them. If you scratch this you see that under its selfish-looking skin is the profound observation that no person finds meaning until his life is oriented around some other person—or for us it may be some other physical thing such as our work or education. The old man is telling his boys that their lives will be cursed if they dedicate them to their own pleasures. Their lives will be blessed if they lose their personal goals and ambitions in those of another.

This old man doesn't really think that he alone is the selfish recipient of his sons' homage and devotion. He thinks in terms of the tribe and his dying directives are such that will bring good, as he sees it, to the family and also to the tribe. The laws he makes, and in fact, those laws followed by the tribe in general, are devised to form a brotherhood or "family of the faithful" firstly within the old man's own village, secondly, within his clan, and thirdly, within his tribe. Any outside this tribe is not under the protective banners of the old one's directives.

The old man knows with the keen perception of the dying that his sons will not dedicate themselves to the welfare of the family. He can see lurking within them that individuality, that appetite for their own exultation, that passion to break the yoke from off their necks—in short, that thing which if carried to its ultimate conclusion will destroy the very things which gave them birth in the first place. He sees them straying from the way of life to the way of death. He wants to prevent this so he erects a wall and that wall is his curse. This sounds like the Old Testament where the law and the curse were the wall that bound the people of God to that discipline which would give them significance. Without that very severe discipline they would never have been able to be God's instrument for the bringing of blessing to all of us. Without that discipline they would have died as an entity long ago.

The New Testament tells us about a power that takes the place of that wall of law and curse. It is power found through blood. It is called grace and its marks are love. This new message comes to the old dying man and tells him that his rules and his curses really weren't able to keep his young men faithful, and even if they were able, it was a faithfulness born of fear and not of love. It tells him that in this new way there is a power that can make his young men faithful through love. It tells him that if his sons have found this new way then he can die in peace, knowing that they will submit their personal ambitions to the good of the clan, to the good of which gave them life in the first place, or we may say to the good of the mother.

If the old man has eyes to see it, he also realizes that the new way is far more encompassing than the old one. He used to think in terms of the good of his immediate family, of his clan, and of his tribe. He now finds that this new way makes all of mankind his brother. The laws he handed down to his sons, which governed their relationship to the community now, apply to the world community of every tongue and tribe and nation.

The Christian comes to this with a new twist. He finds that God is the mother in the ultimate sense, but He is the mother who has birthed that which has birthed the Christian. The Christian therefore has the same commitment to his family (extended to include the world brotherhood but specifically the physical family and the church) that the old man has to his. But the Christian has a further commitment, which is to the ultimate mother. These too at times cause a conflict and where they do conflict, the ultimate mother must be the one submitted to. Why, again, must the individual lose himself in service and commitment to the mother? It is because the mother has birthed him and has given him meaning (a man in isolation is not a man). The other is however dependent on him for its very continued existence. So, if the man is not going to give life to the mother then the mother will die and with it will die the man too.

I am sure that the above has driven you to despair over your brother who has got to trying to get his arms around everybody! If you carry the argument to its conclusion you find that death only awaits he who has gone to the ultimate in giving of himself to others. One cannot exist and at the same time be fully committed to the mother. Yet the paradox is that it is in this death that life takes on its relevance. Here you find meaning because it is through death that life is born. I think that Jesus is the ultimate example of what I am trying to say. He was the "Man for Others" and it cost him his life, yet in laying down his life he was able to bring new life to the world and new life even to heaven. So, there, Mr. Eby, how does that suit you!?

The other day Pastor (one of the theological school students) told me that the Wakiroba people have a proverb that says that a person's mind is like a thicket. This means that within it lurk many unknown and contradictory things. A thicket may have leopards, hyenas, buffalo, rabbits, fruit, shade, thorn—all in the same thicket. I found the saying very apt at least in so far as I have observed Africans. It's interesting that the personality of the class can change from warm acceptance to veiled hostility with no visible external reasons. The other week for a few days Pastor was really foul. One incident I remember was that he would not accept that God turned his back on Jesus on the cross. The darkness showed God's loving concern and watchful care over his son. I had never intended discussing the sayings on the cross that morning but the heat got so great that I could not be kept away from it. The particularly bothersome saying was Jesus' cry about being forsaken. Pastor had been sort of against everything said in class for a few days; this morning he was strongly against anything I had to say. Eventually we went for tea but I told them that right after tea I wanted someone to tell me what did it mean when Jesus cried, "Eli, Eli, *lama sabachthany*" if it didn't mean that God has turned his hand on his son. Right after tea Stefano was given the floor to explain. He made a strong case to indicate that Jesus' statement proved beyond doubt that Jesus was not any part God, but only a dying man. He continued to wrest any scripture on Christ's divinity that I gave to him, so that it would fit into this heretical idea that Jesus was only a man. Truly men's minds are thickets.

The weird thing is that had the class been in its normal mood none of this discussion would have developed. Now that the pastor and the *mzee* were leading the pack it was impossible to continue any sort of teaching because all I was getting was a wall. Finally, I said that I did not know how it was that Satan gets into situations to keep us from being able to talk. I said that we had got worlds apart in our positions, and I could see no way for us to move together so that we could then let the matter rest. Surprisingly, that turned the tables and at once Pastor became just as adamant in arguing that Satan wasn't dirtying our discussion, that it was only the students eager for learning from their teacher who were asking perplexing questions so that the teacher could teach them the truth which was what they after all were in school for anyway. This gave me the floor, and from then on I could teach again and the situation remained clear until they left for holidays yesterday.

I write all this because it points up bafflement for me which I have encountered again and again with Africans. There is that untrue streak which crops up occasionally. There doesn't seem to be a course to which the men are true when the chips are down. You can suddenly expect anything. Pastor, for example, was always so warm a brother who attended fellowship regularly and was continually speaking of brotherhood and the need for forgiveness. Then one day he got mad in prayer meeting and in the past two months he's been in fellowship only once. Did I tell you earlier about the incident? Pastor was giving a prayer request and as is his manner he wasn't very loud, and he was sitting in the front of the church. Suddenly Opanga opened up from the back of the room. "Why are you up there talking to yourself? Speak so we can hear." Dead silence followed which finally got long enough to make it necessary that someone break it. So Pastor made an annoyed sound and said, "I said that now is the time for prayer requests, so if anyone has one to make he is to make it!"

Another example is the Bible School graduate who gave away a plot of a church compound to a stranger for building a house.

It's true, as the Wakiroba observe: man's mind does not tick according to a pattern, but wildly gyrates. One day a person appears with a new personality that no one has seen before. Partly, I think, that the African is regulated by relationships more than we Europeans are. When the students decided to be mad at me—not consciously, I'm sure—no logic or argument could budge them. But in a moment, the air changed, and I could say anything and it was accepted without question. Does this mean that the African will learn philosophy by his relationship to his teacher rather than by his intellectual reasoning? Is theology, orthodoxy vs. heresy, subject to uncharted seas of interpersonal relationships and not to the exercise of the mind and accumulated revelations that the mind has put into writing for us?

But when I take this a step farther and ask if our minds to them seem to be thickets, too, then I fear that we too seem to be thickets to them. I guess they often find in us totally inexplicable behavior and attitudes. So, I go back to ask if what makes them tick is different from what makes us tick. We are generally true to a system of ethic and logic and our theology is strongly colored by what we call the protestant work ethic. Some of our older people who were in missionary schools thirty years ago tend to have it tattooed on their souls that there are primitives and civilized. Now, if one understands each of the above, then I think that what we whites find ourselves doing will, to us, not be too far from what we would have expected. I have tried to search for the key that would open up the African personality so that he would be predictable within at least a certain margin of error.

If there is a key, i.e., if Pastor is wrong in saying that man's mind is like a thicket, then maybe the key is the drive to live here and hereafter. If I use this yardstick then it does explain some of the thicket. Take it that the African whose life's effort is devoted to becoming the head of an important family. He wants power. The old Mzanaki wants the white cow's tail, the forked stick, the leather pouch, a dozen wives, scores of children, lots of strong sons who will pray to him after he dies and who will make offerings which will help his spirit to remain powerful. He searches for the power to dominate the spirits, both those of the departed and those of the living. The African has a strong kind of spiritual capitalism. It seems that maybe this drive to a spiritual capital is a law that, if understood, will make an African's mind predictable, at least within limits. By spiritual capitalism I mean the desire to dominate other spirits.

Let's fit this into the classroom experience of the other week. I know that Pastor has been feeling increasingly that he is slipping in the ranks. The English is getting tougher, his responsibilities at home are getting heavier, and his influence on the station is not rising very fast. The other day there was a formal request lodged with the Bishop that Pastor be given the station superintendentship, as he is pastor of this district. A week later the Bishop was talking about how Pastor must move back to Nyankanga to shepherd that flock, just as soon as he is through school. Also, came the rebuke in prayer meeting. Also, Pastor began to come half way through chapels, partly because he was having trouble at home with a far-advanced pregnant wife, but also I think to sort of show that he was not bound to the same discipline as the other students. I never mentioned it to him, but I think that the students may have made a few remarks. They had been rather hard on him earlier about similar things. Mixed in with all this was the fact that tests are coming up and his English is so poor that he can't study his own notes. So all along the line you have a slippage and what you can expect is that he will lash out against those above him so as to prove to them that they are wrong about something. He will act as though he is on the top, even though he is slipping.

I am sure that the Lord does mellow these things in us, but when the chips are down our true colors so often come blazing through. I propose that an understanding of the African's drive for spiritual capitalism will help us to know when the chips are getting down for him and it will help us to predict how he will react or at least it will throw light on the reaction. As long as the African doesn't know what makes us tick when our chips are down, then we shall continue to have thickety minds in his view of things.

There, Mr. Eby, how does that suit you?! Edith thinks I should edit this stuff as she thinks I don't know what I'm saying myself. But isn't it true that great writing can't ever be fully understood? And you do want me to write great stuff, don't you?

April 14, 1968

We came back from Nairobi by MAF plane early on Thursday morning. It was a lovely clear day. Right after take off we could see Mt. Kenya glistening in the morning sun. Then, as we flew west and the ground dropped away from beneath us, the clouds slowly started filling in below until they got so thick that we had to go down below them. The pilot found a hole and we spiraled down through. Now we discovered ourselves to be over the western reaches of Serengeti. The rivers were overflowing. The grass was abundant and swished over everywhere. Almost immediately we spotted six hippo in a big pool. This was followed by great herds of zebra and buffalo. At times the zebra herds were sprinkled with eland in their rich reddish brown and black hides. It all, we spotted five rhino, including one baby. We were flying just over the treetops, and I got some twenty pictures, which I hope will turn out good. The animals finally gave way to a single isolated plowed field, and this was then followed by more fields and scattered villages. Then we got into the Kisaka area and the intensive agriculture practice there these days. The amazing thing was that everything was rain-soaked. One village on a rise of land was completely surrounded by water. Behind the village was a river and before it was miles and miles of flooded flat land. The thorn-bush cattle enclosure was flooded out, and the cattle milled around the house. Everywhere the fields were sopping with water. Musoma seems to be spared the heavy dunking that most of the rest of the country is experiencing. Dar was cut off from the rest of the country for nearly a week a few days ago. Everywhere bridges are out. We haven't been able to drive to Mwanza for over a month. But here in Musoma, the rains have been moderate this season.

April 21, 1968

Peace has again settled down around our house. A week or more ago I put up a great variety of swinging things in some old stinky-bomb trees out back of the outdoor toilet. There are two regular swings, one chinning bar, very adaptable for skinning the cat, one rope ladder with eight wooden rungs on it, and one knotted rope with a square board on the bottom for swinging. This afternoon we must have attracted a dozen kids, and their arguments got pretty hot, sometimes as to who would swing on which swing and how the swinging should be done. Just a few minutes ago it started to rain and that drove the children away. Now it is quiet again.

April 30, 1968

The church here lost members, so far as overall tallies go. It seems that we don't have enough of a holding structure, so the membership fluctuates according to how the spirit is working at that particular time. Baptisms in some places have dropped off drastically. The other Sunday there were only two baptized here at Bukiroba, and I think the catechism class has about two or three in it. On the capitalism vs. socialism bit, I really got an eye-opener last Sunday. The Bishop made a few remarks after the sermon. He said, "I took over from the missionaries and some of what was done then I knew nothing about at all. Just this past week I discovered that Bible School graduates and other works at the church are not getting a share of the overseas budget. From the beginning, this budget was to be shared among all of us. It was the practice that all Bible School graduates got Shs 10/=. How it has come to be that only a few TMCers now get a cut, I don't know. This came as such a shock to me to discover that everyone wasn't sharing in this money that I could not sleep for two nights. Therefore, I decided to call a special executive committee meeting. I directed that ways be found to give everyone a cut of the budget. I directed that if this cannot be done without having our own salaries cut, then our salaries are to be cut. This whole matter has now been turned over to the finance committee for them to see what can be done. This came as a tremendous shock to me to find that everyone was not sharing alike in this overseas money. Truly, some few of us have become "*kabalia*" (bluebloods) and "*bepare*" (capitalists). But when I decided that this money must be shared alike, then I felt at peace about it." What the Bishop is really saying is that the last white bishop made changes to the budget without informing anyone, and only now is he, the first African bishop discovering the mischief!

Tonight Daddy had to drive out to Bumangi to get a check signed for MEDA—Tanzania! Can you imagine having to drive 18 miles out into the bush just to get a check signed? He left at six and should be back around ten.

I find that during our study of the resurrection the students often sit with mouths agape in complete amazement at what the scriptural records says. They seem not to have read the account. Repeatedly I find amazing gaps in their Biblical knowledge, which makes one wonder if there ever was even rudimentary understanding of what the Christian Church is all about. When you have such put into a situation whose curriculum is designedly liberating and which provides no guidelines for moral behavior then you can quickly have some pretty wide aberrations taking place, even at a theological college.

I'm tempted to draw up a list of rules as guidelines for what is considered good behavior for theological students. But on second thought I felt that this would be self-defeating, in the light of the wider objectives we have here. Therefore, I have thrown the thing over to the students and have told them to sit down in a council and draw up their own guidelines.

Pastor thinks I don't like him because I gave him such low grades on his exams. The school captain also feels that his grades are lower than his rank among students demands!

May 10, 1968

Our rains are impossible. It hasn't rained worth a thing for nearly two weeks. This wrecked our plans for putting another crop of beans into our college garden. Yet, at the same time, the lake has suddenly taken to rising six inches per fortnight, so now our entire garden is under water.

Last evening was the first I'd been down to the garden for two weeks. I went with a couple of other students with the instructions to dig out some sweet potatoes. To my surprise we had to go through water to even get to the garden. All but the tops of a few ridges in the garden were under water. We spent an hour rescuing what could be harvested. The potatoes would come out with a slurping sound and a whiff of rot.

As I tramped dejectedly about the garden, the mud sucking at my boots, I came to appreciate in a small way what it means to a small farmer to have his gardens destroyed. The almost cheerful approach to the problem of the students with me must have been born of their long acquaintance with the way the land fights back in this huge untamed continent.

May 18, 1968

About Daddy and Mother's farewell from this station, as they leave to take up their post in Kenya. A big station tea behind Miss Yoder's house. Lots of tea and delicious stuff made by domestic science girls. Lots and lots of speeches. The Bishop's speech centered around the idea that we missionaries will be remembered in Africa not for what we have done but for how well we have gotten on with the Africans. He pointed out that people quickly forget what we have done, but it is how we lived with them that they will remember for a long, long time. In a sense, it said that it doesn't matter what we do just so long as we get on well. But as Maynard pointed out, what we need to do is to get a lot done and get on both!

One of the students who lives here with his wife borrowed Daddy's old accordion. He's been practicing for the past months. He keeps at it bravely, and by now he can play a number of hymns rather well. A few weeks ago he felt strong enough to try out his skill in a church. He's been assigned to Nyankanga, a small village out at the cut off for the Kirumi Ferry. He and another student attend there regularly. On this particular Sunday they must have been a howling success. They came back just glowing. If I ever glowed half as much as Jackson glowed, I'd have a headache so bad I'd have to go to bed. He glowed so that his eyes seemed to stand out in his head. The story went that never before had the people at that church invited them to their homes but on this Sunday they got invited to three homes for food. Never before had anyone gone with them to the bus, but on this Sunday they went with them to the bus, carrying all their things. It was truly a fresh exciting discovery that Jackson made about himself. He announced on that Sunday that the next Sunday he would go to another church. This was promptly vetoed. They left him to understand that the college had seconded him to their congregation and that he was therefore their property. If some leader at another church wanted them to go there then he must send a written request to the leader at Nyankanga. Jackson told them that the next Sunday he wanted to see the church full and overflowing. He wanted to see people sitting outside. Everyone was directed to bring some one else along for the following Sunday.

What could I do in the face of all this excitement but join ranks! Therefore, I went to Musoma and bought a guitar. The students wanted a loudspeaker attached to it. I don't know if we'll try that. Personally I'd rather buy them another guitar. Daddy's old trumpet still hasn't begun to disturb our quiet. I rather think that none of the students have the gumption to try to get it to blasting. It takes a powerful lung to just get it to squeak!

June 21, 1968

Three boys, one very small and two rather bigger, have crept in through the open office door. Right now they're gathered around the desk, watching intently how this machine works. They've come in silently; neither they nor I exist in each other's worlds. They are fascinated by the way this typewriter works, and I am fascinated at their fascination. They're also just a bit distracting and make letter composition a bit difficult. Wouldn't you like a couple of street urchins looking around your elbow as you type out your MCC news on Biafra and Vietnam?

I guess writing is like love. Sometimes you have it and have it so bad it hurts and other times you just don't have it. (One of the boys touched a piece of paper on the desk, and the others quickly reproached him). Anyway, for the last month I just haven't had the itch to write. Part of this is because Edith has been away, having gone on the first of June, and part of it is that I have been rather busy since she's left. I've sort of tried to make myself busy and have been at all kinds of things off and on. (Right now I'm typing while I look out the window so as to further impress these boys watching me. They are indeed impressed that I can type and not look at the machine; they've started nudging each other about this). Paul Miller from Goshen seminary was here for a week; I was at his side most of the time, translating. And I've driven the Bishop and secretary and treasurer out to Majita A district—out and back in the same day, a long ride.

I've lost three of my close emotional units of relationship, the first being Edith, the second being my daughters who are staying with the Petersheims, and the third is my parents. Edith left on Saturday; my parents were here for the weekend, but they left on Tuesday. So all of these close bonds have been severed and severed at the same time. These have left me grappling for a fresh groove in which to slip and the emotional search for other patterns has left me with nothing for you. It's interesting how I feel. I feel bitter sometimes towards Edith, for not being sufficiently sorry for me in my loneliness, for being so big and clumsy with this baby who pushes me away when I want to embrace her. I feel sorry for and guilty about the children, wondering if they get good enough treatment, hoping that they won't forget their own parents, worrying about their getting sick, and wondering what demons in me make me so harsh with them when they're home. And I worry about my parents and feel guilty for not writing to them and don't write because it takes so long for them to get the letter and feeling that they are so very lonely for their children and grandchildren, while our response does not match their reaching for a haven of family togetherness in these tired years. And I worry about them, especially since Daddy has been so sick. The last letter he reports being very low, with a fluttering heart. I wonder if it is an emotional condition brought on by heartbreak, or if it is just something wrong with his metabolism. I wish I could run up to Kenya and visit them, but I'm tied up all Sundays and my *piki* still doesn't run.

Paul Miller says that the African doesn't plan ahead; he just waits for something to happen and then he reacts to what has happened. I guess I'm sort of falling into that pattern because that is certainly how I acted this weekend. I just waited for the next bad thing to happen, and then I reacted in the manner most appropriate at the time!

June 24, 1968

I got a birthday card and a nice letter from my parents. It took ten days to get here from just over the border in Kenya! I decided that if at all possible I must get up to see them. The Bishop has been much concerned about them, and he too wanted to have someone go see them and let them know that others are thinking of and praying for them daily. The Bishop is particularly concerned that they don't work too hard, even after Daddy is feeling better. But I left it with the Lord as to whether a way would open that I could go.

The way at that point was blocked by my *piki* still not working. In brief, its history is that I finally ordered new wires for it. I could still get sputteringly around on it, but it wasn't satisfactory and was using about a gallon of gas for 30 miles. These wires finally came last Tuesday and I tore out the old wiring right away, only to discover afterwards that they had not sent switches and that their wires could not possibly fit my old switches. This I felt was rather grim, as the diagram of what I ordered included switches. I called Edith in Nairobi and asked her to get switches and a rectifier and to tell Ali the mechanic to put them on the airplane. So, in my prayer Friday night I prayed that if the parts did come on that Friday's plane, then I'd know that the Lord wanted me to try to get to see the folks. Saturday morning I went in to Musoma to pick up the girls from Petersheims and then they went with me to do some shopping and to see if Musoma Emporium had the parts. Behold, they had arrived! So, after finishing up the other shopping I bought a huge whole-nut chocolate bar for Daddy and came home to fix the cycle. The girls came along, the agreement being that if I went up to Migori, then I'd take them back to Musoma.

Characteristically Ali had to have done something wrong, and this time it was that the plastic bag containing the fixtures (little metal ends for the wires and those little rubber-coated clips) for joining one of the switches to the wiring had been opened and all the stuff used. By clipping the metal ends off the old wiring and melting the wires out of them, I managed to get enough ends to fix up the new wiring. Joyce held the metal tips with pliers while I soldered in the new ones. She did it very well, in fact.

So by 4:15 I was on my way to Migori with considerable loads on the back of the motorcycle. I didn't know if they'd have extra sleeping places so I took an air mattress and a sleeping bag. I also had a good bit of second class post for them, along with my tool bag and a suitcase. The cycle was working well, for the first time in over a month, and I was feeling good. I had to wait at the ferry for a while, so I didn't get away from there before 5:00 p.m. But then the engine began to act up. At first it only hit partly, giving less power, but then it began to miss again.

When I got to Utegi, the stores had already been closed, and I figured that it would take a while to get the petrol man out so I figured that I could make it on to Tarime. By this time there was a black mist looming over the Tarime hills, and it began to look as though it might rain. The *piki* was working fairly well, managing up to 40 mph, and I was nearing Tarime, and it still wasn't on reserve so my hopes were high. Then, just as it began sprinkling, the gas got all. I put it on reserve, by leaning it over on its side and went on. I had hardly gone a half-mile before the cycle stopped. I was still about three miles out of Tarime and now it began to rain. I could see nothing to do other than to push the cycle into Tarime.

Some of those hills are so steep and I couldn't push straight up. I'd go back and forth across the slope of the road and in that way manage slowly to get to the top. Then I'd coast down the other side and rest, only to have to fight up the next hill. By the time I got to the entrance of Tarime town, I was so bushed that I knew that I could not go another yard. I was sure that I'd throw up. So I stood the *piki* there in the road and went over to the side of the road and leaned against a tree. Then I just sat down and let the cool rain revive me. After a little while I felt up to it again and pushed on into town. A woman there woke the petrol attendant who was sleeping in a truck; he got me a tank of gas.

By this time it was beginning to seem foolish to keep on. The rain was coming down hard, the *piki* was missing, night had fallen. I began to fear that the police at the border wouldn't feel kindly toward someone coming through after eight at night and in a driving rain. But I hoped that it hadn't rained too much further on. So I started out again.

By the time I got to the top of the first long hill, about three miles north of Tarime, it was raining buckets and the road was so slick that I could hardly manage to stay upright. I went into several really severe spins and only by some miracle managed not to fall. Finally, I realized that I was not to go to Migori, so I turned around. Now the motorcycle lights started to give me trouble. They were getting dimmer and dimmer.

I forgot to mention that after buying the petrol in Tarime, I couldn't start the cycle and found that the petcock had been snapped shut. When I had leaned the cycle over it got snapped shut, so I really wasn't out of petrol after all and probably would have had enough to get into Tarime, had I known the reason for running out of gas.

My problem was now whether to sleep in Tarime or to get back to Utegi. I decided to get back to Utegi, if possible, and maybe go in to Shirati for the night. I hoped that it hadn't rained on the other side of Tarime. But I found that it had rained and the road was a sea of mud. I figured that if I could hold on long enough I'd eventually get to Utegi.

Now the rain was settling into just a heavy drizzle, the lights were dim enough, so that when the road was lit by the frequent flashes of lightning I was temporarily unable to see until my eyes adjusted back to my dim candle. It was impossible to use more than second gear and much of the time I had to be in first gear with both legs propping me up, sort of like skids sticking out on each side of the *piki*. But now the *piki* started to "*zimika*" as the Africans say. It'd stop running and after starting it again, I'd have to keep it pretty well wide open in order to keep it sputtering. The throttle cable also started sticking and I still don't know why that was. But it was still going a bit and I kept thinking that any time now I must be nearing Utegi. Starting up the next hill the motor stopped again; this time it would not spark one spark. So I started pushing. I had a flashlight and between it and the lightning flashes I could tell where to push. Every once in a while I'd slip into a slushy rut, but it really went rather well for some time.

Before long the road got worse, and I got to the end of my strength. I figured that Utegi must be around the next bend, so I just leaned the *piki* against the side of the road and left it there. I didn't even take any of the load off, as they were heavy, for one thing, and for another, I figured that I'd just scout out the road ahead and after finding Utegi I'd come back for everything. So I started walking and I walked and walked. I checked the time before starting, and it took about fifty minutes to get to town. I crossed two rivers. But then it was about 9:30 and fortunately a hotel was open. The owner is a relative of Daniel Opanga, so I felt sort of at home. He had tea, and I drank three cups, a bottle of Fanta orange, and two *mandazies*. He gave me a bed for Shs 5/= and by ten I was asleep. I checked the time about every hour and at 4:30 I got my shoes on and started back for the cycle. I wanted to get there before early morning travelers. Even before I'd got up I heard intermittent drumming, and now I found that it was coming from up the road. It kept getting nearer and nearer and I finally realized that it was coming from on the road. Here was a young man followed by about six other men, walking single file down the mud-slippery road. He had a beautiful little rhythm, and he was doing very well in spite of the mud. He did occasionally knock his sticks together in the dark. The stars were out brightly and a sliver of red moon was still up.

I came on the cycle suddenly. It loomed like a piece of shiny junk by the side of the road. I stabbed the flashlight at it to see what had fallen there and to my surprise it was my *piki*. It had taken me forty-five minutes to get back to it. Everything was still there! This is something to be very grateful for. A number of people who passed later, before sunrise, were surprised to hear my story, that I had left a cycle there during the night and that I found everything the next morning. A group of young men went past about fifteen minutes after I got there, and I rather feel that they may have considered it fair game. They could not have got the *piki* itself very far, but they could have taken the other stuff.

I was in the middle of a long stretch of soupy road. Before long I heard a truck roar and it turned out to be three big ten-tonners, one right after the other, grinding along in low gear, slithering and jouncing from rut to rut and from hole to hole. The amazing thing to me was that they kept on the road. I flashed my taillight so they wouldn't run me down. So there I sat by the side of the road, which had not dried off enough to make the mud stick, and the cycle still would not start. Had it started maybe between its strength and mine we could have made some headway, but it was just impossible to push. Finally, at about eight, a man who had heard me in the night came by and offered to help me get it up on the bank where I could push it through the grass. This we did and after once again digging the mud out of the fenders with a stick, I managed to push it until the bank forced me back on to the road. But here it was better, and I got down to the first little river. I tried to wash out the mud again and then tried pushing the cycle down the graveled slop on the other side but this would not work. Therefore, I decided to take the seat off and see if I could find anything there which could be wrong. I took all the loads off and got out the tools and went to work, but with no success. So, I put the seat back on, tied on the bundles and started pushing some more. After going about one hundred yards, the road got impossibly steep, so I rested about fifteen minutes. Then, seeing some young men walking up the hill towards me, I decided to have another try in the hope that they'd take pity on me and help. Sure enough they stopped to talk to this panting European and to hear his sorry story and then after about fifteen minutes, one of them offered to help. So off we went again for about twenty yards, and the four of us just couldn't go anymore. It was up hill and ahead the whole road was a sea of mud, and this mud was now so sticky that walking in it nearly pulled your shoes off. The front fender fits snuggly around the tire and it was packed tight full with mud. Try as we might we couldn't dig out enough mud to allow us to go more than a yard or two before the wheel would stop going around. At this place it was impossible to get up on the bank so I asked the men if they'd help me to carry my stuff into Utegi. They consented and one of them went with me.

On the way into town we met three boys and a young man who had been told of my plight by a fellow who had passed earlier with milk cans on his bicycle. I asked him to see if he could get someone from the place I had slept to come and help push. These were the ones he had found, but they were from a different hotel. I told them that it was impossible, but they still wanted to try, so I went on to town and they went back after the cycle. I found that the fellows had pushed it about 100 yards and then it had got into gear and they probably thought that had broken something. In any case, I never saw any of them again. They got the cycle to a place in the road where one could get up on the bank and had pushed it into the grass. Right there the road was in really bad shape. When I got back to that location, a bus was stuck sideways in the road. All the passengers were out helping to push it.

Getting around this last muddy spot, I found the road to be better. I was able to push without too much difficulty. In fact, the road sloped down to the last stream before Utegi, and here I ran with it three times just as hard as I could in the hope that I could get it to start. But it never fired one stroke. It was completely stone dead. At the stream I worked quite a while until I got most of the mud out of the fenders and then it went very easily up the last hill and finally into Utegi. I got into town, dripping sweat from every pore, but was very happy for an ice-cold Fanta at one of the *dukas*.

I left the cycle at the hotel and went to find the church leader in Utegi. I found that they were still in church, although it was now 11:45. The church is a mile out the other side of town, so I walked out there and found them finishing up the morning service. I walked home with the leader and they gave me a couch to lie on so I could snooze until dinner. We had a great dinner of chicken and *ugali*. The leader and I then went for the cycle in order to put it in his house until I could come ask for it sometime. The people in the town had been telling me that there was a *"fundi"* in town and that he was good. But I didn't wish to spend more money on mechanics who didn't know anything about cycles and so put them off. We happened to meet the *fundi* on the street and he, of course, noticed that we were pushing a cycle. I, of course, had to tell him what was wrong and he of course had to tell me that he was just then working on a BSA 250cc and that he could check out my trouble for me. He seemed to know what he was talking about and he wasn't too greasy, which seemed to say that he was an orderly sort of fellow, so I accepted to stop at his shack on my way to the leader's house. Here, for once, was an African who knew just what he was about. He had the proper combination of good electrical knowledge combined with the right amount of bailer-twine skill that is needed in the bush far away from spares. In about fifteen minutes he had the cycle running, but it was still not running smoothly. He was sure that given more time he could get it to spark correctly. He had even heard me pass the night before and knew at once that my cycle needed his attention. So he convinced me that maybe he did know what he was about, and I left it with him. I'll try to go after it on Wednesday afternoon after classes.

By this time it was bus time. The first afternoon bus went at 3:30. There had been a number of buses in the morning, but I was always still stuck with the cycle in the mud. So I got the loads tied up and got them perched on the edge of the ditch that runs along the edge of the road and sat down on the muddy porch stoop of a little *duka* on the other side of the ditch and waited. At 4:20 I went for another cup of tea and finally at 4:30 the bus came. This wasn't the first bus. That one must have gotten lost somewhere. So there being only one bus made it double full of people. I knew that it would be full and rushed to be first in line. I wasn't quite first, but after it had disgorged about twenty people, I was one of the first to get on and got a good seat. The narrow isle slowly filled up with baskets and people until by the time we pulled out every seat was full and the isle was packed from one end to the other.

Fortunately, more people got off then got on, as we headed out toward Kirumi, so the press got slowly less and less, but at no time was no one standing. The funny thing at the ferry was that one of the passengers got left behind and the bus waited for the ferry to go back after him. A number of the passengers were about to start a riot when he finally got there, bowing and demanding everyone's forgiveness. We got here at Bukiroba at seven. I'd been invited to Alliance Secondary for a picnic supper. So I got bathed and dressed just as fast as I could and then hunted up a car so I could get over to Alliance. They were all amazed to see me. Dianne wondered if I'd take her home with me now. After worship Hilda served coffee and a lovely layer cake done in white icing with green lettering saying, "Happy Birthday, Joe". It was all very nice. The girls stayed on between the Petersheims and the Kurtzes. I came on home and got a good night's sleep. THE END!

July 2, 1968

What is a brother for? I mean, this is really a philosophical question. Is a brother to be a sort of policeman to keep one from going astray, to keep feeding you light as you seem to be in need of it? Is a brother essentially one who forgives he who is his brother for his various follies? Is a brother the one who carries the burden of whatever needs carrying on the part of he to whom he is brother?

I left a missionary here read my letter about my recent motorcycle adventures. His comment: the letter was a transparent request for finances to buy a new cycle! So I thought maybe I'd better remain quiet, lest writing about these things be construed to be a begging for money.

But the more I thought about it, the more I felt that if a brother can't share the desperation of his soul in extremities, then of what use is that brother? Yet if the soul becomes a beggar for bits of this world's goods, or if his inner sighings are so construed as to so appear, then the result would likely be a straining of the relationship. Strained because the soul would feel beholden and because the brother would feel sucked, to use a Swahili term.

Having said all this, let me continue to chronicle to you my joys and sorrows, and if you find it in your heart to rejoice and weep, then I shall feel brothered. Whatever is more than this is playing with fire.

As I winged my way east from Shirati last Wednesday morning and saw lying to the north the sleepy little town of Migori (in Kenya) and saw the couple of little shacks nestled along the edge of the little hill rising to the east of the town, and thought that my parents had not heard a peep out of anyone in Tanzania, myself included, every since they left on June 5, and knew that Daddy had not been well, I breathed a little prayer of gratitude that I had found someone to whom I could pour out my troubles, someone who might in some later unforeseen eventuality provide the element of human compassion which would make it possible to go on. I am not a sufficiently healthy Christian to find all the solace my soul needs from merely His, "Well done."

July 10, 1968

I am writing this while sitting in a classroom. Giving exams is always a time of low student-teacher relationship and that is what we are doing now. I guess it is the one time when I've got them over the barrel and can force them into my mold—the understanding of sophisticated questions, the keeping to a set time, taking me seriously in their studies. So, I turn the screws, and all they can do is be mad and take it.

Your letter about your job assessment—those things always make me feel like dying. I remember the first one ever done on me. It was at the end of my first year of teaching. I figured that I was just about the grandest tiger in the jungle. When I found that I was rated only "average" with an occasional "below average" it just about killed me. Those scars must still make me wince when I see personal evaluation forms. The kind of evaluation I like is the kind Bishop Kisare gave a retired missionary in the July *Missionary Messenger*—and not the kind that the Bishop and the church secretary and the treasurer gave him on our way home from a conference one time. The treasurer says, "But in spite of how he was, he had a keen mind and he had good thoughts. If you were able to listen to him, then he had wonderful things to teach." Secretary: "Like what?" Roars and knee slapping and joking for several miles, with an occasional burst from someone, "Like what?" In another few miles—the end of the conversation on the retired missionary.

Can you stand women's affairs? How about an extrapolation from my wife's last letter? She had gone into mild labor the night of the third and at around 11:00 she called the nurse and they took her to the labor ward. But didn't prep her. The baby had worked its way around to head down position again, and the doctor had given her castor oil. She'd been the hospital about five days. Then she went to sleep until around 1:00, when she awoke with really powerful contractions. She rang the bell with no response, and rang again, and then just held it on. Finally three nurses came running and pronto there in the bed was a yelling baby. The doctor got there after it was all over. But the baby's head had been crooked and accordingly Edith was torn quite badly. They took her to the delivery room and the doctor started sewing her up. Edith tried to count the stitches but eventually lost track. Anyway, he sewed for half an hour! They then gave her tea, a bath, and a look at newborn Rosemary Jo.

What are my thoughts on fatherhood? I think of myself—in the deep secret parts of my personality—as being sort of effeminate and my third daughter now confirms that feeling. To be amiable to women, to bend to their quirks and foibles. To enjoy their enjoyments. To learn the names of their dolls. To joy in their sewing and cooking. To anticipate with them the day when they will have breasts. To be the fixer who keeps their world happy. I've got a conservative view of the male. Upon him rests the responsibility for the direction of the issues of the day. He is the front to the world—the shield behind which his wife and children live their joys and sorrows. The female is the mother whether in the past, present, or future. It's the man's task to ease her way and make her happy and he in this achieves a fulfillment. But creation is man's highest fulfillment, his sweetest delights and responsibility. Some men don't get the privilege of creating other men. They may create women—a difficult task when one isn't a woman, although for a womanish man, it may be partially possible. Or they may simply spend their lives fulfilling their role of protector and joy-giver, creative functions, no doubt, but of a markedly secondary nature. Even this ceases to be creativity if it loses its spontaneity and becomes an others-imposed task.

To have created men is a cancer which slowly kills a man. If he has created women—good, beautiful, skillful, mother-potential women—then, the Africans say, his death will be preceded by a blaze of wealthy glory. The American doesn't even have this consolation.

Could I adopt my daughters' husbands as sons? Maybe in the role of their now being, in the dusk of my masculinity, my protectors and joy-givers. But I can't be their creative father; to attempt to do so would be poaching. They have already been created and the glory of that work must rest with its rightful owner.

How about all that bombastic spiel?

July 16, 1968

I got word on Saturday afternoon that there was a new cycle available in Nairobi, as soon as I could get up for it. So, I got the children arranged for with Stella and packed up and went off on the boat that night. Earlier in the week I worked at getting more shelves put up in our bedroom, along with fixing a good top on a couple of barrels for a sort of baby's changing station. I think it's fixed up now for a minimum of bother.

I took a cabin on the boat to Kisumu, feeling that anyone who could afford a new cycle could afford to sleep in a bed. Bad thing about the room, someone previously had pissed on the floor. I found half my stuff suitably moistened upon arrival in Nairobi. I'd one of our canvas-type suitcases, so it soaked through. Fortunately my suit was untouched, but the sweater got it.

At Kisumu we got a Peugeot taxi. A beautiful day and an enjoyable ride. Going out of Kericho the driver was careening down one snaky hill full of potholes at about 70 mph. I finally called his attention to his excessive speed and threatened to report him. I could just see all of us floating off the road, somersaulting through the air, should one of the front tires have blown. The driver quickly assured us that "it was impossible for the car to go over 60. It had a governor put on it so it couldn't go over 60. Long ago they used to be able to go 90 down the hills, but now they could only go 60. Of course, on the steep hills it was still possible to go 70." So, we continued to go down all the steep hills at 70. Going down the escarpment, which drops one into Nakuru, he was hitting between 60 and 70 the whole way.

Rosemary is just the sweetest! Edith's description no longer fits at all. She is sort of Buddhist in her whole visage. Not the fat Buddha type that you once thought Joyce resembled. I am referring to the Buddhist theology, which extols the middle road. Rose has no features which are grotesque either by their size or color or presence or absence. Her face is a perfect oval with black eyes. Her hair is neither absent nor abundant. Her nose is moderate, as are her ears and mouth and chin. She is thin with very long fingers. She is content most of the time. Everyone who sees her remarks on how pretty she is. Edith and I cooed and cuddled her as though we had never had a baby before. One experienced couple even asked after observing us with Rose, if this was our firstborn.

Boy, was it a thrill to drive the new motorcycle around the block, first time. I got to thinking that this purchase is just a bit financially irresponsible. But I soon smothered my fears by reminding myself that many, many people in the US are paying (on installment) for most of what they have. And so I hope it will be with this cycle. But at no time have I felt that it was the wrong thing to do.

So, with a new baby, a new wife, new lights in the house, new shelves, a whole holiday free from school, and a new cycle—my cup of joy is just about full.

I got up at 5:30 this morning, had prayers with Edith, kissed my sweethearts goodbye and headed home from Nairobi. The cycle can't be driven faster than 40 mph for the first 1,000 miles and not over 50 mph for the next 500. So I had to poke the whole way home. Still I took an hour at Migori to see Daddy and Mother. Mother got me a wonderful dinner. Just as I was finishing up, Daddy said, "You know, Joseph, it is easier to pray for money than it is to pray for the soul of a person." I at once thought that he was going to challenge me to care more for people than for money. But his was no challenge to pray for souls, it was really how he felt about the matter. He said, "When you pray for a person it involves volition. God can only go so far in answering that prayer. But when you pray for money, then God can much more easily answer the prayer." So he challenged me to pray more that the Lord will pay this loan. I assured him that we were praying.

Tonight after greeting the Bishop and other appropriate persons, I checked my post. In one letter was a pledge to send us within a month $225. This from an old non-Mennonite friend of Edith's mother. She apparently had been shown a carbon of my letter to you about my attempted cycle trip to Migori the other month. So, I was sort of stunned and got on the cycle and rode over to Secondary Alliance to beg supper from the Kurtzes. He gave me your letter. We wondered why you'd use the secondary post office box number, agreed you'd forgotten. I called Maynard back and showed him the pertinent paragraph. I'm afraid I couldn't say much. Firstly, there isn't any thing that can be said that expresses what you feel, and secondly, should you want to try there would be tears, and we are too sophisticated for tears. These two checks almost cover the total amount, which we borrowed to buy the cycle!

Then going home in the dark, I nearly ploughed into a half-grown cow with my new cycle and I shivered for a mile. About all I could say was, "The Lord giveth and the Lord taketh away; blessed be the name of the Lord!"

July 21, 1968

I sort of salve my conscience on writing to you so often by thinking of this as a sort of journal.

Thoughts on turning thirty:

When I turned twenty there seemed to be a new phase of life opening up for me. I suddenly felt like an adult, or at least I stopped feeling like a boy. I suddenly started having more confidence in my own judgment, and I felt that people started listening to me as though my thoughts had some validity.

The years since have been marked by periods of intense self-doubt. These came especially when in confrontations, such as between Shellard at Secondary Alliance and TMC, over placing Josiah there as a teacher. Or when a student won't do as he's told, or a rebuke by someone in authority. There's the inability to stand fast, unshaken and calm. Firstly, I have difficulty finding a place to stand fast, being easily swayed from place to place, and secondly, I go to pieces emotionally very easily.

Also in the years since, there's been that boyishness which seems to me to have hung on far longer than in other men. There's the eagerness to rush into new things. There's the eagerness to dash away on the slightest pretext. There's the constant search for how I may fit into others' plans, rather than commitment to my own goals. Most men you quickly define as being of this or that nature, as being committed to this or that endeavor, as being easily annoyed by this or that occurrence. But to my own eyes I have seemed to not be so easily defined, meaning that I am still a boy. I agree too easily with everyone. I am Phoebe's boy, I am George's boy, I am the Bishop's boy, I am

Dorothy's boy, I am Nyabweki's boy, and when not being the others' man, I am my wife's. But I don't think that I have been very much my own man. In policy decisions, I am the fluid factor whether it is which classes shall be taught or who shall be principal or how much money shall be in the college budget or whether or not a film shall be shown in church.

Also in the years since, there has been this great sexual drive undiminished since adolescence. There have even been fantasies of new modes of sexual fulfillment. Also of who would take my wife's place should she die. There's been the driving heat at work, in the morning, in the night, especially when something altered the routine, like a cycle trip somewhere.

In the years since there's been a spiritual search but a search cooling in intensity. Periods spent in private prayer have fallen far off. Edith and I read the scriptures together only two or three times a week. Prayer has become a tired thing, right before dropping off to sleep. I discovered that there is a Christianity outside the clear-cut, logical, historical, defined-in-time-and-space Christianity which I grew up with. I have peered into the abyss of theological thinking cut loose from St. Paul and the early church fathers. I've felt the breath of what "objectivity" means and have understood dimly. There has been a more permeating consciousness of God's presence. There has been an assurance that my life has been led by Him. There has been a comfort in feeling an acceptance of sorts in this African community.

But now, as I've turned thirty, there seems to have been a new door opened. I find myself discovering some things that I have taught but whose supporting evidence has not until now triggered personal conclusions. These things are difficult to say, because they come as dim inarticulate flickerings of truth that slip into and out of consciousness. One that I might try to articulate is that of the old Chinese proverb: "This too shall pass." All foundations are fluid, particularly those relating to the non-physical world. In geology we learned how the physical erodes and develops again into new forms, but these are the more permanent of things. Man's structures of ownership, of values, of government, etc., are much more fluid. The paradox is that the setters of standards speak as though their creations had eternal values or would be in eternal evidence. The word "forever" is used so much. Today, particularly, we live when these forevers pass, several of them, before us in one man's short life span. No doubt there are some "forevers" but at this point I see more of the decay than of the eternal.

I have increasingly sensed the futility of teaching. A lot can be taught, but most of it doesn't matter, i.e., there are the two kinds of learning, that of rote memorizing and that of putting learned facts and experiences together to form conclusions. It is the second that matters and it is this that is so hard to teach. Why? Because before it can be done there must be so much of the first, and the first takes a very, very long time to do, and it can't be done by one person; it must be done through the critical reading of hundreds of books, and by living.

But the new door seems to open more than to anything else to the promise of adulthood. There is the assuming of responsibility, responsibility for the lives of thousands within TMC, as those lives will be touched by the students here in the theological college. Don't take me boastfully. The issues that I feel strongly about or don't feel strongly about will shadow the thinking of these men, of that I'm quite sure. There is the necessity to know where I am and to be able to articulate it honestly. With this there is the continued disappointment, the disappointment that seems only to get worse rather than better. There are the puzzles. Take this one for example. Phoebe challenges me for going to visit the Bishop when he comes back from a safari. Firstly, I may go to build up my political standing. Secondly, that political standing may be in a church appearing to be going to pot. Thirdly, that political standing may be purposefully gained at the expense of my fellow missionaries who don't go to visit the Bishop out of conviction. These things bring a preoccupation that does not give room for the delights and flittings hither and yon of boyhood.

I see through this door a tremendous sobering sexually. I wonder if I am growing old, if none of the old excitement will ever grip me again. Is it because I am old or is it because I have got involved in so much more than I don't have time to lie around in bed? Maybe this week has been just particularly full of other things. Maybe my having got a new motorcycle, a lovely new daughter, a slim beautiful wife, and my two daughters back home all in six days have drained me to where I am emotionally exhausted. But I think this exhaustion is indicative of the pace to be paced over the next decade.

But with the sobering has come too a new quietness of warmth and love for Edith and the girls. A quiet conviction that making them happy is maybe more important than a lot of other things.

August 8, 1968

At retreat, Jacobs seemed preoccupied with getting unattached from just about everything. His lecture on the Holy Spirit and Culture pointed up that very little is sacred, and we have to be prepared to see the old landmarks disappear. His communion message had to do with the clouds of depression that the Lord would see us through. His final closing words spoke of cutting ourselves off—launching out into the deep. All this is good and right, but my soul somehow likes to keep a few familiar landmarks around. Sometime I'd like to have a long chew with someone on whether the way to build church-life is to emphasize the transient, shifting nature of things and the necessary disengagement of ourselves from things, or if the better way is to work out a pattern easily understood and followed. Do we do best to teach people that most of what we are is an unsacred culture that we must be prepared to help people to view as such or do we do our best to put sacredness into our culture, or what I mean to say is to work to establish among our church people certain sacred pillars? Anyway, I think Jacobs was primarily trying to get himself through a new at sea-ness, which he is currently experiencing. He was shaken, I think, to find that among the youth in America there is now a sub-culture, which he doesn't understand. He hasn't cracked that system. I remember that two years ago his concern was to pick up the youth-lingo, but this time it seems that the youth-lingo is about as hidden as the early African rites were. He told also of some fellow in Goshen, Indiana, who has his basement full of guns and ammo ready to stave off some invasion of blacks into his community. He told of a Mennonite preacher in Virginia who has converted all his assets into silver bars and who has enough petrol in jerry tins down in his basement to get him to Canada when the communists take over America. The world is shifting, and it will be a new system in which our kids will live. (Edith noticed that Jacob's daughter is now wearing lipstick, and that rather shook her. Someday, no doubt, Joyce will wear rings and beads and lipstick. What shook me were Jacob's pricey shoes. I guess some people buy motorcycles and some buy shoes!)

August 12, 1968

Let me comment on your observation that "we must be men, hard and sophisticated, for it is a hard and sophisticated world, even in the church. Right?" Does your "Right?" call for debate? Anyway I would make the rebuttal, that the church is hard and sophisticated, but that it does not follow that we as Christians need also to be so. We all have a threshold of frustration, some higher and some lower. Ought we not to try to keep it high and accept to be walked on some. What I mean is that it seems that an alternative to being also "men" we might be "children" and consciously absorb some of the abrasion meted out by the communities in which we live. Even among the students in the theological college, I know which ones can be bent to almost any shape and the ones who are sort of flinty; it's the flinty ones I look out for. They're the ones who count, when a meeting is on. The others are sort of children who don't yet know where they stand. They're the fearful and timid who are bent because admitting that this is true, isn't there still a place for the Christian to accept being walked on?

We get a lot of this noise in the African revival about being broken, but I suspect that most of it is because we have no alternative, so we find a good way to accept it with honor. To announce to people that I have become broken to a very difficult thing is really collecting a bit of glory from the shambles of defeat. What I'm saying is that I get your point, but I keep going back to the other alternative and wondering if it may not be a possible honest position.

One last word on the new motorcycle. I appreciate your reluctance to have it known that you helped, but it is just impossible not to share it. Mind you, I don't mean to throw pearls to swine, but this sort of thing just can't be put under a bushel. It is partly the way we live here. Quite a number of people, five or six, knew that I was borrowing money to pay for the cycle and now that it is paid for they are rejoicing with me. It is surprising how many people ask how much the cycle cost. When I say Shs 6,000/=, they are a bit taken aback, but when I tell them that the Lord paid for half of it, then they can take it better.

Another matter that could be discussed at great length: How much of what goes on with you do you share with others? Ought one to be pretty quiet about the ebb and flow of his private world, or is there a place for sharing with the immediate circle of fellow believers. Some of these people I get to know on the money end right down to how many pounds of cotton they sold and how much money they got to help send one of their family to a distant hospital for some kind of treatment. I remember one fellow confessing to me that he got more expensive shoes after he had shown me the ones he was getting. It is with people like this that I find that a sort of trust is broken when I clam up on my cycles and how it is that I happen to have come across that amount of money. Not only this, but there are needs here in the community, and people feel that I may know how to write to certain contacts so that I can get money for them too. So then there is a discussion of how money comes and how it was that I got money if they can't.

August 27, 1968

Today I spent a good bit of time helping to bury an old grandmother who was a Mennonite Christian. Yesterday word came to the pastor here that she had died. He is a student in the theological college, so he waited to go until mid-afternoon and then I took him on my motorcycle. We found that some relatives still hadn't come so they decided to wait a day. I got the students this morning to resurrecting our school garden, which had been under the lake for several months after the rains. Now the water has gone down and we are going to try to hack it out of the weeds again. Their going to the garden meant that there would be no morning classes, so the pastor and I went again to the funeral. It was a big funeral, with about one hundred people present. We found all the women at one little village while the men were at another little village across some hoed fields. The second village was the grandmother's home and they were digging the grave out in front of the door to her house. I helped a good bit, and I also got a fine sunburn. It was a fiercely bright day and the digging had to be done with a pick.

Once the grave was ready, and this took a number of hours, during which the pastor got a good opportunity to talk with a lot of people—everyone was sitting around under whatever shade they could find. They brought the body on a rough stretcher from the first house. I was one of three in the grave to receive the body. She was sewed into a sheet with the face open and then wrapped in two new blankets. We tried to make the body comfortable and then got out of the grave. We had scripture, a sermon and a prayer. Then everyone helped fill in the grave, after which all the men brought a stone each to cover the top of the earth mound. Then there were closing comments and a young steer was slaughtered in preparation for making a meal for all the guests. At this point we begged off because my daughters were alone at home. I found them eating dinner alone, which had been prepared for them by the girl who works for us. This evening I bartered a tray of ice cream for an invitation to have supper with Stella and Evelyn. My girls love having supper with Stella.

Out at Mugumu I conducted my first communion service. It was a bit scary, doing all the stuff for the first time. I guess the leader thought I needed some help; he made a little speech before turning the service over to me. He warned people not to participate if they weren't living right. I felt that we had a warm meeting. The student who played the accordion commented afterwards that he had felt a warmth of fellowship which he hasn't often experienced. His music contributed to a good meeting. It is a tiny church, having a capacity of about eighty people, if its jammed full. It was over half full. One of the mud walls is threatening to fall down, and they have it propped up on the outside with a good stout log. The seats are just rows of mud bricks that are not even plastered on the top. Another first for me was a young couple wanting their son dedicated. I said a few words about the difference between baptizing and dedicating a child.

In a couple of days Joyce will be going off to boarding school. The other morning I was having a fatherly chat with her on my knee before the rest of the house was awake. I asked her whatever we would do without her here at home. Her reply, "Well, maybe it will be better because now you won't have to get so cross with me anymore." She was entirely innocent of how what she said struck me. Her thinking was that she is a bone in our throat so much that it will be nicer for us to have her in school. She is a girl extremely sensitive to the feelings of others. She shows remarkable maturity in her being able to think of the other's wellbeing rather than her own. She must get her maturity from her mom. I remember that Edith's principal in high school said that she was the most mature student he ever had.

September 10, 1968

We are in the midst of the refresher course for students' wives. Right now there are about fifty people in the mess hall! Assorted kids accompanied. Also now is the time for annual meetings all over the place, and college men are in high demand for singing. We are out of funds, but still we manage to show up in more or less numbers at most of these meetings. A gripe: the Bishop keeps putting people into the refresher course without my knowledge. That's okay, as he is the instigator of the whole thing. He is simply bringing his course to the school campus. But I've got stuck with housing for the women, and it is a bit embarrassing when a woman shows up a week late, when the Bishop isn't around, and says that she has been told to come for the course, and we don't have a place to put her. Furthermore, we didn't welcome her. She had to come to us and say, "Here I am." And we say, "Who are you?"

Paul Kraybill (mission board executive) was here and he said some pretty tough things. For example, he laid down stiff guidelines for who can go to the States for six-month leadership training. Also, stiff guidelines were presented for who may go as a trainee, and who gets money loaned to him for building a house. The biggest bomb: starting with 1970 the Mission Board will say what percentages of the budget will be used for what, and in 1973 the budget from the mission board will be cut in half. The cry all along here was that if you give us something then we want to do with it as we like. Don't go giving us something and stipulating how it is to be used. It is my thesis that more purchases by the educational secretary for rabbits should slowly teach the reasons for why stipulations are necessary.

There was a tremendous effort here at Bukiroba to host Kraybill. Steady infighting among the citizens for opportunities to slaughter chickens and goats. Two brethren nearly lost their love for each other over who would be honored. Things were in such a frenzy of feasting that only a couple of hours were given to meeting with the church's executive committee. I'm sure that by that time Kraybill should have been beaten into a submissive and helpless pulp. But I think it speaks well of Kraybill's resilience and buoyancy, not to mention his youth. In spite of the fearless efforts on TMC's part, one senses that it is the closing of an era. We all went off to town, including the college men, to respectfully bury Kraybill in the departing airplane!

I forgot—when Kraybill was here, he told me that he is now appointing me as mission representative. I asked him whatever that meant. He said that it meant that I was to be a sort of father confessor to the missionaries and help Stella with whatever she needed advice on. Therefore, I set out early the next morning to see if Stella and Evelyn had anything to confess. To my surprise, they threw me out on my ear, so that was the end of that!

John and I got a little hike in. I had wanted to go climb that ridge back on the edge of the Serengeti, but he wasn't in the mood, so in typical Shenk fashion we just sort of grumbled around at each other until at last I decided we go climb Bugoshi again. I wanted badly to go off with him somewhere because I don't think that you really get to talk unless you set aside a time when circumstances throw you together for a while, circumstances which do not demand any mental effort. You are then free to be silent or to talk and usually one talks with the conversation ranging over many subjects, alighting sometimes for long periods on something of special importance to the hikers. There is also a lot of small talk, not forced, but freely flowing, about all the things which make up a personality and as the day progresses one comes to know again him with whom he hikes. And so it was with us, in the end, and it was nice, and I've found John again, and just maybe he has found me.

October 3, 1968

I think I'm losing my cool. Things bother me much more than they used to, and I find myself getting sharp with people. In part, maybe it is because when we first got here we left everything slide, not know at all how the land lay. Now that we know a bit more how it does lie, and we have got a feel for where our position is in relation to the rest, we feel a bit freer to start pressuring. So we sort of keep up a constant pressure along various lines, and the result is a straining of the good happy-go-lucky atmosphere. Then in part, it is just that I have been getting old and I have been getting tired and grouchy.

Did I tell you that at the beginning of the term when I announced that we are going to keep track of absentees from now on that the pastor stood right up and declared that if we're going to have school for little kids instead of for adults then he was going to quit now!

The other night we had the married students at the house for homemade ice cream. The pastor refused to come, feigning illness, and I'm still a bit put out about it. Anyway, the students got to talking about how it would be if one of them would help with the serving at their home, such as I was helping Edith. In the ensuing conversation, Clifford said, "Before I became converted I had begun to think that the following would be a pretty good way for me to live: I would have my wife bring my food before me and then after putting it down, she should sit at a respectful distance to keep alert to any of my needs. Should I need water, she would be quick to notice and bring it without my having to mention it. Should the meat become low she could supply quickly from the kitchen a new supply for me. Should a dog under the table bother us, she would chase it away without my saying anything to her. Later if it developed that should the work of the house become too demanding so that one could not fulfill all the functions required of a wife to her husband then one would simply take a second wife, and later, a third wife, and so forth, for however many are needed to keep the husband properly treated."

I suppose my distaste for this arrangement is bred from my not ever having had the delicious experience of being pedestaled. I've been reading an unexpurgated version of "Arabian Night," and I have been finding some things that fit into the above view a man may come to have of himself. I guess we guys from the West just don't rate. Firstly, we don't have anyway near as an exalted view of ourselves as we should have, and secondly, our women have an even lower opinion of our uniqueness among God's creatures than we do. It's really rather sad when you think of it and I suppose the best way to get over the gloom is to bury oneself in work!

Today I got a bit of an insight into some of my Swahili grammatical goofs. A student told me that sometimes in my prayers I say "*Tomba*"—shortening of "*Tuomba*" instead of saying "*Twaomba*". The dictionary says, "to have sexual intercourse, copulate of the male, commonly avoided as vulgar." The one chap filled me in on the English, by saying that it means, "fucking." How he came to know what that word means in English, I hadn't the nerve to ask him. Secondly, they told me that when I preached about the church of Smyrna, I used the English pronunciation. The Swahili pronunciation is something like "*Simna*". Anyway, in Kijita, Smyrna apparently also means "fucking." Further, I found out that the word "manna," for the food that fell from heaven, is also written "*mana*" in KiSwahili, but that in Kijita also means "fucking." In fact, the Jita who told me this was so in fear of the word that in our entire conversation he wouldn't actually use the word. Further, the name of the church leader at Utegi, Manain, is also a prohibited word in Kijita. So, today I got my head full of dirty Jita words.

October 17, 1968

These days I find myself a bit short with my fellow mortals, for example, what happened yesterday between Pastor and me. He's been thrown off stride because his wife had gone to Shirati Hospital. He missed classes, came late, skipped chapel, etc. After tea today he came in a period late as I was beginning a review of Paul's second missionary journey.

Pastor: Say, what are you doing up there? Are you writing notes or what? I haven't heard that you are writing notes, and I don't even have my note-book here.
Shenk: If you want to know what is going on here, why don't you attend classes. How many classes have you attended in two weeks? Only two?
Class: Tittering and laughter all around.
Pastor: What I asked was if you are writing notes.
Shenk: It looks as though I am writing notes.
Pastor: (He gets up and exits the room, not to appear until the next day and true to form, he was ten minutes late for chapel.)

That evening pastor spoke in prayer meeting, extolling Moses, who wasn't happy when the Lord got angry with Israel. We, too, shouldn't be happy when our brother has trouble. He then asked Brother Principal to close the prayers, so the Brother Principal prayed a long, long prayer. It seemed to clear the air, and only once today did pastor try to give me the conclusion of the matter, something which among us lesser humans he finds it impossible to refrain from doing.

I've got a theory about when African pastors get to the States: they should remember to keep their sermons simple. No matter how profound they may become (knowing the limitations that our present pastors have) they still can't begin to touch the profundity of their audience. If they want to do something better than the audience, then they should try to get simpler. They may be able to get simpler than the simplest of their audiences and by out-simplifying them, they may be able to get around the audience's profundity. You beat them by getting simpler than they can get. You can't touch their profundity, so don't try to compete on that score. Thus I advise!

Yesterday I was teaching away to the women when I noticed that some were intently looking out the window and door. I asked what was wrong and one of them said, "That boy was in our toilet." I looked and saw a fourteen-year-old schoolboy sauntering down across the lawn. I lit into him and told him not to ever again use the women's toilet. The women informed that his companion was still in their toilet, and the lad outside confirmed it. So I took off on a run across the lawn and burst into the toilet and surprised this fellow squatting over the hole. I laid two good barehanded smacks on his posterior before he got his pants up, and out the door he shot buttoning his shorts as he ran. I shouted several threats after him and returned to teaching. I still haven't got bashed down by anyone about that matter. But it's one of those things which you could never make stick should the community decide to unstick it for you. It's still better to be weak than to be strong—here, at least.

Yesterday I thought I was going psychic. In the morning was this tremendous confrontation of wills between the pastor and me. He came in with all the bravado he displays and began at once to take command of the classroom. I rejected his advance. He at once rejected me as his teacher, if I wasn't going to let him dominate the show. He did well in leaving, because even had he stayed he wouldn't have been able to think for an hour, and he would have charged the situation so much that it would have colored the whole situation for the class. He left with the twitter of other students in his ears, and to return without an apology from us was to ask of him quite a bit. That afternoon we got to talking about the dead and their affect on our lives. I tried to approach the matter from the viewpoint of the psychic power of influence which one well may have on another. We got this thing going so deep and the fellows were so deeply involved in belief and emotion, the situation being heightened by the already tense psychic conflict of the morning class, which still wasn't resolved, that I got to feeling that there were forces pushing to the surface here which were beyond rational control. I suddenly wondered if I might have a strong psychic domination on those who cross my path. This the African interprets as witchcraft. I got to wondering if I might be an unwitting witch. I even got to wondering if I might drive the pastor to suicide, my unrelenting insistence on his not dominating the class. I felt on the threshold of something mysterious and fearful.

I went home after classes determined to go and beg the pastor forgiveness for causing the students to laugh at him. Then I felt the cloud of the evil lift a bit. At prayer meeting I sensed that the pastor's conflict had passed, so I just gave him a cordial greeting and the high tide of psychic conflict ebbed away.

October 21, 1968

I guess I'm too proud to have many kings. I did have some, but more recently I've been more intent on killing them off than on having them. I search for their clay feet until I find them, and then I'm content that they haven't got anything over me. Isn't that a terrible attitude to take toward people?

Maybe what I mean is that I don't have any kings anymore like that, i.e. like the kings who could do no wrong. But I do have kings of another sort, the kind who do wrong and know it and live in repentance for that wrong. It seems that most of them are little people who haven't left any great mark nor done a superhuman thing. They're people who have come to a position of humility about who they are, people who live repentingly. I do still stand in awe at the accomplishments of some Homo sapiens and these I don't want to diminish as they have performed tremendous services. But such men may be only like machines, which can turn out more of a better criterion whereby we differentiate between God's people and the world's people. So, in the Christian's perspective, it really isn't too important.

It seems to me that what is distinctive about Christians is that they are aware both of their own clay feet and of the clay feet of which they are part owner due to the fact of their being part of humanity. How's that? I mean that the more organized we become the less latitude we have for independent action and therefore the more we share in the collective sins of our fellows to whom we are bound by the system. So we sin individually and we sin collectively, and the Christian is sorry about it while the non-Christian doesn't realize that anything is amiss. I don't mean that the Christian is morbid about his repenting. I just mean that he is aware and that being aware he orders his life as much as possible toward rectifying what is wrong. But what is wrong is basically that the system, and we as individuals, force our fellows into rigid patterns of existence, isn't it? So the Christian's repentant act can't be the devising of new forms of imposing rigid control over his fellows. His acts have to be ordered toward the end of setting men free. This the Christian probably can't do, but he can at least be sensitive about it.

So wouldn't these be the kings, no not the kings. These would be the brothers and through them we see the King?

Let me go over this again. I have just been reading Jacques Ellul's, *The Presence of the Kingdom.* I am finding it really stimulating. Some of what he is saying seems to me to be that: The movement of history seems to be toward the enslavement of man. He continually has less and less freedom to control his own affairs. It seems that most of the revolutionary forces in the world today are simply working to enslave man more. It is sort of a contest to see who can enslave him the most. This is because you can't crack the system without getting one that works better, i.e., that enslaves more fully. It is that old Hitler thing, which goes that the US beat Hitler, but in doing so it had to get like Hitler, so now the world is more Hitlerian than before we fought him. This man points out that both western capitalism and Russian communism are dedicated to enslaving men so as to produce more goods. The US does it for the benefit of the capitalist, while Russia does it for the State. He says that to be truly revolutionary we must work toward the destruction of this grip on men. But paradoxically this can't be done because of the way to do it would be to develop a better way of enslaving men, so that you could use their combined power to overthrow the enslaving system. So the Christian works at it spiritually, and I'm not sure yet how this is to be done. But it would seem to me that the former point is taken, i.e., that the criterion for measuring a Christian is not how good a slave he is but how repentant he is about his own sin and maybe more importantly about his own role in the enslaving process.

It is this spirit which to me makes a man to be of significance. If this spirit is happily combined with great intellect and physical stamina then you get something like a Hammarskjold. But it seems further that this spirit in most men is a fleeting thing. We see it and then it disappears and we live in disappointment of him and then again it flares brightly again. So that even these if examined for long periods lose their luster. I've stopped and tried to think of whom specifically I am writing about—and I can't think of anyone in particular.

But let me give you an example of what happened today between the pastor and me. Again he came to chapel ten minutes late and interrupted the speech I was making as he found his seat. Then, after chapel, he was again late to class because of his having to return to his house for something. So when he got back from his house, I met him on the path and I challenged him about this trouble of his. So, we began to talk, a bit harshly on my part I fear. In a couple of moments a church leader rode up on his bicycle and I left them, but when they were through the pastor came to my office and we spent the entire following two periods before tea talking. This time there was no heat, only talk, and both of us said just about everything we had on our minds. The experience for me was one of tremendous release of pressure. I felt free again, sort of like when you get converted. I felt reconciled and there was nothing between us anymore but love. We both prayed and then we left the office with our arms around each other. When we went to my house and parted ways I nearly kissed him, but instead we embraced. Right after tea I made a short statement to the students, confessing my tension and giving the Lord praise for His release and cleansing. Pastor then followed with a few words, and so we proceeded to the classroom business. Both he and I had felt that the other was trying to "enslave" him, and what happened, I don't know, but the result was that both of us took down the walls and set the other free. In so doing we were again brethren. We admitted to each other that given our pride, ambition, and propinquity and given our oscillating roles where I am under him outside the classroom and he is under me in the classroom, we will definitely find the problem attempting to recur. Whether or not it gets as bad as it did depends on our repentance.

So these are the people I have been touched by and through whom I see the King. And if I see Jacobs allowing the machinery to stop a bit while he repents and gets a new vision of the Christian ministry, then I see the King in him too.

But returning to the matter of the US and Russia enslaving their millions, let me quote a few lines from Tanzania's President Nyerere's fifth booklet "Freedom and Development."

"If the aim of development is to make freedom and the life of the people bountiful, it cannot be implemented by force. There is a proverb which says that you can force an ass to the pond but you cannot force him to drink.

"By order, or slavery, you can erect pyramids and build giant roads; you can expand *shambas*, or increase the output from your factories. These and many other things can be attained by using force; but they do not bring development to people."

Nyerere is a Christian statesman!

Another quote: "Leadership means talking to people, exchanging views with them, telling and encouraging them. It means giving worthwhile proposals, working together with them, showing them by actions what you suggest they should do. It means to be one of the people and to understand that they are people like you."

The other evening I concluded that I am not a good administrator. Edith concluded this a very long time ago. Also, Edith thinks she could stand another five-year tour here, if she could get away to Nairobi every so often to have another baby!

November 17, 1968

Thursday the water on the station went off. It was said that a hippo must have broken off the pipe because it was pumping stuff too big to have been able to get through the sieve on the end of the pipe. Early Friday morning I went down to the lake with Kishamuli, the young mechanic, to see what was to be done. Kishamuli wanted to move the whole pipe to another location, where we'd not have to go through so many lake reeds in order to get out to the water. I was against this move because it would mean so much longer a supply line. But as we stood discussing all this I looked out over the reeds to see how things were and behold a massive floating island of reeds now rested right over the old pipe stand. So then it was a floating island and not a hippo which had done the damage. So the old route was closed to us, and we then decided to try the new one.

We worked on pulling out the old pipe and putting it together again in the new direction. We needed a good bit more pipe and fortunately a lot had been bought from the old gold mine at Kabasa, so we had just enough. We must have strung out twenty lengths of pipe in the new direction. Then about four in the afternoon we had a terrific storm, which we waited out in the station wagon. When the storm passed we discovered that the floating island of reeds was now moving majestically off across the way. So the main reason for moving the pipe was removed. By six we had the new pipe all joined up and we then started trying to get the pump running. We tried but failed and as it had got dark, we decided to let it go until tomorrow. The pump apparently had sand in it.

The next morning I learned that the Bishop had sent Kishamuli to Shirati with a number of his children and his wife to visit the village in which his wife's older brother had just died. So that meant that if we were to have water for the station, I'd have to do it. Then at breakfast our milkman came, asking that I loan him a truck to haul timbers and *bati* for his house. I sent him to the church secretary, but the secretary sent the milkman back to me, saying he could use the truck, but I'd have to drive him. Daddy and Mother were visiting for a few days. They returned home by bus. I walked them up to the bus stop. On the way we stopped in at the Bishop's to greet him. He told me that he needed me to drive him to town in connection with a problem that pastor was having with the police. And so it goes! And these are the holidays when I was hoping to spend more time with the family and jobs about our house.

December 6, 1968

The other day I had another of those more-interesting-than-usual experiences, and I thought I might as well let you know about it. See if you can't get it published in the SatEvePost!

The Kirumi Ferry snapped its cables the day before we were to take the kids back to school in Nairobi. Actually only one snapped, but they could find no cable to replace it anywhere. Reportedly, they had ordered new cables to be sent from Dar six months ago, but they still had not arrived. So the talk is of the ferry being out for another six months. Understandably, the owner doesn't want to fix it up because the government has promised to put one of their ferries in by last August! So it looked as though our kids just would not be able to get to school. (The Petersheim's two kids and our Joyce.) I got the idea that we could get to Nairobi by going through the northern arm of the Serengeti Park. One can get a track to Kenya from somewhere near the Banagi Gate. Daddy reportedly came through there once back in the 1930s and burnt out clutches and so forth. More recently we'd heard that a new road had been built into Seronera from Kenya along that northern arm of the park. Leroy Petersheim jumped at the idea, and we left here at about noon, much too late, but that's as long as it took to find out for sure what bad shape the ferry was in and evolve an alternative way to get the kids out of here.

Edith had planned to go along and get some dental work done, but Dianne had been sick for a week and the day before she suddenly got a lot worse, so we figured that Edith had better say at home with Dianne. So it was Leroy and me with the three children. It was really quite exciting, not knowing where we were going or what we would see nor when we would get into Nairobi. For my part, I was happy to have Leroy along. He didn't want to do much driving, but he has a strong back and he has a head full of practical ideas for emergencies. We took along tire patching equipment and an extra tin of petrol, but we didn't have any shovels, *pangas*, or hoes, omissions, which I'm sure Daddy would have felt to be criminally negligent.

The road out to Banagi is much better than in 1963. All the rivers have passable bridges over them. Just the same, it is a long hard hundred miles, and the road is the worst we encountered on the whole safari. We saw very few animals before Banagi. There we discover the new road we'd heard about, stretching out to the north. It's quite straight, well graded, and so new that it has few holes or corrugations in it.

Here we saw quite a few herds of elephants, five huge ones which had just crossed the road before we came upon them. The animals seemed tamer and we could get quite close to them. Maybe they were breeding and that was what made them so tame. Most of the zebra seemed to be in pairs, and they would stand and watch us instead of dashing off. The impala were in rather large herds of either female or males. Several groups we passed must have had about thirty to forty does, zealously guarded by only one buck. Then other groups would have ten to twenty beautiful bucks, all with splendid racks. We saw a good many buffalo also.

We got to the Serengeti gate, Kleins Camp, at about 4:30. The guard urged us to push along, so that we wouldn't have to sleep at Keekorok Lodge, a very swanky outfit. On that stretch through the Serengeti we got into one of the worst thunderstorms I've ever been in. It just got absolutely dark, and it poured rain like doomsday. I was a bit unnerved by it, I must admit. Everywhere there were sheets of water. Sheets of water over the road, sheets of water on both sides, and sheets of water coming down. I was glad Leroy was along. Fortunately it hadn't been raining for a month or more, so the road stayed firm and we got through before the water collected in the low spots. It was a very flat area and that too probably helped us to get through. Leroy's son Robbie was in his glory. He was hoping we'd have some extraordinary adventures.

To my surprise we got into a Kenya park just as soon as we got out of Tanzania. I thought it was a border check for entering Kenya and when the chap told me to cough up Shs 30/=, I thought he was pulling my leg. So he got very sober and notified me that they didn't want any trouble. In the end, for the privilege of driving through about thirty miles of sparse animal country, we forked over the money and got receipts. The rest of that day we had to stop at five check points, all for parks or hunting. At one place I had to sign a book indicating that we were photographing animals rather than shooting them. Lucky thing I had a camera along or we would have had no excuse at all for being in the park.

The road in Kenya evolved from gravel to dust for the most part, rather good, but made us all very filthy with dust. We got to Narok at about eight, bought petrol, and pushed on. Leroy drove that bit from Narok into Nairobi. We got there at about eleven—about eleven hours after we'd left home. To our happy surprise the trip was thirty miles shorter than the normal way.

Two days later we left Nairobi, waiting until 11:00, until Miss Wenger, who was in Nairobi, to be finished at the dentist. The ferry was still closed, so it was a retracing of our steps back through the wilderness. We got one flat, but Leroy got it changed almost before we knew what had happened.

This time the worst road was at the end of that stretch from Banagi to Ikizu. Shortly after Banagi I eased into a rock-filled mud hole, but just as the front wheels got into it something went wrong with the drive mechanism. It felt as though the axle had broken. Leroy jumped out and pronounced us hung up on the differential. Sure enough we hung up on a high clay center. Leroy got a pole and tried to pry us off, but the pole was rotten and broke, so we jacked up each side of the vehicle and filled in under the wheels with a log and some flat rocks we got out of the mud hole. Then while Leroy and I pushed, Rhoda drove it through. It all looked like a simple and harmless operation, but what we didn't know was that a small stone in the clay had punched a hole the size of the end of your thumb into the soft aluminum underbelly of the differential.

We were unaware and just kept pushing on. We got to within five miles of a place called Mugeta. I suddenly felt a sort of rhythmic grinding, and told Leroy to get ready to fix a flat as our spare was already used. There was no flat, so we started off again, but almost at once came that peculiar sound. Just then we were passing through a tiny village of about six houses, two of which had pressure lanterns, so we stopped. It turned out that we have a church there, and a number of people knew us. They quickly provided some flashlights and we jacked up a wheel to see if something might be wrong with the differential, from which the sound seemed to be coming. We couldn't find anything conclusive except that I got to touching the axle housing and found it too hot to touch. So we figured that someone hadn't put oil in the dif. Just then a lorry from the Emporium came along. He was a few hours late on his return from a day of selling supplies to dukas out toward Isenye. I flagged him down and he readily consented to take us home. We parked the car behind a little duka and climbed aboard. It was still 47 miles to Bukiroba. We got there at about eleven, some twelve hours after leaving Nairobi. It seemed that the Lord had that differential programmed to go dry at the best possible time and at the best possible place.

The day we got back was a Friday, and I agreed to go with the mechanic to see what was wrong with the car. At first I had wanted to go by *piki* with another driver, but Daddy and Mother were here when I got back, having got across the bay in a rickety old boat. They felt we should go in the mechanic's Chevy pickup truck. So that's how we went off at about noon. Some two hours later we were nearing Mugeta when I suddenly remembered that I had forgotten the keys to the Peugeot wagon. We had thoroughly locked up everything. So we stopped and discussed it and the mechanic felt we should go and give it a try before driving the whole way back for the keys. He had a pair of keys to another Peugeot and with them he got one front door open. So he got to work on the rear end while I got to work on the steering column.

Before long he discovered that the differential had a hole in it but he couldn't discover any large amount of damage done. For my part, I could take the switch apart and thus start the car, but do what I may I could not unlock the steering column. So at about quarter to four it was decided that I go back for the keys. I drove that old Chevy just as hard as I could and by eight that night I was back with the keys. I think the only time I have ever felt more stupid in my life was the time Jacobs took me to Nairobi, over the time Edith was sick, the other year. We left Bukiroba at about 2:30 in the afternoon. A couple miles south of the border I remembered that I had forgotten my passport. It was almost too late to get back across the ferry. That time Jacobs managed to talk the officials into letting me through, but Daddy had to bring my passport to the border the next day. Brother was I embarrassed!

The mechanic stuffed some rubber into the hole and had tied a pad under the dif with strings that went up over it. He then filled it with oil and as soon as I got there we set out. After about eight miles of driving, we stopped to have a look, and his entire repair job had been scraped off and all the oil had run out again. So lying there, astride a gully, we redid the whole thing. This time we drove very slowly and tried to avoid even the grass in the middle of the road. This time it worked longer. We stopped several times to check; it was still holding. But down toward Nyankanga the road is such a mass of sand ridges that it was hard to keep the wheels in the sand and the undercarriage over the ruts. I was also getting so sleepy that I could hardly keep awake. We were also driving faster on the better road. When we stopped at Nyankanga we found the new plug gone. The oil was still draining out, so we took off and got home a bit before ten thirty.

On Monday morning the mechanics repeated the rubber stopper stunt and drove it into the garage at Musoma. They welded an aluminum patch on and hung a crude patch on under the dif for future protection. Next week the Shirati people want to take the car to Dar, and they want to go across the *pori* on their way. I figured that I'd better put a proper shield on it. That is what I was doing all day yesterday. What took so long was that the only metal around which was suitable was a plate $3/16^{th}$ inches thick, and the only thing to cut it out with was a hacksaw and a cold chisel. And molding the contours could only be done by heating it red hot.

That's one of the things about being a missionary. Some days it seems that your whole time is swallowed up just by repairing and maintaining the stuff that we need to live with. I think sociologists call that kind of living "subsistence level living." If I hadn't been at the car, I would have been helping the mechanic fix the station electrical system. We developed a massive short somewhere the other night, and he spent all day Saturday looking for it. Most of our light bulbs were only half lit, this for a week. But it is only once in a while that these things get us down. Most of the time being a missionary is a jolly good life.

December 20, 1968

I am getting up in the world. I now have a seat on the bookshop committee! I am mission representative, having co-responsibility with Stella. I am secretary of Musoma Alliance Secondary School. I have been elected on to some ad hoc committee of the Tanzania Mennonite Church Youth League. The Alliance board thing is sort of a testing ground for me. I can queer the pitch and that will be the last that Joe will be heard of. Or I can do a good job and sometime be given more responsibility. It makes me feel just a bit as though I am about to take an exam which will tell me something about myself and I am not at all sure what I shall discover. I know that during the past year I have done far too much garden work and far too little desk-work. Now I have got to get my files straight and try to keep track of this administrative chick which has hatched. But brother I don't hanker to administer anything. I like the freedom to run around that it sometimes gives and I like the publicity but I don't like the work. I like to teach amidst the cluttered pile of old papers all over my office and desk!

At annual conference the discussion of National Service came up. We got the same old rehash about how Bishop Jacobs and certain others visited someone once in Dar es Salaam. Pastor Muganda said, "If I were a youth I'd want to be in National Service because I could give testimony while there that I do not fight. Now you people of Shirati, why did you bring this question? We were taught to beware of military training."

The Bishop attempted to make a distinction between the army and national service. The man in Dar is reported to have said, "Wait until there is a war and then come and talk about it again." The word even seems that it would be a good thing for our youth who are prospective pastors to pass though National Service. Another brother said, "Because of putting immature youth into this sort of a place, I also warn about being prepared before the time comes."

"Let's be careful of opening this word again with the government, as it will be like stirring up a bees' nest."

Finally the Bishop said, "I've done my part, I went with Jacobs, etc." He repeated the story again. "My conscience is clear because I've done my part. If war comes then I will say to the government that they be sympathetic to the consciences of our Christians but I will not ask for the Mennonites to be excused. I'll ask that they get a sympathetic ear. So we must teach our children now so that should war come they will be prepared to stand for themselves before the government."

Lengthy discussion continued on both pro and con about serving in National Service. We got some conservative opinions, but it appears mostly that we are scared of stirring up the government needlessly.

On another issue: If our daughters are married by a polygamist, are we or are we not to accept cattle for them? One pastor said, "Yes, we should collect the cattle because they are our daughters." Everybody wants to collect cattle, so the matter is closed. It looks as though Shenk was going to say something, but another brother spoke first. There is pressure to get the discussions shut off. Then Pastor Igira came out to be against accepting the cattle. Elder Migire is also against accepting cattle! Shenk then got the floor. He, too, does not want the cattle. Sarya is very strong for getting the cattle. Mato didn't take cattle but now he hears that it is no matter and we can give our daughters to polygamists! Great noise followed. The Bishop says that we refuse them to be so married, but if they get so married, then collect the cattle too. If you don't take the cows it is a curse on your daughter. Later, in the men's toilet—a great racket over the topic. I now have three daughters!

December 27, 1968

Jacobs gave me *The Presence of the Kingdom* by Jacques Ellul, a 1967 edition. He is very good at analyzing the problems that face the modern man in a technological society, and he presents constructive patterns of intellectual attitude for the healthy Christian thinker. He doesn't hesitate to indicate that he is writing as an intellectual to other intellectuals. I am not one, and so it went slowly for me, but it was very worth while.

He seems to be saying that we shouldn't let facts become our masters. In that regard, TMC is not in slavery to fact. Or at least not the sort of fact to which most of the world bows. The men at the helm know practically nothing about the facts which the world worships. If they're bound to anything (I am speaking here of that extra to the spiritual commitment to Christ which they necessarily have—of that stream of motivation which runs deep and strong and almost primordial whose currents carry us even when we are not aware of it). It is a sense of commitment to the well-being of their extended family, which in the case of the Christians, become those of your own tribe who have become Christians and whose responsibilities in the church place them in contact with you. A person is elected to office not because of his ability but because of his amenability to your pursuit of your own well being and interchangeability. The secretary for youth is appointed by conference as a sort of big brother to watch over the affairs of the church youth. The youth don't like the present secretary and further he doesn't do his job. But he has placed himself in a position of subservience to the elders. For example, yesterday, they threw a feast at his home for the TMC wheel and a number of the missionaries. The only possible reason I can figure out for the feat is to keep his passionate dream for going to the states as current thinking among his elders. He serves them and they are bound in turn to serve him. His name is *Bwana* A. M. N. K. Nyakiakikomati. I'm sure you shall hear much more of him.

But getting back to the worship of facts. Since the African church doesn't bow down to facts maybe they are freer than we are. But maybe bondage to one's extended family is a greater slavery than that to facts. Just the same, there does seem to be a freedom here. But my thinking has now gone beyond that freedom to the bondage imposed by one's associates. Question: How much shall I enslave myself so as to be in a position to exert revolutionary pressure? Answer: Probably none at all.

Over this Christmas time I got the first opportunity in my life here to give a series of messages in church. I have been preaching maybe once or twice a month, and sometimes not that often. Over Christmas the Musoma Church had a three-day series of meetings and they cast about even to the AIM for speakers but could find nobody but the Bishop of TMC. Accordingly, they contacted me, told me the sorry story of a search for speakers and asked that I help them out of their difficulty as I was after all one of them! So I consented.

There were very few people there the first two days, but Christmas morning there was a packed church. I got to preach four times and each time took a different aspect of Advent. After the first session, the Bishop got me to speak first and he then sort of underlined and commented on what I had said. The point is that both he and Muganda seemed to be quite impressed. In a way, I felt a bit badly because I felt that I had over-shadowed the Bishop. So I sound like boasting and maybe I am, but I don't intend it that way. For me it was like the first time Jack Shellard had me preach at Alliance Secondary, and he was favorably impressed. Now it was TMC's turn. Maybe it means that I may be given an opportunity to speak more often although more likely it may be an even greater reason to avoid me.

How much shall I write about our latest *safari* to climb Mt. Kilimanjaro? It was fun but too expensive. It snowed the night we climbed the mountain and it snowed the whole way up to the top. The guide was about as bushed as were the rest of us. He said that if there had been more snow we would not have made it. All of us finally did get to the top. I pounded steps for Cora for the last hour or so as she had a stiff leg and climbing had got very difficult for her. I carried my black-white camera along with the slide one and got a series of excellent pictures. Unfortunately, the focus mechanism froze up and I broke it before I knew what was wrong. Just the same, I could shut the shutter to 22 and got excellent pictures anyway. Dick and the first guide made it about a half-hour before Cora and me, and we made it about a half-hour before Naomi and the second guide. We found both Dick and the guide fast asleep. Dick was really blue, so blue, in fact, that he looked black. Nobody remembers how I looked. It was gusting while we were on the top, and at times it would clear so we could see across the crater, but at no time could we see across to Mawenzi nor down to where we had come from.

Dick is not a talker, so I mostly had to talk to myself or just banter about this and that. I'm sure they all got slightly tired hearing Joe talk about how it was and how it will be and what to do and not to do. Dick was about as determined to get up the mountain, as he was to pass his medical boards. Naomi said her parents would be horrified should they realize what she went through on this climb. Cora was a real plodder, but her stiff leg sort of put us out of stride on the way down.

On the matter of ever publishing any of this stuff, I say right away that none of mine is publishable. I view our conversation in three ways. (1) It is fun and stimulating to write to someone who will read the stuff and care about it and sometimes respond specifically to it. It also insures that I get an occasional letter that is stimulating and interesting. Something more than how many cans of peaches got canned. It gives me a sounding board on which I can throw my quirks and foibles to see how they come out when treated by another. And it is just a bit of my caring enough about my brother to keep in touch with him. (2) These letters are on file, as you have often let me know. So I admit that some of my writing is sort of journalistic, i.e., it is a sort of journal that another keeps for me. I would hope that sometime in my old age I would be interested in reviewing these few years spent at Bukiroba. On the other hand, maybe I won't be able to face what I was and won't be interested in reading them. (3) You are a writer. You need to have a thorough exposure to life as it is lived so that your writing about Africa is relevant. A writer usually has his own life and experience on which to draw for relevance in his own writing. I have got the idea that maybe my writing to you can (a) expose you to yet another life met in the flesh not between the covers of a book written by another, and can (b) provide you with an experience different from that you experience in the American swirl of living. Maybe I can help your writing to be more relevant. I know that this last idea is a bit wild and a bit hubristic on my part, but in my conceited little soul it is how I think about it. So here it is!

1969

January 19, 1969

Our good Mennonite nurturing is standing us in good stead this year in Tanzania. The TANU Youth league, with the approval of the government, has launched a drive to clean up the dress habits of their fellow citizens. Such items as mini-skirts, tight skirts, tight trousers, short Bermudas, wide belts, skin lighteners, wigs, and outlandish shoes and hats are banned. Already several men and women have had their trousers and skirts slit in Musoma by vigilant government youth. I don't anticipate that Edith or I shall have any trouble.

Joyce is beginning her second term of school at the Rosslyn Academy near Nairobi. Dianne is learning to speak Swahili in Joyce's absence, as she has no other English-speaking playmates. We all look forward eagerly to Joyce's weekly letters with her dictated news and a few imaginative drawings.

The Theological College students have just begun their third and last year of training. Sixteen of the original twenty are still sticking with it. Pray with us that these men may be "the salt of the earth" and "the light of the world" and that they may be willing to work as "sheep among wolves."

January 20, 1969

The graduation of the nursing school at Shirati Hospital was this past Saturday. As has been the practice in the past, invitations were sent to a great number of people. One also was sent to the Regional Commissioner and the Regional Chair of TANU. No one gave any thought about what they would do should the RC come. In fact, Sister Tutor made the graduation plans without any consultation with the hospital administrator. He was not even kept posted on who the speaker was. Sister Tutor does not like too much outside meddling into her affairs; this attitude kept anyone from acting independently. It seems incredible but apparently no Africans were involved in planning the program, at least no African with a veto voice. So then, the day was mapped out with no thought whatsoever as to what would be done should the RC turn up as invited. That no RC had ever come to graduation before seemed sure evidence that this one would not come.

The procession had formed and had actually begun walking when the RC drove up in his official car with flags flying, accompanied by a government information officer. The doctor saw him drive in and remarked to the hospital administrator that the RC is here and wondered what should be done. The administrator sent a nurse to show the RC into the auditorium. She took him through the back door and seated him over halfway back in the audience. All the chairs for the official guests were filled, and not a soul thought to bring additional chairs. After the procession got into the church, someone up front sent an usher back to whisper a welcome to the RC to come up front. He, of course, at this point declined, saying later that he didn't want to create a disturbance in a meeting which he could clearly see hadn't really intended that he be there.

So the meeting continued from start to finish without a soul bestirring himself, more than to acknowledge at the beginning of speeches, that the RC was among them. The chair of the meeting was an African and numerous African pastors were in the audience. Yet no one bestirred themselves. I should mention that the Regional Chairman of TANU carries the weight in politics. In fact, in political meetings the Regional Commissioner becomes the Regional Secretary of the Regional Chairman. The Chairman is elected, which makes him the representative of the people. So the offense was compounded!

At the end of the ceremony an invitation was given to all those who had special cards, in addition to the regular invitation, to come to tea. On the end of this announcement an appendage was placed a note indicating that the RC and his party were also invited for tea. The amazing thing is that someone should be invited by letter to a graduation and then barred from having tea because he hadn't got a second invitation to tea. The church secretary wondered just how expensive their tea was at Shirati! This is an aside, but it points up again a great gap in understanding on the part of the missionaries as to what is kosher and what isn't among the Africans.

The RC stood outside waiting for someone to greet him and to show him to where tea was to be served. Nobody so much as gave him a hand.

Therefore, he decided that he had better get on home. Accordingly he got into his car. At that point the hospital administrator ran after the car and knocked on his door and asked him if he wasn't going to drink some tea. "Or, are you very busy?" The RC conceded that he was indeed busy and off they drove. Even then, except for a few Africans and a couple of missionary nurses, no one at Shirati felt that things had gone too badly. The feeling was that there might have been some slight protocol offense but what can one expect from Americans who can't become Africans. The RC must realize that Americans are just different.

On Monday morning, the RC summoned the Bishop to his office. The Bishop was away at a funeral. So a pastor and the church secretary went instead. Both the Regional Commissioner and the Regional Chairman of TANU met them and it was one hot hour. They told our men that they at first felt like simply declaring the whole Tanzania Mennonite Church illegal. Many hard things were said. The Bishop got home toward evening and went right away into town, but the RC had left. The next morning a messenger came and summoned him to a 9:00 o'clock meeting with the RC. They had a long round, but not so hard as the first. The Bishop begged for mercy and pled with the RC not to include the whole church in this one mistake. The Bishop acknowledged that Shirati has long been a hot bed of trouble. He acknowledged that the Shirati area does not have much sense of national involvement. He admitted that Americanism there has gone deep and the people are as their teachers have taught them to be. No doubt it would have been better not to have isolated a segment of the church, but when you are getting the third degree, it's only natural to try to isolate the cancer and to cut it out, if necessary, rather than kill the whole body.

The RC's complaints fell under two headings. The first is that there is only an American spirit at Shirati. The Americans are not liked in the world these days. He sees that they have managed to keep their loyalties there. He was sure that had a representative of President Nixon shown up at the graduation ceremony he would have been given highest honors. But when a representative of Tanzania's President Nyerere shows up, and invited at that, no one so much as bats an eye. The second point was that none of the Africans there have any sense of national involvement or concern. This they have got from their American teachers. The government has now become aware of these two characteristics of the Mennonites. The government is therefore going to put the Mennonites under surveillance. Security officers will be in Shirati area daily from now on. They will look into every nick and cranny of the Mennonite operations. They are going to crush this thing. They are not only going to put their men in Shirati, they are going to put them in Bukiroba and any other place where there are Mennonites. No wonder the Bishop trembled.

So the Bishop drove to Shirati on Wednesday. He had a round with me on Tuesday evening, and I wondered what I could do to be of help. He asked me to go along to say in English what he could say only in Swahili. He said he didn't want his words to be twisted out of context. So he and the church secretary and I went. There was a meeting with all hospital staff and missionaries and pastors and elders. The Bishop read the passage about the householder who went on a safari and whose servants didn't know when he was going to come home. He then prayed, and in his quiet way, he asked for love and forgiveness for anger. Then he began to have his say. I felt that on the whole he was very gentle. He did pin some of the nurses down (Sister Tutor wasn't there—which pretty well brought everyone to nervous collapse). But he didn't castigate anyone. He laughed at the absurdities of American protocol, and I am sure that in some of this the missionaries knew they had been ridiculous, but they were not just sure what had been ridiculous. He did not isolate the missionaries from the other staff. He did not denounce the Americans. In fact, he praised them for their sense of national involvement. He did not castigate the Shirati church. When he asked the church elders questions, however, they just fell all over themselves to put the blame on the side of missionaries. And the church secretary took the missionaries to task for not showing more respect to the Bishop when he comes to Shirati. He took them to task for not having Africans involved in the planning of such things as a graduation. He took them to task on a number of points of protocol. He insisted that any future programs and arrangements are to be cleared with the church office before they are officially announced.

I then had my say. I tried to say what the offense had been by way of identifying who the guests were and trying to explain a bit of what proper protocol would have been. I tried to explain what the results might be in terms of long term government scrutiny of the hospital. I tried to point out where our attitude has been wrong. I tried to use the "we" rather than the "you." If I know my heart I do not think I have isolated myself from the Shirati people. The surgeon thanked me for coming. None of the other missionaries expressed how they felt.

Afterwards, the Bishop laid out his program for reconciliation. He wants the hospital administrator and the surgeon to come to Musoma and meet the Regional Commissioner with him. Then there is going to be a reckoning day with the RC at Shirati. He wants statements to be read from every institution in Shirati area. He then wants the RC to be given his chance to say what needs to be said. If these plans work out, I feel that the ulcer may be healed in its totality. But I do not think that this will clear the air for some individuals. We are in for a period of close scrutiny, to say the least.

We are all individually put together in our own special way. For everyone there is that threshold beyond which he cannot be pushed and still retain his internal structure. Either the structure falls to pieces and he goes mad, or he commits suicide, or he fights and prefers to have his enemy kill him rather than dissolve inside. To say it another way—you cannot push a man beyond the threshold of his internal credibility without destroying his integrity.

Finally, it should be noted, the Regional Commissioner warmly praised the speech he heard at the nursing graduation. I was surprised and deeply humbled to learn of this.

March 17, 1969

I believe I once told you to keep alert to the name Nyakiakikomati, as you might meet him in the states sometime. He's the church's secretary for youth and Sunday school. He was appointed to be a sort of watch dog over the youth. Many can't stand him.

When Orie Miller (the mission board's overseas secretary) was here, Nyakiakikomati insisted on having him for dinner. So the Bishop, the pastor, the church secretary, and I were also invited. The meal was the sort one could write a book about.

First, we had sesame seeds with conversation. This gave way to corn on the cob with conversation. This gave way to beautiful white hominy with some of the best chicken I've ever eaten. This was followed by delicious goat meat perfectly cooked and with any cut of meat you wanted. I've never eaten goat stomachs which were so well cleaned or so well cooked. It was really a masterpiece. To go with the goat meat were Irish potatoes, rice, and *ugali*. For the end of the meal there were cakes, candies (a sort of peanut brittle), *mandazies*, doughnuts, and peanuts. Then there was hot water and milk with little tins of coca, coffee and tea. After all of this there were fizzy drinks for any who could manage it. Long speeches followed, and then we came home. Orie got a letter along with his invitation inquiring into the possibilities for Mr. Nyakiakikomati's going to the States. At the feast Orie handed all this correspondence over to the Bishop!

When I got home, I staggered down to the men's dormitory where a clutch of students was eagerly awaiting news of the feast. I explained the whole thing, from beginning to end. About all the men could do was shake their heads. Such feasts have been known to have been produced before, but they have always been done by a group of people. Never has it been known that one man will put himself out in that way for people who are not his relatives. They all agreed that poor Orie has no idea of the tremendous debt which now hangs heavily over him, since he has accepted the feast and apparently enjoyed it so much. Had he known it, Orie practically mortgaged his family's whole shoe business for that one grand hour of feasting. But alas, Orie is blissfully ignorant. One of the students summed it up by saying, "Now, no one can complain about Nyakiakikomati to the elders. Anyone who says a word against him might as well try to overthrow the whole church hierarchy."

Nothing much happened at the recent pastors' meeting. Just one observation. I felt that the climate drifted farther from acceptance of the youth, than in previous meetings. The Bishop made a strong plea for youth at the beginning of the meeting and that toned down some criticism. Just the same, by the end, there were rather free expressions downgrading education and youth. One pastor was very strong for his two deacons, one of whom is illiterate, and rather negative towards the theological college graduate who has been placed in his district as an assistant to him. He was sticking up for his deacons who feel badly about the assistant getting closer to the top than they. Particularly they feel bad about his getting a salary while they do not.

We had a bit of witchcraft here at the college over the time of the pastors' meeting. Behold, the morning that the college men moved out of the college dorm, a short developed in the electric line which affected only the dorm and the chapel. We searched and discovered that a massive short had developed outside the dormitory, at the terminus of the underground cable. We fixed that, but something was still shorted out. We searched again and found an underground connection near my office, which had shorted so badly that the insulation was melted back four to six inches on the lines. So we fixed that too. Then the chapel lights lit very nicely, by then it was nearly evening. When the lights for the night were turned on, however, we discovered that the dorm still did not have lights. That night we could find no trouble, and every day since the mechanics have spent at least a little time on the wiring. By today, they said that something must be burnt out in the wiring of the fuse box but still no light on what is actually wrong. The dorm, therefore, is still dark with the exception of a pressure lantern.

Rejoice with them that rejoice! Last month we finished paying off the cycle and we finished paying for our December holiday. Edie's mother's faithful friend sent us $225 which put us in the clear. Over the past couple of months

I was pretty scared as never have I been so deeply in debt in relation to my ability to pay. A MEDA person who stayed here gave Edith $50 for ironing his shirts! She's hoarding it for a ball the next time we go up to Nairobi.

April 6, 1969

When we got back from Nairobi we found the Bishop sick with a heavy cold and fever. That was Wednesday night. I messed around here Thursday morning, and then Thursday afternoon went to Buhemba to see into a farmers' training course. When I got back I found that a Mr. Barns had come whom I had met in Nairobi. So my evening was taken up with taking him to Musoma to meet the Catholic bishop. Before we went, I took him to meet our bishop. The Bishop then wondered if it would be possible for the Shirati doctor to come see him. Since our inter-station radio is not working, I decided to try to go for the doctor the next morning. I got back from Musoma after lights out that night and told Edith that I would be off for Shirati early the next morning. The Bishop offered me his car in case the doctor wouldn't have one to use. So by first ferry crossing, I was on my way to Shirati with Joyce and Dianne. We got there at about eight-thirty and found the doctor had gone on a *safari*.

I spoke with the hospital administrator, and he was a bit put out: having a doctor make a 130-mile round-trip to see just one man! He located the doctor and loaned me his personal motorcycle to go for him.

It was nine miles into the bush, toward Utegi, then another fourteen miles back a track towards the lake. I got there a bit before noon. I guess everyone thought that someone had died. The doctor was floored when he heard what I had come about. However, he figured that when they were finished at that place he would come with me. They were giving measles shots and attending to incidental medical cases. They finished up early afternoon, and I took the doctor back with me to the hospital. The doctor had a heavy operation schedule for Saturday morning and felt that he must get to Bukiroba and back the same day. But the more we looked at it the more ridiculous it seemed. Therefore, we finally decided that I'd return with the car and the doctor come down with his family on Saturday afternoon and make clinic visits on Monday, to make it a legitimate hospital *safari*.

About ten miles out of Shirati on the way back the muffler fell off the car. Actually it was the entire tail pipe. It fell off right at the manifold. Wow!! What a racket!! I wired it up so I would not lose it. The car engine had been missing on the way up and by the time I got back it was hitting on only three cylinders. I also got a flat at the ferry. I limped into Bukiroba at about five, sounding like an airplane! The doctor got there the next evening and pronounced the Bishop very ill, having suffered a heart attack. That diagnosis is now quite clear. On the bus run between Dodoma and Singida it occurred at about midnight. The dear man stuck to his guns until he got here late the next day! It is really surprising that he didn't die. Now he is responding to drugs and the doctor hopes that in a month he will be up and about again.

May 4, 1969

I'm trying to remember if anything exciting happened last month. Oh, yes, I fixed up the pastor's sewer system. We cleaned it out earlier. Then it backed up again. So I decided to put in a soak pit. Over the last holidays the cooks dug the pit. One day I was helping. My job was shoveling out the gravel. Once I decided to do a bit of picking as well. The hole was rather narrow. I raised the pick over my head and drove it powerfully into the ground. Only, instead of going into the ground, the front edge of the pick struck a rock in the wall of the pit which threw the force of the pick back on the other arm, the result being that I got a terrible whack on the head. Boy, was I embarrassed when I got out of the pit with blood streaming down my face. I washed off the blood and clapped my hat hard against the wound and so was able to get up to the house without further incident. The pastor can now use his *choo.*

That's my trouble! I do too much of that sort of thing while I should be at my desk writing letters about stuff or making out lecture outlines or planning new exciting things for the college men to do. I've got my excuses though, mainly that the people don't see one's deskwork, and so basically what counts with the people is not the deskwork but the other stuff. I know that is baloney, but it's the only excuse I've got.

May 15, 1969

You wonder if we'll know each other after four years. You were brave enough to admit that sloshing through mud and digging trucks out of bogs leaves you cold. I had a long think on that one and came to the conclusion that you must be getting like your clever daughter who had her Uncle Joe stereotyped as the man who is always making ice cream for everyone. Now you have got a fixation of my being a missionary who is always stuck in the mud. The more I thought about it the more convinced I got that you really don't know me at all. In fact, I haven't had any mud stories in a very, very long time. In addition to that, I don't really like mud. So, having got it settled in my own mind that I'm not really a mud man, I went out the next day and got stuck with the church lorry! Since mud gives you the creeps I'll make this one short.

It was a Saturday, and for a week I and the fellows who go to services over at that place you dubbed Twin Breasts had been planning to take some water there to wet down the dusty floor of their new church. One of the men got tied up with something else, so it was just two of us. Dianne wanted to go along, so we took her, too. We filled three barrels with water and set out in the mission lorry. But the night before it had rained heavily, especially over at the Twin Breasts. The road was terrible, but somehow we managed to get there. We leveled off the floor, mixed a bag of cement in with the top half inch of dust and gravel and put on our three barrels of water. But it still wasn't quite enough, so we went down to a dam and filled our barrels. But when we attempted to leave we found that the wheels had been slowly sinking into the soft soil and it was impossible to move. We off-loaded and tried digging out behind and before the tires and putting in tree twigs and branches for traction, which was a terrible mess, because there were swarms of safari ants all over the place; these kept swarming up our legs. But to no avail. So we had to jack up the lorry, only to find we had no jack. There were no bicycles available, so we walked home. Dianne ran about half the way; we carried her the remainer. We got home about one thirty. We got some lunch, got some jacks and boards, got two more students, and returned in a VW. We got the lorry out, backed in towards the dam at another place where the earth was good and firm, something I should have done in the first place—filled our barrels and poured this on the church floor and got home with both vehicles by dusk. So there it is again, another mud story!

But I don't really consider myself a mud person. I have a carefully thought out theory for the *shamba* work that I do. The getting stuck stuff is usually just stupidity and so doesn't need a theory for supporting it. But the *shamba* theory goes this way: Given the amount of influence which we expatriates are able to wield by way of policy-making and execution, such people as I must come to the conclusions that it isn't worth the time. The place we can make an impact is in the minds of the African community. This can only be done through a medium which the African community can understand. They can't understand what it is these *wazungu* do behind desks all the time—sometimes I wonder myself. So I figure that I should spend at least some time doing what in their eyes is legitimate labor.

For the second time in two months we can't get any more money out of the church office. I'm in a bit of a panic, as I spent some Shs 800/= of my own cash. We've been awaiting a hospital check from the government. As the Shirati Hospital moneys are in the same account as the church's it is possible to borrow Shirati credit balances to give us cash. This has kept the church work floating for about a year now, but now even that system is not working. There will be no more money from the States until near the end of the month. I just hope that we can finish the year before things bust. This year we are worse off than any other. It seems that the church panicked when the American mission executives started suggesting guidelines for the budget for next year. Everyone seems to have tried to get his share this year. The church bought two new cars—well, practically new. Neither of them is used much at all. The pickup already has its one door bent and is in the garage for repairs. Someone backed up when the door was open and bent the door and hinge. No one seems to know who did it. The church lorry had its differential stripped the day after I got it out of the mud. It was taken for a wedding and got stuck and the driver had never driven a lorry before. The mechanic thinks we'll need to get parts from Nairobi.

Our poor pastor nearly got jailed. The school radio was stolen. It got tracked down, but the chaps who took it wouldn't admit that they had sold it to a relative for a bull. So the matter went to court. It's still in courts, and our men from the college have had to make six trips to testify. The first to be called was a student. He was told to swear on a Bible, but he refused, saying that his faith does not allow him to swear. They had a go-around for five minutes. Finally he was told that he is to confess that he swore under duress and not of his own free will. So he swore and gave his testimony about the theft. The second to be called was the Pastor. He also refused to swear. Court officials tried the same pressure on him, but he wouldn't cave in. The court stopped for forty minutes while the judge argued with him, but to no avail whatsoever. Finally they decided to throw the book at the Pastor. They adjourned the court for ten minutes, and told Pastor to go talk with his fellow testifiers. Then, if he would still refuse to swear, he would be charged with contempt of court and be jailed. Further, the prosecution would be charged with the expenses of the trail and the case would be dismissed. In addition, the accused could now accuse their accusers of libel and take them to court. One of our teachers advised Pastor to swear, which he did. Now he says he couldn't sleep that night.

When he got home he went to see the Bishop about the matter. The Bishop is reported to have said, "It's good to take some brethren with you at times likes this, so that they may counsel you what to do." They said that the court was packed and that everyone outside and inside became aware of the fact that Mennonites do not swear. I can't help but feel that Pastor still feels a bit cheated out of a good chance to get put into jail. The chaps who were accused of stealing the radio have got a lawyer for Shs 700/= to represent them. I understand the case will be opened again later this month. In the meantime, the college men have my personal radio. Any world news?!

One of the pastors would make an excellent story for you. You'll remember that early story about an old woman who attempted to bewitch Daddy and an African man for cutting down a sacred tree and nothing ever came of it. Maybe! The pastor's wife has often been unfaithful. He pastored the tiniest district in TMC, so small in fact, that in the Bishop's latest report, he didn't even have a membership figure for the district. The pastor prospers on his farm, using a MEDAT loan to get ahead economically. But he got jailed a half year ago, and he feels that it is directly related to jealousy over his prosperity. Also, none of his daughter has got married yet. They are beautiful women, but it seems men think of them as potential whores instead of wives. I asked another pastor about it once. I had placed the reason of their still being single on the fact that their father probably had not allowed them to be circumcised, and wondered if this may have kept the young men away. But the other pastor didn't feel at all that the reason lay there. He said that many Zanakies say that it is the curse of that old woman coming home to the next generation.

June 3, 1969

I'm remembering a conversation I once had with Paul Miller, that Elkhart seminary prof on a study leave in East Africa. He was feeling a bit sorry for us all here, and I managed to say that I guess here is as a nice place to exist as any. He looked just a bit taken aback and remarked that if that was how I felt, it was okay by him. I could discount his feelings as being culture shock or maybe simple self-hatred regarding Mennonites in general and Lancaster offspring in particular or maybe just an atmosphere at variance to his cool academic halls in Elkhart.

These days I'm not feeling well. Maybe I have a bug sticking in me. But I dream such long convoluted dreams, and you are usually mixed up in them somehow. I can't even reconstruct any of them now; all that is left is a feeling. I used to have David in my distressed dreams, but now it has got to be you. Only with David I used to be fighting, but with you it seems to be something about traveling or being sick.

Phoebe left. And she left without so much as a cup of tea in her honor. She just left. She didn't even pack much. She left being sure that she is coming back in a couple of months. She left with all of us being quite sure that she won't get back at all. Jacobs will see that someone examines her in the States and pronounces her unfit to come back to Africa. That woman did scads and scads of good in this country. There must be a hundred people whom she helped significantly in one way or another. And she left without a cup of tea, knowing that she was coming back. The doctor sent a letter to her brother, telling him that Phoebe was medically unfit to return to Africa. We all knew it. The "neutral" doctor in the States will clinically pass on to Phoebe the news that she cannot come back. And she left without so much as a cup of tea.

Brother, does TMC have financial troubles. We're at the place where on the first of the month I go to the treasurer for money enough to see us through ten days of the new month, an amount of Shs 1300/=. She shows me that there's only Shs 3000/= in the bank for the whole church! Our next remittance from Salunga doesn't come until the end of the month. Shirati Hospital has its money in the church accounts. Why? Because we need their money. We have used a lot of their money already; the treasurer refuses to say how much. The church expects some money soon from the government for the hospital. But we are going to use some of that too. Some day the hospital administrator will want some money and discover there is none. Then we'll have a court case or something. We've vastly overspent, vastly overspent, vastly overspent! No matter what we do next year, it will take a terrific slice out of the budget just simply to repay these debts. A lot of money has gone out on loans, some of them sort of private arrangements. One pastor borrowed money to buy a car, which he is repaying in monthly installments at the rate of Shs 50/= per month. At that rate it will take eleven years to just repay the capital, let alone any interest.

The amazing thing to me is that no one was specifically trained to do anything when this place was handed over from missionaries to Africans. There are lots of good schools of commerce around. Why wasn't someone sent to one of these schools long ago?

Sometimes I have to admit that about the only thing we have succeeded in doing is educating people. We've got quite a number educated now, but we have no money to employ them. We've not grown economically at all. We still make out an annual budget that takes into account ONLY Salunga's money. I can't think of one thing which is really surging ahead, besides the small time farming of the little farmer. Our water pump runs only five hours a day. The electricity is constantly shorting out. The mechanic's garage is a mess. The Musoma Bookshop is going into a hole. Church cars and lorries are going to pot. Anyway, there simply is not enough money in the bank to write checks!

Now all of this would be bad enough as it is. But to get your letter on the eve of the day when one is low saying among other things that you're "tired of the perpetual preoccupation that missionaries have with the small allowances, the perpetual mental squalor of worrying over money, of having not to offend other missionaries who treat their allowances differently, of being misunderstood that since we didn't always talk about our salaries we must have had secret sources of perpetual incomes." So, this is the truth? I used to try to shake it all off, thinking it a sort of paranoia, but now you've got me to thinking that maybe it is true.

Sometimes I get to thinking that I have been ordained to preside over the finishing of things. I become secretary of the Musoma Alliance Secondary Board only to find that in a year the board may be legislated out of existence by the government. I become principal of a silly little theological college only to see it evaporate as soon as the first batch of students gets through. I get ordained only to wind up shepherding a handful of women and school kids out back at Nyamitwebiri. I get a degree and study church growth only to be completely ignored when any discussion of that is about. I am asked to preach at Bukiroba Sunday morning only to be given a note asking me to start the water pump, which takes an hour, until you find a container for fuel, borrow a truck to carry the fuel to the machine, get it going, only to find that someone had a faucet running all during church, so that after church we still don't have any water, and to boot, I didn't preach anyway because an elder came and sat on the bench and he was asked. I join the Association of East African Theological colleges only to have our school drop out of it as soon as I get to know those people. I am mission representative at the time when hospital staff listens to their administrator, secondary school staff listens to their headmaster, and the Bukiroba missionary community is stripped to one secretary and my family. Everything seems to be dying and I can't get a hold on anything that grows.

June 17, 1969

I just don't get fired up anymore about things. I had my first round over Josiah when I saw every dream of the past two years go smashing to the ground. I felt that I must do something. I was sure that had I been in the correct position, I could have done something about that situation. But now I see that there was nothing anyone could do but wait out the Fate ordained for us and then fit into whatever pattern that may offer. That thing has repeated itself many times over, and I have got to where I don't care. When Barak was assigned to us here, he didn't want to teach because he didn't get enough money. I hatched up all kinds of schemes to help him out, but in the end none of them worked. He didn't stay on the staff more than a term, yet my budget kept right on paying him for the entire year. But so what. If I hadn't been paying him, then the church would not have given me all my budget, so what is the difference. Now I fear that the next chap will not teach unless he gets Shs 70/= more per month.

I'm not interested in going back to teaching in a secondary school. You cannot jump from place to place forever. I was pulled out of the secular academic community and put into Bible, and that is where I shall stay. I might get hooked up with another theological college in East Africa. But right now what I'd like to do is be chaplain over at Alliance Secondary. There's a wide open door for teaching Bible and denominational doctrine in that secondary school. However, I would not want to be considered part of a school staff!

When you get to the basic psychology of things, I think that it is something like this: TMC wasn't entirely convinced at any time that it needed all these trained high-powered leaders. They weren't convinced that they need them and they are quite convinced that they don't have the money to pay them. So the school, this round anyway, was a sort of status symbol in which a number of reasonably dedicated and ambitious young men could be given the opportunity to get ahead. It was quite definitely felt that the school would change into a secondary school by this time. The rational for the school has always been more on the side of "helping our children to get ahead" rather than on "making a significant contribution towards church programs and growth." And when you look at this, I am never sure if our rationale comes out the way it does because that is how we feel on the principle of the thing or because of a pragmatically-attuned sixth sense which knows that this is how it is going to come out anyway.

The student group can be classified into three sections. There are those who have always been church leaders and will go back to church work along with subsistence farming and will stick with it no matter what the cash returns. There is the second group who is anxious to make a contribution to their home district but on certain conditions, such as a decent salary. But the districts are a bit afraid of most of these men. They think that they may take the few cents of offering money that now go to the old men of long service with big families. Definitely, there is jealousy of these younger men. And they are feared not only because of the financial threat but also because of the political power, which their education has given them. When pastors speak of their students in theological college there is often a strong emphasis on making it understood that these are "our children." I heard one pastor, who is just now coming into grandfather-hood, repeatedly refer to a student who has fifteen to sixteen-year-old children as "my child." There is the third group who has always viewed the college only as a stepping stone to study in the states. Their pastors tend to say, "Well, you wanted them in your school, so we allowed them to come, and now what will you do with them?"

Now the first group the church isn't worried about. They'll fit in, even without any more training. The third group would like Showalter Foundation funds to start the scramble up the long ladder towards a degree in the States. But it is the second group that offers the most challenge. I have faith that they are sincere about church work. But they want some extra training to give them financial leverage. The church jumps at the chance to get them out of its hair. The church is very reluctant to make any commitments about their role when they are finished here, partly because things are in such a state of flux that there is no certainty and partly because the church isn't sure that they want them back. So further training becomes the way to get both the church and them off the hook. They can then get the better standard of living, which they have come to taste while here and the church gets rid of any commitment toward them. Of course, the option remains open that for some, the end result will be a wedding between them and the church, but it remains clearly an option to which the church is not willing to commit itself. Jacobs had the same problem with the first set of students. But he took the pressure off the church by sending a number to the States. This solved some problems, but it magnified others. We still have not decided what to do with these men. The main difference the church sees between them then and now is that now they're very much more expensive and certainly much more revolutionary. I'm not saying that this is either bad or good, but at least that is the result. So, we're in the same position again. What are we to do to get these chaps out of our hair?

We run into a different set of problems when we begin to consider a year of training here rather than in the States. This is a socialist country and the options for individual initiative are very limited. So, sometimes a student will opt for what he can get rather than for what he wants. For example, it is practically impossible to get any agriculture training of the nature that we want. All ag schools train government workers who come directly from those schools and who are appointed by government after they leave. I've said all this so that you have an idea of how the land lies in this matter.

When Paul Miller was here he urged the students to consider self-supported church service. The students cried that they had no skills with which they could be self-supporting and asked us to teach them skills. We can't do that here, so I got the idea of using Showalter Foundation Funds to give them a skill in a fourth year of training. This discussion has been going on now for about a year, and we have got to the place where a tentative budget has been submitted to Salunga. Kraybill insisted that the skill be one which can be used in the student's home districts and that there be an agreement between the student and the district that following his completion of the course, the student will serve the church for a stated number of years. And that TMC foot one-third of the bill. TMC is reluctant about all that. My problem is: What will happen if this thing falls through? These guys will probably kill me!

I don't always write how I feel; I'm always just a bit afraid that some day a letter will go astray. You may have noted that I did not have a standard return address on the previous letter. And now again. I think I'll go and take a phenobarb!

July 4, 1969

Now what did happen to Phoebe is this: Phoebe is a senior missionary who is very attached to her appointed field of service. When she was accepted for foreign service she had to declare before God and these witnesses that she was intending to be a missionary "for life" and she meant it. Now she is at retirement age and still was in very good shape physically up to about a year ago. It is the policy of the mission board to deal with missionaries through the national church, so when Phoebe declared herself to be anxious to make good her vows of thirty some years ago, it was the national church which had to act on it. The mission board could not tell her to come home because there was no reason for her coming home other than a silly retirement age arrived at. They couldn't even terminate her assignment because for the past five years or so she hasn't had an assignment from either the board or the church. They had nothing to say about money because never in all her years of service has she cost the mission board or the church one cent, other than housing here. Neither could the mission board tell her to stay on because that was the prerogative of the African church. The church, for its part, could absolutely not tell her to not come back. What ingrates they would appear to be throwing out the woman who was responsible for the education of many of the church brass. It is like killing your mother, and no one could bear the guilt of doing that. Therefore she had to be accepted back. No matter which way you look at it, she had to be accepted back. The only alternative would be a very big stink. If the board had told her not to come back they would have been accused of meddling in a sphere not theirs. And you'd have written them a very stiff note wondering why they have forced a good and loyal lady to premature burial in some old people's home in the States. If the church would have told her not to come back then it would have been interpreted as a white paper explaining that the church is not in the least grateful for all that has been done here by the missionaries of the decades. Everyone would refer to the Phoebe rejection for decades as evidence of the greed for housing that the new church leaders have in the early years of their independence from the mission board.

All of this is fine except for one thing. Phoebe did definitely deteriorate during the last year she was here. She is a very determined personality, however. She never asked for one word of advice from anyone. The only information the missionary community had about her was her happy announcement that she is "coming back in September." She never talked about her going, only about her coming back. No one was ever given the chance for an opinion. But her health had deteriorated. So what should we do? Tell the church? They'd say, "It wasn't our idea that she comes back." Tell the mission board? They'd say, "We have not authority over Phoebe. If the church wants her we can't refuse." So, before anyone knew what had happened she was gone.

You're hard to figure out. You say at one time that I should show more fire and stop oozing optimism and sweet reasonableness all the time. Yet, if I do get excited about something, the first thing that happens is that my mother worries about the bad news my sister is hearing from me. Or if I try to spice up an incident, I find Harold Miller lecturing on the unfairness of exploiting a foreign culture for kicks. He doesn't think it is right to get a bang out of something that is not bangy to people of like precious culture, so we foreigners should be careful how interested we allow ourselves to be about things which to our culture are oddities. You carry this a step further and come to the conclusion that no group of people have a homogeneous culture and therefore anything funny that we may see in anyone is really an exploitation of his difference which is not fair to him as to him what happened is all very straight forward. So I suppose I shall have to go back to oozing more oozily than before. I can imagine Harold claiming that I have misread him!

Last week I went by bus to for a committee on Swahili textbooks. It was fun, in that the bus driver (the same man going and coming) was cracking good. Only once in the whole trip did he hit a bump so hard that the suitcases bounced in the racks. Fun, too, in that we saw two lions beside the road; and it was cold and windy at Arusha; and that the meeting was held at the Baptist Seminary. These Baptists certainly do believe in leaving none of the amenities of North American civilization behind. I was reminded of that chap in "The Sound of Music" who declared between mouthfuls of rich pastries, that he loves rich friends. I'm to return to Arusha later this month for a weeklong seminar on theology and theological training. My thought on it is that this is the Lutheran reaction to the frustration they feel towards the work Paul Miller did here. The seminar asks the very same set of questions that Miller was supposed to have found answers to in his two years he was here. Yet, Miller is not mentioned once in the whole program. I have got a dozen lectures to study through before the meeting. This thing will be fun in that it should stimulate my recently latent theological brain cells and in that there will be a very large number of precious theological college people there.

Tomorrow I want to go down to Mugango, eight miles beyond. One of our students, Jackson Magangira, whose wife works for us, has been rebuilding a church down there during the past school term. Everyone laughed at him, including his pastor, when he started. There used to be a thriving church there, but the leader moved away and it fell to pieces. So Magangira decided to go and revive it. He has actually got a new church built and got the congregation revived. He wants me to go see it. I am really quite excited about his efforts.

Our tomato *shamba* is getting revived. Today the bishop, the secretary and the treasurer were down to see it and to be counseled on whether they would allow our tapping an irrigation system off the water pump that supplies the station. They agreed but reminded us who had given the permission and who was therefore entitled to a few extra tomatoes. Now you can take that two ways. We down there today took it all with a very good laugh. Tomorrow I want to be up at the crack of dawn to set up the system. I hope to have it working before we leave to visit that little church. Today I bought Shs 125/= worth of spigots and stuff.

July 20, 1969

From Makumira Theological College, Usa River, Arusha. I've just come back from a five-mile hike up the slopes of Mt. Meru. It would have been wonderful hiking round there with you. As it was, I was with a Norwegian about half the way, and we were joined by an East Berliner for the last half. I am beginning to see why Jacobs loves these jaunts away from Bukiroba so much. It's really pretty wonderful to get away from everything for a week, especially if you get away to a place as nice as Makumira. I wish Edie could do this once in a while.

After the hike I had an icy shower. The dorm I'm in has no hot water. Other items: I've been drinking ten cups of tea or coffee per day. This is the eighth day of "Theological Faculty Conference" sponsored by Lutheran World Service and the Theological education Fund, and attended by teachers from the fifteen Lutheran theological colleges in Africa and Madagascar. There are about seventy people here, the most famous being Doctor Professor Bishop Bengt Sundkler, former bishop of Bukoba and present professor of mission at Uppsala. Unfortunately, I am not much impressed. There are nationals here from Tanzania, South Africa, Madagascar, Sierra Leone, Ethiopia, Uganda, E. Germany, W. Germany, Sweden, Norway, Rhodesia, Cameroon, and the USA. Not one Englishman!

One of the things that has impressed me here has been an underlying anti-European spirit shown by people from Central and Southern Tanzania. There must still be some domineering whites in their areas. Also interesting is that the African static one picks up about church finances is remarkably similar to the kind of thing we get in Musoma. There was one particularly interesting exchange in a panel discussion. Bishop Sundkler had been saying that possibly some Europeans had not been allowing full development of African creative initiative. He proposed offering a Bachelor of Divinity in Swahili. The discussion got warm and there was a lot of laughing on the African end of the panel (Africans always laugh when things get too serious so as to smooth the clashes). The chairman, a huge fat jolly Moravian bishop whom some whites found particularly irritating, got to his feet to shut off the discussion. Sundkler felt he wasn't being taken seriously; he popped to his feet, he is a short, intense, white-haired man, shouting that "this is serious." The African bishop simply put his hand on his shoulder and pushed the great doctor bishop professor back into his seat, saying, "Sit down, sit down!" The Moravian bishop got a lot of mileage out of that with the younger bucks.

July 22, 1969

Let this be an itemization of what we know up to now. I was in Arusha as you know and I got the word last evening. Then this morning Victor Dorsch and family came for me by car. We were back in Nairobi by 1:00 p.m.

Monday, July 21: The MAF (Missionary Aviation Fellowship) plane left Wilson airport at about 7:30 a.m. In it were the pilot, three architects for the

Shirati Hospital and Mother. They did not radio back, but Wilson assumed the transmission was faulty. Apparently around 11:00 the Shirati Hospital administrator radioed from Shirati wondering when the plane was coming. So one of the MAF pilots went up to hunt; after a time he found the wreckage in the Ngong Hills, about 25 miles west of Nairobi. Normally the plane passes to the north of these hills, but this time it was on the south. It seems that the plane was too low, possibly because of clouds, and it simply crashed straight into the hills. The searching pilot continued circling in the area until a rescue party could be got together. The crash was in a place some five miles from the nearest road and the Land-Rovers couldn't get nearer than a couple of miles. By 3:00 word got out that there were no survivors. It took them until dusk to get the bodies out, and even then a herd of buffalo and a couple of rhino cleared out the rest of the rescue party until the next morning.

The hospital administrator got word around noon that the plane was down and he with the doctor set out to try to find Daddy, who was on an evangelistic *safari* somewhere in South Nyanza. They located him, and brought him to sleep at Shirati.

Helen Rufenacht, the Nairobi administrative assistant, was magnificent. She sat on the news, with the exception of the hospital administrator, until it was clear that all were killed. Jacobs was in Mombasa and could not be located until midnight, so Helen carried the whole brunt of the burden of notifying our relatives. She got to me by 7:30 and to the States by 12:30. She worked on Addis and Mogadiscio, and by today she had sent cables to others. We have words that Paul Kraybill will be here for the funeral.

Tuesday, July 22: Helen got no sleep and continued at it all day today. Abe Godshall in Nairobi was working with police and the morgue. I went with him this afternoon and by God's grace, Mother was given an autopsy today and therefore was released for embalming. None of the other bodies have any assurance of being released before Thursday, as the doctor has a court case tomorrow, and he wouldn't do any more today.

I was present at the identification. Her face looked strained, but there were no gashes. Aside from bruises, she didn't look too bad. Abe had seen all the bodies earlier and he said that Mother had a compound fracture on her left arm. But her face was much better than any of the others. Apparently she was sitting in the back seat. The autopsy report is not out yet, but it appears that they were all killed instantly.

Anna Ruth Jacobs gave me a lovely dress this evening, which we shall use for Mother. We plan to have an open casket at the Shirati memorial service. The plan is to bury her at Shirati, which I think is a good idea. Daddy has been there since Monday evening, and Tuesday evening Edie and others went up to Shirati. The plan now is to take the body to Shirati tomorrow, just as soon as we can get it from the morgue. George Smoker, Abe Godshall, possibly Victor Dorsch, and I will take it down in the Rosslyn Academy truck, actually a small school bus. The funeral will be Thursday afternoon, after people from Nairobi have arrived.

David has been asked to come from Mogadiscio; he is expected to arrive tomorrow night. He should make it in time for the funeral.

Sitting here beside me is Joyce's koala bear which Mother had with her. Joyce was so nearly on the plane. We had asked Petersheims to bring Joyce home with them overland. But they wanted to have a family holiday enroute home, spending time at Keekorok Lodge and on the Serengeti. Abe couldn't find Joyce's passport and couldn't get a new one in time from the immigration officials. Mother would be leaving Nairobi in two days, flying back via MAF. Abe advised Joyce wait and fly with Mother, but Leroy wanted to take her because he felt sure that in going through the bush country, she'd not need a passport. So in the end, Joyce went with the Petersheims. Had Hershey Leaman not accompanied Lois and John home to the States, he, too, would have been on that plane.

Mother had bought hundreds of little gospels in Swahili and Luo. These were scattered all about on the Ngong hill; many had blood on them, according to the newspaper article. I now have over a hundred of them stacked in a cupboard here in my room.

Mother was wearing her beautiful blue jersey that she often wore with a white sweater. When Dorsch came for me, Mrs. Dorsch was sitting in the back seat with a blue jersey and white sweater. It looked just like Mother, and I had to wonder for a moment, if I had been dreaming all night (after receiving word of Mother's death!)

It's expected that the missionaries will get together Thursday night following the funeral. They'll disband then on Friday.

My counsel at this point is that Daddy stays here with us here at Bukiroba, until he can get reoriented. Pray for Daddy.

August 5, 1969

Estimates of the crowd at the funeral ranged up to 1,800. People came from all over the church districts. The grave was dug by Christian men who were anxious to show some token of appreciation. I have never seen a grave dug so deep in Africa. The ground was very hard. After the graveside ceremony the grave was filled in again by brethren. We all stayed until it was completely filled. It was so dry that the earth made great clouds of red smoky dust; those who were particularly active in filling in the grave were brown with dust.

It is the custom in Africa that when a parent is in difficulty one of the sons takes over. Therefore, it seems particularly appropriate to the Africans that Daddy came here to live with us. We also feel that this is the only path open to us now. We cleaned out our guestroom and put in a desk, bed, easy chair, Daddy's file, a bureau, etc. He seems to be very happy with the arrangement. He still doesn't sleep all night through, but he is getting more comfortable.

One of the things we have had to cope with since Mother's passing is a continuous stream of visitors. In the US we send cards, but here you go to visit. During each visit the entire story is recounted again, and it often ends in prayer and a reading from the scripture. Daddy must have told his story a hundred times by now. Today a group of seven lepers from the leper colony four miles from here came on foot to greet him. They had come, 12 of them the first time, on Monday before we had come back from Migori, Kenya. This time I knew they were coming and had bought five loaves of bread and a big can of jam in anticipation. They brought us a chicken and Shs 6/[60]! For them, it was truly a fantastic sum. We gave them all the tea and jam and bread they could eat.

Daddy's future is clear in some respects. He will be staying with us for a couple of months. During this time he will make at least two trips to Migori. Then he wants to spend a month in Somalia with Davids on his way to the States for a furlough. He hopes to be home by Thanksgiving at the earliest and by Christmas at the latest. They had been planning their furlough, and dear Mother was afraid that she would not be able to fit into the new America that we hear has developed.

It looks to me as though this crash could have been avoided. This makes us a bit bitter at times. Daddy was particularly bitter for a time, but the Lord has taken it away and he has a testimony of forgiveness and peace now again. It does seem ironic that the man whose name has come to be a synonym for exacting care and caution where danger is present lost his wife through the apparent carelessness of someone else. How did it happen? Well, it seems that there were clouds covering the Ngong Hills just outside of Nairobi. Nairobi is built on a plain that ends in hills just before land drops away to the Rift Valley. These hills that lie to the west of Nairobi are often in clouds, but then it is usually clear on the side facing the Rift Valley. It is against MAF (Missionary Aviation Fellowship) policy to ever lose sight of the ground. So if the hills are fogged in, it is policy to land again until one can get over them visually. This pilot did at times fly blind. Just the day before he had come from Somalia with some Mennonite missionaries and he flew above the unbroken cloud layer all the way into Kenya. When he figures he was at Nairobi he just dropped through again. That is okay if you know that the clouds are off the ground, but in any case, it is against MAF policy to fly in that manner. The gauges on the plane stuck, showing that everything was functioning normally. The only thing was that the altimeter showed 7,500 feet, while the hills are 8,000 feet. So one can guess that the pilot was trying the best of two worlds, trying first to keep in sight of the ground and upon finding that the hills were indeed solidly fogged over, deciding to fly over them blind after all. Why he didn't circle and gain altitude before punching the cloud covering is anybody's guess. Probably he was tired or something. It was his eighth straight day of flying, which is also against MAF regulations. But another pilot's wife was taken suddenly ill and he had to take her to the hospital. So he begged the young chap to take this trip for him.

This pilot got himself into a couple of little scrapes previously, when he was doing medical flying for us. Once he landed at Shirati Hospital, and before he could taxi to the parking place his motor conked out because he had run out of gas. There were a few other such incidents. Jacobs lodged a complaint with MAF. They were sympathetic with his complaint but were unable to do anything about it. The pilot was a very likeable chap, always courteous, always happy, always willing to do anything one asked of him, always with a bright Christian testimony—a Baptist preacher from Scotland.

Although the plane crashed only some twenty miles from the Wilson airport, it was in heavy forest and rescue operations were hampered by a herd of buffalo and a rhino. They got the bodies carried out by nightfall. The nearest road was five miles away, but the Land-Rovers could get nearer than that.

It will be lonely indeed for our children without their grandmother around. She was a real pillar whenever we needed help. The girls loved her dearly. Although she never said it, I always felt closer to her than any of us children. Maybe we all feel that way. She wrote me such a lovely birthday letter. Then again, I got a letter here almost a week after her death which she had written to me when I was in Arusha. I guess my sentiments are this way because the Africans always said that David was the spitting image of his Dad while I resembled Mother. Anyway all of us miss her very much.

I think there is a difference how Americans feel about death and how Africans feel. Americans are probably more secular in their souls and therefore do not fear death as much as people here do. Americans tend to convince themselves that there is nothing after death, and I assume this conviction carries over to the deathbed. The African has no doubts about his living after death. I think for the non-Christian, death is more frightening for them. I am guessing here and should really not presume to speak for the non-Christian.

Death affects the living also as well as the dying. For the living, I think that death is more traumatic in the States than it is for Africans. They have a big extended family and there are rules for settling every matter upon the death of any member of the family. The bonds between people are many. Some sociologists show that the possibilities for meaningful relationships between people in a primary group is diminished according to the inverse square of the increase in the number of persons in the group. That is, if you have a family of four, the relationship between each member is sixteen times richer or stronger than that which exists between any two members of a sixteen-member family. So, in the extended family, no one person has terribly strong ties with any one other person. Therefore, if a member drops out, it is not too traumatic for those who remain. For Americans, however, who put so very much into a two-person bond, the loss of one member of the bond is indeed traumatic in the extreme. And on this score I really think that Daddy has been hit just about as hard as a person can be hit. Fortunately, he has his children to fall back on, but it is almost as though he is only half a personality. He once confided to me that he really has not developed any truly deep relationship with another person.

Now all of the above is speaking in terms of the person who does not know Christ. In Christ, all of this takes on a new perspective. I think God was trying to teach Abraham this perspective when he asked Abraham to sacrifice his son. I really believe that Daddy's bond between his Savior was stronger than that between his wife. I think that it is this truth which has made his testimony so effective. It was a fact of both Daddy and Mother's lives that they had a stronger bond between themselves and our Lord than they had between themselves. We have all sensed this. And I know that I am in Africa today because I know they weren't phonies. So, I would say that Daddy has a bond which has kept him through this experience. And I really don't think that it makes much difference on that score if one lives in Lancaster or in Musoma.

August 6, 1969

There have been visitors and more visitors and telling and retelling of the details of the accident. These past two days people from Kisaka have been here and they sit for a couple of hours and they really are our guests, having no one else to go to. But our house is full and so we finally ease them off to the dormitory or to others of their friends.

Daddy seems to be happy living here with us. In a couple of weeks he'll move all his stuff back down here from Migori. Then he'll probably start living in the small trailer again. For now, he is in our guestroom. We, too, are happy and very comfortable with him.

Annie said in her memorial speech at Millersville Mennonite Church that she was so happy Mother is at rest and told about how Mother never had many nice things. Daddy at Migori was ashamed of now tacky her things were. He said, "She just doesn't have anything nice." He had got her a lovely gift from each country he visited while on the Israel tour. He got her a very lovely tablecloth with matching napkins. She used it only once when Lois visited them.

August 24, 1969

My one item of creative effort, making a multi-cage rabbit pen, has finally got finished. I started it several weeks before Mother's death. I'm not even sure the students will eat rabbit! Maybe the *wazungu* will eat them!

We had visitors from the Kinshasa meeting of the presidium of the Mennonite World Conference. The man from Brazil was asked by the Musoma Emporium owner to post a letter for him in South America. He agreed to do so, but I think it was filled with illegal cash. Anyway, I didn't say anything. But a couple of days later, when J. C. Wenger was going out, I put a bug in his ear. Sure enough there was another envelope for him. Wenger asked if it was legal and the Emporium chap said that he would post it tomorrow instead. The Bishop was there and he said I am to tell Emporium not to bother our Mennonite guests anymore about such things. But I have reason to believe this Indian merchant has used other Mennonite missionaries for his money schemes.

Some CID (Tanzania's FBI) were investigating shops at Shirati for illegal goods from Kenya, and the citizens finally jumped on them and very nearly killed one of them. Both were beaten severely. After they were taken to the Tarime hospital, the citizens rifled their van and stole everything the CID had confiscated. Two hospital workers were party to the theft, but they were hauled before the police and made to return everything and make a full confession.

J. C. Wenger was a tremendous help to Daddy. They just fit like two brothers, or better. I think it was a Godsend for Wenger to be here just when he was. Daddy left for Migori the day Wenger left, and we don't expect

Daddy back for another week. He is putting on a church roof somewhere in South Nyanza. The beautiful thing about Daddy is that he is so adjustable on almost any matter that does not infringe on his faith. In matters of faith he is stalwart, but on others he is very pliable. I saw through that just today in a clearer light than ever before.

J. C. Wenger thinks I should go to seminary. Paul Kraybill thinks I should work towards my Ph.D. Paul Miller thinks I should go to seminary. Jacobs doesn't see that M.Div's have ever done anything. What do you think?

There is a wild cat scratching at our rabbit cage. But I don't think he'll be able to get any of them.

August 28, 1969

I explained the circumstances of Mother's death to an African friend. He told me that in their culture the rest of the surviving sons could never forgive the son in whose service their mother perished.

Which brings me to the MAF pilot again. His wife's faith led her to tell the man who brought the news of her husband's death that he should not grieve. No matter what would have happened, none of those five on the plane would have been alive by evening. God made no mistakes when he took them. It was written that on that day they would die.

Now maybe the pilot's wife was right. But was she? And if she wasn't, does that shatter our faith? I believe I came to some sort of conclusion on this while hippo hunting with the doctor down at the lake one night. I said something to the effect that man in his blundering foolishness and in his sinfulness sometimes utterly fouls up God's plan and purpose. And when man mucks up God's program, then God has to work out alternatives. For those with faith he takes even the shattered ruins of the catastrophe and makes out of it a thing of beauty. And there is where I have come to rest on this matter.

Now let me tell you about finances. I hadn't made a report for four months. I should have made it at the beginning of the last holiday. But then came Mother's death and all the confusion that brought. I found that I completely disintegrate insofar as the daily intricacies of operation go. So, when I finally did get to making out my report, I discovered that I was about Shs 400/= short. So we used some of our tithe and some other things and got it down to about Shs 60/=, which was within one percent of the amount spent during those months! Why do I feel so relieved? It's just that all my money worries are over for another month. I sweated over this one for two days, and I feel like exams are over for another term. You know, sort of like you can make love again!

Daddy is back home with us from Kenya. The other night he said he dreamed that Mother came to him. They exchanged a few words before the shock woke him up. I also dreamed last night that it was Mother who came back from Kenya rather than Daddy. It shocked me awake also.

September 16, 1969

Sometime ago the Bishop told me that he is tempted to be bitter because he bore mostly daughters. He said that boys do the same things that girls do but they don't get caught because they don't get pregnant. Therefore, no one notices it. But the girls are noticed. So, if he would have boys, then they would still do the same but no one would know so it would not be a shame.

At the conference in Kenya, the Bishop gave a testimony in Luo instead of Swahili. Pastor told me later what the Bishop said. He confessed to the fear of being bewitched. He said that Satan gets him to thinking that someone has prepared medicine for him and it is now bewitching him. He said that he gets thinner and has more ill health while others get fatter and prosper. Pastor Muganda was there but he couldn't understand Luo. But the impression I got is that the Bishop is sometimes tempted to think that Muganda is bewitching him. He and Muganda make tremendous statements about one another in public, and each is careful to give all deference to the other. The Bishop says that Muganda and he are such good friends that they would split a fly tongue between them. This means that even if what they had was as little as a fly tongue they would share it. It also means that they eat from the same plate. Yet the two will not sleep in the same room. Pastor told me that if you really want to make trouble try putting them in the same room to sleep.

I attended the first board meeting of Musoma Alliance Secondary School since my installation as secretary. At lunch at the Headmaster's house, the education secretary for the Seventh Day Adventist got to praising South Africa. He had been there for four years of schooling. He has a son in university at Salisbury, Rhodesia. He could not get over praising the excellent condition of things in South Africa and Rhodesia. He praised their wealth, their opportunities, their peacefulness, and so on and so on. He also touched on their military might. Yet, he was the one who made the clinching speech to not ask one of the old American teachers to return.

Sometimes I think that our thinking is just a bit skitzo. I also think that our missionary rationale on policy will steadily shift year-by-year. I have just had to work out some sort of rationale about our school garden. For three years now we've had a *Bwana Shamba* who is responsible for seeing to it that our vegetable garden is kept operating. Yet, in all these years, I have still to teach him that when you start a new bed of seedlings you need to water them daily and after four days take off the sacks with which you have covered the seeds from the sun. I gave him great credit for coming to me last week and asking for more tomato seeds. So we planted them together on the evening of the 19th. Now, some five days later, I am sure that he hasn't visited the seedbed once. This happens every time we plant seeds and I have grown tired of getting after him to water. This all has a very nice rationale and having rationalized it, I can be enthusiastic about *Bwana Shamba* once more. The rationale is that *Bwana Shamba's* calling is not gardening. This I figured out on my own and one of the oldest of the students agreed with me when I discussed the matter with him. But we won't drop *Bwana Shamba* from his job because he himself does not realize that this is not his calling, and to drop him would be an embarrassment to him. What we have to do then is appoint an assistant whose calling is *shambas*. Is that thinking skitzo?

October 13, 1969

I must tell you about taking the theological college men on a trip to Nairobi. Well, only a few select incidents.

We stopped briefly in Migori (Kenya) to see Daddy and then drove leisurely on to Kisii. The men were truly amazed at the meticulous farming of the Wakisii. It's always a fresh marvel to me also. Kisii was awfully cold, and the shower water was icy. So we men shamed each other into taking a bath; there were lots of shouting and shivering during the process. At Kericho we had an appointment at one of the tea factories. Our guide was a pert little miss which impressed all of us young men. She showed us the whole process from picking tea in the field to the final packaging for shipment.

In Nairobi we went out to Shauri Moyo to the YMCA Hostel. Unfortunately, a police group who was to have left the hostel stayed on another night, which necessitated our sleeping in the mess hall. The next morning we went to the Nairobi Farm Show. I think one of the greatest attractions for the men were the rock bands; they had amplified instruments and were crooning Congo and American rock and roll. All of us were much impressed by how much in command of everything the Europeans still are. Even the top police at the show were Europeans. The presidential section of the bleachers at the stadium was about three-fourths filled with Europeans.

We left the farm show in time for an early supper. We planned to go to a drive-in movie that night. "Bonnie and Clyde." From what I'd read of the movie it was a bit bloody, but I didn't think much more. Hershey seemed to think it was okay.

But during supper Hershey came to plan the next day. He told me that Jacobs objected to our going to that movie. He was under the impression that there was a lot of nudity and sex in it. This was a surprise to me, but I dutifully reported that the show was off and gave the men three alternatives. I saw that the men's palaver was going very much against changing the plans. I got Hershey to telephone Jacobs. Word came back that he was adamant that we not go. The school captain reported to me that the group had decided that we either go to that particular movie or we do nothing.

There was nothing I dreaded more than sitting with a bunch of sullen men all evening. I decided to drive back into town, pay for the mileage out of my own pocket. But only half went along. We walked around, window shopped for an hour, and then I bought everyone ice-cream cones and we went home.

When we returned to our quarters, the captain announced that we were to plan for the next day. This met with a blank wall. Then someone suggested that maybe their principal should be clued in. There began the worse grilling I have ever had in my life. Speech after speech after speech. The upshot was: I was a traitor for having, in the first place, meddled with the plans laid out for the trip. But this was nothing compared with my taking a chosen group with me to town where we must have planned some sinister plot against the ones who chose to remain behind. About three or four speeches strongly urged that we go straight home tomorrow, as I had caused a mutiny, and no telling what else would happen.

I managed to make a very broken and contrite speech, acknowledging that I had done wrong to break the plans. I also suggested that we go home tomorrow. My speech only earned the sarcastic remarks that some people are very clever at repenting at the right time. So, it went on and on. I was awfully happy that I had three years of experience with these men under my belt. We'd been through a lot together, and I was sure that it would come out right in the end. Actually it seemed to me that I was taking the full heat, but there was some infighting in the group too. There was also a lot of ill will against Jacobs. About 11:30 p.m. some men began to complain about wanting to get some sleep. The driver declared that he would never, never have come on this trip, if he'd known how things would turn out. Pastor kept calling for prayer, but this made a number mad because they declared that they were just as much praying Christians as he was. Eventually a speech was made to the effects that everything must now be forgiven. None seemed to get the idea that I was to forgive anyone, only that I was to be forgiven. After a couple more speeches, Pastor led us in the evening "Grace."

Don't ask me to analyze all that! The next morning it was clear we had had a fall-out. A somber silence hung over everything. I was happy to note, however, that the men were back to calling me *Mwalimu*, instead of just Joseph. Everyone was very correct, shaking my hand and asking how I had slept. As the day progressed, we slowly loosened up, and by evening happy banter was going on once more. We got a newspaper and discovered that "Bonnie and Clyde" was still playing, so it was immediately decided that we'd go see it that evening.

Next day we visited the cathedral and the university, a museum and a snake farm. At Parliament a couple of us got turned away because we were not wearing coats. Sweaters over shirts did not count! The hottest topics were: registration of voters in the Luo district; the expulsion of three British journalists from Kenya, and secret tribal oathings going on prior to elections.

All the students declared, on seeing the movie that they had got a good subject for a sermon: "Crime Never Pays!"

Jacobs arranged for the Nairobi Mennonites to meet at Rosslyn Academy for the evening; we were to give a program. Joyce found me and stuck right by me the whole evening. Really nice to be with her again. But when I had to leave Joyce got to crying. So I got her together with her cousins Karen and Doris and ran for it. We drove home via Narok through six-inch dust. The next day we didn't have school. Everyone was almost sick with fatigue; at least I was. But I would gladly take the men again.

Daddy is in Kenya this week, visiting all the churches up there one last time before he leaves for the States on November 10. Rosemary has got over a week of diarrhea. Dianne is a cute little green-eyed girl. We've got rabbits now and we're trying to breed them. No success after a month. Maybe I'll have to borrow an old bloke in Petersheim's herd. His place is crawling with rabbits.

October 14, 1969

Today and yesterday the church executive committee met. Two young men recently graduated and returned from studies in the US asked for an opportunity to greet the executive committee. They told their elders everything that the elders wanted to hear. The elders are not to put up with missionaries they don't like; they are not to take Salunga seriously about wanting the budget reorganized; they are to tell Salunga now is the time for expansion not contraction; Kenya is a new field but one for which TMC has no financial obligations; MEDA loans never need to be repaid with interest; that there are piles and piles of money in the States just for the asking, etc., etc., etc. The elders were overjoyed. Nothing but visions of sugarplums danced in their heads. "Imagine it! A professor of economics, one of our own, tells us that what we've been wanting all along is to be had by pressuring and here these whites have been pulling fast ones behind our backs."

The thing that laid me low was that the committee never got around to saying anything about the future of the college students soon to graduate. The executive committee seems determined not to give any budget money to these men. Increasingly it has become Shenk's project, and for that reason, I can see the handwriting on the wall. Where will these men go? Many were in Bible School before coming here for theological studies; some have been in school for five years. The rest have been here for three. But now they want some indication of what they are to do. And there is no word out of the church's executive committee.

Later I asked the Bishop what I am to say to the students. He said to tell them to keep calm. So somehow the word got out that every Israelite is to go home and sit under his own fig tree. It's surprising how quiet everyone is about this matter. Compared to the noise in Nairobi over a movie, this is absolute silence. I guess the men know whom they can peck and whom they can't peck!

Last night I didn't sleep until I took a pill, and then I didn't sleep for another hour, until sometime after two. Everything looked pretty dark and confused; I could see rather clearly what was going to collide with what. It made me fearful.

November 2, 1969

We are on the threshold of a very busy week, Graduation on Wednesday. A farewell to the Smokers. And a farewell to Daddy. And a Musoma Alliance Secondary School board meeting to discuss a furious exchange of letters over the firing of a senior missionary teacher.

A great deal of my time is taken up with listening to the stories of students who come to ask me what they are to do. They come one at a time and pour out how they aren't sleeping or eating and wonder if I have any good ideas on what they should do about the future. At a long student council meeting

I was requested to go and tell the Bishop to come speak to the students. He refused, so it took another two hours to decide in a meeting of the student body to accept the fact that the Bishop would not come.

I should be able to pull myself together and make a cogent appraisal of all this. But I still don't know what will shape up so that I know enough about what is happening to make an appraisal. All I can say is: "There, sir, is a sample of my present confusion!"

Oh, yes! Recently a young woman here declared that an older woman got power from our senior woman theology teacher to bewitch her. My colleague groaned, "What a way to end twenty-six years of missionary service."

December 11, 1969

We flew back from Nairobi yesterday. We were the first Shenks to fly MAF since Mother's death, and for me it was a terrible experience. It still makes me sick to think about all of it. We got a number of bombshells upon our return from holiday, which I'll set forth here:

— We're supposed to move into the Smoker house which they vacated on their retirement last month. It is full of stuff they left behind; our house is full of stuff Daddy left; plus our own stuff!
— Theological college is off for the foreseeable future. Plans now for a Bible school which will also teach a trade: carpentry, bookkeeping, typewriting, etc. Scheduled to open September 1970.
— The church's monthly newsletter has fallen on my desk. The former editor briefed me all of five minutes.
— Jacobs suggests that I do an in-depth study of TMC, touching on the themes of growth, nurture, leadership, church-state relations, etc., etc. At first I thought he meant a short history. But he suggested I do a research of themes which would be "for the whole world of missions." Recently I learned that the church secretary is doing a history. I am to help him—but I am not to travel to the districts and gather information.
— Joseph Shenk was assigned Smoker's former church district. A district that is about five thousand square miles and lies one hundred miles south east of where I live!-Before he left Dad resigned from MEDAT, with a long list as to why a white should no longer manage such money affairs for an African church. So the executive committee assigned that dirty work to Joe.

— Phoebe has returned and recently wrecked her car. She won't talk, but the account of Africans riding with her is that she didn't see gravel piles alongside the road. She drove over the edge of these, throwing the occupants of the car against the ceiling. The car then went out of control and plowed into a stout tree. No one was hurt, but the car is garaged. I must go down and take a look and give advice.

— Jacobs wants me to take over the supervision of building a hostel in Musoma.

I find it interesting that all the things the Smokers and Dad were doing have now been assigned to me—except Dad's pastoring the Migori District in Kenya. Only this morning, a representative of Migori was in my living room wondering if I might not be able to take over that district in the absence of my father.

I feel as though I'm getting strapped into being what I never intended to be. I feel that I'm getting increasingly buried. I am happy that furlough is only two years away and supposedly at that time I'll have a brief say about my next assignment. But I am happy!

1970

January 1, 1970

The balance has certainly been upset here again and just how many pieces will fall and what the new pattern will be is quite unknown. (Every time I sit down to write I end up with a sob story.) I guess I am just demoralized. Maybe I am just for the first time in my life coming to grips with what life is like for me.

I can't present a very good case to anyone for staying on here at Bukiroba, now that the theological class graduated and they've not taken in a new one. I don't know if you ever observed a "missionary" closely in his daily round of duties. But the thing which most impressed me when I spent a week at Kisaka following my dad around was just how very much time went into keeping himself maintained. Here it is different because I haven't any responsibilities, i.e., stuff which I am responsible to maintain, but just the same it does take an awful lot of time just to keep ticking and the tough thing is that without a regular assignment you just soak up more and more stuff to maintain. We now have rabbits, chickens, gardens, two desks in my office, a motorcycle, about thirty rose bushes, eight guest beds, battery lights on a grand scale, and so forth. I can, of course, soak up a lot more to keep ship shape; in fact, I can become a fulltime handy man around here.

On the other hand, if we weren't here, who would edit the little magazine, "Mjumbe"? Who would see after the building of the hostel in Musoma? Who would get the chapel in order for annual conference? Who would take care of the guests? Who would do the Radio Tanzania programs? Who would keep the missionary women company? Who would take care of MEDAT? The obvious answer is that we are not indispensable and that which crashes when we leave might as well crash. I, however, do not fully subscribe to the theory that all crashes are good for what ails an institution. The theory is that after the crash the local people will build out of the wreckage something new and thoroughly relative to the local scene. I'd like to propose that very often nothing gets put in the place of what crashes. Take Mara Hills, the former school for missionary children. The executive committee hasn't even been able to get a delegation chosen from its own ranks to go to Mara Hills to take an inventory of what they've acquired.

Now, in spite of all I have said about keeping things ticking, there is a streak of laziness in me and I know that my day's schedule will be something like this: 7:00 arise and listen to BBC; 8:00 breakfast; 8:30 attend to various chores; 10:00 tea; 10:45 go to town or lounge about the house reading; 1:00 eat lunch; 1:30 take a nap: 2:30 read or desk work; 4:00 tea: 4:30 station prayer meeting, fellowship or visiting; 5:30 rabbits and chickens; 7:30 supper; 8:15 put the kids to bed; 9:00 read until lights go out; 11:00 listen to BBC; 11:15 make love; 11:45 read or go to sleep. Now isn't that just a grand life to live! I must add, however, that all of the above is subject to sudden, unexpected visits by all manner of people and trips to all manner of places, which throws the eating schedule out of kilter and drives my good wife up the wall.

But possibly the thing that most distresses me is my discovery that very very few people are honest. I wonder if it is the same way in the States. Seldom is the reason for an action stated and usually the judgement given for taking an action is a judgement very strongly colored by personal considerations. One never knows if what someone is saying is the truth or not. Of course, the Africans repeatedly accuse the missionary of having been the same sort of animal, and maybe they learned it from us, but I doubt it. The more I think about it the more I don't wonder that the kids of churchmen so often go wild. They see the hypocrisy underlying the whole game and it makes them sick. I used to take all this stuff about "brokeness," and "service," and "brotherhood," and "preferring each above oneself," and "giving selflessly," and so on, seriously, and I always figured that many among God's people did so too. But I am now not as sure.

I drove the Bishop, the church secretary, and a pastor across Serengeti to Arusha to meet with Jacobs to lay plans for the new church center to be built there. About ten miles out of Bukiroba the tail pipe broke off, up at the manifold, and the Bishop wanted to come home and get it fixed in town. But we managed to persuade him to carry on, which we did, until Seronera. Wow! What a racket!

I can never get enough of the magnificent view from the top of the Ngorongoro range. It's a grand spread of contoured farming, with sugar cane rows between the contours, surrounded by great jagged mountains. We passed through in the evening again when the afternoon rays of the sun offset the greens, browns, and mountain grays. The Bishop had to keep reminding the others not to point out the scene to me, as I had to be watching the road! (Just a week after Mother's passing, a tourist microbus fell down into the crater from off this road and killed some eight passengers.)

This center in Arusha was first thought of as a pastor's house with an outside kitchen, and assistant's house with outside kitchen, and a church. This TMC had negotiated with the Arusha Town Council without consultation with any Salunga representatives. Now TMC is faced with paying for it, and Jacobs has suggested that it be a four-apartment building for renting, a two-apartment building for the pastor and his assistant, and a two-room chapel-nursery combination. This, of course, changes the nature of our request, so we have to start all over again with the Arusha Town Council. I hope TMC puts someone good in there. But no thoughts about whom until the place is ready for habitation.

Is there any church in East Africa which is moving ahead in the spirit of Jesus Christ, as servants in the community? Well, consider the Mennonites. We have a rapidly expanding membership. We have been training leadership at a rate unprecedented in any other church. Our rate has been a graduate per every 1,500 church population per year. Other churches do well to get the ratio up to one per every 10,000 population per year. When you consider the AIM of Kenya, the ratio must be around one per 100,000. We are way ahead of most other churches on Africanization. In fact, I think that we are close to becoming like the so-called "Independent Churches," in that our leadership fits their pattern and our distaste for constitutions, etc., is akin to theirs. We are making capital expansions everywhere. A new cement block church is to be built at Mugango in the near future. A hostel is being built in Musoma. This center for Arusha. The Shirati Hospital has a four million shilling expansion program half completed—and that operation is so successful that they yearly run sizable bank balances. We are expanding rapidly into Kenya. No church in East Africa has the proportion of external aid that this church has. For what are strictly church operations, TMC gets about Shs 10/= to match every Shs 1/= of local funds. I am sure you'll be hard pressed to find a hub station in East Africa where there is the amount of peace and good will in evidence as here. Where, for example, could you rebuff the entire student body of the highest training institution the church operates and still have no evident repercussions. So, you must never misunderstand my healthy self-criticism, a necessity for any rapidly expanding institution.

February 21, 1970

I'm writing from the Christian Council Conference Centre, Dodoma. I've been reading *African Genesis* these days, and I'm fascinated by the role which dominance plays in the world of the primates and among peoples. We were talking here in a bull session about the Reformation. Someone used the illustration of father and son to explain who was wrong. A new member joined the group and to make the point clear, the following conversation took place:

Question: In your home, do you have a son?
Answers: Yes.
Question: If you tell your son to do anything, he must obey?
Answer: Yes.
Question: What if your son refuses to obey you, his father?
Answer: (Incredulous blinking!) Why then he is not my son, if he does not obey me!

Great roars of approval all around. The point being: the Catholics should have damned Luther and his cronies!

I draw a number of conclusions here. One is that if you understand this thing of dominance, then you have a key for understanding a good bit of what goes on in the church. In fact, I would like to venture the guess that a jolly lot of positive program enacted by the church is related to dominance. The negative pronouncements are also dominance related. For example, the closing of the theological college is just full of dominance theme. Kembo, an unordained man, wants to dominate the ordained, by taking away their salaries, and he can begin by creating a school that produces self-supporting leaders. Second he envies my position of influence as head of a highly popular institution. In order for him to keep from being eclipsed I must be blocked.

(An aside on this is that if I can avoid giving the appearance of a prime mover then okay, but if I get too prominent, then either an arrangement must be made where my glory filters to Kembo, directly or indirectly, or there will be a good drubbing in store for me some day). Thirdly, the church brass was threatened by the theological graduates and by my popularity among the youth. So they must go and I must go. The whole decision had nothing to do with the nurture program of the church.

Now the second line of thought which I develop here is that we expatriates have to of necessity be placed so far down the pecking order that we appear to be human freaks—bland operators. That is, we get castrated, man!

The next thing about *African Genesis* is this bit about the female being the prime mover in sexual matters. The male is supposed to be concerned about territory and the pecking order while the female sees to it that sex isn't forgotten. That idea about sex is wacky, as seen by us who have the double standard loaded to say that men naturally must seek sex but it is shameful for women to seek it—even abnormal—and therefore women who have illicit sex are considered abnormal and fit to be punished—sort of as if they are witches. But in all my discussions with Africans, the assumption has been that women are the originators of the act. The Pastor once asked me: "How soon after the birth of a child do you begin sexual relations again?" I said, "Oh, about six weeks later." He queried, "But what if she wants you before then?" Then, I smirked inside thinking "You big prancing goat, persuading your wife to let you in early." Now, I am beginning to think differently. Africans take it as a matter of course that their wives will go searching for other men unless they are beaten and made to fear the consequences more than the pleasure. Ardry supports the supposition. But then, what is wrong with our women? Or aren't we men properly tuned in?

I read *Christ the Tiger* on the way down here in the bus. I want to read the closing chapter again. But the impression I got bouncing along in the bus was that he has rightly put his finger on the futility of life and if life is so futile then why should I worry about myself at Bukiroba. I get good food. I have maximum of freedom to come and go (at least within a certain radius), my wife loves me and keeps our home attractive. I've got three lovely daughters. I've got a brother who cares enough to write once in a while—so what am I fussing about?

There is no comprehensive syllabus for teaching religion in Tanzanian schools. The Lutherans finally got to doing something and they pulled the Christian Council of Tanzania in on the act. This meeting is the second in the series, the first being simply a consultation. There is a Dr. Shaeffer from Geneva (Lutheran World Federation) whose business is to nurse this kind of thing along all over Asia and Africa. He's really a good chap—intensively brilliant, huge (about 6'2", 250 lbs.), a pipe smoker, ten languages under the belt, born in India; missionary in India, Ethiopia, Lebanon and now works out of Geneva—46 years old! He was a personal friend of Ghandi. Reads the sacred Indian writings in Sanskrit, etc., etc. Yet, he is a very simple chap. He shows us step-by-step how to go about what we're doing. So far, we've got a general objective for all Christian Education; a general objective for Christian Education in Schools; age level characteristics through Standard Seven. Etc., etc. Actually, it is fantastic how everything falls together; all twenty of us are having a great bang out of the meeting. There will be a longer writers' workshop slotted in October or November. I hope I can attend that one, too.

One of the funny things to watch is our new church secretary here, his theological and historical naiveté! He is always in the center of a passel of wildly gesticulating, passionately articulating young Lutheran reverends who are trying to illuminate him on some issue. He's never heard of the Apocrypha, Apostolic Succession, or liturgy; he thinks all Protestants are Lutherans. He, of course, counterblasts his persecutors by insisting that they don't know about feet washing, and that Luther after all was a rebellious son who should have been tipped out of the church on his ear. Boy, is it great fun!

April 23, 1970

I bought a bunch of books when I was in Kampala (Uganda). One was the New English Bible which Edith and I have been enjoying at evenings. We have got through Genesis, so far. One of the fresh discoveries for me was that Potiphar, the chap who bought Joseph in Egypt, was a eunuch. Now how could a eunuch have a wife? And if in fact he was a eunuch and he did also have a wife, then it would be rather understandable that she should seek the company of a young man in her husband's household. Anyway, the library of the Mennonite Theological College is not adequate for the pursuance of such lines of inquiry. Just possibly you may have happened upon access to resources able to illuminate that passage, and if so please illuminate me.

May, 1970

Today I must have malaria. I woke with a headache and by this evening I have taken about eight pills, and it still persists. So, I finally started on Chloroquin and now I feel somewhat better already. This afternoon I spent two hours with Catholic Brother Richard and an African padre, going over the Secondary School syllabus for religion that he is working on full time now. It was a pleasant afternoon, but my head kept splitting in with its matter of fact warnings that all is not well.

It was of interest to me to see what static you picked up reference Kraybill's trip here in June. I think that the choice of Ira Buckwalter (mission treasurer) as companion is quite transparent in its intent. Kraybill is sort of bringing along an elder statesman who (1) won't embarrass him as Orie O. Miller might do and that (2) he'd be counted on to keep the atmosphere dignified and solemnly Christian throughout their visit. This is all okay, provided Kraybill comes with his mind fully made up to do constructive bargaining. However, from this end, it is expected that he will come full of arguments. The Bishop told me today that he has asked Kraybill to come on the 23rd. "That is the day for argumentative clashes. I told Orie that Kraybill is full of arguments and Orie laughed and told me that I understood Kraybill." The Bishop today also monologued on the failure of Mennonite mission boards to attract outside funds. He sat a great while before he started talking and then he spoke very slowly, as though trying to put together a feeling that he has had for some time. He sees that other church's bishops have been able to tap into large foreign resources, while we Mennonites have just stuck with our Salunga donations. I came up with something about the Mennonites being isolationist with a reluctance to see spiritual value in the bodies which have large amounts of money. Secondly, they are reluctant to get money from outside sources. Thirdly, being a simple people, we have been reluctant to get into complicated projects. Fourthly, we are too small to attract too much capital, and fifthly, we have attracted a fair amount of capital during the Jacobs era.

The traditional Luo approach to the white is to get from him absolutely as much as possible, to ask for the sky and to be satisfied with whatever he gets. As two or three speakers said in the last conference: "If they don't give us anything, why we can always eat cassava. After all, that is what we have always eaten."

May 14, 1970

Daddy by nature is just a bit gloomy, but I felt that it got worse over his last months here. Yet, when he'd get on the job, he'd be quite as happy as the next person. But conversation always turned gloomy. It is this sort of gloom and a sense that something sinister is about to happen or is happening behind your back that just depresses me too much. I think a missionary should be buoyant. In fact, one of the main pressures I felt for staying on here was to help to make Daddy and Mother's lives happy and buoyant. If they aren't here anymore, much of my feeling of responsibility for TMC will fade away. At the same time it takes an awful lot out of one, if the people who are dear to you are gloomy all the time. You feel that you must lift their gloom somehow.

In one of mission secretary Kraybill's letters he mused aloud on the idea of terminating all Salunga budget and personnel to TMC for awhile. Then hope to pick up somewhere later. I think that sort of thing would cause such a serious rift that no one could ever pick up again. In fact, the church might just cease to exist. Kraybill did seem to take me seriously about my beginning to look for a way out. But at the same time I will not feel badly about staying on here for a while. My relationships with the church are excellent. I have plenty, plenty to do—in fact, more than can be done. I see no one on the horizon to take over the MEDAT account, and that one too might fall on my desk. Further, I think that some sort of connection should be maintained between the mission board and an independent church. There are still a couple of Mennonite missionaries around for whom I do feel responsible.

David Augsburger was here from Mennonite Broadcasts. I got him to sit down and bat out two twelve-minute radio programs. Which he did, without even preparing. It was of interest to me that he spoke on love, which I couldn't help recalling was Elmer Gantry's favorite theme! But that aside, I admire and respect the man very much. He just can't help it that he's so smart. He asked me what was the most important thing I'd learned through years of being in Africa. I told him I had learned not to care!

It's great that you're returning to Africa on a two-year term. And going into a new situation cold. I wish sometimes I were "colder" here. It would be so much easier to disengage oneself. I know, for example, that the Bishop has never given a thought to the fact that Joseph might not be here forever. I am just part of the woodwork. Keep yourself from becoming that. I managed quite well, as long as I had a school to hide in, but now with that closed, Wow! If you were coming here, I'd say that you should never present a solution to a problem before the church. All you are allowed to do is pose problems. Even the simplest thing is posed as a problem: "Where would you like your car parked today, Bishop?" "What do you think about my fixing my chicken house today, Bishop?" "What would you like for me to get for you in town today, Bishop?"

June 1, 1970

Today I set out rather early for Mrangi to pay my sympathies to Stanislaus Majinge Karuguru, otherwise known in the college as "the long man." His older sister had died, and he wrote to inform me. So, I figured this was a good excuse for me to go and see an old friend. I didn't want to go empty handed, so I took a freshly pregnant rabbit in her little box, and in town, I purchased the equivalent of eight lengths of cypress and a six-foot sheet of roofing. Made quite a load, and the road was quite potted so I had to drive very carefully. I also had to take care so as not to side swipe anyone along the side of the road. When I got within five miles of where he lives, I stopped to ask directions and found that there was a meeting of all the Majita A district up on the hill at the pastor's house. So I went up there and got Stanislaus out of the meeting. They then got me into the meeting, and then both of us got out again and went on to his place. It was still crawling with people giving him condolences on the death. After being introduced to the main members of the family, we sat in his house for an hour and talked. Then we had dinner and after that got to pounding the rabbit hutch together. I had a plan to go by, and in an hour and a half, we had it pretty well together. Some of it remains for them to finish with local materials, but it was well enough along that we could put our rabbit into it. She is a great big pure white one. Afterwards we gathered around outside and had a little worship period. I got home at seven in the evening. I am really pooped.

Last week returning from Kenya, the church secretary began pushing the Kenya inspector of baggage to hurry it up a bit. He took offence and signaled out the secretary's bags for an extra special searching, all the while apologizing to me for holding up the works. So I sort of lamely put in a word about this man with me is the Top Secretary in our church and that the other gentleman is our Bishop, and that all work together. I knew that Kenyans are very respectful of clergymen. Anyway, much to our dismay, the official began discovering medicines in the secretary's hand case. He started to show this stuff to the Bishop and me, so that we could be witnesses to the fact that the secretary was transporting medicines across the border. He had medicines in vials, in bottles, in envelopes, in little scraps of paper. In all, I counted fifteen different medicine containers, including two bottles of snakebite medicine. The secretary had to explain that he was sick and that they were on a two-week trip. Eventually we were allowed to pack up again with the warning that the next time he travels he should get a doctor's prescription for all these medicines. In the event of crossing the border again, before he got a letter he was to hide them. At which point the secretary, self-confidence well restored retorted, "I will never hide these, as that would be dishonest!" The inspector at that point just sighed and waved us through.

June 8, 1970

Recently I read an article by Colin Morris. I suppose that when I get back to the States and occupy some pulpit I shall be equally enthusiastic about what is going on here in Africa. Morris wasn't really enthusiastic, but he just was full of hope and he saw room for active effort in the struggle to solve the country's problems. Reading this and other things recently have driven me to think over again quite thoroughly my own involvement in Africa, so I'd like once again to think on paper.

Two things here at TMC have reduced me to impotence. The first: I really do believe that the TMC brass around me here really believe that I love the church, and they depend on me to stick with the situation. In any situation, someone has to believe in whatever is happening sufficiently to carry the banner. When the banner is carried, the troop follows, usually without too many questions. I say it very humbly, and I wouldn't say it to another soul other than you, but I really think that TMC looks to me as one of their banner bearers. So that is number one. Number two is that I am sitting here with nothing to do. I do have picky, busy work, but it isn't anything significant. This MEDAT thing has cooled off, and now for two months I have had practically nothing to do on that. The magazine is going, but it is nothing anywhere near a full-time job. The hostel is now nearly completed and takes less of my time. In brief, what I have extra could most of the time be squeezed into the cracks of a full-time occupation. For two weeks now I've done practically nothing. I go to town, I go to Tarani, I read, and in the afternoons I sleep. Even the picky little jobs I should be doing lie untouched on my desk. Mine is not a personality which thrives on picky problems. I like a theme on which I can concentrate for large blocks of time.

Now then, apply over these two fundamental facts the overall assessment of the present TMC leadership and that is where I get the bind. The secretary knows nothing about program. When he thinks of positions, he thinks in terms of whom you peck when you are in that position. He does not think in terms of the responsibility of work production. He does work, mind you, but it is all rote work, nothing creative. The treasurer is using his office for personal advancement. Thus, finance is in a real mess, and I see no plans underway to start un-messing it. The last finance committee that met simply added on vast new sums for spending. The Bishop is an excellent man with insight and spiritual stature, but he sometimes gets discouraged. He looks longingly toward the Catholics or Anglicans, and he has got fed up with this little Mennonite station. He has still got reserves of fortitude, but I know that he feels hopeless sometimes.

Now it might be that just around the corner there is someone who will come and dedicate himself to getting the church moving again, but I don't see him. Now then, my problem is how can I sit here and vegetate with nothing to do? I myself cannot take a leadership role, for reasons discussed sufficiently in other letters, and I really do not see other leadership on the horizon.

At the same time I am convinced that the church is on the right track. We have to discover what constitutes good leadership, and we can't find that out before we make some mistakes. We can't be committed to the church until we have tried other possibilities. We can't see the need for balancing the budget until we have got our checks bouncing. All of this is normal and must be passed through as a phase, I suppose. So, I am not against what is going on; it is just that I would like to be doing something and I see no openings.

So you say, I should ask to quit and to move on to something else. Here is my problem. I have got to the place at this ripe old age of 32 where I can't make any decisions. I think that there are really only two major decisions that I ever made in my life. The second one was to ask Edith to marry me—and that one could assume was inevitable. The first was my decision to become a teacher. From then on my life has been a series of accepting someone else's decisions. And indeed sir, that is how one operates in Africa. So I've got some of this rubbed off onto me. I am not like you, able to quit at Musoma Alliance Secondary after only one year and then negotiate a return to Africa after three years in the States. I am just not that bold and I am also not nearly that self-confident about my ability to survive anywhere else. In fact, over the past months I have been having repeated attacks of self-doubt.

So, I don't know if I want to quit this scene! We live in a lovely community. The people here are more my family than any other community on earth could ever be. The people respect us and we respect them. And in time, I am sure we will get the Bible school opened again.

I think that I need one of two things, either to be told to get out or to be told that it doesn't matter if I am not working—that to vegetate for a cause is noble and good and right. But then wouldn't I vegetate anywhere else, too? I get far too preoccupied with the hopelessness of things these days. I have a real thing on economic development. But nothing works. We fed these rabbits one hundred shillings worth of food and have put in countless man-hours caring for them and what do you get? A spot of flavor in the stew! I also have a thing on controlling each other. I feel controlled and I then sense that the younger missionaries think that I am dominating them as well. (I dreamed the other night that there was a compartment in my pocket watch in which, horrors, I discovered a little smiling baby, about Rosy's age, whose job it was to keep my watch wound up. Counter to that is a horrible dream I had several months ago that I watched the church secretary beat Dianne to death. That one woke me up so thoroughly I couldn't sleep for hours. I had the insight that possibly psychologically at least I may be destroying part of my family by my insistence on meekly following along in the pattern of the directives handed down from others.)

September 26, 1970

Here I sit and listen to the lake flies swarming about the door, with an occasional one making its way inside to swirl crazily about my lamp and eventually diving down my collar. I don't know where to begin writing, much less where to head for. I've been sort of waiting for the sap to start flowing again, sort of like waiting for a new birth, so that my letters may once again be buoyant and full of purpose and life. For too long I have leaked drudgery and discontent through my typewriter. If life is joy and happiness then so it should be in all circumstances and yet I find it not. Whenever I think of writing again it is just the sad and bitter tales of discontent that troop through my mind, waiting to be put on board paper and shipped to you. Occasionally I do get a sniff of freshness and my spirit finds peace and I want to let these moments find their expression in my letters and in my life. But I also want to be open and free and true with you. I think I have more than made my point that life here has its tough spots so that by now you know how it is and I know how it is and both of us know why it is as well as the conditions for getting out or staying on. This is clear to us and so for a time I'd like to leave that whole sphere of discussion and work rather on the beauty evident everywhere, on the little gems of precious experiences that trip through our lives once a day. I am tired of pain, and I have burdened myself too long with it.

We've finally figured out why we have only girls. There's an article in a LOOK magazine that Maynard dashed over to us the night I got home from a nine-day safari, just in case we might need it that night! The article explains how to have boys or girls. After I read it, I must admit that it makes some sense. The general idea is that small sperm counts tend to have a certain acidity or something which can't overcome the alkaline in the vagina and which therefore ensures that only girl sperms survive. Boy sperms survive more readily if there is a large sperm count and also the mother's secretions tend to kill girl sperms if she had an orgasm prior to the sperm infusion. All of this means roughly that people who have intercourse every day or two have small sperm counts and an unresponsive woman, who has had too much of a good thing. Consequently one gets girls. Anyone who keeps away from his wife for the entire period between onset of menses and ovulation will find a very high sperm count and a very responsive wife who hasn't had enough of a good thing. The result is PRESTO—A BOY! This whole thing can be further ensured if one uses certain kinds of douches, one for boys and another for girls. I think it is vinegar for girls and soda for boys. I'm not sure I have got what it takes to make boys—

September 30, 1970

One particularly beautiful spot on my last safari I wish I could share with you. You'll remember Chamuliho, that ride on which the old German lighthouse stood, to where we once climbed. If one proceeds toward the plains from there for some twenty miles you get to Issenye, the first of my little string of churches. There's a lovely full primary school in the village, situated on the edge of a high bluff which overlooks the plain lying between there and Chamuliho. We were up at the school, setting up our equipment one evening just as the sun broke through the clouds low in the sky over beyond the escarpment. The scene was one of vast and primitive emptiness, the whole panorama empty and silent and at rest. They had some rain, so the expanse was tinged with green. On the horizon Chamuliho rose abruptly out of the plain, as did the neighboring ridges, which fell away west towards Lake Victoria. I separated myself from the activity of setting up camp and enjoyed the solitude and silence for some minutes. A little lark came chirping through some of the shrubs nearby. It was then that I began to feel that there may be new life yet for me, if I but look for it. The next day I even began to look at the birds again.

Later we came upon two female lions watching over a dying male. He lay on his side with his neck twisted round so that we could see the bottom of his throat. He was nothing but a skeleton; the only evidence of life was the occasional heaving of his rib cage. Both females were on the same side and had their haunches drawn up under them. Both had their noses against their male companion and both snarled menacingly. Little cubs were mewing about through the grass. Eventually one tried to get close to the male. The cub approached between the females and they put their heads together and thus prevented the cub from touching the male. Eventually one female began to suckle four of the cubs, which she did by rolling over on her back with her legs widespread. She growled menacingly whenever any of the other three cubs tried to approach her, and we suppose that they may have belonged to the other female who appeared dry. Anyway, all of them were thin and some of the cubs were practically gaunt. There is practically no game around Seronera just now.

We slept in an empty two-room apartment; it also had a shower and a kitchen. We were really glad to get clean again. The pastor smelled something strange and got to investigating. Here in the kitchen pantry he found a half-barrel of bubbling banana beer. We had lots of jokes about that. To our keen disappointment, it disappeared while we were out the next day. It looked to me as though the neighbors didn't know that the anticipated guests would be preachers and a white man.

Our trip to Biharamulo was excellent. This *Ujamaa* Village is situated just inside the climatic division between Atlantic oriented weather systems and the Indian oriented systems. Bukoba has about 80 inches of rain per year while our Bukiroba averages about 34 inches. This village lies in fairly dense forest but the forest only begins some ten miles before getting to the village. Probably for the same reason, the air is perpetually calm. Morning, afternoon, night, always a silent stillness over the whole area. It is really an ideal place to live. The grass grows taller than a man and the people use ebony logs in their walls. The corn grows taller than two men, and the cassava grows into great thickets beyond description. There is plenty of rain and it never gets very hot.

We baptized 28 adults and took four others into fellowship. There are now plans to open congregations in other areas, namely the towns Biharamulo and Chato, lying 45 miles from each other with the *Ujamaa* Village (Ichwankima by name) lying midway between them.

Last night Pastor wanted to treat our station to what we were doing for a week and a half out in the Mugumu district. So we set up just as we had on safari. From eight to ten we saturated the entire station with the stories of the ancient men of faith. Our loud speaker was hung up outside the dispensary; we projected the pictures against the wall of the mess hall. The narrator's voice then was blasted over to the office buildings from which it rolled back past our little party to the broad sides of the theological buildings from which it again bounced back to us, mockingly in the gaps between words. Edith said that she could follow every word clearly from inside our house!

Last night a man came to the door all distraught, having alighted from a bus which awaited him here by our front door. His trouble was that he had left his very important package on a Tarime-bound bus from which he had disembarked at Nyankanga. His wallet was open displaying layers of bills which he was eager to press on anyone who would lend him a car and driver so as to give chase after the bus. I counseled him to go by *piki* and he dashed off to release the waiting bus while I got my motorcycle cranked up. I have never driven at such sustained speeds over such terrible roads, even when alone. In fact, I didn't know that the BSA would go so fast. We literally flew with my companion tightly clutching my waist. Repeatedly both of us would bounce off the seat, but with my firm hold on the handgrips we always landed in the saddle again. My companion got to enjoying the little aerial flights that he even tried bouncing when there weren't any bumps, but consideration must be given to the fact that he may have been in a state of mild inebriation. We got to Kirumi ferry in something less than fifteen minutes, just as the bus driver was revving his engine in preparation for boarding the pontoon. Two minutes later and we would have been too late! Something right out of "Rough Rider?"

October 18, 1970

I'm writing again from the Christian Conference Centre at Dodoma. Another round of workshops on this syllabus for teaching religion in the state primary schools. It's a delightfully beautiful Sunday morning with a cool breeze and crystal clear blue skies.

Dr. Shaeffer is back and yesterday I translated for him. Then after the meeting we had tea together and got to talking. I told him about Mother's passing (and incidentally I dreamed about her last night; she was really sweet but had on a terribly old and patched dress) and he told me how his first wife died and this lead into discussion of theological issues reference God and his care for us. And this led on and on until I began to tell him about my present dilemma at Bukiroba. We had got really into this one when some fellow whites spied us and soon we were six instead of two and the conversation reverted to inanities. I was disappointed, as I wanted to see where he would come out on this one, but the atmosphere was such as to make talk in depth impossible. Maybe the moment is lost forever with him. One thing which he said earlier on is that God never calls us from something but to something. This, if I accept, does set a sort of direction to my wanderings. Let me lay to rest the idea that God may be calling me from Bukiroba. This he will not do, but he may be calling me to something else. And I don't want to leave Bukiroba until he has called me elsewhere.

Here's the essence of what I recently wrote home to the mission board. I went over the problem of being a non-specialist in Africa today. Harold Miller feels that one must be a specialist in order to survive. I asked him why and he just said that all non-specialists whom he knows have washed out. This seemed contrary to what I had always felt about Africa. Africa has so few trained people that one will be best suited to serve if one has a broad spectrum over which he may be free to operate. Then, whatever the present need is you are equipped to do a little about it. But when Miller first told me this we didn't go into the whys. Now I'm beginning to understand. If one is too scattered in his skills or too adaptable then the result is that he never knows where he is. It is okay to be adaptable if you are on top directing the show. Then you can have a finger in everything because the actual slog you delegate to your underlings. But when you yourself are responsible for the slog and you are an underling yourself who takes overseeing, then indeed you get lost in the confusion, particularly if you are the only one around. Therefore, if one is a non-specialist in Africa and if one is not on top but down on the slogging level then the only way to survive is to put a great hedge about yourself so that your area of slog is defined. That is my first point: A non-specialist has to have an area of specialization identified for him.

The next point has to do with profession. What is my profession? I am a missionary. What is that? Jacobs leads us to believe that the missionary worthy of the name in today's world needs to be a specialist who is transplanted for the moment into the foreign culture. His task as a missionary is little different from his role at home. This sort of person is defined as the "new Breed" of missionary. He is contemporary, reference his home country. His wife is chic and his children are raised in a sort of hot house of the home country. His salary should enable him to live close to the same level of comfort enjoyed at home. The New Breed's emotional alignment to his new culture may be defined as "academically curious." His long range values reference his assignment are that it will better equip him to be a better contemporary in his home society. It will round out his personality and give him an international perspective.

So, I am a missionary by profession. But I don't think Jacobs' definition fits "missionary by profession" but rather "missionary for exposure." In any case, I cannot fit his definition. My orientation makes it impossible. So how would I define a missionary? Whether I am right or wrong, I cannot say, although most likely I am wrong, and this I expect to be told, i.e., that I am wrong. However, the wrongness or rightness is an intellectual matter. Intellect should rule over emotion; it must always check emotion to see if it is on the right course. But for the moment I lay intellect aside and speak of my concept of a missionary, emotionally. This is how I feel in my bones—whether right or wrong.

A missionary's first concern should not be about himself, professionally or otherwise. He does have a responsibility to his family and in one compartment of my mind I put this responsibility as priority. As a missionary he is primarily responsible to the community in which he lives as a missionary. In another compartment of my mind this is priority. These two priorities give me, on occasion, a considerable amount of pain, when they conflict. But let's leave the family out for the moment. I think I should feel comfortable with the people to whom I am sent as a missionary. I should be comfortable with their food and customs. I should negate by my own example the stereotyped concepts they have of people of my race. When among them, their customs and priorities should come first. So much for attitude. My function as a missionary should be to do that which those to whom I am sent want me to do. If they want me to dig ditches then that is exactly what I am to do. I am a tool given to them for their use. To be a missionary means that I will develop those qualities which will make me a useful tool in whatever capacity the church wants to use me. I must realize that sometimes tools are incorrectly used or one tool may be used for a task for which it was not designed. This I must realize and my own training as a missionary should equip me to accept this sort of use and to accept it cheerfully. If I do not accept it cheerfully then I give the impression to the church that their judgments of my value are not good ones and thereby I instill in them an inferiority complex and such a complex will always keep them from growing in the ability to make sound judgments. They should be assured that I do not stand in judgment of their priorities. A stereotype they have of whites is that whites judge harshly any creative instigation of activity and so they are in perpetual self-doubt. I need to accept without exacerbating the already sensitive issue. In all of this the missionary should do well any task he is given. In time there will build up a body of understanding in the church that this particular tool is capable of a great variety of activity and hopefully in time the more difficult tasks will be assigned to the missionary. "He who is faithful in little will be faithful also in much." The missionary should not feel discouraged if at any one point in his career he is being used "foolishly." Seasons come and go. Ideas come and go. Tasks come and go. What is today is not an indication of what will be ten days from now. So the missionary needs to be patient. Moses was patient in the desert for forty years. If the missionary is young when he starts, then he has a good chance of working under a half dozen administrations in his lifetime. Michelangelo was used by some six or eight popes and some used him well while other used him poorly. Daniel was in three administrations at least. So if this particular administration is inept, then be patient and wait for the next one. And through all of this doing of that and this, the missionary must know by his life that Jesus is saving him from futility and frustration. Futility cannot be escaped by man's effort. Solomon tried to escape futility but in the end he said that all was vanity. If anyone could have escaped futility it should have been Solomon. So then to escape futility is a spiritual quality and not dependent on what one is actually doing. Therefore one can just as easily be saved from futility when one is doing nothing as he can be saved from it when he is doing something of great importance. The missionary should train himself to live a full and happy life no matter what his particular activity at the moment is.

So then, this is what a professional missionary should be. He should be firstly at the disposal of the people with whom he works. If a missionary is one for life in a given situation then what I have just described works very well. The missionary keeps himself honed to the sort of needs which arise in his community. But the problem arises when you try to make the missionary responsible to two communities. You tell him that he is not an African but an American. In my case, I am not really a member of the Tanzania Mennonite Church but rather a member of Lancaster Conference. At any time my assignment in TMC may be terminated and I shall be thrown back into the lap of my true parent. So then the missionary has two places to which he must be responsible, or should I say "relevant." At any time he must be able to drop back into Lancaster and fit. So then Lancaster is a very competitive place. Any and all tools are very highly specialized. Whereas in Africa you may use a pliers to open a tin of food, extract a tooth, take a tire off the rim, straighten your sunglasses, hammer a nail, trim your toenails, scrape the grease off your motor cycle engine, do any variety of prying. In the Lancaster area a pliers is used for only one purpose, holding something that is difficult to hold with your fingers. And the chances are that should one in Lancaster be given a battle-scared pliers from Africa he will discard it altogether, even for holding things, and get himself a new pliers whose teeth are better aligned. You see the problem now lies in that the missionary needs to be ready to be of use both in Africa and in America. If he keeps only the Africa part in mind then some bright day he will find himself consigned to the dustbin.

What is the solution? The proposed solution is that one begins by stipulating a certain spectrum of activity to which he will allow his pliers to be directed on the mission field. What I mean is: That he will decide just what sort of instrument he is, whether it be pliers, hammer, spanner, or screw driver. Then he will stipulate that on the mission field he will engage only in that spectrum of activity which suits his tool. In this way it is hoped that when he returns to the States he will still be somewhat relevant, although never will he be as relevant as he would have been had he never gone, only somewhat relevant. So here we get into a sort of second level of professionalism. The missionary, such as I, is a professional missionary but he is also a professional at something else, which is supposedly marketable in his home country.

So then both the arguments about the problem of a non-specialist in Africa and the one about the missionary profession, both of these point to the fact that the missionary needs to have his activity defined within certain limits. That definition may be built into his own abilities or it may need to be defined in terms of the work assignment.

I wrote to the mission board that I prefer to define my area of specialization as the "academic end of church involvement," preferably as a teacher in a Bible school or seminary. I also said that I would be interested secondly in pastoring, but not in Africa. So then, when on furlough, I would like to go to seminary as well as get to know some segment of Lancaster in a pastoral capacity, preferably in a single congregation, as an assistant pastor. This would indicate school in Philadelphia, near to Lancaster. I also went on to say that I see no point in my returning to Africa if a Bible school does not materialize.

I came down to Dodoma this time by third class train. I got into Mwanza by bus from Musoma. I was late getting to the railroad station, so I had to travel third class. But I want to, in order to get the experience. It really wasn't bad, after you had a community established. But in the beginning it was a bit of a strain for me lugging my three cases into a compartment and then looking for a place to sit. I tried this and that, only to be told that they were occupied. Finally an old woman with a child gave me a piece of her seat. So I was then seated, but I was still in the foreign bubble I had brought with me into the coach. So I just sat and let good old group dynamics do its work. After about a half-hour I ventured to ask the woman beside me where she was bound for, and then slowly the people around me warmed to the white stranger and let him into their community. We were in such good spirits that by the next morning when we arrived in Tabora I was going off to fill the ladies' thermoses with chai and a disembarking man offered me his excellently situated seat. So I was all set for a good run into Dodoma when a whole swarm of nation Service men came smashing into our coach with their baggage ordering everyone out. That was really a mess because all embarking people had already gotten on and that meant that all of us had to find seats in an already full coach. It took me five hours before I got a seat again. And then again group dynamics did its work, and by the time we got to Dodoma a Muslim woman with a small child asked to come under my patronage until she disembarked and had located her whereabouts in Dodoma. This I was happy to do and shortly after disembarking, she found someone who could direct her to where she wanted to go. My main gripe with the rail trip is that it takes 26 hours from Mwanza to Dodoma. In that time a through bus would take you from Musoma to Dodoma. The worst is the night when it is pure agony along about three in the morning, trying to sleep while sitting up. Some people spread a cloth under the seat and slept on the floor.

"Jesus loves me this I know." This got impressed on me the other day. I had wanted to come to this workshop very badly. I enjoyed the other one; it was something academic. It got me away from the gyrations of Bukiroba. Anyway, word came that the Christian Council had decided that each delegate's expenses were to be paid by his own church. The Bishop disclaimed any knowledge of how or when this was decided, although he was at the last CCT meeting. So I proposed that I personally pay half and TMC foot half. Still the Bishop, the secretary and treasurer would not okay the use of the money until I would go to see Elisha Meso out at Bumangi and get his permission. This is how tight money has come here! About noon on the day before I was to leave I got on the cycle and headed to Bumangi. Going up the long stretch at the top of which the road divides, I noticed that the cycle wasn't handling properly. But I kept on going until I got to the top of the long hill. I stopped and found that the rear tire was nearly flat. It was about noon, and I had no tools whatsoever. I took off my helmet and wondered whatever to do. Just then I saw a truck coming which looked like Meso's. Sure enough that is who it was! He was nearly empty and was on his way to Bukiroba. So we put my cycle in the back of his truck. In less than an hour after my leaving home I was back again with the mission accomplished!

I wonder about your life at Kitwe (Africa Literature Centre, Mindolo Ecumenical Centre, Kitwe, Zambia). Maybe we'll come to see you!

October 31, 1970

The board for theological education met last week. I prepared a written statement of about three pages in which I outlined my own position on a number of things and then said what could be done by way of having a school, namely that we have one three-year stream, and another six-month stream. We wound up having a one-year stream with promises from the elders that they would get the executive committee to find an extra Shs10,000/= for us, as well as another teacher. Anyway, the thing I wanted to especially say was that there seems to be no bridges across which to build understanding reference my involvement here. I can speak with you and to us it makes sense. I can speak to the Bishop and to him it makes sense. But I cannot talk the Bishop's talk to you and have it make sense and neither can I talk your talk to the Bishop and have it make sense. It is the strangest thing. He was rather sharp with me in the meeting for my declaration that I didn't feel free to continue indefinitely as I had this past year. He had picked up this talk from others and he felt that I was slandering him behind his back. Further, he quoted me earlier in the year as saying that I wanted to be given something to do and now I complain that I have too much to do! I finally did score a point when I pointed out that my American friends laugh at me, one who claims to be a Bible teacher and not teaching Bible. I pointed out that being here I am slipping behind. This he understood by way of making concessions to my foreign roots but the matter would not have held water for him in a purely African context. He wanted to know what I was going to study on furlough. When I said that I planned to attend seminary, he was satisfied that I had said the truth about my wanting to teach Bible. They think that I am finding an excuse for picking a quarrel with them so that I can leave and in leaving fix the blame on them. Anyway, that evening I went to see the Bishop again and declared before him my fidelity and high regard for him and my commitment to TMC. However, I repeated my desire to teach and then pointed out again how I am not able to do properly all I have to do. I told him how the secretary attempts to rope me into his orbit. When I said this at once my whole story began to make sense to the Bishop. He declared himself a wall of protection against any inroads which the secretary might make. He reciprocated my statement of fidelity by having me drive him to town the next evening for a leisurely shopping tour, with my carrying his basket. Now to you that doesn't make any sense, but to him it did, and to me in this context it made sense too.

November 18, 1970

These days things are catching up with me. There is just one continuous round of activity and most of it is significant. What has balled things up is that first the mission board reps were here and the very day they left a batch of pastors came in for a refresher course in marriage and family. Between the two I have been absolutely flat out! I've also been getting pressured for carrying through on MEDAT matters, and Mugumu folks have been wondering why I don't carry on properly as their pastor. Now, too, the refresher course blokes are wondering why I am not producing more for them, and so on, until you get just too tired.

Early Sunday morning I leave for Nairobi and a two-day consultation with reps from the mission board, Ethiopia and Somalia, and the Nairobi brass. We then leave for holiday and return late December. We hope to have the school functioning by mid-January. The school is to be a one-year affair and the church has promised to keep it functioning even when I leave in July. And then when I come back, just as that one is nearing completion we start out on another three-year stint, hopefully with the one-year thing still in tact. That is, I run both! Salunga promised to find another Bible teacher by the time I leave so there won't be a missionary lacking on the place while we're away. Hopefully that bloke would then also be able to carry on later when I retire (in my private thoughts!). So, it looks like I'm stuck here until 1975! Boy, am I tired.

December 6, 1970

I'm writing from the Mennonite Guest House, Nairobi. I mentioned to you once before that when my letters leave me they are no longer mine and at your discretion you may do with them as you like. (Don't, of course, feel obligated to do anything with them. But please don't burn them, as I haven't any copies and in my old age your file may prove interesting reminiscing.) Your being with us here in Tanzania those weeks en route to your assignment in Zambia highlighted for me that something must be wrong with me, with my situation here. Maybe I wanted sympathy from you and therefore exposed to you my rotten break in life. Maybe I feared that you had created me in your own image and that exposure to me in the flesh would reveal basic flaws and so I was prepared to let all the flaws appear, particularly my intellectual and professional ones, even the personal one, too. I had hoped, of course, that we could find a block of time together for brothering, although too much of that I also feared and still do. Why? Because of what you may find and because of what I may find. The sterility of most of our association during those weeks you were here depresses me. I admire you more than I can easily say. Yet, when we are together the admiration sort of contrives to be a one-way street, my accepting your sincere admiration for the earthly skills I have, while at the same time failing to express to you the sincere admiration I feel in reference to your more relevant talents and insights. I come to have an inkling that I am an interesting curiosity to you in my ability to cut down trees, make camp fires and drive motorcycles (all of which is irrelevant in your world)—a curiosity lacking in those gifts one normally looks for in professional people, and therefore you over-value my world and not yours. And so the upshot is something deeply sincere yet unbalanced and therefore incomplete and maybe at times a little dangerous.

I am going home on furlough fully expecting to be a curiosity and that is okay if one isn't brothering—but when brothering, it becomes bothersome. (Where have I gone to here!? I am "feeling" myself out on paper and feeling isn't logical, and so let me start again at why I wrote that letter about being a missionary).

I felt that I must explain to you how I feel about my role as a missionary so you may understand even if you disagree and even if I am wrong. I wanted you to know how I tick so that in knowing, you could be sympathetic with what I am doing and so that in your weaker moments you may not throw me out with the bath water. I also did it so that I, too, would know better where I stand.

I do hope that in time I may be able to affect bureaucratic decisions but not as I think you mean. For instance, the Bishop drew up a beautiful five-year plan for TMC. The only problem is that the plan and the church finances are on two completely disassociated levels. For the plan to work, the Finance Committee must accept it and form priorities which takes it into account. Maybe in time a missionary could help to identify for the church where the problem of implementation lies. The missionary might become a sort of technocrat who would help to implement the church's program. He may also be able to separate in program the feasible from the infeasible. This is the sort of thing I have in mind.

We (my family) have been in Nairobi about a week. Tomorrow we go out to TAP (Teachers Abroad Program) retreat where I am to have three of the six Bible studies (The Rev. Tom Houston, preacher at Nairobi Baptist, has the other three). After completing my assignment our family is off to Mombasa for a week.

Daddy and Aunt Miriam are to return for a three-year evangelistic mission in Kenya. Up until 2:15 a.m. reading *Airport.* Yesterday went to the races at Nakuru—cars and motorcycles, the BSA doing very well!

December 24, 1970

Christmas Eve! The living room is all decked out, Christmas music is playing, the gifts are arranged on the coffee table, and now there is a lull before supper, so I felt like a conversation.

When do we get to Kitwe to see you? I checked with Menno Travel Service, when we were in Nairobi. We could get to Kitwe and then on through West

Africa for a very minimal extra fee. That would, of course, knock out Europe, but I guess that is just as well. We'll try to see Europe sometime when the children are older and can enjoy it and profit by it.

It still isn't clear if we'll have a Bible school this year. The secretary has circulated a letter asking for names from each district. But neither finance nor executive committee have met since we left, so it's still not clear if in fact we will have a school. My assumption for now is that we will. It is to be two terms, and I would hope to leave after the first term. We, of course, have a hell of a house to clean up and pack away and my guess is that we would get moving out of here by the end of July. That should give us time to get home and into seminary somewhere.

When in Moshi, the Housmans took us out to see the new Kilimanjaro Christian Medical Centre. I got a vision of that place turning out to be a sort of Mindolo Ecumenical Centre, where you're at. These days I've been reading Updike's *Couples* and that fits into Kitwe and KCMC, too. This KCMC place has rows of houses to be inhabited by these high-powered people from Europe and the States. If there ever was an island that surely has the makings of one.

I gave Harold Miller a copy of my observations on being a missionary. He said our ideas are far apart. His point is that the main task of the missionary is to be an educator of the sending body. That is, the missionary is here in order to keep Salunga informed and to sort of redound to their benefit. This being the opposite of my view, being here to be of some benefit to the TMC. I like Harold's idea and think it a good one, but I am sufficiently hubristic in my outlook to wonder how I can communicate anything of value home to the mission board, about my TMC experience. If what we are to do is to communicate to Salunga insights into foreign cultures and systems of operation then wouldn't one be better able to do this some other place rather than Bukiroba? I got a beaming comment out of a Somali missionary in Nairobi: "TMC is using money in an African way and we need to learn their way." My comment was that however TMC was using its money wasn't worthy of being called African. There are hundreds of wrong ways to do things. I don't know as the world will be any the better for having learned more of them or not.

We had a nice holiday this year, motoring 2,700 miles throughout East Africa. (Not one flat tire or motor trouble!) About a dozen TAPers climbed Longenot Mountain, and I with them. It was a good hike with about eight of us going right around the top. The only trouble was that I could hardly walk for a couple of days afterwards. Then, too, I sunburned my legs so badly that my ankles swelled and I ran a mild fever for several days. That time I was hunting shells with Joyce and Dianne out on the reef at Mombasa. I had difficulty walking and after sitting or lying down it took a couple of minutes until I could stand up. The change in blood pressure in the lower legs would cause muscle cramps and extreme pain. As soon as that started clearing up I went snorkeling; this time with long johns on! Still I singed my back and again ran a bit of fever. I guess my system is just getting older. The next day I agreed to help make up a party of three for deep-sea fishing. The terrible thing of it is that of five strikes I got the one which held. For about a minute that old sailfish yanked out spasm after spasm of line, leaping three or four times clear out of the water, shaking his head angrily at the restraining steel and then suddenly all went quiet. It was a great disappointment. The hook had torn loose. We didn't get another strike. So after four and half-hour we called it quits and headed for shore. The next day, the same boat brought in a 67-pound sailfish, which must have been about seven feet long!

It was good to get back home. My office is still an absolute riot, having been out of it for about two and a half months. The Bishop and others are worried about their half-finished houses. He wants me to start pressuring Salunga for money to finish them, etc., etc. Still, it's nice to be home.

1971

February 1, 1971

The Bishop wanted to go to Nairobi for a few days to be Dr. Jacobs' guest. So he started looking for a driver, but Mama Bishop said that she believes in only one driver, namely Joseph Shenk! But he told her that he couldn't ask Joe; he'd look a fool asking him to go to Nairobi just one week before Bible school opens. But Mama wasn't to be put off, so she came to see Edith while she was doing the washing and asked her if she would like to have a few days in Nairobi to see her daughters at school. Mama said that she and the Bishop were going and she wondered if Edith would like to accompany them. So Edith came to me all starry-eyed about going to Nairobi with the Bishop and his wife. So I went to the Bishop and asked him what all this was about between our wives. Out came the whole story, his version being just about identical to what my previously conjured version was. Therefore we had a week away from the place, going up last Tuesday and returning today. It was really a very nice thing.

Saw Harold Miller. Our main discussion centered on what to say when we go home and as to whether any of our efforts as whites here in Africa were getting anywhere. One idea was that the idea of any relationship between us and Africans in which the African seems to take an initiative always results in the African's making a request for money or services. Then, after either you have given him what he wanted or refused the request, at that point the relationship which had been developing deteriorates. One gets the feeling that Africans see you only as someone who can be milked and after you have been milked dry then they have no more use for you. My only comment on all that is that it is terribly true! At least it is true for me. I have even gone a step farther and come to feel that the only way that an African can express appreciation for a white is to ask him for something. During a bad personal relationship period no one asks for anything. But at a time when tensions are easing and there is a warm brotherly feeling all round, then the demands skyrocket.

Tonight the old lady in the tumbledown shack across the way came to greet me. We chatted and then she rose to go. I told her to go out to the kitchen to see Edith. There she saw some ground cherries we had brought along from Nairobi. So I told her to take some. Edith gave her a little handful so there were enough for each of the kids at her village to get a taste. Then I went out on the porch to say good-bye and we chatted amiably for a bit. I could tell that she was feeling really good about our relationship and sure enough just before she turned to go she suddenly said, "Oh, yes, I forgot. We do need some kerosene for the lamp. Shall I send a child over for some?" I, of course, insisted that she take it in a tin can and spare the child a trip. Anyway, that is just the way it is. Genuine friendship breeds it and avarice also breeds it. I know no other kind of relationship with Africans. I remember once when I needed to clear with the Bishop why I was making such a point of saying that I wasn't interested in coming back to Bukiroba if I couldn't be a Bible teacher. We had a long chat and I assured him that I respected him and even loved him and that my talk about not coming back had nothing to do with him but only with my profession. For the next three days I spent my mornings driving him to town. For him, there was no other way to show me that he appreciated what I had said.

Are we Mennonites going to become Quakers? The minds that I admire and look to for inspiration are moving in that direction. It troubles me that I haven't begun to try to form a cogent position on anything. I feel that either I am just too dumb to see to the bottom of these things or else my personality is too unstable. I have never been deeply distressed by the fact that churchly people are not very much better than others and that what they do in light of what they profess is a scandal. (I've been reading Updike's *Couples*; the churchly ones there are just as bad or worse than the others!)

March 6, 1971

We have settled into a rather dull routine which makes it difficult to get material to put in letters. For those first three years I wrote about my observations of TMC and my fellow missionaries. It was sort of an effort at discovering what lay here and reporting the discovering to you. Now that has worn out. First, I know what lies under the surface and I guess you know too, having had it reported so faithfully. But secondly, I am now part of the system and being now an insider makes my picking at the system not so interesting as it once was. And therefore from my end at least, I need to find a new area to explore. This new interest hasn't opened up yet, for me at least, but I do really hope that it will, for otherwise I fear that I shall stagnate.

It's most terribly hot these days. The sun blazes across a smoggy sky, scorching the hazy earth. All vegetation around here has turned a sort of gray. One blessing is the hard wind that blows relentlessly from off the lake all afternoon. But there is little air movement at night. So, we pray for rain and look at the sky but most of the time there isn't a distinguishable cloud from horizon to horizon. I have got myself to thinking that if the rains come then I shall get the energy and interest to tackle my deskwork once again. But indeed so much is pending here that my thinking about it frightens me. I need someone to give me a kick in the pants. As it is Bible school takes all my time and then there are so often people here in the living room waiting to see me about something—and that is the end of my efforts!

Our furlough plans are still not clear. I am feeling a bit grim; however, in that it may be that our leaving dates will conflict with your holiday dates in Zambia. Hopefully sometime during the next month the church should give us more direction reference when they want us to leave and then we can talk shop with you. Victor Dorsch, from Somalia, seems more and more likely to be our replacement.

March 14, 1971

Bible school is in full swing. We have 19 students and there was the possibility of getting one more. The skills part of the program is coming along remarkably well. I am teaching typing, and I find that it's a lot of fun. Some of the chaps are just a bit old for learning typing skills. Ten are taking typing and nine are taking sewing. As a miracle would have it, one of the students is a tailor and he is also a brother of about 50 years of age. So the whole thing works very beautifully with him as the tailoring teacher. We take turns with domestic science students, using their sewing machines. So glad that aspect of skills training has come off without a hitch whatsoever. Next year I'd like to add carpentry to the list of skills. I am, therefore, excited about what is happening. Reference my own time—the bind is greater than I like. Hopefully when I go on furlough some of my responsibilities will get shifted onto others. Then when I return I can spend most of my time in the school.

The big "stinky bomb" tree outside our house died. One day I guess it will fall over on my motorcycle. I must be hexed on these trees, seeing that a similar tree died down at the other house where we lived.

Last weekend was one of those beautiful experiences where you get back in off the beaten track far enough so that you catch a glimpse of life in God's garden, where the people are recently new arrivals, to have prevented them from destroying nature's vigorous vitality, and yet where they have tamed the wild sufficiently to wrest from it an ample livelihood. It was an area about ten miles to the left of Chamuliho Mt. Ayoo and I drove in from Issenye by *piki* some ten miles. No car could have gotten within seven miles of where we were. The virgin trees were still standing and although it is dry in many places, the ground was moist, black and fertile. The people were vigorous in body and mind and their swarms of little and medium-sized kids were a delight to behold, crowding around the *piki*, sitting patiently through the religious service, getting up at one point practically in mass to dash outside and spend the remainder of the worship period chasing each other in wild abandon up and down the footpath out at the end of the church's little yard, pummeling each other and then racing with such vigor that the drumming of their feet could be felt in the church.

All those present brought something to eat. So after communion and foot-washing and filling in the fellowship cards and counting the money (Shs 27/^{50}) we left the church—a new-built thatch hut with such small windows that even at midday one had to tilt his Bible toward the light streaming in the door to be able to read. We ate at the leader's house, emptied except for a table and a large earthen water pot. Being one of the dignitaries I got first taste of everything. Then those outside, then the women and children. The chicken fell off the bone it was so thoroughly seethed; a thin *ulezi* gruel prepared with yeast, giving it about a two per cent alcoholic content; a glass of thick milk; sweet potatoes— which the folk call "nylon" on account of their delicate texture and flavor. Here "smooth as silk" becomes "smooth as nylon." Corn on the cob. And, of course, finishing off with lots of tea!

April 16, 1971

I have taken a fall. The way they tell me about it makes me grateful that I'm still alive and well. We were working on the radio-call aerial. It had got crooked somehow and Rywangaria wanted to straighten it out. We tied a rope around it and tried to let it down the same way we put it up. But the stem snapped at a joint in the pipe. To avoid its snapping on the way up we made a seven-foot frame from which I held it. But when the pole got beyond my reach it suddenly split. I got hit in the forehead by one of the tubes, which poked me on the forehead just above my right eye. This blow on the head knocked me over backwards off the frame. I did a half somersault in the air and landed on my shoulder. I had the wind knocked out of me but didn't lose consciousness. One of the missionary women looking on was sure that I had been killed. All the Bible school students were stunned for a few moments until they all got the idea that I should be held down. The executive committee was meeting, and before I knew it they were all present. The Bishop suggested I get up and walk to the medical dispensary to avoid a further congregational gathering. The nurse soon fixed me up. I feel rather bushed but have managed to keep functioning. People have been coming to the house all the time to give me sympathy and are stunned to hear that I am off to the classroom!

Today we planted 26 guava trees. Our *shamba* of beans, potatoes and other vegetables is doing well. The rains have come again. After 30 rainless days we've got about three inches.

Tomorrow I must be at an all-day seminar in Musoma. I am on a youth team which is to spend this weekend and the next two weekends giving seminars to selected youth leaders in three church districts. How do I teach Bible school and hold seminars? It's sort of like a war where we operate on more fronts than we have equipment for.

I have been looking for a very dumb photo I took of Edith in the nude and couldn't find it. I fear that it got stuck in one of those books I gave you. I'm of course very embarrassed about it and hope that if you got it you have long since destroyed it. Thank you very much.

I was thinking the other day about community. Someone said that for development to occur one must have a community. Community is a group of people who trust each other, who are willing to make sacrifices for each other, who have a defined pecking order of sorts and who respect that order, and who would hold community interests above personal interests. I felt that we had this sort of thing here at Bukiroba a few years ago, but it collapsed around the end of 1969. I think that now again this sort of thing is reforming here on the station. We have clay in the ranks, of course, but no longer do we hear key persons such as the Bishop and the mechanic making plans to leave. The prerequisite for such a community is that you have a core of dedicated persons who are willing to go beyond the call of duty in ministering to community needs. The place where I try to develop community is in the Bible school. I think it is forming a bit now again with this new group.

I've begun doing a very dangerous thing. Ever so often I write a long letter to the home mission director, just to clear the air on various matters here. For instance, at our Nairobi consultation last year someone allowed a comment to creep into the minutes to the effect that an African said, "Missionaries are needed but not wanted." The Bishop has taken offence at that and wants to know to whom to write his protest. He is anxious to have more rather than fewer missionaries. At one point he thanked me for keeping him posted on things and commented, "I appreciate your loyalty, but I think you have to help the church in America to understand our needs and point of view on this kind of thing, just as much as you help us to understand how the American church feels. I know you do this, Joe, and simply hope that in the process you attempt to represent our concerns as well as your own."

So what is my position here? The church feels that I am seconded to them and that I work under them, that I am their servant. They recognize that, to put it in their phraseology, "I wear an African hat," and they therefore use this as a tool in making themselves understood. I become an interpreter of TMC to Salunga. However, when you turn the thing around and say, "Joe wears an African hat," then I would function as an interpreter of America to TMC. But the psychology of the thing is that when one hears TMC coming from me, one naturally feels that I am in the "enemy" camp. TMC even more so sees me as being in the enemy camp if I put myself out to make Salunga's position clear to them. TMC at once assumes that I have gone over to the other side. If I spout Salunga here the human thing is to assume that I also advise Salunga contrary to TMC's best interest. It is natural, of course, that I understand Salunga's thinking better than I do TMC's, and in order to offset this disequilibrium I need to be particularly careful how enthusiastically I speak for Salunga to the leaders here. So, to volunteer unsolicited explanations places me in a position where TMC's confidence in my loyalty is undermined.

I would add another dimension in saying that if I am to truly represent the TMC interest as the church wants me to then I must understand it sufficiently well as to make it appear that their position is indeed mine. If I don't do so then I run the grave risk of being branded a traitor. So when that rich Mennonite businessman was visiting and asked: "Joe, do you really think there should be a new church building at Shirati?" I knew that I was effectively interpreting. TMC does not want me to decide whether or not a new church should be built at Shirati. They want me to communicate effectively to the States their ideas to whether they want a new church or not.

One little comment on John Knowles' *A Separate Peace*. Here is an interesting story on human relationships. More than interesting—also deep and in a sense untouchable, something which one wonders about and turns over in his mind and then lays aside again. Maybe I lay it aside because I am afraid and don't want to engage in a relationship deeper than so deep, maybe it is that probing hurts, maybe, too, it is that some things are more beautiful in their mystery.

June 8, 1971

Bible school is closed for a recess. I had looked forward for some time to its closing, but now that it is a reality I find some sort of latent psychosis coming to the surface. I've driven the Bishop to Seronera, and spent two mornings driving him to Musoma. Along with this business of being rapidly sucked back into the Bishop's orbit I have a clear-headed wife reminding me for months of all that must be done by way of packing up to go home. Dorsches are moving their stuff down, so we will have to move out. I also have a backlog of deskwork. And exams which haven't been touched yet. Getting funds and purchasing equipment for our next skill training here at the Bible school—and so on.

I've finally decided to try to get into grad school. Why Temple? Edith refused to live alone in Lancaster while I'd be off in New York full time. But appendages to this are that I didn't really want to do full time study anyway and wanted some place within commuting distance of Lancaster. It was only in the last months that I began to seriously think about registering as a full-time student studying for a doctorate. Full-time is anything over six semester hours. David's dropping out sort of pushed me on this one. I know it sounds funny to you but as long as David was getting such a degree I sort of felt that it was enough for our family. Now that his is in doubt, at least for now, I sort of feel that I owe it to Daddy to try to get another degree. It is a deep wish of his that at least one of his son's gets to attach "Dr." to his name. Insufficient reason, of course, I admit.

I'm sort of feeling blue. I'm entering a period of serious self-doubt. Maybe it's because the Bishop has been sort of slipping of late and having previously sold my soul to him I am now powerless to do anything constructive. Maybe it has been the role I have played in making well-constructed English pitches to the States as ghost writer for the Bishop—pitches which I have not felt to always be quite square. Maybe it's a fierce letter I wrote to Salunga about missionaries. Maybe it is just that we will be going home in a while and I fear either that people in knowledgeable circles will have sold me out for my identification with TMC, or that they will put me on a pedestal for my unique contribution to this or that—a contribution which they must discover upon further scrutiny has simply been a capacity for slavish devotion to the powers that be here and a skill at slipping between the power wheels without actually getting sufficiently involved in any one to make my own position evident. I can imagine no greater horror than to have Salunga ask my advice on any of the issues confronting TMC and EMBMC. I have absolutely no idea of which way to move on any of these issues. Surely some day I will get crushed. So far I have walked a tight rope, but some day the picnic must end. Look—take all of this with a grain of salt!

June 23, 1971

Today is my birthday. It is a clear, cool, crisp, dry morning. The children are all home from boarding school. My Bible school exams are almost corrected. Our plans for leaving are jelling. This is how it looks just now:

> Tuesday, 3rd August—Musoma to Nairobi
> Wednesday, 4th—Nairobi to Lusaka
> Thursday, 5th—Lusaka to Kitwe
> Friday to Sunday—Kitwe
> Monday, 9th—Kitwe to Lusaka
> Tuesday 10th—Lusaka to Douala (Cameroon)
> Wednesday 11th—Douala to New York

Then after a couple of days in Lancaster to get our balance we want to make a ten-day trip out to Michigan and Indiana by car. I must be back in Lancaster by the first of September for registration at Temple University. I find myself getting apprehensive about going home. I even feel paranoid about going home. I am getting to feel like that priest in *The Power and the Glory.*

July 2, 1971

We ARE coming to see you in Zambia, thus making convoluted missives superfluous. We will be dependent on you for sustenance, both physical and spiritual.

On my studying for a PhD: I think I finally discovered the key to my about face on this topic. I was reading in *Time* that there are three kinds of children: the problem child, the ordinary wonderful bothersome child, and the slow-starter child. I think I am a slow starter. I really do—don't laugh. I always hesitate about any new thing and almost need to be pushed. But once I have got over that, then I can function perfectly well. There have been lots of examples and one of them is this education bit. Now suddenly all of the problems which loomed so threateningly ahead seem to be nothing at all. I am anxious to get back into school. If pushed, I would even consider doing school full time. It is in my genes, inherited from my mother, a certain hesitancy about anything new and untried. My brother David, inherited not one trace of that particular gene. Isn't there any validity to thinking in terms of social units rather than in terms of only individual units?

Today we found Dianne squatted by the garbage pan picking mango seeds out of the slop and chewing on them. Good grief!

July 7, 1971

Just a line—my last from Bukiroba, for a while.

I finished reading that book on Lawrence of Arabia, and now I don't know what to think of him. Sometimes I saw Jacobs in him, sometimes I saw myself, some places I saw you in him. Doubtless he was a great man. Anyway, I must let it soak a while and maybe we can talk about him when we're together.

Discovered that we have $350 more in our States checking account than we had at first thought! That should see us through Zambia and Michigan! Go plan something fun—but not expensive. I find myself very, very tired these days.

Lancaster / Philadelphia

1916 Lincoln Highway East
2026 North Broad Street

August 1971-June 1972

1971

September 1, 1971

Life has been one grand whirl with no let up whatsoever, since we got here in the States. The ten days in Michigan (Edith's home) was the only exception.

I was down at Temple University yesterday and have now got registered. I've registered in the Department of Religion in the College of Liberal Arts, three courses, totaling nine hours. They are: Seminar in Relation of Church and State by Dr. Franklin H. Littell, an expert on Anabaptists and director of graduate religious studies; Proseminar in Formation of the Gospels and their Interpretation by Dr. Gerard S. Sloyan, chair of the department; and a Proseminar in Method of Study of Religion, by Dr. Striker, about whom I know nothing. I must take four proseminars, one in the religious tradition that I am familiar with, one in a non-Semitic religious tradition, one in how religion confronts the modern world, and one in a religion that is Semitic in origin but not familiar to me.

Temple impresses me as being a very nice place. Much of it is new and there are beautiful malls and little gardens here and there. Many of the trees are youngish looking, as they were planted only a couple of years ago. Temple did change its status from that of a private university to that of a member in the Commonwealth system, in 1965. Maybe that's why the place looks impressive now compared to the feeling I had about it back when I finished at EMC.

My classes are on Mondays and Tuesdays. My idea is to go down by train on Monday morning and stay there until Wednesday afternoon. Then I should have a couple of days in Lancaster to study before the weekend catches up with us. I need to find a place somewhere at Temple for a cot!

Your car (1967 VW Squareback wagon) is the berries. I get about 20 miles to the gallon. It's very nice for children with that lay down seat in the back. The finish had got really bad by the time we got hold of it. I worked a day getting it shined up. Someone had a mini-accident with it, and smashed the right front fender. You can tell that bodywork was done on it. The rear tires have been going out. On the PA Turnpike a fellow tried to get me to buy a new rear tire. I wouldn't listen, but when I got to Indiana I discovered that indeed the cords were starting to come through! Altogether it is really a marvelous little machine.

I had sort of thought that any number of congregations would be willing or happy to have us be part of their system for a year. The truth of it is that congregations have their pastors and as is true in Lancaster Conference many congregations have two pastors already. Furthermore I have not gone through the lot for ordination and have therefore sort of got into the pulpit through the back door. My asking for congregational involvement sort of looks like I'm angling for some pastor's position, and maybe for some money as well. So it boils down to people being very happy to have us be members of their congregations but not as part of their leadership. On the other hand, in some cases, the congregation wants outside stimulation while the leadership feels that such would be a threat and possibly detrimental. Therefore if anyone is to get into congregational leadership he has to either have been ordained there through the lot or he needs to be invited after about a year of delicate negotiations has been carried out.

Bishop Landis remembered that the Mellingers congregation has a study commission working on ways to improve the congregation's vitality and he decided to jump in with both feet and suggest to them that they invite me in for a year. The commission accepted the idea; I am told they were enthusiastic about it. However, when the idea was presented to the ministry, one pastor said I'd be welcome to attend but he was not going to give up any of his preaching Sundays for me! This brought the idea to an impasse, but the commission insisted that the matter be taken to the congregation for a vote. Bishop Landis suggested that the Sunday before the vote we attend Mellingers. Accordingly we attended and sat up near the front as a family. I got invited to the pulpit to pronounce the closing benediction. Afterwards I kissed the brethren and made harmless noises about our need of a place to identify with.

When we were in Michigan we got a letter from Bishop Landis saying that the Mellingers' ministry met with the congregational ministry and it was agreed to invite us to attend Mellingers. Each minister would give me one of his mornings to preach per quarter. I was happy to hear that the matter had been resolved without a war. So, I'll attend the second and third Sundays of each month. The fourth Sunday I'll be posted to another congregation in the district. The fifth Sunday I am to hold open for an assignment from the Bishop. The first Sunday I am to be free to sleep in—if I like—or take appointments elsewhere.

My brother Danny has been over a number of times. Just this evening he came on a big BMW 650-cc motorcycle, which he let me take out for a spin. We've had a number of long talks. At first I sort of felt that he had to occasionally give a condescending smile when he felt constrained to explain something to us lesser mortals, or should I say to us mortals from some other world. I've been impressed by the soundness of his thinking and the maturity of his emotional responses. He brought us a whole stack of phonograph records. I noted that he had two gospel song records in the pile. He said that he brought all he has of that kind, thinking that we must groove on that stuff!

What about the university? Most students make a point of being unsophisticated. It seemed to my unpracticed eye that fully 75 percent of the students at Temple wear blue jeans. I was down there in my safari suit with a white shirt and tie and felt like a professor. In two days only one person took a second look at me, and I think he was a homo. There was this one gal wearing a blouse over her yellow bathing suit, at least the bottom didn't cover more than a bathing suit—maybe it was just yellow panties. Most of the gals still seem to wear bras. Everyone seems courteous and good-humored. People are very civil with each other. Everything around Temple is written over with aerosol spray paint. Most of it hasn't been gone over twice, so it is a bit artistic. You can't read most of it. The city traffic got to me. I am beginning to get used to it now, but for a while I was a little psychotic about it. I think the traffic is sort of a reflection of the whole American society. You get into the river and then swim for dear life. Any slowing down ensures that your place will soon be swallowed up by another, and it is likely that you will get run over.

We had our physicals and as far as we know everything is okay. For some reason I have a "boggy" prostate gland. The doctor recommends regular and frequent intercourse in order to keep the gland drained and thus increase its general health. He repeated this prescription twice to me and another time in Edith's presence! Nothing like having sympathetic doctors.

September 12, 1971

I've been trying to analyze my writing now that I have found that America does not provide the sort of matrix for writing that I had in Africa. I am sort of coming to appreciate why you didn't write often during your three years at MCC, Akron. For one thing, one is a good bit busier here than in Africa. For another, I find that I am under considerable less strain here than at Bukiroba and further the strain I am under is not romantic and therefore rather dull stuff to write about. I do sort of need to be feeling in need of a pat on the back to get the best writing out of me, or maybe I should say, "a sympathetic tear," in order to drive me to the typewriter. And you know the American scene so I don't need to explain that to you.

Everywhere I go in this Kaunda Safari suit I bought in Kitwe—it just becomes the rage. Edith's sister's husband insists that you buy him one and ship it home—size 38. In the hospital elevator a lady asked me what kind of uniform I had on and remarked it was very handsome. At a shoe store the clerk told me not to wear that round Lancaster or I'd have everyone wearing the same thing. I wear it when we have an evening presentation on Africa and it always goes over big. So rest assured that you'll not go wrong by getting a couple more before coming home. Actually there is something about that suit which makes me feel very self-confident. It adds about fifty percent to my poise. It was sort of funny over here at Mellingers church. I showed up to preach in my old plain suit, the one I got married in. The pants have these very wide legs with big cuffs. It's a dark blue, the kind of which just is not worn anywhere anymore.

Another thing about images is this missionary guesthouse we live in behind Mellingers church. The furniture in the living room was castoffs twenty years ago, stuff that even Mother (when they lived here years ago) remarked on as being unfit for a girl to bring her date home to. There is one glass cup and one glass mug. The rest is stained pink and black plastic. There are a dozen spoons, but only six forks and knives. The living room rug is worn through. Upstairs the bedrooms have rough plank floors with throw rugs. The shades are tattered. The wallpaper is coming off in several places. The paint is chipped and dirty. A piece of clothesline is the bathroom towel rack. Earlier missionaries living here on furlough fussed about it. The Mellingers' deacon took a look and promised that a crew would spruce up the place. They painted the windowsills. So at least they are nice and white. Oh, I forgot to say that every drinking glass is plastic and the only flower vases are old canning jars. There wasn't even a coffee percolator, until we bought one. The one tablecloth has holes in it.

Don't go and think that Joe has gone dotty about how he thinks furloughing missionaries should be treated. We are abundantly happy here and enjoy every minute of it without malice in our hearts towards anyone.

How is it going at Mellingers? This morning we had council meeting (prior to communion) and everyone went out into the anterooms to give an expression of peace. I was invited into one of the anterooms, the old ladies' one, and got to shake hands with all the old grandmothers. Rows on rows of them. I couldn't get over it; there must have been over fifty grandmothers! Apparently over the past ten years most of the marrying young people have discontinued attending Mellingers.

We still have not got under the Mellingers skin and probably won't. I attended a mid-week prayer meet and was shocked at the fact that only about twenty grandparents attended. I helped give the church its annual cleaning, and was shocked again that only about twenty people showed up, some younger ones. I've been impressed that whenever there is any church activity afoot, Sanford High is bound to be there and contributing. I have a thesis, but it is too early to know how true it is. Thesis: "Sanford High, more than the ordained ministry, is the guiding spirit behind the Mellingers congregation."

Yesterday afternoon Danny called to say he was going over to the farm orchard to pick up dropped apples. So we put all the children in the car and spent the afternoon in the orchard. The orchard found no takers this year, so it has been entirely neglected, with the exception of the cherries. The trees are laden with fruit for the most part, but there is no picking. We just helped ourselves to the Macintosh, which are dropping all over the place just now. Danny got seven bushels; we got sixteen. We just couldn't stop picking! Then when we went to come down from the orchard, I saw that the one tire to the trailer behind the tractor was flat. Danny assured me that the trailer is customarily pulled with a flat tire. Just the same I felt that we should put some of the crates in the car so as to spare the tire too much trauma. So, your car got converted into a farm truck. These apples are to be made into cider.

All this reminds me—someone from Mellingers did bring us something. When we got back from the orchard we found a gallon of cider on the kitchen table. That really warmed our hearts. We put the children to bed and then came down for a glass of cold cider before going to bed ourselves. I got out the ice tray and filled two glasses with cubes. Then went to pour them full of cider. The stuff was very thick, so I tasted it. It was honey. A whole gallon of honey. Later a senior deacon phoned and told us that one of the members every year gives a gallon of honey to each of the ministers, and this year he gave one for us too. So, we have lots of honey!

September 27, 1971

The flush of newness is wearing off. I've preached three times at Mellingers. I've traveled the trains and subways sufficiently to be assured of no longer getting lost. I've got the measure of the profs and know in what direction the classes will go. All that remains is to do the slog. I come and go here at the Messiah College Hostel, spending most of my time in the city locked within the three-room suites, reading and writing and sleeping. I have read enough to take the edge off the wild strangeness of the religious field of study. Although the professors still correct me on an English pronunciation from time to time, in short, routine has set in and I am settling myself for the long drag.

It's about time to hit the road for Lancaster. I must still take a bath, undo the bed for the chap coming in later this night who uses the apartment on Wednesdays—Don Kraybill by name.

October 20, 1971

I am no longer a doctoral student. I'm not so sure about being home two years to complete the thing. You mustn't imagine that EMBMC is that interested in me or has a program that requires such degreed people around. They don't really know what I am doing down here at Temple. I went to see the director of grad religious studies—Dr. Littell, who made Anabaptist respectable back in the 1950s with his sympathetic research into the matter. He is now my adviser. The point of the conference was to point out to me that I must have two languages under my belt for a Ph.D., and that I must take 18 hrs of grad study after having passed the second language. Temple does not give a Swahili exam, but I may be free to go to NYU and take the exam and then have them transfer that information to Temple. German I must take in a crash course next summer a U. of PA. They practically guarantee that one will pass the exam after their six-week crash course. That means that after that language exam I shall still have to take my preliminary exams and do 18 more hours of study. Therefore the conclusion to the whole matter is that I get an MA which can be secured with my Swahili, take a crash course language exam this summer and put the whole thing on ice for another five years. Then next furlough maybe . . . . Frankly, I feel just a little discouraged about all this. There is a provision that one needs only one language if he is fluent enough to lecture in it and carry on a discussion. But Littell points out that that is a general university statement and that the religion department does not accept it. So, now I'm sweating for a glittering MA ahead of me, and frankly it doesn't glitter so much. I need to do a sort of extended research paper of about sixty pages. I'll do something on the indigenization of the mission churches.

About your library. I'm sorry it got moved from the house to the attic of the garage/chicken house. I've had a look. They're all lying out flat and covered with plastic sheeting. I think the terrific heat of summer will be harder on them than the cold of winter. I'll go revisit them again during the winter.

The Doctor who recommended intercourse for curing a soggy prostate pointed out that traveling salesmen are frequented with this affliction. I supposed that he had a recommendation as to what such should do about it, but my not having inquired, he didn't divulge!

Another thing I must philosophize at greater length is these Lancaster Mennonites. They are really freaking me out. These people are antiseptic. I am in Philly three days and the color of the world begins to rub off on to me, but after being back in Lancaster for four days I begin to feel that one should perform intercourse with all his clothes on. It is really something I haven't figured out yet!

November 10, 1971

We had a Shenk get-together the other evening at David's place. It was John's birthday and Lois made up a beautiful cake. We used the occasion to discuss Daddy's letter about what we think should be done with the insurance money from Mother's death settlement. Jacobs, too, had informed us as to why the latest settlement is only $7,000, rather than the previous $25,000. We discussed at great length, but in the end couldn't arrive at any consensus. We did settle on three alternatives which we pass along for your comments.

1. Cut the pie six ways: In this case the money would be divided into six equal shares and each child would be given one share, the sixth being designated for doing something in South Nyanza as Daddy suggested in his letter. The understanding would be that each child would then use his share in a way which he personally would feel would speak most clearly to him of Mother's life and love. In some cases this money would be used for some project, possibly African, although not necessarily, which would be in accordance with the life Mother lived. In other cases the money would be used by the child for some personal memento to him of Mother's love and concern for her children, such would include possibly a library, education for grandchildren, a trip to Africa, etc.
2. An Alta Shenk Memorial Fund: In this case, a memorial fund would be set up with the entire amount. This would be used as a core amount that might attract more money from friends and relatives of Mother's. The fund would have a constitution with guide lines providing that the money be used for evangelism, building of church houses, and leadership training for the Mennonite church in East Africa, which Mother served so faithfully. It would be set up so that the controlling group would be in the States and certainly for the near future one of us children would carry the ball on getting the thing up and functioning.

This idea has been discussed with the mission board treasurer and he encourages it, in that he feels there are a lot of monies around in the county which are not being tapped due to the feeling among our people that the board is becoming too socially oriented. He points out, though, the fact that it must be properly organized. Further, we would not mount a big campaign but simply make the matter known over a period of a week or two by way of fliers or spots in the *Missionary Messenger.*

3. Cut the pie seven ways: This is a compromise effort. In this case the package would be divided into seven, giving $1,000 to each child and leaving $2,000 for the creation of a memorial fund. Each child would be completely free to do with his share as indicated in #1 above. However, one possibility would be to put the personal share into the memorial fund on a voluntary basis. We discussed this one at considerable length, noting that it does have built into it a possibility for later recrimination, knowing how human nature works. (If one child would use his share for a library while the rest put theirs into the memorial fund, it could be a divisive force between us. We noted that such a procedure might have adverse publicity, reference the fund itself. In spite of these cautions the third option is still on our books as being a middle way between the first two.)

We had a good discussion all round, thoroughly discussing all aspects of each and it just seemed that the Spirit was not yet ready to give us a consensus on the matter. So we decided to let it rest for a while so we can give it a good think.

November 30, 1971

I must tell you how I came to pray for you in tongues! The Messiah students here at the hostel participate in a Wednesday evening prayer meeting at a large Negro church about a block away. I went along for fun and to see how a Negro church does things. The Messiah group planned a song service which lasted about a half-hour and then the meeting was turned back to the pastor. Few Negroes were present, about one to four of us whites. The pastor read the scriptures and then he told us that we were to pray out aloud during the following prayer time. He explained that everyone was to pray and not to mind his neighbor. After a rather lengthy coaching session, he intoned, "Now, let us pray." Absolute silence filled the hall. I had a spasm in a neck muscle over the anxiety of wondering how to pray out loud with people packed all around me. Suddenly I struck on the idea of praying in Swahili. So I waded in and prayed a good long prayer for my brother in Zambia. No sooner had I got started than all around me voices struck up other prayers and soon the whole hall got a mumbling. Slowly the voices stopped and I also quit. Finally even the pastor stopped with a final Amen, and it was over. So there, you see I prayed in tongues and interpreted for myself, and I am sure God heard.

I went to see "Jesus Christ Super Star." It was put on down in South Philadelphia for a number of nights in a big hockey arena. The Messiah students went, so I tagged along, too. It cost me $5.00 for a ticket and $1.00 for transport. It would have been wonderful having a peer along to discuss the thing with. Danny has the records and he brought them over to our Lancaster house, but I had heard only about half of it. The event was really counter culture in that the music and lighting was psychedelic, but I enjoyed it very much. The ending is peaceful and they had a mechanism for bathing the entire arena in swirling dots of psychedelic light, but the resurrection is not included. This, I think, is because just before the death of Jesus the chorus sings a song asking if Jesus knew who he was and what was happening. The question still hangs unanswered at the close. To have portrayed the resurrection would be a statement of faith, which the musical does not purport to give. I was disturbed by the manner in which Herod was portrayed. He mocked Jesus during the night of the trial. But he hammed it up so much that he sent the arena wild. There is an almost orgasmic frenzy with which these mobs of people respond to a stamping gyrating figure on the stage. It was a bit like when the Alliance Secondary boys used to go off the deep end, but this time it was thousands of people. I thought it was most inappropriate for the mob to ham it up over Herod when he was taunting Jesus. He should not have portrayed Herod in such a way. It just destroyed the whole continuity of the musical.

I had decided to quit at Temple. But now I am back into it again. My application to use Swahili for my first language was rejected. It must be German. I felt that the way for me to conserve my credits would be to get a second MA, but with the language problem, that meant that I'd need to go to school full time from now on to near the end of furlough. I just don't have stomach for that kind of things. But when I told my adviser that I was quitting, he soon persuaded me that that would be the wrong thing to do. So now the idea is that I take just the same load I have and transfer some credits from NYU and take the language this summer and thereby get out of Unit I of the Ph.D. program. There are still two more units to go, a year of study and a year of dissertation. So, in my mind, it is still all pretty hopeless, but at least I am keeping the door open. I can't stay here though because they are filling up with their own students. So I guess I'll ride the subways at nights. For one thing I will be here only one night per week. There are various things opening up in Lancaster, and I want to spend more time being involved there this next term. Further, I have found that some of my time here has been spent doing nothing.

1972

January 3, 1972

En route to Indiana we spent a night with Harold and Annetta (Miller) in Pittsburgh. We talked until midnight—talk about faith and Africa and the church. He is a great one for setting the problem down in a logical systematic fashion, but this one just would not untangle for him. He said that all night he was studying this book which lay open before him, but he just could not make out what was written therein!

We spent five days with Edith's sister and husband. Gil went coon hunting almost every night. He did take off for the Christmas party. I agreed to go along once, the only night they got anything the whole week. It was a big male. I've got a memento of him. A coon's penis is mostly bone. The hunters cut out this bone when skinning the animal and save it as a talisman of some sort!

Back in Lancaster we had a very blessed Christmas, one that we will remember for a long time. We had a tree with lights, which the children just loved. Danny helped David's children put up the tree. David is busy with his dissertation. We spent the entire Christmas Eve out driving around looking at lights.

This year at home now has a psychology with me of sliding down hill. In a few more months it will be over and we will have to get back to work again. I hope to have a good New Year.

January 14, 1972

I went to Washington D.C. with Daniel last Saturday. We really had a nice time. For me, it was a time to get to know this brother better. We did some shopping—I got a brilliant maxi-skirt for Edith—saw various tourist attractions, spent an hour at the Potter's House and saw a movie, "The Last

Show." A black-and-white low budget production but very thought provoking. It speaks to the problems of depersonalization. Danny says, "Love Story" isn't worth seeing.

I start back to school on Monday (I got Bs on my three courses last term). In addition to that we're getting busier at other things. I am to write a script for a Tanzania filmstrip. The speaking appointments are racking up, and I am taking in several seminars.

This summer we have accepted to be at Laurelville Camp for July and August. Then we plan about three weeks in Michigan with Edith's folks before going back to Bukiroba—probably for another five-year term.

John is consumed these days by a passion to discover his ancestral roots. Every day he drags in fresh supplies of ancient photos, old documents, and ancestral trees. It's really interesting. Our house is becoming a sort of clearinghouse for him and Daniel.

January 29, 1972

Winter finally visited us here in Lancaster, with two inches of powdery snow. The night it snowed Edith and I tucked the kids into bed and then we went sledding down the macadam lane out in the new part of Mellingers' cemetery. After that we went out and slid in our shoes across Rt.30. The highway was a sheet of ice and made for easy sliding. It was almost a full moon, so, although it was snowing heavily we could read the tombstones. We found Clarence Shenk's stone, grandpa's brother. I made up a little story about the blizzard of '72 as we bent into the wind in our return walk home.

Today we finally fulfilled our long-standing pledge, now that winter has finally started, to visit your books and do some Hail Marys over them. They are clean with newspaper and plastic over them. There is positively no evidence of rats and mice about the place. I pulled the corner off and looked at some of the titles and truly I felt a sort of deep sorrow that this library shall slip through my fingers this winter. But other than that feeling of inaccessibility, I assure you that the books seem to be in good shape.

When will you come home to the States? I'm concerned that we're going to miss each other. We are so busy it's terrible. In fact, I've reached the sad state of feeling that I can't really clue you in without some talk. There is stuff about preaching and missions and church and family and university and future and Danny and Daddy, etc., etc. But maybe you're tired of my world and would like to talk about yours in Zambia. You know, you are the one who set me free from myself. For the past five years you provided a sounding board which kept me sane. And now I would just like to digest with you a whole new craw full of stuff.

By the end of September we'll be back in good old Bukiroba!

February 10, 1972

I went out and washed your car. It had got absolutely crudded with salt and stuff from the last one-inch snow we had. It's been fantastically cold, and we have been equally busy, so your poor old car just rusted away. This term I am really giving it a beating, in that my schedule in Philly requires that I be there three or four days a week, and my Lancaster schedule requires that I be here a good many evenings, so I've been driving into Philly, which is 120 miles and three hours per go. I am about insane!

I have moved beyond the dream for an eventual Ph.D. I expect to go back to Africa with my work still six hours short of another MA. Should I ever be able to complete that work, I shall be content. This I say because, gracious, there are so many reasons. The biggest reason is that I have come to see that I am a humble traveler along life's way, and my work has been and likely always will be among humble folk (educationally), and a Ph.D. would only be a barrier. If I pushed it and if I could get the encouragement from Bishop Kisare, I could possibly get an extension of furlough until next Christmas so as to finish my second MA.

How long should we be in Africa this next time? I very much like the idea of being home for a year, and this is why I hold out for longer terms in Africa. If we go for only three years, then we are home for only three months. That is absolutely too short a time to do anything. Only now am I beginning to get under this Lancaster skin. If fact, last night I got sufficiently under the skin for it to bother me considerably. I was at Winter Bible School in a church and this Brother Kolb was pounding the pulpit about sins against the spirit, which were indicated as being such things as voting the women's covering out of some of our congregations, and no longer doing foot-washing. I had come up from school and hadn't even come home for supper and was therefore still in my blue shirt and sport jacket with khaki pants. I teach a class before this plenary lecture. So after the lecture, a sister grabbed my arm and gushed how much she appreciated the message. I thanked her because she was in my class and then she pointed out that it was Kolb's message she appreciated. Interestingly, the youth class in Bible School was down to one student last night, and yet, just droves of kids from church poured in for choir practice as we were going out. So all of us pious plain-suited stalwarts could greet the uncovered chicks coming in. For the first time since getting back here I felt like going off and forgetting about Lancaster. Now in just three months of furlough you wouldn't get that far under their skin.

My talk these days has been about the fiasco of some North American Mennonite study team that breezed through East Africa. It's all so astonishing that I can't comprehend it. This team went to Bukiroba and proceeded to throw its weight around, demanding that this or that be done for them. TMC had a tight schedule arranged for them which they wanted to throw out. They wanted to get a high government official out from Musoma whom they could cross-reference the sins of the church. This the Bishop was not happy to arrange, so the visiting team got him into one of their meetings and gave him the third degree. They chaired the meeting! Good old Africa professional, Dr. Elmer Neufeld, chaired the meeting, and they proceeded to double cross Kisare. They eventually got him backed into the corner where he would answer only in crisp two-word sentences. Finally, he observed that the group was not a "learning" committee and that when he comes to our country he is our guest and that he thinks the meeting is over. The crazy American visitors thereupon arranged to have another meeting with the pastor, without the Bishop's blessing. That pastor has been a critic of the Bishop, so the whole thing developed into a very bad picture for the Bishop. But it developed into an even worse picture of Americans on the part of the Bishop. Of course, I must admit that part of my rage against Neufeld and company is my basic inferiority complex which is so absolutely delighted to discover such asinine stupidity issuing from one whom the Mennonite world views as a great authority on mission and service.

I want to write you a longish letter some time on a new idea I have been working on. It is "liminality." It is what the hippies are; only they are liminal in a vacuum. It is what Gandhi was and Jesus and Buddha and St. Francis. It is the person who drops out of the system. In the church, it is the person who accepts to let his life be, in fact, what we have been preaching. More on that some other time. It is fraught with pitfalls.

May 8, 1972

For the first time in my life I stayed up all night in Lancaster with my studies. My last paper (I had seven of various lengths for this term). My prof said I could bring it in Saturday morning to his home in North Philly. So, I got the old typewriter to smoking and it just smoked right through the night to the finishing touches at 7:30 a.m. I then took it over to Millersville State

College to get it photographed, and Edith and I took it to Philly. Thus ends my American experience as a grad student! Hooray!

It's good to be in the States for a whole year. You get to know how the land lies, and more than that, you get a feel for who you really are. So, since I have me on the brain, let me talk a bit about that.

When one first gets back in the States, one is lost completely. I didn't know where my place was on the ladder. An example of this is that as late as last month a dear elderly sister, perfectly capable and intelligent came to the door with a cake she had baked for Edith because Edith had taught the Sunday school class she is in here at Mellingers a few times. I chatted with her for a bit, and then she asked me who I was and where I was from. Now mind you, she is a Mellingers sister and I have preached here about six times this year. So I told her that we once lived out on the New Danville Pike, and the she wondered if I was Clyde Shenk's son, the man who had just married Miriam Wenger. "Oh, so that is who you father is!" Now that is all okay, but the point I got was that I am still a vagabond on the earth, which of course is true. Were I over at Millersville Church, they would all know me. Anyway, after being here a while I slowly got to feel that I knew where I was coming out. For one thing, we began to be asked to give our Africa program at a number of churches and several Sunday School classes asked us to have special Bible studies or a banquet with them. In fact, I must give you the itinerary of one weekend. We put on our Africa show, a family affair, at Andrew's Bridge, a little congregation some fifteen miles south of Strasburg, on Friday night. On Saturday night we put on the Africa show again for a Sunday school picnic at Byerland. Sunday morning I went to Erbs for a sunrise service and a breakfast. Sunday morning worship was at E. Petersburg, my having come home for the family in the meantime. Then Sunday evening was down at Dawsonville, Maryland, where we again put on our Africa show. We got home around midnight, and I had to be in Philly for class at 8:30 on Monday. That, brother, was the worst blast we had this year. Just the same, it has gotten to be a normal procedure for us to take our sleepy-weepy kids out of the back of the car and up the steps as a sort of Sunday night anti-climax to the weekend race. What I am saying is: that all of this has sort of proved to me that we, as a family, could possibly get onto the ladder and find a place in this community. It took us some six to eight months to find that out.

Who am I anyway? Every man must have some yardstick whereby he measures his personal worth and quality as over against that of his fellows. It is a human problem. If I were in a school, then I would find a place there to "channel my intensity," as Danny puts it. If I were in business I could measure it by my expanding capital. If I were a laborer I could measure it by my rising check and by promotions. As a student, I measure it by where I got my papers done on time and what grades the profs assigned me. But in school a grade is again contingent more on who you are than on how you produce. And that Temple University just isn't my pond. Every way I look at it, I am at a disadvantage there, except for the fact that I have a job and know where I'll be next year. So, the truth of it, as I see it, is that I find my worth by how Lancaster rates me. That is why speaking engagements are important to me. Speaking is my way of "expressing my intensity." Please don't be too hard on me for being happy that during this furlough I discovered that I come off with an above 50 percent rating on speaking!

Another aspect of this is that in Africa I have no way to channel my intensity so that I get feedback that is ego satisfying. Jacobs used to write and say I was on the ball, but soon he's gone from Africa. Anyway, in Africa I must always slink along in the shadows, and this is why furlough has been so important for me.

Now that the school year is almost out, there is of course the period of truth that one must go through. I must admit that it has all been a game, and a fun game at this, but a game which is now over. It was a flash in the pan for this brief period. Even if we stayed on, I would soon be strangled by the vested interests that are hereabouts and by my own latecomer status. I got a notion the other day of where I stand when I got my first concrete job offer. The Locust Grove School offered me a teaching position, at exactly half the salary John makes at High's Steel. Funny thing is that we are already the poorest people attending Mellingers in terms of worldly goods, and so, of course, why not offer us a job with a salary in line with the poverty station of our life. The man who offered me the job is a very wealthy farmer from Mellingers!

The second thing that opened my eyes to who I am was that twice I have been the featured speaker at banquets. The first was a MEDA-Africa thing. All the big brass was there, and I got dressed up and gave them what I considered to be a tolerable lecture on development in the third world and their role as businessmen in helping their poor brothers to get going. The speech was well received. But there wasn't one red cent in remuneration. I guess the point is that this missionary is in there plugging for his product and he should be happy that we gave him free commercial time along with a free dinner to boot, with his wife thrown in! Okay, I let that one pass. Then I got invited to be a guest speaker at the annual "wife's night" banquet of the Mennonite Christian Businessmen's Association. This is an outfit that was started by Lancaster Conference but once started it has been conducted by the businessmen themselves. It was really a big bash, man with some three hundred and fifty people at the dinner. Flowers all over the place! Special music by a choir which is going to Mennonite World Conference! And again I gave what I considered to be a good lecture. Everyone listened attentively to my thirty minutes and quite a number came around to pay what they said were sincere complements and appreciations. But again, not one red cent. Edith did get one of the bouquets which filled our house with fragrance for a week afterwards. I suppose that the idea was again that as a mission board representative, I should consider myself lucky to have been given commercial time before all those big wheels. But to me, their not giving me something says that they have made a value judgment on my services and in terms of their yardstick they have rated me with a zero. I also gave a lecture at the Locust Grove Parent-Teachers-Fellowship, which went unremunerated. But I let that one pass; they're like the mission board, dependent on charity themselves.

Myron Augsburger will be giving a lecture in the community at a banquet this month. My guess is that he will be amply repaid because he is Myron and he doesn't do things in a missionarying sort of way! Anyway, now that I've got the venom out to you I am sure that I won't say anything inappropriate to anyone else. Why is it that when I get up tight I write to you? What would ever have become of me if I wouldn't have had you? Thanks.

Now I want to write about the psychology of public figures. There was one meeting this year when people came to the meeting just because our family had the program. What I mean is that usually you speak to a captive audience. At a banquet, for example, the whole mob came for the food and you get to shoot at them before they are let out. But one night we were on here at Mellingers for the regular Sunday night services and people turned out in rather large numbers. There were as many there as at the morning service and some people came from other congregations. Suddenly I began to feel what it must be to be a public figure who people go to hear. It is a very frightening thing because you realize that people are now looking at you for some sort of sustenance and for a word on how to go about living. You become a prophet and you get quoted and people look up to you as some person who knows more about it than they do. I've been studying this sort of thing at Temple. Now to taste it a bit, sort of makes the "who" thing personal. The point is that when a prophet arises, people look to him and put him on a pedestal and hang on his words. But the truth of it is that the prophet is just another poor bod who happens to have a gift for oratory and who glories in being in the public eye. He becomes terrible with his children in his attempt to maintain his public image, and he lets his family relationships deteriorate so that he can attend all the speaking engagements offered him. He is then so presented and he has such a commanding pulpit performance that everyone "worships" him. The thing is that if you are so good at holding an audience spellbound and if you can with conviction point them to the right way then you become sort of a Bible for people. They come to you to have their questions answered. Your words then become more pronouncements than dialogue and you lose your ability to be a conversationalist. In fact, if you have got the right public image, people shy away from you as a conversational partner. Further, to be conversational, you must show a genuine interest in the person to whom you are talking and this soon becomes impossible as you get to know more and more people at more and more meetings. Your interest in other people then becomes a sham. Lurking in the background of all of this are people like you in the audience who can see what's going on and mock it!

Example: Myron Augsburger was a teacher for three days at Keystone Bible Institute, which Lancaster Conference ran this winter. It was a one-week deal. Well, for the first day Myron just told story after story about his experiences. He told about how the students pressured him into going to Berkley U, about the rich businessmen who give him money, about how he can frighten form-critics out of their liberal stances reference the Scripture, how a women's Bible study group told him they place his writings on par with St. Paul's writings, and so on and on. Everyone really lapped it up. The second day his stories dealt more with how tough it is to be a preacher. His emotion the first day doubtless was to establish his position as the biggest baboon present, and having done that, his emotion the second day led him to feel sorry for himself and to cast aside his achievements and ask for sympathy from the audience. The third day I forget! But a further observation was that he didn't eat lunch with us. We were in the basement of a motel restaurant and he disappeared after his morning lecture. I discovered later that Augsburger was eating upstairs. I got to talk with one of the men on a walking exercise in the parking lot. He told me that long ago the Lord showed Myron that he must watch his diet. Myron burns up much more energy than an ordinary person, and if he is to maintain his health for his ministry he must keep strictly to a high protein diet. And that is why he always goes elsewhere as to order the right kind of food. So the explanation to me was that Myron finds that he cannot maintain his public image and at the same time mix with the hoi polloi afterwards. Imagine what a conversation would be like if we had sat together at dinner. I could have been hard pressed to ask him enough questions on which he could make intelligent pronouncements. So, of course, he had to have a way out of the mingling and his way out would need to be one which would further enhance his image as a public figure. Nothing better than to say that he needs a high protein diet. My parking lot walker believed this all implicitly. I have a guess that evil little Joe was the only person in the camp who would have thought differently. You know, at first I was very critical of him, but as I thought about it and tasted myself a bit of the dilemma he is in I came to see that just maybe he did the best thing after all. I only hope that deep in his soul there is an humble awareness that he is only a man and that he excuses his various defensive mechanisms as devices which help to protect one of God's humble message bearers from the democratization which could ruin his ministry.

On another tack now: I found too on furlough that people, if they knew you at all before going overseas, now still remember you back at that stage five years ago. It is sort of like having your emotions stop developing somewhere along the line. The relationships I had with people way back then are the ones they pick up today. So, one day I was substituting at LMS and old Laban Peachy was there. If fact, he sat across the table from me at lunch. In picking up the conversation he got back to some of the rough times I had at EMC in my freshman year. He had called me into his office to talk to me about boiling urine in someone's room and about cooking and eating my goldfish before Christmas break. To him that was me. I hadn't changed for these whole fifteen years since, and if he wished to give someone an intimate introduction concerning me he'd start off with college escapades. The conversation moved quickly to when I'd be going back to Africa and the suggestion that I must be dying to get back, and with that the talk swirled in another direction.

A confession—now that we're going through my bitter soul this bright spring morning. Everyone, I guess has his defensive mechanisms which he uses to protect himself against the outside world. For me, it is the fact that I cannot urinate in public. My father can't either, for that matter, so maybe it is inherited. But anybody whom I fear or am not perfectly comfortable with tightens me up to the point where I cannot urinate in his presence. The thing grows on itself because an admission that you can't would free me of the inability, yet such an admission would be a queer point chalked up in the mind of the person I'm trying to impress in the first place. For example, I know that Dad can't urinate in public because I first discovered it from a missionary colleague who was laughing about it one time. He had discovered it when Daddy admitted it on a motorcycle trip they had once; Daddy had to go far into the bush and thus in peace urinate. So if I tell friends about it then they will in turn further undercut my image which will make it worse in the end. Anyway, down at Temple these toilets are just plastered with the awfullest stuff scrawled all over the walls. Even in the study carrel there is gobs of stuff. One thing I picked up on a study carrel was "Don't change Dicks in the middle of a screw, vote for Nixon in seventy-two." Another was, "The only thing wrong with Temple is that the final exams are orals. I got a 69." Or, "Oral sex is best but it gives you bad breath." And so on ad infinitum. Anyway, in these toilets there is usually some quiet guy sitting. He sits there forever and I can't keep going in and out every ten minutes until I find the place empty. In time, I discovered a couple of toilets scattered around the campus which were relatively clean and rarely inhabited.

This problem makes me frightened of traveling with groups of people. When and where will I urinate? At each stop the toilet is jammed with people. So you become secretive and try to find ways out of the problem. You sit on the john and that works sometimes. Or you just watch how much coffee and water you drink and hold the bag for a half-day. But I find that the sheer problem of searching for a way to urinate gives me the mentality of a spy. I discovered a whole world which is closed to people like that missionary colleague who has no such problem. I keep hoping that sometime the whole thing will get relieved as I become more comfortable with people. The university was the worst. Second worst is with people I know personally. Third worst is with people I don't know, even in clean places like a turnpike rest stop.

All of this I've been finding out about myself during this yearlong furlough! Now, I am ready to go back to Africa for another five years. Which reminds me about my blasting off about that Dr. Elmer Neufeld affair. I feel that the climate in Africa is such that were we to ask them questions that need to be asked, then they should in turn ask their set of questions of us which needs asking, and that the result would be a fine stalemate. We must remember, too, that the climate in Africa just now is not democratic. That is enough I think! I should add, though, that even as this letter has indicated, there is deep within my psyche a feeling of suspicion and resentment against the great ones of this world, my unconscious assumption being that they are out to enhance themselves at the expense of us other nonentities. For some reason I felt that the Peace Study tour was made up of guys looking for a chance to put their names on maps and that they were more interested in telling people what to do than in listening to what people had to say to them. I thought about this at great length one day and came to the conclusion that Jesus himself had suspicions about the credibility of the great ones as a class. So maybe part of my emotion is Christ, after all, but part of it I am sure lies in that I realize how I personally come through the grid of the great ones. This reinforces my theory that most of the bitterness in the US isn't about wealth and job opportunities. It's about recognition. If everybody would suddenly start treating his inferiors like legitimate human beings, then I think 90 percent of America's race tension would evaporate. I mean by that specifically that if the guy in charge of the peace trip to Africa which was to spend time in TMC would have asked the EMBMC mission representative to that church about what the situation there was, that I would then be emotionally prepared to forgive everything that happened. Remember, of course, that this group was hosted by the whites everywhere but at Musoma, and that whites readily understand what their fellow whites are up to. But when Kisare was in Nairobi with Jacobs prior to the coming of the troupe, Kisare was trying to find out from Jacobs who these people were, who sent them, and what they were doing in Africa. Somebody didn't do good groundwork on that one. Further, there was a white (ME) in the States at that time who has entrée into the confidential circles of TMC and whose word about who was coming would have been accepted and who was in fact ignored entirely. The mission board sent a photographer to TMC just after the Peace Committee went through. I wrote a personal letter to the Bishop explaining everything and telling him what pictures were suggested and begging the Bishop to take the chap in hand. So presto, it worked! Toot! Toot!

TMC will be sending two delegates to World Conference in Brazil. The Bishop and the Secretary. Neither can speak English well enough to take care of themselves, so an interpreter must accompany them. There's a possibility that I might be chosen as that person. In fact, the Bishop wrote to me saying that he hoped I'd be the one, as he felt I'd look after him appropriately. That should be a lark, except for two difficulties. I'll miss seeing you on your arrival from Zambia, and wherever shall I urinate for ten days!

I nearly forgot! We've gone bananas. Edith is expecting—November!

May 14, 1972

David and I spent two days in Virginia with Daniel where he works at the prison. I was impressed. Danny is maturing and I feel that he is going in the right direction. On the trip back to Lancaster I did get to asking myself these questions: Will I always look on him as my little brother who sort of needs the watchful oversight and fraternal interest of his big brothers? Will I always feel that I sort of have a responsibility to drop in on him in an effort to help him sort himself out, or will the time come when I can set him free to be himself without any emotional reservations on my part? I got to thinking that he is now the age that Daddy was when he went to Africa the first time and everyone, of course, considered him a capable adult sufficiently mature to be entrusted with the responsibility of guiding others to a new faith and a new life style in Africa. At Danny's age I was licensed to preach, and a year later, I was ordained I guess in spite of it all, though, I shall always think of him as my younger brother. Anyway, our time in Virginia with him helped me to see him as a responsible, mature adult who is no longer a child.

The most significant thing that happened for me while at the prison was a rap session on Friday night. A chaplain had arranged to bring some businessmen from Emporia to rap with some of the prisoners. But neither he nor the guests showed up, so it turned out to be a rap between about a dozen prisoners and us three Shenk brothers. Aunt Ruth had sent some cookies down with us. The guys tore into those cookies with a desperation as though they symbolized a breath of freedom wafting from rural America into their prison compound. So, we ate cookies and drank coffee and most of the guys chain-smoked. The meeting was a bit like an East African Fellowship meeting. First, each of us gave our names, home, and reason for being in prison. The fellows were really honest in telling why they were in jail and what their sentence was. I guess men who are penned up like that just get more honest with each other. We also found the session to be extremely tense. For over three hours we were on an emotional high, as questions were fired around and men emotionally stated their cases. I suppose a good bit of the tension—or intensity—as Danny says, was due to sexual intensity levels. In any case, it certainly was a sight different from the Sunday school class I taught yesterday in a Mennonite church.

What did we talk about? First, they wanted to know about Africa. David carried the ball all evening, with my filling in once in a while. It worked best that way, because with two of us responding it became scattered rather than constructive. They wanted to know about drugs in Africa. Many of the chaps were in for drug offences. One chap was in for blowing up the ROTC building somewhere in Virginia. He got six years. Others were in for possession of marijuana and got from 15 to 30 years! It is fantastic, but if you want a good long jail sentence, just walk around with marijuana in your pocket. Then they wanted to know about marriage in Africa. Both of these questions led to discussion of America's problems. Later we asked them to tell us about prison life and how they cope with their sentences. This led to a good discussion with the chaps quite knowledgeable about defensive mechanisms for coping with incarceration. Then we asked them what they would tell a class of high school grads were they given the opportunity. Surprisingly, their prison experience didn't seem to have altered their view of life any. We got responses that generally indicated that you should just eat, drink, and be merry, for tomorrow we die. We talked about God and found them quite convinced about all this superstition. "Do your thing, as long as you don't hurt anyone," was the standard creed. Finally at ten to eleven the guard came to turn us out so the men would be in their cells for an eleven o'clock count. The guys were young, from 18 to 25, and it was almost impossible to think of them as prisoners. Even now, I keep thinking of them as students.

That prison session really brought home to me the truth of something I've been learning this year. It's almost impossible to witness in a convincing manner to someone who is not part of your spider web. People who are historically related or connected to us will listen to our message and fairly readily heed it. The web of primary relationships is the web along which the gospel flows. Most other witness is just water over the dam. I felt that if any of those men took us at all seriously that night it was because they knew Danny before hand. But even that was tenuous. To me it was so terribly clear that faith for us three brothers was so very much easier, almost an unavoidable thing, because we were connected to each other and to a faith community through historical circumstances. But faith for these men who have no faith community, into which they are historically plugged, whose spider web of relationships contains so very little faith, is now practically an impossibility. I've been telling people here in the Lancaster churches that if they want to get serious about witnessing they should get into seeing their unchurched relatives and unchurched former-Mennonites. These are still within our web and they can be won. They in turn have others in their webs whom they can win, but whom we cannot reach. I must admit that the more I think about it, the more I gravitate toward a concept of the church, which is more akin to Lutheranism or Catholicism than Pentecostalism. Maybe it is America's lack of community which causes religion to appear doomed.

Looks as though I'll be going to Brazil for Mennonite World Conference.

May 24, 1972

Summer is upon us. I'm getting lazy, not having a structured job to get me up in the morning and keep me going all day. Edith is quite busy attending seminars and getting us packed up to go back to Africa for another five years.

I must say a bit about our expecting another child. You won't believe me, but this was really more Edith's idea than mine. I was pretty well agreed to calling it quits once we got to Lancaster and nothing further developed. (I was sure she would be on the way after that wild night in the Cameroon on the way to the States!) We did sort of take precautions, using the Catholic method. Then one fine day, surprise, she is overdue. So we accept this as sort of an act of God. It wasn't planned; in fact it was avoided. But it wasn't rigorously avoided, and now that it has happened without our employing the sophisticated methods designed to produce a boy, we have completely resigned ourselves to whatever is God's will. If it is a boy, Edith will be overjoyed, and if it is a girl, I have a theory that it is the girls who count anyway. See, I have developed this new theory that says the transmitters of values from generation to generation are the mothers rather than the fathers. So if one feels a need to transmit himself to future generations you will probably get farther concentrating on girls rather than on boys. How's that for another crazy idea?

Now about the need I feel to succeed at some sort of public display. I think it is that it's my vocation. I am a teacher and to me being acknowledged as a good teacher is very gratifying. The guy who builds a boat I am sure is equally gratified but I have this strong sense that community is where it is at. For me, building a boat could only be gratifying if my friends would come to admire it and if I could then take them all for rides in it so that their lives could be happier for my having made a boat. I also respond on another wavelength. Here in the States the principle criteria whereby people measure worth and success is money and the display of things which money buys. These virility symbols say that one is an authentic creature. For me who has none of these symbols the acknowledgement of my teaching or preaching ability becomes a substitute. One of the nicest experiences we have had this year just happened this weekend. A Sunday school class, a group of 30 to 40 year old couples, asked us to have a Bible study with them this past Sunday afternoon and evening. We had another with them earlier and we used St. Mark. This time we used the Corinthian correspondence. Actually it turned out so well that on Monday I was picking up complements from people who weren't even there. I had blocked out diagrammatically the four phases of the correspondence, indicating the amount of space devoted to the subjects Paul covered. First, I went over the whole thing, then handed out the diagram and then we did a little five-scene play that I had written. Then we picked at random a passage dealing with gifts of the spirit and discussed that for a while. In all of this, the thorn in the flesh is that the Lancaster businessmen for whom I produced what I consider my best speech did not respond in the language which speaks to the businessmen. On the other side, I am finding that it is most rewarding being with a small group whom I know.

I'm afraid that my letters have sounded a trifle bitter here at the end of this furlough; certainly they should not. We've had a most wonderful furlough experience. It is just that as the time nears the end one once more realizes where he is in the structure of things. Particularly money-wise, one sees that the gap is very great indeed. I am sure though that once we have cut away, there will be blessings even of money which we don't know about. I guess that something might be forthcoming from the Mellingers district for services rendered, for example. You see, I think I am going through the middle-age blues when the awful truth finally dawns about who one is and where he is going, and I think all men must experience such blues. And I think that the end of a furlough is the natural time to experience them. So continue to bear the burden of hearing confession, which you have borne so admirably thus far.

The Brazil thing looks firmed up. And things are shaping up for us to be in Michigan the first half of September. Then back to Lancaster, and two farewell meetings. Mellingers in the morning; Millersville in the evening. Then off to Amsterdam and on to Nairobi on September 28th.

Mennonite Theological College of East Africa

Bukiroba/Nyabange II

October 1972-July 1976

1972

October 5, 1972

We're back at Nyabange/Bukiroba. Very comfortable, except for the stifling heat and parched dryness everywhere. We came down from Nairobi by car because no air traffic was allowed around Musoma due to a bombing scare. Musoma was pretty well emptied of people scurrying for the bush, but now they're filtering back. There was a blackout for a while, but now it is back to normal again.

We had an excellent trip. Rosy was sick with a fever and vomiting in Amsterdam, but we wrapped her up in a big sweater and went touring anyway. She slowly pulled out of it and is her vivacious self again. We didn't have to open a single suitcase since we left Lancaster. No questions asked anywhere. We were also some twenty pounds overweight, but that didn't cost us even a raised eyebrow either. There was tight security reference hand baggage and in Amsterdam there was a thorough physical search also. It took over an hour to load the plane.

We spent a night at Migori. It was really great to be there with Daddy and Miriam, but from the long conversations we had I gather a bit of disquiet about their returning for another term. If Daddy could be boss of the district for another eight years, he'd be very happy here. But if he comes under the jurisdiction of an African pastor, I feel that it is best they come home. But that's just a feeling.

Musoma stores look terribly barren, but I'm told that things are much better than they were six months ago. There are a number of new buses now that the government has declined to nationalize. The big problem in Musoma is meat. There's meat available for about an hour two mornings a week; there is a minor war to see who can get an order in. Today I entered the pushing throng and fortunately some chap up near the window helped me get four kilo of bony meat.

Our barrels were all here waiting for us. The stuff stored in the attic had been brought down to our house. So by tonight we're pretty well settled in. Tomorrow I leave for a three-day meeting at Mugumu which culminates in the ordination of a new pastor for there. Daniel Imori, the Bible college principal, has planted trees all over the place. I am his servant for now, so I can stay out of the church secretary's hair!

October 12, 1972

It is raining!!!! This is the first substantial shower this place has had since last May!

It seems I always have reentry problems, but tonight I feel free and happy. Part of it is the rain, part is the good book I am reading, *Passions of the Mind* by Irving Stone about Sigmund Freud, part of it is the excellent ground cherry pie we had for dessert, part of it is the nostalgic music we're playing from the LMS Choraleers, part of it is that I have been doing a little teaching again and thrill to the interest of the students.

Last evening I climbed up our little hill back of the station and heisted myself up on the Giant's Shoe rock and just looked at the station for a long time and thought. I remember Andrew Wyeth's comment in your book of his paintings to the effect that he had traveled a lot in Chad's Ford, or was he quoting Thoreau? Seems I traveled a lot in Bukiroba. What's new just now is that the paths have had their stones replenished and straightened and whitewashed. So that from the Shoe they look like little bright spots of light twinkling all over the place. Funny how I wished someone was with me for thought banter, but the solitude was therapeutic, too. A little chap had made himself a little car of soft wood, which he pulled on the end of a long string. I spied him first racing along the footpath leading from the school kitchen, his little chariot churning swirls of dust.

Rosemary has got to prefacing her bedtime prayers with the statement, "Dear Jesus, I believe you; you are stronger than Satan." I sort of like that simple faith.

I am a stranger in Musoma. Everything has changed since a year ago. I went for meat the other day, not that I wanted to, but my wife had to have some kind of meat or she was going to be incapacitated. There are ten stalls at the Musoma meat market which are supplied by a great white van with *N'gombe* over its sides in great red letters. Each stand was so jammed with people that I decided I could more easily face my wife than all that and went off to other business. But a half-hour later I returned and one of the outlets was still supplying meat and the crush wasn't too bad so I gave it a try. It proved not so bad an experience. A young man in a floppy red hat was maintaining his position in the crowd by leaning over the people jammed around the window, hand propped against one window strut. His free hand held a cigarette with which he burned a hole in the kerchief of an unsuspecting girl who got in his way, and he got one man angrily rubbing a burn on his forearm. His value to me and to others was that he would decide whose cause he should help along and then he'd do the shouting for us. He soon got on to me and after finding that I wanted four kilos (chopped bones with meat is the only fare these days) he began shouting. Before long, four kilos came through the window which I received by squeezing my basket between pressed bodies to where the chunk of newspaper-wrapped flesh and bones could be dropped off the window ledge into the basket. Then I had to pay, so I gave my benefactor fifteen shillings which he wrapped into a little scroll and poked it through a small hole in the screen above everyone's head—a hole poked through for the purpose. Before long four silver shillings appeared pinched between two black fingers on the inside of the hole and my friend transferred the change to me. I thanked him and departed. While I was there a small frail housewife moved off to a second window which also still had some meat. I called after her because she was there long before me. "But," she said, "I can't get service over there."

Another day I went to the "Mennonite" window where a certain Joseph inside was being implored. This time I waited my turn, there being no benefactor to shout out my case. The Bishop was over at the door, calling occasionally to Joseph so that he'd know that a Mennonite stood without in the throng. For some time Joseph served only people crushed at the outside window which faced the street outside the market. We inside the market, we at the Mennonite window, numbered about a dozen and we were in no line at all—just loosely on the outside of the small crowd and not wishing for too much body contact kept about four to six inches between myself and those ahead and on both sides. Imagine my surprise when a little woman squeezed her butt in between the others and me. Thereby I learned that contact must be maintained with the surrounding folk if one desires to reach the window. Shortly, Joseph turned his attention to our window and then the pushing got intense. As soon as one person was served the idea was to occupy his place at the window without backing off to let him out because backing off to let him out would allow someone to squeeze into the space you had backed off from. Again I noticed that I was getting ahead of a frail girl in a pink dress who was standing beside the window but hadn't the strength to get over in front of it. I discovered that yesterday's benefactor system of leaning over the people and resting a hand on the window strut helped to give one extra leverage in keeping off the thrusting bodies behind you. Just as soon as Joseph began giving meat out through our window a great blowzy woman rushed up and tried to bore her way to the front, shouting all the while that she had been there all day and that Joseph was never going to pay her any attention. She managed to get her hand to within inches of the window, a hand clutching a five-spot between thumb and forefinger, but I kept her bulk from getting past my hips. The little girl then slipped in sideways in front of me and managed to get served between my two orders. The whole thing took about a half hour and although Edith decried the bone and gristle I had brought home, she was mollified by my assurance that it was better than a lot that went out the window before mine. If one goes for the physical contact and for stew meat full of bone splinters it isn't too bad, but on the other hand maybe the Seventh Day Adventists missionaries with their vegetarian diet have a point after all!

The first weekend back I drove the Bishop out to Mugumu, nearly a hundred miles one way, for the ordination of a pastor to carry on with that district. The Bishop went hunting and thus used up our spare fuel, so we had to buy some at the Ikizu School on the way back. Marko, the newly-ordained, shot an impala. The hunting party of the previous day had got three animals. Anyway, the point isn't that. It was a good show; the ordination was, but very much as others that I've described. On the way home, as we neared Bukiroba, we were clonking along in the old Toyota jeep when a beautiful new yellow Tusker Beer truck whisked around us and was soon so far ahead that its dust didn't even linger on the road. The Bishop remarked, "That one is still new." On our trip we had seen three wrecked or broken-down buses and a fourth one came to some minor grief that Saturday we were out there. The week before a large truck ran off the road between here and Musoma. Yesterday when I drove into town there lay the lovely Tusker Beer truck on its ribs at the sharp turn where you make a right at the end of the salt marsh and head in for town. The stores in town are pitifully empty. Just now the acute shortage is cloth and flour. Petrol too was rationed over the time of the Uganda scare. Yet we are told that the town is in much better shape than it was six months ago.

The East African Airways DC-3 flights have resumed, following the Uganda disturbance, but the last one that came in here last Saturday had three bursts of some kind of automatic fire sprayed at it as it came in for landing. The poor white pilot was reported to be hopping mad and absolutely insistent on being returned to Nairobi by road. He had some passengers on board. There is no report of the plane having actually been hit, but some heard bursts of fire. Africans disappeared, but the Asian women came out of their houses to see what was going on. Eventually the pilot agreed to take his plane up again, but whether he'll return on Saturday is still unknown. It is reported that during the scare, three folk were shot here in Musoma. The blame is put on the Chinese rifles, which are said to go off without provocation. A number of our missionaries have been pretty well shaken up at roadblocks. I have always shut off the motor and acted very willing about everything at the roadblock leading into Musoma and have always been treated with the utmost courtesy.

So that is the Musoma that greets us. The graphs are still going downward and my guess is that the kind of Musoma we knew won't be back for another decade. (I'm negotiating with the Bank of Tanzania in Dar es Salaam for permission to import a used BSA motorcycle from Kenya.) But as we get used to the restricted way of life and to the paucity of good following our American furlough, we find that life is still good. The skies have been a perfectly brilliant blue.

October 15, 1972

Yesterday and today a carload of us went up to Nyabasi to visit Elva Landis. The excuse we had for the trip was that her house roof leaks and Victor (Dorsch) decided to go fix it. I'll spare you the details of fixing roofs. It is beautiful up at Nyabasi, with the heavy spicy aroma of pine and cypress quickening the step and clearing the mind. Last night I went outside for a bit and just stood listening and looking. There wasn't a breath of air, yet it was cool and pleasant. A quarter moon hung low in the sky, and bright stars scattered their twinkles over the dome of heaven. Around on three sides were traces of clouds blocking out the lower stars. There was no sound whatsoever anywhere indicating any sort of human habitation throughout the whole land; only crickets chirped, some three or four varieties giving a sort of musical range of pitch and meter to their joy. Then after a bit a dog far down in the valley began barking. There was nothing else; no sound of machinery, no human voice; no smell of fossil fuels burning; no human light stabbing the dark; just a silent peaceful calm. I went into the house and slept soundly the night through.

There has been a civil war raging for the past month between the Kuria and Ngurimi peoples. The fighting is apparently at times intense beyond Kisaka. When we were out in Mugumu we heard that the war had spread also to the Iko and Maragoli peoples. Apparently someone started stealing cattle and the mutual recriminations just kept snowballing. There are verbal reports of some thousand people killed, very much cattle displaced, and villages burnt. It was intense for the police to be using our radio contact with Kisaka for a number of days last week. It is a strange sort of war—completely local and tribal, which makes it seem unreal and distant to us here who are less than a hundred miles away. Interestingly, too, is that the conflict is going on in the areas which have just recently (during the past 15 years) been settled and it is amongst the major tribal groupings who have moved in to the fertile country beyond Kisaka.

Hunting has become the rage since we left last year. Just this past week the Migire brothers went through here on their way to the *pori* to hunt. On

Friday the Stoltzfus brothers and wives went on a two-day safari, coming back with three animals for the annual church conference at Shirati next weekend. The stuff is to be dried. Tonight Ken and the African mechanic left for the *pori*, expecting to be back sometime tomorrow with a load of meat. Twice when I was out at Mugumu, hunting parties went out—all African parties. It's the scarcity of beef.

Nothing profound to write about. Nothing but a steady rain dripping on our tin roof, whispering comfort and the promise of good sleep.

1973

January 6, 1973

I had a barrel of fun these last four days. A shipment had come for various people and was waiting in Arusha to be picked up. The Bishop had a trip planned for Arusha anyway, and he wanted me to go along. I persuaded the Bishop that we should go with the church truck, that old Bedford. The old "*chuma*" is awfully battled-scared, but it still works pretty well. The mechanic was put on a two-day concentration of the truck, and the Bishop with the Treasurer and I set out early Wednesday morning. Amazingly the rains are still hanging on this year and it was drizzly until close to Seronera on the Serengeti. Then, of course, Ngorongoro was wet and in places the road was very slick. The Bishop was full of "*wasi-wasi*" and so was I a few times when we started skidding but actually everything went nicely. That whole wheat-growing country of Mbulu, which you can see from the top of Ngorongoro, is now in the plowing stage and it was really a magnificent sight.

Driving the truck was something else! It rides fairly well and the road had been repaired in places because President Nyerere was coming through, but it is such a long journey and one has to keep pushing all the time in order to make it in a day. Our charger didn't work, so the mechanic gave us two batteries. We started back at five in the morning with the second battery, which went dim by dawn, so we knew we had to make it home by sunset. As it was, it was too dark to see the road for the last two miles, and we had to use what lights were left to keep from going off into the bush. But using lights killed our spark so the engine wouldn't run well. By gearing down and keeping the motor racing, we managed to get both a bit of power and a dull red glow in front of our noses. We finally made it home.

For three days I had no discourse with another white person. I've found again that living three days as servant to Africans points up for me the basic differences which lie between us!

Things since getting back have been very very low key. Victor has continued to play a dominant role with the Fraternal workers. I've been slow about jumping into school while the African principal is still here. He leaves now in a few days for national service, and it looks as though he will be back in June. My relationship to the church office is even more tenuous than before, which probably means that the church is functioning without missionary involvement. There are the missionary secretaries in the office, and that's about it. The Bishop having got his own driver helps a lot too. But increasingly it looks as though it may be possible to get compartmentalized and not do much outside of the classroom. So, I'm planning on putting in a lively year in the classroom and let the rest of the world go by.

These days the ferry across the Mara River doesn't use cables but has two big engines, one on each side. We went up to Migori, but we had trouble at the ferry. The family had given up on us and went ahead with the turkey dinner. So by the time we walked in the turkey was a shambles. But there was plenty left so we sat down and had supper all over again!

This was the first time we've paid a visit to Daddy and Miriam since they moved to Migori. We just ate and ate and listened to Daddy's tapes and talked and walked around. It just seemed like they should stay on there forever. Truly they are the ideal people to be there by the side of the road to help us who travel, and their station is just blooming with trees and flowers and gardens. But it is also true that the Bishop doesn't trust whites as heads of parishes. So there is sort of an unwritten agreement that as long as Daddy is there, no African will be ordained. But Jacobs envisions ordaining two to four Africans in the next several years with Daddy as sort of the catalyst for development and expansion of the Mennonite work in Kenya. Jacobs wishes for a one thousand percent increase in membership over the next five years! From the white perspective Clyde and Miriam are the ideal missionary couple doing the ideal kind of missionary service at an ideal station.

Did I tell you about my new cycle? It's orange with chrome fenders, and it is a year newer than my last one. But it is considerably more worn than the other. Obviously, it has been taken apart many times. Still, it is more snappy than the other one. It also leaks oil. On balance, it is just a middle-age cycle.

The lake is blue and still this afternoon. The rains are gone and the sky is crystal blue all day. Here at school I am in charge of building a women's dormitory for domestic science. That keeps me tired.

January 18, 1973

Thanks for your sympathy about a son. It would be nice to have a son because I feel that it would develop a whole new love relationship in my experience. But I really feel that the one most disappointed about it was Edith. But to be very frank with you, we are happy with our four beautiful daughters. I really think that Rebecca looks like Mother. She has that sort of bemused grin that Mother used to have, and she is more ruddy of complexion than her sisters. She'll probably have something of green in her eyes.

I am beginning to get under the surface of things here, and it is becoming apparent to me that my role is very limited. I've said this before, but always with some hope in reserve that I may be able to break out of the crust and take a hand in helping to run this church. But it is not to be. At conference this year, for example, my name was on the slate for only one committee, the Musoma Bookshop. That one I won handily! The bookshop is also bankrupt and we must find a way to close it quickly. Even with our low profile, some three statements were made in conference about the whites not knowing Africa and therefore not being able to function effectively. Dr. Brubaker is regional leprosy officer and as such he has tried to maintain some autonomy. Fifteen minutes were spent discussing how to wrest his independence from him. Two reports castigated the ag boys for their ineffectual contributions. But Daddy won a seat on the Executive Committee, as well as on the evangelism committee.

Today we opened Bible school with eight pastors and deacons present; two or three are still to come. We are to provide them with blankets and soap, among other things. So I had these things on hand to distribute, only to discover that the blankets are of a quality that none but the lowest strata of society uses them, and which in fact is dangerous to health. The soap I had got for bathing, a Tanzanian variety of Lifebouy, turned out to be what some people use only for washing clothes. I just didn't know any of this.

March 8, 1973

Don't we take on the coloration of our surroundings and doesn't that mean that there is a sort of binding and loosing going on, causing one to be judged differently, depending on his environment? Take me, this year, for example, when I was teaching ten pastors with an average age of fifty. Today they were talking about drinking and smoking. It almost got me to worrying about the wine I drank in Amsterdam, and the three cigarettes I have smoked in my life. It turned out to be the same problem that we used to have with the plain suit. I remember that in 1966 I was wearing a tie to church in New York City and at Millersville, back in Lancaster County, the Bishop was refusing communion to men wearing a long tie. Then when I came home once he had me help him to serve communion!

Nelson Litwiller passed through here. I was his chauffeur and we got to talking. In 1970 he got an in-filling of the Holy Spirit. This grew out of his concern that something had gone wrong in the Latin American mission effort of the Mennonites, as indicated by their very slow rate of church growth. He was to go on a preaching assignment in Europe in 1970 and felt that he had absolutely nothing to say. He began reading about the work of the spirit and one writer was a Catholic working at Notre Dame, in South Bend, Indiana, near his Goshen residence. So he and his wife began attending a Wednesday night prayer meeting with this Catholic group. In time he asked for help and was told to attend instruction, which he did for two weeks. Instruction, however, was terribly elementary and his Europe trip was coming up, so he asked if they could hurry it up. So after the regular prayer meeting, he and a number of others stayed and they prayed for him with the laying on of hands, and he was filled with the Holy Spirit. His experience in Europe was tremendous. He has subsequently kept up his contact with the Catholics and has been used of the Lord here and there in a very powerful ministry.

He came here because someone invited him to Somalia for a retreat, then later to Ethiopia, South Africa, Nigeria, and Ghana. He also visited the Mennonite missionaries in Israel en route to Africa.

We wanted to hold our spiritual retreat at Shirati but political pressure there is such that missionaries meeting alone creates too much noise among the African church. So, in the end we decided to have it here at Bukiroba and to include all the TMC pastors as well. Viola (Dorsch) masterminded the cooking, Victor the sleeping, and I the cow. We cooked in the college kitchen and in the domestic science kitchen. We ate in the college classroom, with the kids eating in the typing room. The meetings were held in the college chapel. Mary Oyer was our song leader. The morning before the meetings began she spent with the college men, talking about music and doing some singing. Pastor Jona sat there with tears trickling down his face as Mary sang Negro spirituals. She is really something else. I wish she would give two years sometime to helping TMC's music get on its feet. There were between 70 and 80 participants in the retreat, about a dozen of who were Africans and about 15 kids.

We started Friday night, and it seemed that there was a steadily mounting awareness by Saturday afternoon that something good was going to happen.

Then a storm began to blow in from off old Bugoshi Mountain and during the singing it began to rain. Slowly the rain built up to where you had trouble hearing Mary's music directions. The distraction was the noise of the rain on the roof. Then, just like a flash, the room was suddenly filled with huge drops of water raining down from everywhere. With one accord everyone rushed for cover, but there wasn't much cover to be had. Most of us hid behind the stage entrances and the rest crowded in the back, behind the entrance juts into the building. It was weird, with it raining about as hard inside as out. I was looking up at the ceiling and a mist of rain was swirling about there like it does in a driving rain along the ground outside. It seems that the wind outside just lifted the rain backward through the louvers in the walls. There were puddles on the floor even the next day. As soon as the noise subsided a bit, a teacher who loves Jesus got out his guitar and a clutch of younger folk got to singing in one corner. As soon as the rain inside subsided we wiped off the chairs and went back to having our meeting. Litwiller spoke on devils which live in us, such as chronic fear or hate or jealousy or lust. It was a powerful sermon, and just as soon as he was finished the Bishop stood up and confessed to chronic fear so that he cannot sleep, along with self-doubt and an inferiority complex, along with propensity to anger in his relationships with others. It was a sincere confession with all the stops out. As soon as he got done, Litwiller put his arms around the Bishop and asked if he might pray for him. The Bishop agreed, so Litwiller got a chair, sat the Bishop in it and called several people to come help and began to pray. His method was to lay hands on the one seeking release and to pray in three steps. First was a prayer calling on Jesus' name and invoking the authority inherent in His shed blood and binding Satan and thrusting him out. All the oppressing devils that the Bishop had mentioned were mentioned by name. The second was the prayer for the filling of the Holy Spirit, and the third was thanksgiving with the person being prayed for urged to verbalize his own thanks. I could tell that Litwiller hoped someone would burst out in tongues during this thanksgiving, but through out the meetings no one did. He himself did several times softly, so that only he who was looking for it detected what was going on. Well, when the Bishop got up, he was a new man and so he has continued to be ever since. But after that, until suppertime, people came just as fast as opportunity afforded. It seemed that the Spirit broke in upon us like the storm had. It swept in with such fury that it just carried all before it and none could resist. Later that night and on Sunday, the initial fury of the storm subsided and it was just a good soaking rain. By the time we were finished on Sunday, all but two pastors had had hands laid on them, and all but a dozen of the missionaries. Neither Edith nor I responded. I was translating the whole time, and it seemed that I had to get my blessing vicariously through what happened to those for whom I was interpreting.

In the last session we held hands, forming a huge circle and prayed that Litwiller would get a visa to enter Somalia. Now, just this evening we heard from Nairobi that he did indeed get permission; they left this morning. We also had a communion service to wrap up things.

From Bukiroba the Litwillers went up to Shirati Hospital; there again was a minor breakthrough. While no tears and no soul-wrenching confessions, there was some genuine seeking of the Lord afresh. That same weekend the first Christian at Shirati died out near the Kenya border. Some 500 people showed up for the funeral with powerful preaching and ringing testimonies. There was no wailing whatsoever, which is a first for here. So all around us there seems to be a fresh wind blowing since the other weekend. God's people have a new look in their eye. And not only that, the Regional commissioner has heard that some missionaries have been subject to harassment by local officials, particularly reference border guards. He asked for an opportunity to make a courtesy call designed to buck up our morale. For my part, at least, I haven't had so much fun in a long time.

Here's what I did with the fifty dollars. I bought a blanket for an old man. He is the husband of a woman who wanted to borrow Shs 350/= from me to pay someone to resurrect her dead son. The husband's youngest kids run naked, and the old man is finally reduced to wearing only a blanket. I gave him another one to help with the kids. It was a deed of mercy, but at the same time I don't feel awfully sorry for the man, as I feel he got himself into his poverty mess—a story in itself. I used some of the gift to help a young man pay the fees for his wife to attend the six-month domestic science course. The rest I added to our family's tithing tin for further use.

I think of the conversations we could have if you were here. Yet, when our paths did cross, we were busy and didn't converse that much anyway. I've thought about it over the past years, and I feel that maybe I converse better in letters. Then, too, I have thought that one never reaches his desired perfect state of conversation or loving or understanding or caring or giving. We always strive for it, and in moments of reflection we glimpse its glory, but it always lies beyond our grasp. Yet, I think it isn't entirely elusive; we seek and find in bits and flashes, and as we live, these are more frequent and more satisfying and more genuine. Yet, the ultimate expression of love eludes us until death.

July 2, 1973

What have I been doing? End of May took the Bishop to Nairobi for his several days of vacation. Early June went with Edith to Nairobi to bring back the school kids, spending one night at Migori to visit the parents. A trip to Moburu Bay for a weekend dedication conference of the Nyangwayo church, taking all but two of the Bible school college students. This past week I drove the Bishop to Seronera and camped two nights there (Serengeti Plains) with Edith and the girls. Then the first weeks of this month I'll again be in Dodoma for editorial work on the school syllabus for religious knowledge. At the same time I've been holding down this full teaching load. In the cracks I supervise work on a dormitory and carpenter's shop on the grounds. And a lot of time goes into doing what the church secretary should be doing, but he is never in the office. About all he does for the Bishop is to buy bus tickets for him.

Another excuse for not writing: I haven't got either sufficiently excited or depressed to need an audience. It seems last term that things were going down in flames all around us, and it was sort of fun to chronicle the wonder of it in a sort of incredulous tale. But now, all that is past and we bump along on the bottom of things with not much hope for anything too great coming along. Our generator went bust the other week, so we're now back to doing without lights or washing machines or electric irons, not to mention battery chargers and film projectors. I am typing with a candle waxed to the top of the typewriter. Shirati Hospital lost something near Shs 400,000/= in the past couple of years. The big road from the upper crossroads to Bunda these days is being repaired by crews with hoes, as in the early fifties. Some places the church is going, but in others it is a dim affair. The Bishop took this trip to Seronera with nine adults and three kids in an old Toyota, ostensibly for evangelism. He must have expected to have hordes of eager Mennonites descend on his sleeping quarters to submit their problems to his wisdom. We finally started the worship service Sunday morning with one teenager present, and ended up with four local people making it in time for communion. These got scolded for their efforts.

The big political word these days out of Dar es Salaam is "*Hakuna nyapala, wote ni wafanyakazi.*" ("There is no boss, all are workers.") This means that all across the board we lead by persuasion and example, which is good. But there is no way to knock things into shape. There is sort of a massive inertia that has set it. You cannot fight the sea; it is too great for you. And of course, the continual corrosion of the infrastructure continues. Take the history of the Pastor's battery. His car has been sitting here for over a half year, now having been driven out here by me one memorable afternoon; he wanted it in safe quarters. The thing had a good battery, so in due course, when the Bishop's battery gave out, his car got the Pastor's battery and continued so for several months, until the Bishop discovered whose battery he had and therefore dropped it. I had been using the radio battery in the truck for hauling sand and stuff needed for these buildings, but it has got scratched up and pressure was mounting for me not to continue, so I took to using the Pastor's battery for the truck. The principal's car was needed for a wedding, and as his battery is bad, he got the Pastor's battery and has now had it for a week. The car we went to the *pori* in had been sitting for six months due to not having a windshield. When we started out, we couldn't get to the top of our hill here by the station due to water in the petrol from its having sat without a cover on the tank for six months. It took three hours to clean out everything, giving us a really late start. Then we left with one of the back wheels from the immobilized Shirati Toyota as a spare and then we got a blow out within 25 miles out. Fortunately we had a hand tire pump.

So you see to tell you all this is only old hat, and I can't sit down at the typewriter all the time and tell about the four flats we got going to Mohuru Bay, the last one making us late for the Kirumi ferry, so we had to sleep in some drunk's home and stand around a smoky grass fire late that night eating bananas his wife cooked with plenty of pepper since it is so difficult to get salt.

And all this is only one side of the coin. Things are quiet here, in the sense that we could drive all the way from Seronera to Ndabaka gate, seeing the Serengeti swarming with every kind of animal; for one 75 miles stretch we met no other human being. Or in the early morning at our tent site we could watch a male lion following his sweetheart across a mile of burnt meadow and hear not one human sound, other than our own excited whispers. Or even tonight, for example, to step outside and hear not a sound but the squalling of a wild cat. Or again, driving home last night with the whole western sky ablaze with crimson over the vast expanses of kopje, valley, plains mountain-rimmed and falling away to the lake with nothing as far as the eye could reach of any significance made by man except for maize fields among the bush and the little brown huts blended into that whole picture. I told Joyce, who was sitting beside me, "That's Africa." Or where again would you have four great Luo matrons accustomed to singing in quartet, unamplified to large crowds, chanting in full nasal power ancient desert airs set now to words of Christian praise, all emitted in competition with the roaring of our muffler-busted Land-Cruiser, with resonant clapping in wild mixed beat, now fast, now slow, until for 36 hours afterward one's ears still ring? There are times when I am happy here, when I feel that I know the land and its people, and that I am comfortable.

So there are both, the bad and the good, but neither is really why we live or don't. We live because of hope and I think hope sometimes falters with me, and this is more truly the reason why I now write so seldom. A Catholic padre said the other day that for the African, Calvary is more important than the empty tomb; it is most important not that you die but how you die. So, maybe then for the African hope is much tempered by failure and hurt, and submission becomes a powerful theme. And this is what is happening to my hope during these ten years at Bukiroba. Through it I may be becoming more African, at least more the Tanzanian type of African, and I am afraid that I may get crippled for life by it. During these same years other men move from success to success and it colors their approach to life. We become schooled in forgetting initiative and this we can do, but what will we be when we come back to the States?

The problem I find with certain of my fellow missionaries is that they see me as thinking that what has happened to me is firstly not painful for me, and secondly, that I judge them for not having allowed it to happen to them. They think this because I have got an entrée to where the African lives, which they have not, and they are angry with me for having done it, by becoming what they cannot become. Yet, I am too proud to talk their language, also too crippled to, and too proud to try, and then holding tenaciously to my silence and evasiveness, they feel I sit in judgment. And true, I do feel that I hold the trump card, although not judging them for not holding it too. But then I see that the trump card I hold is for a game I cannot even play, for in that game the African is my teacher and the westerners will never need to play. They will not stay here long, a term or two at most, and those who would come back, but without knowing the game, will be asked not to, and those who saw what the game was about will not want to come back.

July 17, 1973

I got my hair cut! I went in to the Musoma barber and egged him on until in the end the longest strand on my head was about one inch! I walked into the house and took off my motorcycle helmet and Rosy's mouth just dropped open. Finally she exclaimed, "Daddy, you look so funny!" Then Edith looked up and pronounced herself shocked. Some three weeks later the Weavers passed through from Shirati Hospital and Ruth couldn't get over trying to analyze why I'd done such a thing. All the white men at Shirati now wear beards. I assured her that I had no reason. The Africans were pleased, it giving them opportunity to talk about the good old missionary men who cut their hair decently. Mine's growing out now, with fuzz around my ears.

These days I've been reading *Sitwell and the American Experience in China* by Barbara Tuchman. I've been reading it for about six months! Sitwell just kept hanging in there with Chiang Kai-shek, expecting that some day he could really get a hold of things. I cannot help but draw parallels between my experience and his. I note that there were a lot of foreigners working for Chiang and that at the bottom of it he hated them all. He allowed Sitwell to operate, not because he believed in him or wanted him to work with Chinese troops but because Chiang felt that that way he could get America to keep sending him material. Just today a man from Majita told me that they have invited Daddy to preach at their annual meetings, and that they want him to bring his loud speakers, lights, and films. Then he re-emphasized that Daddy is invited to be one of the speakers. It is clear to me that what they want is the equipment but in order to get Clyde to go to the bother to bring that, they have to put up with his preaching. I am used here as a means for getting material out of Salunga. But I keep telling myself that I am on the verge of some breakthrough and that some day soon I shall be able to function in a creative capacity. The Bishop tells me clearly that the reason missionaries at Shirati have been allowed back into the decision-making orbit is that they complained so much that he got afraid they might all go home. There is no hint of supposition on his part that their being readmitted may help to make better decisions, only that their egos will be satisfied and they will stick with their jobs. But Sitwell still hoped until he was finally recalled, and I expect that I shall keep on hoping also until recalled. But in the meantime, I fear that I shall have become crippled and will wind up incapable of doing anything. I have put all priority into adapting to this situation in the hope that some day it will win for me an opportunity to provide creative leadership. Yet, it is a striving after wind, and in the end I shall be nothing in the States because I haven't developed the requisite equipment.

I get to feeling like that priest in Greene's novel *The Power and the Glory*. Cheer me up with a letter.

August 3, 1973

Nate Showalter and his parents were here for two nights. The first evening we got into a discussion where it was evident that when it came to African matters—political, sociological, historical, he considers himself considerably more enlightened than us old fuddy-duddy missionaries. Yet, the next morning I had to rescue him from a jeep full of angry special police. I was behind the house seeing about a water problem when someone from the garage came and advised me to go rescue "my friend," as the police are after him and he isn't answering respectfully. They were in front of the Dorsch house going at each other at a great rate. Fortunately, the police contingent was an outfit which I had helped with petrol up near Tarime once, and they welcomed me into the spat like a long lost friend. It turned out that Nate and his dad were going to Musoma and on the way remembered that they needed to cash traveler's checks and would need their passports. So they turned round to come back. But just before that a Special Forces unit had passed them going toward town. Seeing this Kenyan car turn round and head back just after being passed by the police alerted the police to check out what was up. Then Nate didn't stop for a while after they tried to stop him, thus increasing their suspicion of him. When he finally did stop they asked for his passport and his driver's license. Since Nate's dad didn't have his passport, they all came back to Bukiroba in convoy. Then, while the dad was in the house getting his passport, Nate began taking the police to task for messing with him. The fat was in the fire then. If I hadn't been near, I am sure the Showalter men would have spent the day in the police station.

Finally, good old TMC is hitting rock bottom. I guess the good life is drawing to a close. What brought all this on suddenly was that the Salunga treasurer took out half of investment repayments owed in 1973. He took it out in one monthly remittance. Secondly, Shirati Hospital ordered some Shs 20,000/= worth of stuff through Salunga, which Salunga also lopped from last month's remittance. So these two things on consecutive months have pretty well brought things to a halt. But Daniel Mtoka is safely back from national service; he's again installed in the principal's office at the theological college. I am honestly and sincerely happy about that matter.

September 2, 1973

This evening we did something new. We all went fishing, the whole family. We cut poles from our mulberry trees, bought hooks at a penny apiece from a little country shop that has "borrow tomorrow" painted on its wooden window shutter, got some nylon twine from Mr. Rabbit's shop, borrowed Ryangaria's Peugeot pickup, and with a picnic supper we went in to town to the old wharf. Everyone but Becky (nine months) caught fish, a total of 56! We put them in a quart tin, which filled it half full. Tiny things. They're great fun to catch and not bad eating, but, as a young African who was watching us remarked, "You don't get too much fish for your effort." We sure got a lot of fun for our effort.

We're planning to be with Daddy and Miriam at Migori for Thanksgiving. Then in Nairobi for a while, and then spend a week with Davids at Mombasa. Wish you could join us.

November 30, 1973

I'm writing from the Nairobi Mennonite Guest House. It seems that my journal hasn't done much this year. I think it is due largely from being too tired. I can't push myself anymore; it makes my chest hurt and my ears buzz, so I try to stay away from writing. Congratulations on the birth of Omar Lawrence. I'm guessing that you'll call him Lawrence, and I'm guessing too that he's been named for that illustrious Englishman of Arabia. I like both names—they've got a little salt to them, as good names should. Now you all have got sons but us. All Africans think we should try again.

I went book shopping. I browse and buy sort of hit and miss. Bought Doris Lessing's last in her trilogy, *The Four Gated City. Future Shock* by Alvin Toffler, and *How Young they Died* by Stuart Cloete on WW I. You'll note that my reading runs towards historical fiction. That way I learn some history and get some fun in the bargain.

What's on my mind these days is this Mellingers thing. For a while I thought I wouldn't write about it, but there is nothing to be gained by that except a notion that by not writing you will credit me with self-effacement or with nonchalance. Actually the thing is eating at me more than I had imagined. I've been dreaming. The first night it was that after twenty years I came back to Africa and was greeted somewhere by an old leper, a quiet, lonely old man with the toes off one foot and one crippled hand. His one foot was so bad he had his shoe on backward. He looked familiar and I checked his face for a scar on the right nostril, and sure enough it was Pastor Jona still living with his wife in some obscure village, still warm and truly spiritually, but with no active ministry. We embraced and I could tell without his speaking that he loved me as ever and that my being away had been a heavy burden for him. Jona was my student last year, he at 61 years. More than any other student he allowed me into his life. He put the roofs on those buildings we put up and I helped him as a son. I often took him home by motorcycle. He had cattle problems again this year, and I advised him profitably at one point and drove him around looking for his escaped cattle. I have such a warm spot in my heart for him because I grew up as a boy under his wing at Bumangi, but more because up to now his community has rejected him for his forthright stand against the traditional religion. Yet, his faith is as pure as the day he believed. We have often talked together in a sort of analytical way about his experiences. I got to thinking that probably he was entrusting to me more than he entrusted to his own family, and it came clear to me that this is the new family that Jesus talked about. What was the implication of my dream?

The second night I dreamed that we were at the meeting for casting the lots for minister at Mellingers. First went a fifty-ish dairy farmer, prosperous and happy, typical middle class American. He took the left book. I was next and suspected the slip to be in the right book, but took the middle one. Then the Hoover brother took the right book, a salesman by trade. Then we riffled through our Bibles looking for the slip. Mine didn't have it, so I watched my neighbors from the corner of my eyes. Hoover had the lot.

The third night I dreamed I was making love to my wife—very good making love, too, but she got impatient over my taking so long so I took longer than ever and eventually woke myself up. Then I dreamed again that someone had given me a life size poster of a *Playboy* centerfold. It was folded up and I never did get home with it to see what she looked like. The last dreams I attribute at least in part to the impact of the eroticism of a tourist city after a year of Musoma. So the result today is a somewhat guilty feeling about my worthiness to lead other people to God, and with it an understanding that my personality and its drives are what they are and are not likely to change much, except as I wear out. (Like the old man who congratulated himself on the fact that he was leaving his lusts behind, while, in fact, it was his lusts which were leaving him!)

Bishop Landis at Mellingers wants a commitment (for my being in the lot) by Monday night. But I said I must see Bishop Kisare first. We at three in the morning, Hershey and I left for Musoma. We had breakfast with the parents at Migori and gave them the news. They, of course, both feel strongly in favor of the lot going my way. They were afraid Bishop Kisare would block it.

The Bishop was surprised to see me so suddenly returned from Nairobi. I told him all about it in his office, then left him to discuss it with the secretary and treasurer. After lunch he came over to Victor's house to give their response. First he said that had he had long hair it would have stood straight up. Then he conceded that we didn't want to be like two dogs fighting over one bone, and then gave his testimony of being at peace about it, knowing that the Lord will make His will known. That was about it, an assurance that he and the church were prepared to accept the Lord's will when that became known. We prayed and started back to Nairobi.

I've been determined not to get all fired up about this, to avoid that raising of eyebrows when the slip isn't in my book. But I must confess that it is a traumatic experience. Both alternatives have so many implications that thinking about them leaves me tired and giddy. I've tried to think what you feel. I came up with an observation such as, "Good grief, Joe, why are you accepting to dump your position as transcultural-interpreter and go-between just when another four years are open to you. Further, I'm sure you have no idea what an albatross that ingrown old congregation would be around your neck, with one on the bench blocking your every initiative."

(Later) The ordination went as I dreamed! I had expressed to Edith that basically I hope I get it, but when I learned the results, I was greatly relieved.

1974

January 2, 1974

We climbed the Aberdares (northwest of Nairobi). David with his three oldest and me with my two oldest, with kid brother Daniel. Guided by Ron, a Baptist missionary who took his two children along. We left his place out near Thika around 8:00 a.m. in two short-wheel base Toyota Land-cruisers from his mission. It took two hours to get to where the trail began. A good bit of that driving was on a fantastic mountain road, a partly overgrown track, incredibly steep in places. Just before we got to the trail, Ron heard an elephant trumpeting. We saw none, but a big herd had just come down off the mountain, following the trail that we followed up. They made a real muddy slurp out of a lot of the trail. In places the elephants had sunk up to their knees! The trail most of the way up the mountain is through a bamboo forest so dense one can seldom see out. Elephant trails crisscross all over the place, so that without a guide one could get lost. By noon we were up on the ridge where there is a small cabin. The last mile or so is through scrub cedar. It's quite steep, with more and more strawflowers the higher one goes. There are little red lilies, too. The Aberdares are much more picturesque than Kilimanjaro. Nowhere are they so high that you are above the scrub line. Further on they becomes a whole mass of peaks running for fifty miles north-south. So one gets the feeling of their cragginess. Maybe, to, it was just the time of year, but there was an abundance of flowers. I picked eight different kinds of strawflowers.

We ate lunch at the hut and then most of us scouted back through the mountains. The particular set of peaks we were on reaches to about 12,000 feet. Five peaks are easily accessible. Then you hike down into the valley again and back up the second set of peaks, which reaches to 13,000 feet. This second jaunt is about six miles, and you can do it only if you spend the night. So we just hiked back in to the fourth peak. We were surrounded by mountains in there, and if you shouted it echoed like the Alps. I wished I knew how to yodel. Just opposite us was a sheer rock face with the patterns of ancient lava flows clearly distinguishable. Far down in the valley to the west we could see buffalo. From the east the mists flowed through the passes and pushing up, over, and around the area we were in. About 2:00 p.m. we decided the children should start back down. Daniel and I wanted to go on to the fifth peak, highest in our group of humps, so David started back with the children, Ron having stayed at the cabin with his youngest daughter. That last peak was the most beautiful of all.

Daniel and I went through swirling fog and climbed a nearly vertical wall of rock ledges with little cedar scrub. The whole wall was covered with a thick mat of orange moss. By thick, I mean that it was a foot deep in places. About half way up we noticed a large golden strawflower that grew out of the steepest places almost as though the flower knew it was lovelier than any of its cousins. We came out on the top on to a narrow ridge some fifty yards in length and ten yards in width, covered with cedar scrub. On all sides it dropped off steeply, at least a thousand feet.

The clouds were everywhere by then, and at time we couldn't even see the opposite cliff. We started back through the cold white mist. Soon it began to sleet, a little at first and then hard, covering the ground with white. This got mixed with rain, so that by the time we got back to the cabin we were soaked through to our underpants.

The day had started out so clear that we could see Mt. Kenya without a trace of haze or cloud anywhere on the horizon. But now the warming day had brought the convection currents which pushed the lower moisture laden air high around the mountain flanks where it got chilled, turned to cloud and spat sleet and rain everywhere.

We caught up with the kids. My daughters had been worried that I would get lost. At one point Dianne had refused to go on until she knew where I was. So when they heard us behind them coming through the cedar they began shouting. Daniel wondered if something was wrong. I told him it was just the happy screaming of one monkey band meeting another!

The bamboo going was no joke. The morning's mud was now worse due to the heavy rain. Even where one could step along side the trail where the bamboo leaves covered the ground, one found that the leaves acted like little toboggans. It became quite a trick to stay upright. Fortunately the children took it to be a lark and they were soon muddy from the waist down, elbows, too. I split my pants from waist to crotch, straining to keep from falling into the mud.

I was cold, as were we all, and not altogether sure that the elephant track we chose at all the junctures was the one with jeeps at the other end. My knees gave out, and it was only with the most acute pain that they continued to ease my weight down and down and down through the red soupy mud. I began to have a horror of what it would be to spend the night in there with all those kids.

Suddenly, some two hours after starting down, we came into a little clearing, and there were our jeeps. Then it was another two more hours of endless driving with a splitting headache with perpetually steaming windows, following our pillar of dust back to Ron's place. By 8:00 p.m. my party was steaming in hot tubs back at the Mennonite Guest House. Edith soaked our muddy duds. And Dale Resslerwent off to Westlands for boxes of Kentucky Fried Chicken.

Edith had decorated our room for Christmas with all the presents on a table by the window, but we were too tired for Christmas. We waited until the next morning, instead of going to church. My bundle of straw flowers are here in the office with me still wrapped in their safari newspaper, but still giving off the most romantic mountain aroma, bringing back all of that great day.

January 14, 1974

I am increasingly converted to the good sense of motorcycle trips. They give you the time to be away from the routine and with whoever is along. I took Daniel out to Kisaka, and we just talked the whole way there and the whole way back, as well as the whole time we were there overnight. Of course, Danny is such a stimulating conversationalist, that all I need to do is listen and just throw in an occasional word of caution here and there. On the way back from Kisaka he drove the *piki* but he still did most of the talking, shouting into the wind now, rather than into my ear.

That trip caused me to yearn for another trip with you. Let's plan on it next time our paths cross. A day in the mountains, in some city, on a farm, anywhere—but let it be a day again for just the two of us. You came up in our conversation on the way home to Bukiroba. He brought up about your being a cynic. He brought it into context of his visiting Dr. Showalter, his feeling that he was better than you because you ought to see a shrink to get over being a cynic. Dan feels you are cynical for some reason that you won't face, and he thinks the solution for you would be his solution, seeing a psychiatrist! I suggested that Dan has no idea what's going on in your head and therefore had no right to pass judgment about what you should or should not do. He did see that his road is his road, and he must be careful not to impose it on others.

While we were out at Kisaka we went to see old Ludia. She wasn't expecting us. No one knew we were coming, and she didn't even know that Dan was in Africa. She greeted him with great dignity in her smoky outside kitchen. We pulled up stools while she finished the sweet potatoes and put on water for tea. Dan talked with her and with Pastor Nyamwino and I talked about my Mellingers going through the lot experience. Ludia was so quiet and full of love and wonder at her Dan being there. Then she had us go over to her house for sweet potatoes and tea. While we ate she just stood there in her long dress and bare feet and looked at Dan. The next day she had chicken fixed with *ugali*. The chicken was in a broth thick with richness and love, and again she just stood and watched. Later when we sat around for prayer she said how angry she had been that others had monopolized all our time so that she just got what was left over, she's Dan's mother and now not able to ask him all about himself, not to be able to just sit and talk! And she told about her dream that night when our Mother had come and stood beside her. When we left Dan kissed her on the cheek; her eyes brimmed over, tears touching her old cheeks. I knew that I had just seen my dream of Pastor Jona now in reality.

There's a growing unease about the mission board's involvement in Africa. So the Nairobi people created a "think tank" and included me. I went up on the cycle, which needed some work done on it. One of the problems: EMBMC has lost the initiative in Africa. Orie Miller pointed the way to the emergence of national churches, and that has happened, and in its happening; the board has become only a resource. A second problem is that these national churches have, for the most part, also lost their initiative. The psychology has been to get all one can out of the Americans, and the vision about church growth and service has faded. That national churches are struggling hopelessly with the problems of administration of institutions they inherited, being neither able to administer them properly nor willing to turn them over to the government.

A third problem is that where EMBMC does attempt to be creative, such as in Swaziland, Botswana, and Sudan, and Northeast Kenya, the board simply acts unilaterally without regard to the fact that somewhere in the fog one may find a church already there which should be involved in what external agencies are doing in Africa. A fourth problem is that the national churches are enclaves completely blind to each other, each with only one overriding concern, their hot line to the Salunga mission board.

The new pattern to emerge goes something like this: The board may seize an initiative by bringing about the new pattern. The local churches may be stimulated to BE the church at home by being helped to be the church on the continent, something in the same way the Mennonite church in the States came to BE the church there, through the sending of aid and missionaries to foreign places. If, for example, TMC could be party to plans for EMBMC's expansion into northern Kenya, and if TMC personnel could be involved, the TMC at home could be stimulated by this experience to reactive their flagging interests in the Kenya Mennonite Church and the Somali Mennonite church. The idea would be that these churches could even sit together and decide together how certain EMBMC's resources could be divided among them. Supposing the board could grant X dollars for special projects in 1977, then these national churches should be able to come to consensus as to how this was to be shared around. Further, any Africans going to the States on visit must be exposed to the black churches, and even to the Amish church. (Harold Miller thinks the Amish and the Africans have a lot of commonality!)

Pastor Muganda died at the home of a "witch doctor" down near the old Shirati town. This caused some scandal, particularly as it was reported in Nairobi by a pastor who wanted to prove that the church of South Mara is apostate.

About a year ago Muganda had surgery in Dar for prostate troubles. They forgot to put in a catheter, so his urine backed up and sent him into a coma. After four days the problem was discovered, a catheter inserted, and the old man came around. But never again did he trust these instruments of Western medicine. It is quite a commentary that just at the time Shirati Hospital is going off the deep end over not being able to maintain the highest standards of Western medicine, the senior pastor in the church dies of hemorrhage in the village of a traditional herbologist, three miles from the hospital. After the Dar experience, Muganda came home, but his health was never right since. He had been to traditional herbalists in Mwanza, but now, he told me, he was going to go to Shirati. Dick was afraid to operate on him, thinking that he may have got messed up at the Dar hospital and could die on the table.

In a few days Muganda was begging to be let out of the hospital. Eventually Dick consented that he go to Tarime to see his daughter, but warned him that he was a sick man. Muganda was at Tarime for a week or two, and then got some intestinal problem. He sent for his wife who was back at Musoma. Then on Friday afternoon he began to hemorrhage through his penis, so they got a car and took him to Shirati. But he directed that they drive past the hospital to the village of this woman whom he had heard knew how to treat male problems. Upon arrival she wondered why they were bringing her a dead man. "I can't do anything for him," she is reported to have declared. So Muganda said they should pray and this he repeated three times. During the third prayer he died. They then sent a runner to the hospital for a vehicle to take the body back to Musoma.

The funeral was planned for Sunday afternoon. There was a debate among Muganda's people as to whether he should be buried at Kwikerege down in Majita or here in the Musoma town cemetery. Eventually the Musoma won out, after his son telephoned from New York. By early Sunday afternoon all the children had come, some from as far away as Dar by plane, others from Arusha by Land-Rover.

Several things about the funeral were outstanding for me. One was the rollicking fun the young men had digging the grave. Stefano was up on the heap of dug out dirt acting as a sort of unofficial emcee of the fun. There was a lot of vying with one another about who was strongest and could dig the hardest. There were plenty of allusions to traditional folklore about death, this in the vernacular, so I couldn't get too much of it. One idea was that it would rain mightily that night because a great seed had been planted in the earth. The fun got sufficiently risqué to have another elder tone it down a bit. But on balance, digging the grave was a carnival. I suppose that it was because Muganda was such a powerful figure. Now with him gone the door opens for all kinds of new power arrangements. Everyone felt free as a lark. I did two spells in the grave, one with a hoe and one with a shovel.

Near the beginning of the grave digging someone came to call me to a meeting of the ordained and senior elders. The problem had to do with how Muganda should be dressed. Never in Africa have I seen a corpse dressed. The idea was that he should be dressed in his clerical collar. This led to a debate as to whether his plain Mennonite suit was also clerical in nature. But what impressed me was the sense of the meeting that we were making historical decisions, which would have ramifications for years to come. One elder said as much, "We today are making history. What we do will be quoted for years." Imagine my surprise when one pastor asked me for my considered opinion,

seeing that I was the only theological college teacher present. I answered that
the truth is ascertained in each generation and in each place by the leading of
the Holy Spirit through the counsel of the brotherhood, and that I could not
see anything wrong about burying Muganda in clerical clothing. So it was
decided that clerical it would be. But then there was a very long discussion
on how the funeral was to be conducted. I was amazed at how at sea everyone
seemed. We have all buried many people, but now with Muganda, it seemed
that we were paralyzed to think and act.

Finally at about three the pastors went over to prepare the body and again
there was all kinds of hesitancy until eventually two old Muslim relatives
stepped in to show how the washing of the body was to be done. Sand was
scooped up outside and a ridge of it was poured all around the bed to soak
up any water. Then the mattress was dug out from beneath the body, leaving
him on some mats and blankets. He was undressed already so it was a matter
of unwrapping him and going to work. All along I was amazed at how the
younger pastors shrank from doing anything in the funeral. Pastor Mabeba
had to chair the morning worship service, the inside funeral service, and the
graveside service. He was suffering from high blood pressure, yet his cries of
illness fell on deaf ears. The bathing then was given to a deacon. He too had
been sick several weeks ago, yet he had to do all of the washing by himself.
Birai and I were appointed to turn the body, but the deacon had to do the
soaping, rubbing, and wiping. It took a long time and obviously the bending
over was painful for him. Once someone offered to help. But the deacon said,
"Let me do it; I'm the last one left. Next it will be me." I really pitied him
and his face was such a contortion of sorrow and dread. It almost seemed to
me like a punishment inflicted on the aged by the younger men all in the
guise of respect for the dead. The whole body appeared to be in good shape.
Someone at the hospital had come over and shot him full of formaldehyde,
so there was only the strong odor of that. Then at the end as we were rolling
him from side to side, thick black blood began to ooze from his genitals.
The old men instructed the deacon to tie them up so it wouldn't leak again.
This he did with a strip of white cloth. A good job, because no blood oozed
through his pants after we got them on.

We then dressed the body. We used no underwear. It was a long-sleeved
black clerical vest with clerical collar. Then trousers with suspenders and the
plain Mennonite coat. I guess we should have slit the uppers but we managed
without. I figured that it was time to quit showing proper respect to the elders
and get the brother dressed. So I sort of took over on that. Everyone was afraid
to touch the dead flesh. It's cold, and very squishy to the touch. Every time I

had them sit him up they would hold onto his clothing which just pulled it up around his neck. So I would have to instruct them to pull on just his bare hands. And then try to work his vestments down around his back.

The worse was getting his arms into the sleeves. Then in the end, they brought his shoes and socks. I was impressed at how difficult it was to put his socks on. I did one foot and it just rolled right up, but another pastor was struggling with the other foot and took forever. I realized then that I have often put socks on my daughters and therefore know how to pull them on to another person. But most likely the pastor had never put a sock on another person in his life. Finally we had the body ready and lugged it off the bed and into the casket. There were two blankets in the bottom. Then the shroud lying in the casket so he could lie in it, and then be covered with it, or sort of folded into it. A third blanket was then tucked in all around. But before tucking him in we had a viewing with people coming in one door and out another. People came for a very long time. Surprisingly, not too many men went through to view, mostly women. Half way through the viewing someone discovered we men hadn't combed his hair, so his wife put on a five-minute search for a comb and eventually combed him.

Carrying the body to the church was a crushing experience. I think everyone wanted to get hold of the casket, so they could get up front in the church. The pastors were supposed to carry him, but few managed. I for one did, but after the service I gave up and got out of the mob. The church was jammed, with that many people again milling around outside. After the grave was filled in, they brought a young bull and borrowed my VW to go and buy a sack of flour. Many of the people here had had only gruel for two days, so people were weak from hunger. Surprisingly, nothing very impressive was said in the service.

The Shirati Hospital is a complex mess. I could give you the Bishop's story and you would be appalled at the stubborn, willful, selfish, provincial missionaries. I could give you the surgeon's story and you would wonder why anyone ever thought the national people should be handed these institutions. Both of them talk to me by the hour about their problems; so far there are few bridges between the two camps. The missionaries are at the point where they won't listen anymore, and the Bishop is at the place where he is tired of trying to accommodate the foreigners. I don't know why they all tell me about it. I'm sick and tired of it all too.

I have been invited to go to Switzerland for the International Congress on World Evangelization, 16-25 July 1974! I don't know how that happened. I'm the only person from TMC who got invited. I took the invitation to the

Bishop to see what he would say. He said I should go. The conference will be at Lausanne.

January 25, 1974

AFRAM. This came at a time when we had been very busy. Victor and I took the college students to Nairobi for seven jam-packed days of travel and activity. Then, just after that we went to Seronera for three days, and then closed school. I worked several days to get a church pickup fixed so we could take a choir; Victor spent the same amount of time welding up the Bishop's car body so we could use that car. Also, we got Kenya cash for what people wanted to spend. Driving up to Nairobi was a hard trip, with a flat and a blowout. Both cars finally pulled into Brackenhurst outside of Nairobi. The schedule there was packed and in the cracks I tried to do things with the choir so that their Nairobi experience could consist of more than the conference. I was translating full time—hearing English and speaking Swahili. So I was tired from that and also didn't get much time for reflective thought. Then, every spare moment outside the assembly people were wanting to speak, either the Bishop or a pastor or a choir member, so I was translating even between sessions. To make matters worse there was a strong undercurrent of tension going on within the Tanzanian delegation. Mtoka and Nyambok had come up a week early to do evangelism in this little Nairobi congregation David is starting. The Bishop wasn't happy about this and for various reasons felt it was time to bring that congregation to heel. So just after he got up there on a Sunday, he cleared the air. This infuriated one pastor. Hershey then told me that the Bishop had given him thirteen points on which he was to straighten out David on. So, after a day of tremendous unease I finally decided to tell the Bishop that I was picking up static detrimental to him, and that I worried about his reputation. I was going to suggest that he and David get together. Daniel had said that David was crushed on that Sunday by the Bishop's pounding on the church elders. The bishop was surprised; he back-peddled, doing all he could to show that he had said or done nothing to elicit any ill will. He declared further than there was no animosity between himself and the congregation. So, in the end, each of the belligerents had seen the Bishop, and all seemed to come away happy. Once the boil got lanced by my telling the Bishop what I was hearing, everyone came up sweetness and light. What I suspect is that there was a change of spirit all around, that the same facts were now spoken but without the incrimination.

It seemed to the Tanzania delegation that the Afro-Americans had come with a set of resolutions readymade up. A resolution committee was appointed, consisting of people who would be favorable to Afro-American concerns, and they did draw up quite a set of resolutions, which were presented, to the plenary on the second to last day. These resolutions in effect spelled out what the mission boards are doing, except that it was now the blacks who would be doing it. I asked whether this meant a new mission board. No, it was only to give direction to the existing boards. Anyway, the African refused to have anything to do with this, saying that they didn't want anything rammed down their throats. But since there were so many Afros there, along with students who had studied in America, they could carry the vote. For a while it looked like they would try to ram it through anyway, in which case I think the Bishop would have gone on record as having had represented another opinion. As it was, they just abstained from voting but did a lot of filibustering.

In the end Powell stood up and announced that AFRAM was dead and that everyone was to go home. He, of course, hoped that people would rally to his side. Instead, the meeting declared that AFRAM was good and that it was to be continued, but that this business of resolutions brought by one side and thrust on the other without adequate understanding was for the birds. So another resolution committee was set up by delegates appointed by each group. Of course the Bishop was the Tanzania representative. But the irony here was that Bishop Kipe of Zambia insisted on reading out his set of resolutions, which he was sure the committee now reconstituted would approve. It was so funny that here were blacks struggling to be authentic people and there was a white insisting that he tell them what they wished to say. They had to really bolt his lid down to keep him from reading the whole bit. In the end it was essentially his statement which was returned by the resolution committee. Good old whitie in there saving the day!

The tragedy of the meeting seemed to me that there were legitimate things the Afros were getting at but somehow in their presentation things got a poison into them that created divisiveness and blockage. I had to wonder how long it would take for these people to be healed of their wounds. It seemed that the more they sought healing the more at war they got. This came crystal clear to me near the end of the meeting when Raymond Jackson attacked Paul Lederach. It was thus:

Lederach was invited to AFRAM to give a paper on developing curriculum for Sunday Schools. Of course, everyone there was too poor to be able to develop such materials. I know a bit of how it is because of my involvement with the Christian Council of Tanzania doing materials for primary schools.

So he simply got to what he considered the core of the matter and said that we must be biblical and if we are biblical than we will be Anabaptists. He went on about this at length with great warmth and feeling. Obviously he had seen a star! In the afternoon plenary session Jackson attacked Lederach by name and proceeded to show the fallacy of his thinking. What I think Jackson was trying to communicate was that we German Mennonites see the Bible through Anabaptist eyes. But he as a black from slave stock sees the Bible through different eyes. It bugs him to have Lederach tell him what he will come up with when he reads the Bible. Why must whities always be ramming the answers down his black throat? So, in the middle of all this Leroy Berry gets up near the back of the auditorium and announces that he has something to read that was written to Christians, and he is assuming that this assembly is Christian. He then read form Colossians the passage about esteeming each other and so forth. This enraged Jackson because it looked like Berry was saying that he wasn't a Christian. Jackson told Berry plainly that whatever spirit was prompting Berry was incompatible with Jackson's spirit, and in as much as told Berry that he was no Christ. Well, after this thing finally got calmed down it was past time to go for a meal; they closed with prayer.

When I put my head down to pray the whole hopelessness of the situation just flooded over me. I felt that Jackson had a very legitimate gripe and that he didn't hate us whites at all. But there was Lederach brought up near Philadelphia where as a child he attended a mission church where blacks were being converted who felt that he was never in the slightest bit prejudiced and who could not see at all why Jackson was so shook up, yet he was epitomizing the exact thing that make blacks so mad. Further, there was good old Leroy Berry who has dumped the whole black thing in favor of becoming white. Berry has forgotten the acute pain of being black, and he would just as soon everyone be German Anabaptist. So there you have all three perfectly right in their position, but unable to communicate it in such a way that others will hear them and so they wind up calling each other the devil.

I felt as though here was AFRAM struggling to be born with fully legitimate aims and concerns but somehow thwarted and crushed even before it was out of the shell. I just broke down and sobbed as if my heart would break. I hadn't cried like that since Mother died, and even then I wasn't so distraught. I was sitting out at the end of the auditorium because the speaker's mike didn't work and I had to rely on straight vocal strength for translating. I just couldn't get hold of myself, so I went back into the dressing room and hid behind the door. Later, someone must have told Jackson that he had caused me to weep and he asked me what was the problem. He wondered if I had been offended. I just told him that it seemed that something didn't want his concern to be understood.

All that provided the background for the breaking that came later, about which I am sure everyone reported faithfully in their church magazines. There was a lot of weeping that night. But again, what was so significant to me was that earlier in the week the Afros were giving us their soul beat in music. One Tanzanian asked me if that is really how they sing, or are they just trying to put on a show. I told him that it how they sing. But on that night of reconciliation not one Afro-beat type of song was sung. We went strictly back to the good old German hymnody. It wasn't until the next day when people were beginning to feel free again that the Afro soul-beat crept back in. Someone said that we have to meet on our common ground and that was German, so back we went to it when we got stuck. But that the hallelujahs on that night of cleansing and forgiveness could not be Afro said to me that there is still a great lot of sense of dignity and personhood that must be birthed before the American blacks become people in their own right. There was such a contrast between all the other blacks and the Ethiopians. They alone stood up as men confident among their peers.

Yesterday we opened Bible School for a new two-year class. Up to now not one student has showed up! We hear from some that they are busy with the *Ujamaa* villages and from others that the notices came out too late. So, we'll just wait and see what happens. The *Ujamaa* village thing hit this region just before December. It has been going on full blast ever since, with over half of the people in the region having to move. It has done havoc to the church's program. Two of the churches in this district are now without people.

March 28, 1974

I guess 1973 was not so good a year for investments. I note that the Mennonite outfit into which the mission board makes deposits against the day I retire lost an eighth of its capital last year. In spite of interest and the board's deposits to my account, I ended the year with only $11.42 more than I had a year ago. I note that the news magazines say my entire investment was inflated about eight percent, so I really lost $156 on that one last year. But that is just symptomatic of what is happening all around us here in Africa. The poor are getting poorer. Of course, we keep getting raises, so we're not so bad off!

A second problem of mine is that I need money, gifts of money! Remember that I am the TMC rep on the workshop that is preparing materials to teach religion in the primary schools. Standard three and seven are selling now, with standards one and five promised by the end of the year. Standards four and six are to come out next year. We will have our last workshop in May. There are 14 books in all, one for teacher and one for student in each grade. Problem of course is that the church had budgeted nothing for this; of course the good missionary stance would be to just stand back and let them stew. But I think if we could stimulate the districts to know that these materials are available then maybe next year something could be budgeted. One set of two, for one standard, costs about $1.50. The man in charge of Bible in schools and I pooled some tithe and ordered two sets, i.e., standards three and seven, for each district, so the pastors can at least see what is coming.

April 30, 1974

(This letter is to be read laconically! JCS). I must tell you about our excellent investment in art. Remember that print of a painting by David Shepherd that we have, two zebras, a limited edition? We got it the Christmas of 1969 for something under Shs 400/=. The other day Edith and I were in Nairobi, taking the kids back to school, and we passed the same art studio and saw our zebras hanging on the wall. So we went in to see what it was selling for. It was their last print and it was selling for Shs 8500/=. Maybe they were just trying to keep it from being sold! Now I've got the notion that for each Christmas we are in Africa, we should get another David Shepherd and then when we get old and die we can give one to each of our daughters for an inheritance.

I think I'm suffering from hysteria. The other day I developed this severe skin pain, like a bad sunburn, under my ribs on the right. But there is no indication at all of any physical disorder, no swelling or inflammation or rash. Let me spin out some of the conflict which I think is causing all this pain.

One thing, I think, has been the fear of the Bishop's coming back from the States. Life was relatively easy while he was away, but now that he's back I'm sure there will be pressures of one sort or another. The Bishop is asking for funds from Germany to build a hospital down in Majita. We filled out a very inadequate form and sent it off. Now while he was away that form came back with many, many pointed questions. These cannot be answered except by a competent medical person and by the government medical officials. But the Bishop doesn't want these people involved in his request because they don't have the same political reasons for wanting to put a hospital at that place. So, I fear that I shall be asked to sit down the Bishop and fill in the forms in a skewed way, hoping that presto one day we may be the happy recipients of US $100,000. Then will come the nightmare of building whatever it is that we have drawn up, not to mention running the place. So derailing that thing or getting it into Shirati's hands or government hands for derailing is a problem.

Another problem is getting a new supply of light bulbs for the station. If I get them, the church hasn't any money to refund me, so it would the missionaries who buy them. And if they buy light bulbs, I will have to sell them. But then I'll be maligned by the African people to the effect that I have hogged the bulbs for my house and I sell them only to my people who can afford to pay for them. Behind the Europeans' back the Africans will say that we don't want them to have lights in their houses. Eventually the Africans will get a martyr complex and sit in their big houses without light bulbs!

The church driver quit while the Bishop was away and stated as his reason that we missionaries have told the Bishop that he is a bad driver, so now the Bishop doesn't trust him anymore.

I'm at the difficult place where I act as servant to two people, both of whom need to have me in tow in order to satisfy their egos. Neither can conceive anything better for me or for my family than that we are in perpetual attendance on their little projects. The principal wants me to spend my holidays painting his buildings and writing more and more letters for cash. The Bishop asks me where I've been just as soon as I've missed a day going up to sit with him and talk. Possibly I am getting to the point where I will have to disengage somehow, but the inevitable then is that good old Joe will be found out that he doesn't really love these people after all.

Then, too, there is the nagging feeling that since the Switzerland thing isn't a TMC thing, it may very well turn out that some other "important" thing will be planned here over the same time and my trip will get derailed. I've been trying to keep myself emotionally prepared for not going to Switzerland.

I have been acquiring an appreciation for the problems that an emotionally exhausted person faces. You get to where your body hurts and your spirit can't cope with any more complexity and still the waves come rolling in. How to cope with copping out or dying out is the question. The funny thing is that all this nervous exhaustion simply cannot be seen by anyone outside of myself. All that I have described has nothing to do with activity; it has to do with standing emotionally in the gap or in the place others scrape together at or trying to play servant to too many chiefs. Of course I also ask myself if I was in the States wouldn't I there too get myself all tied up in knots over things, and if I would, doesn't that say that I haven't the emotional fortitude to be of much consequence. So maybe before too long I'll be looking for some quiet little job that has nothing to do with people.

July 17, 1974

I'm writing to you from Lausanne, Switzerland! I sit eating a half kilo of dark red sweet cherries! In fact, this is the second half-kilo I've gone through since getting here. You can't imagine what a tremendous physical and spiritual thrill it is for me to be here! The drive in from the airport (Geneva to Lausanne) in the quiet tourist bus, driving through the countryside abundant with wheat, corn, oats, vineyards and orchards. Then the abundant food—and delicious! Breakfasts are continental, with bread, jam and black coffee. Wow, is the coffee around here ever heavy stuff. We got here early Sunday morning and the meetings didn't start until Tuesday, so we had a lot of time to walk around the city. Monday evening three of us walked down to the lake, ate ice cream sundaes in a sidewalk café, saw the sail and motor boats, watched fishermen. It was a truly wonderful experience. It was such a quiet evening with the lake smooth, the evening rays of sunlight falling across the lake to light up the sheer, snow-tipped mountains beyond. On Sunday evening we crashed a music program put on for a mini-congress that preceded ours. Young people sang, did skits, gave readings. It was tremendously stimulating. I just find my eyes watering all the time I'm here. I wish you were here. I keep thinking that I see you through the crowd. This is how conversations should be—picked up and dropped as you go through an experience new and different from the ordinary routine. I've been entering into conversations with people at the table—really, it's quite fun. You just wade in on some subject and soon you've had a half-hour of dynamic exchange of views with a person you'll never lay eyes on again. Isn't that weird?

The showers connected to our dormitory of some 150 participants is open only one hour in the morning and an hour in the evenings. So the place is always jammed. It's one big room with doors for the boys and girls dressing rooms opening off the shower rooms. We haven't figured out what age students go to this school, and I guess they shower in shifts. The Asians have never showered in the open, so the poor chaps always shower with their underpants on!

I bought Edith a watch. I'm wearing it now and am still debating with my conscience whether or not I'll report it at Tanzanian customs. My own watch fell in the lake the day when the family was fishing at Musoma. I didn't get to go diving for it until one week later. I'd forgotten the goggles but I went diving for it anyway. On about the fourth dive I spied the strap sticking up behind a rock. I guess a crab had tried to make off with it as it was fairly wedged behind the rock. Anyway, it wouldn't run and just now it is being fixed in Nairobi.

There are so many stories I could tell: like how I started off for this meeting on the motorcycle with Joyce on behind and got into a heavy rain between Tarime and Migori and what terrible mud; like a trip I took by cycle to Mwanza with Dianne on behind, she hanging on for the whole 270 miles! Like the girls' scaring up a huge green mamba on the hill behind our house; like Joyce's badly spraining her foot and needing crutches—

Myron Augsburger wondered if I'd be free to come home next month to take over the student pastorate at EMC. I thanked him very much for the affirmation he gave me, and I really meant that. But it is unthinkable for me at this time to accept anything outside of the TMC orbit. I told Augsburger, "Definitely nothing until '77."

July 31, 1974

I'm back from the glories of Lausanne and trying to catch up with the daily humdrum of Bukiroba.

I thought about this: If you'd listen to what I say to the missionaries, you'll find that it is a call to them to accept the conditions imposed on them by their environment. When someone shows up on our doorstep for a meal we should give it to them. When the doctors complain about their inability to function effectively, I tell them to find ways to live with it. The catch is that for the most part this community does not see or understand our needs as Europeans. They do not realize the intrusion they make into our homes. Oh, of course, they may stop coming into our homes, but they will judge us badly for being so insular. They give more autonomy at Shirati not because they appreciate the missionary's need for this autonomy but because you've got to let the spoiled ones have their way least they run away and never come back. So all of the noise coming from Lausanne and from the mission boards has been to accept this personal destruction in the service of the community. (I don't think many churches or their mission board secretaries realize what the call of Lausanne to the missionary really means.) And this is what I have always felt and it is what I felt called to rededicate my life to at Lausanne. Then, coming back into the situation again and going through what I did in the first three days here brings the whole thing into focus again. It is possibly feasible for me to follow such a call to commitment, but I do wrong in imposing it on my children or the other missionaries or my wife. I come through to the church as accepting things the way they see it, and the church wonders why I can't bring the rest of the missionary community into line. The problem has no doubt been studied and analyzed by psychiatrists. I am stumbling on to it as a sort of personal discovery and am still groping for the machinery to cope with it. Jacobs says that for many things there is no synthesis, just irreconcilable acts, and he says the first way out is to repent of trying to form a synthesis. So possibly the solution is to teach people to consciously compartmentalize themselves?

August 5, 1974

While I was in Lausanne, Jacobs one day was telling me how he had responded to Carr's Lusaka statement. He was referring to the bit about sanctified violence. I responded in all seriousness, "Who is Carr?" This put Jacobs into such a fit of laughter that he couldn't respond for some time. When I got back to Musoma and was reporting to the Bishop on the moratorium on missionaries discussion at Lausanne, he asked the same question, "Who is Carr?" By admitting that I asked the question I reveal just how blind to what's going on I am and I repent of not keeping up on what is going on in the upper echelons of the church's machinery. But the point is that we who are down at the grass roots of what is happening don't get involved in the quarrels of the great ones. Abe Neufeld at the Mennonite caucus at Lausanne was remarking on the wonderful spirit of unity and brotherhood he was feeling and wanted expression of this to be put in the communiqué. Augsburger challenged us not to be naive, seeing how much infighting was going on in the back rooms and coming out here and there in some of the addresses. So some of us go along without noticing very much what it is they are fighting about up there.

I don't want to be taken naively though. I know that the upper discussions do finally reach down into the mass, and I know that leaders define for us what it is that is bugging us before we have defined it ourselves. My point is that all this noise in *Target* (an East African church paper) and the pronouncements of Carr and Gatu should not be taken as a mandate for us to unilaterally pull out of the places we fill today. This sort of thing fosters a psychology of disengagement which can prevent us from being God's people in today's world. Involvement has its price to pay and the easy thing is to say, "Well, Gatu thinks we missionaries shouldn't be here, so I'm going home." Everyone who left Shirati was grandly declaring that it was for the good of the institution, but isn't this imperialism in reverse, for me to tell the church that my not being here is good for them? I'd rather have them say it. Ah, yes, but the African Gatu did say it. But Gatu and the Presbyterians are not Kisare and the Mennonites.

This matter was discussed at great length in the East African caucus at Lausanne. Gatu was there and he was given time to explain himself. He was very very unhappy with the kind of headlines that *Target* gave him. He chalked it up to sensationalism. He said that he never said any missionaries were to go home. What he said was that in some cases it might be well to hold bilateral discussion with sending boards and agree upon a period of disengagement so that the national church could get on its own feet. He said that he believes that in some churches the missionary presence is still so strong that effective leadership is still not in the hands of the nations. In such cases the AACC (All Africa Conference of Churches) felt that "moratorium" should be recommended as an "option." In spite of this beautiful and balanced explanation of what he had intended, African after African rose to challenge Gatu until the gentleman finally had his head down on the desk. The overwhelming response was that Gatu has a problem and he should put his finger on the problem, but his answer to that problem is not Christian. After Gatu was beaten down some Bishops came to his rescue saying that he was after all grappling with live issues which the church must face. But in the final communiqué no mention was made of the word "moratorium" precisely because the group felt it to be inflammatory and they felt it would further play into the hands of such people as Idi Amin, the dictator in Uganda. The communiqué said that where the national church has been having such and such difficulties bilateral talks should take place, etc.

At the East African caucus many bishops pointed out that their churches had formulated a gradual policy of "nationalization" and that church machinery had in this manner been turned over during a period of years. All seemed to feel that to have a "moratorium" would wreck a relationship and that any further relationship in future would necessarily suffer. One African, an international evangelist, pointed out to me privately that just possibly those people who are calling for a moratorium are those people with personal leadership problems. He said than an African leader may want to be using church funds for the wrong thing, for example, and a knowledgeable missionary is exposing him, so he therefore wants to get rid of them. Or again, some churches may still have dominant foreigners with a thumb on the national church leadership and the way to get out of the problem gracefully is to call for a moratorium. I told Bishop Kisare of this observation, and he snapped it right up, saying that such was a typical way for an African to solve such a problem.

I felt through the talks that EMBMC is right on target with the move to transfer power from the missionary to the national. I can hardly believe that some of the stuff Carr says is actually true in Africa today. I have the feeling that he looked pretty hard to get those examples. He cites one missionary aged over seventy who apparently has both the African church and the American churches held tightly in his web. Frankly I find that hard to believe and even if it is true, such a one will soon die. Frankly, Carr sounds to me like a Johnny-come-lately to the business of church-mission relationships. I certainly haven't heard this kind of thing coming from East African churchmen. But no matter what others' problems are, I felt that we are not on the firing line on this one.

But let us not congratulate ourselves too much. I slept in a dormitory room with six other missionaries while at Lausanne. They were: a Baptist pastor from Tanzania, a Lutheran pastor from Finland (Their Finnish mission has been in Tanzania since 1885 and they still have some thirty missionaries working for the African church), a third-term bachelor medical doctor from Uganda (He's English from EMS), a Scottish missionary to Afghanistan, an American second generation missionary working in Upper Volta, a CMS Australian who is chaplain at the University in Dar es Salaam. It was interesting to me that of these six, only the chaplain was an extrovert. The others were soft-spoken, happy, low-tension men who love the Lord and were excited by seeing men and woman "saved." I talked to them about the problems we Mennonites have and those who knew the Mennonites remarked that indeed we are "getting out." The man from Afghanistan spoke of the Mennonites as being of two kinds, those who love the Lord and those rascals who avoid the draft and could care less about church. But all these men either spoke of how their mission is growing from year to year or they spoke of the relationship of trust and good will that existed between them and the churches for which they work. I mentioned the problems our doctors have with professional deterioration and financial stagnation. One of the men shot out that there are greater values than money and wondered if we don't feel the compensatory excitement of seeing a man find Christ. None of these men, not even the extrovert, spoke of the tensions we Mennonites write so many letters about.

Frankly, I didn't feel very happy or proud of who I was. I even got to looking us over here in Tanzania. Of the Lancaster people we still have nine. But you look closer and you see that four caught the vision from another age, not this one. The others were not influenced by the new frontiers for Lancaster. And four are not Mennonite at all.

You see, there is something very fundamental here, I think. We are ahead, or up to, the timetable reference handing over the power to nationals. But if we then disengage, we give the lie to our whole maneuver. We say that they are to do the leading, and that seems right to them too, but then we leave. So what in truth we are saying is either that if we can't lead we don't want to stick around or it is saying that we're tired of it and want you to lead so we can leave. It is a matter of not wanting to get involved if we can't call the shots. And so we Mennonites do all kinds of things all over the world, but not very much of it is involved with national churches because we don't want to relinquish our hold on the rudder. Bishop Kisare says, "You've got to watch it or they will let you standing in the middle of the road holding a bag."

Now, of course, I admit that part of our problem is historical and it will pass as we get over this phase and part of it is the blessing of being stuck here with so many tribes in one church. I also find that I repent of trying to find a solution to our problems and at Lausanne I had to do a lot of repenting of wanting to point to how we have fruitfully served this church and I must repent of the pain of seeing Shirati lurching from crisis to crisis and seeing the church there almost empty on some Sundays, and I must repent of the pain of seeing that all our leaders are first generation Christians.

Why can't our people at least leave in a way that is affirming to the national church?

And that brings me to another whole world. I am stumbling on to some of the personality and psychological problems one has in affirming others. I don't think you can be an effective missionary without affirming the people for whom you work. What then happens in your personality when you are called to affirm one whose personality or psychological make up is foreign to yours? The psychology of leadership here is so different from that in the States. The African is a chief by nature and our American society hates kings. How do you affirm such a one and when you do affirm such it immediately becomes more than words: those affirmed take you at your word and practicalize your words. We need to do some serious thinking about what is involved here.

This is the anguish I feel as I encounter fellow missionaries of other denominations.

August 12, 1974

We had a very relaxed family weekend at Seronera on the Serengeti. The Weavers gave us a bird book for our fourteenth wedding anniversary. Ours has got lost somehow. So for the first time in quite a long time we were back to bird watching. We racked up 45 different kinds on this trip, which isn't awfully great, but there were many we couldn't identify. The grass is very tall all over the park; seeing lion was very chancy. We did have the immense good fortune of chancing on a leopard up a tree with a Tommy whose horns had been wedged into a crotch. We saw a cheetah in an even chancier manner, but it disappeared after giving us all a good stare. We saw some elephants on the way home, down in a distant river valley, and that with binoculars. At the hippo pool we saw a score. But we saw no rhino, which is almost a miracle to spot one from the road. The nights were peaceful with lion roaring in the far distance. But spending two nights with a family our size in one tent has its strains. And everybody got filthy! Afternoon naps were a bit of a hassle with the kids somersaulting around. We took one seat out of the VW and Edith used the space provided as a wind-free kitchen, using her Swedish Primus for heat. These trips, in the end, always leave me just a bit more tired at the end than at the beginning.

About coming to EMC as Campus Pastor: I really feel deeply about what we are into here in Africa. We are part of a community that just now is suffering from factionalism and tribal self-interest. We all suffer together, and those who love the Lord learn together how to allow the Master to be redemptive for us in this situation. I do, now and again, get down in the mouth about how the pressures stack up, but be assured that these pressures are active on all sides and possibly I suffer less than most, having managed to keep free personally from tribal entanglements, a freedom I am sure is noted by the people I work with. There are many places in which I am actively involved although the relationship is informal and unstructured and liable to sudden alteration. But it is a way of life which is quite possible once you understand what is going on. I get a lot of fulfillment out of being the interpreter of the church to those on the outside and only recently have I felt that people on the outside are recognizing me for my ability to make this contribution. Just before going to Lausanne we had three important guests. Reinhold Fast from West Germany, the Howard Charles family and a Mr. and Mrs. Lloyd Fisher. I felt that each visit would have been less fruitful had I not been with them in the interpretive capacity. I get a lot of fulfillment out of this kind of thing and generally I am willing to wait until the occasional opportunity shows itself. I also frankly have the feeling that many people here are happy to have me around. Just seeing the apparent healing of the Bishop's spirit following an anointing service and the fact that he asked me to conduct the service are all pointers that say to me that the community sees that I have a ministry here. Of course they cannot utilize me in the professional way I might be used elsewhere but to ask them to do otherwise is not realistic. At least I am being used in their program. I've been supposed to be working on a translation of a commentary on Revelations for the theological associations' Swahili Textbooks Committee. I am doing some work for David on materials he is supervising, the writing of correspondence courses for Somali believers. I am doing the Swahili translations. So, you see, I do not really think of myself as being in an impossible situation even though in my weaker moments it is good to have your shoulder to cry on.

But all that aside, I've felt quite strongly that for the girls' sake we must terminate our service over here in 1977. This, of course, leaves all the frightening questions. At the end of the last furlough I felt that possibly we could have stayed home and got into a fruitful ministry. But now, after another five years, I fear that I shall be hopelessly out of step, fit only to sweep floors. One of my pet gripes is that we can't build the kingdom if we get too concerned about personal fulfillment. But supposing I do come home and try to do a pastorate, I practically do no counseling here. I try to keep brushed up in my thinking by writing letters. But the only counseling I do is with the missionary community and that is precious little. I rarely preach, other than chapel messages, and a few licks to the kids and old women out at *Uhuru* Church, which is now closed down because of the villagization which moved the people away from that area. My deep emotion about American youth is that they are frivolent, interested in bedding each other, in drinking, in pot, and in a sort of pop Christianity which, as always, makes Jesus into their own image. My feeling about EMC is not a positive one. The place has too many over-layers, or under-layers. I tend to feel bitter towards the people who teach there, seeing them as self-important purveyors of their own brand of cultural Christianity with little notion of what it is all about. I know all of this comes from a fear of people whom I do not understand and that once introduced I would stop stereotyping them. But my memories of Virginia are not very good ones; they are rowdy in youth and too interested in money as they get older.

Given all those hang-ups I am frightened to death then of not being able to perform adequately. Suppose I do become a pastor. I would guess that I would get a pretty good build up by way of introduction. And, to be frank, I am not interested in pastoring a place like Rohrestown or Mountville. So I've got the build up and I've preached them a sermon ten years in my bag and they take me on and then both they and I discover that I am just an African and not able at all to perform adequately in the States, let alone meet up to the expectations trumpeted. Suppose I am taken on as Campus

Pastor at EMC and then discover that Augsburger didn't outline everything to me, that it is rather beyond my ability, and the real church heavies come laughing at me, wondering what I thought I was doing! So I get the feeling that there is a great fall for me somewhere along the line. Things like this, one should work into step-by-step, proving yourself as you go. But now as I near middle age I am not anymore interested in that step-by-step proving yourself; I'll be starting all my life, which is, of course, a fact I had better get used to if I don't want to be frustrated. Maybe I could just have a heart attack in '77 and lay down the burden, my piddly little burden. So we come and we go and in the end does it really make any difference? This is what I am looking for this year, and it was what I went looking for to Lausanne—what is my new mandate? The old ones have served their day; I must find a new reason for existence.

August 13, 1974

About my going to Europe. Everyone from the Bishop on down seemed anxious that my timetable be respected. We were very busy for some time with all the guests, and I'd come home almost too exhausted to talk to Edith. Once I started getting this band of tightness across my chest. I came from the vigorous kind of exchange that was being worked through with MEDAT and TMC. In order to faithfully interpret you must be emotionally involved with both sides, and I guess it was really a bit too much. But I at least had one day to sort myself out before leaving for Lausanne. I haven't been given any opportunity for reporting on the conference to this church community, but then neither did the Bishop or Buteng'e's report on their trip to the States. I just praise the lord for His gift to me to go to Lausanne.

About Mugumu: It lies about half way between Seronera and Kisaka. It is a newly-developing area; one which I served as acting pastor for a year and did a lot of cycling out there on my blue cycle in 1970-71. It's about 90 miles from here at Bukiroba. One goes through a good bit of open country getting there. The water project at Bumangi started out as a local church project, but once we had a few shillings, sixty thousand out of a total of some two million, the government asked us to cog into their scheme. So what we are doing is building the water tank. Water is being piped from Mugango on the lake to Kiabakari, the army camp, to Butiama, the President's village, to Bumangi. In fact, we even gave the government fifty-two thousand shillings out of the total. Their water department is doing the building. We keep a hand in it by doing the transportation with the church lorry.

Your observations about my wanting to believe that my nourishment should come from the African community sort of hit me between the eyes. Possibly I do feel that one should be able to get enough nourishment to survive out of the African community, but frankly I do not relax with these people. My relationships are always carefully monitored. The Yusufu (Joseph) that comes flashing out in good old camaraderie when I encounter Africans is a second part of me which isn't really me. I am two different people, which I am sure you observe when putting together what I write with who the African community observes me as being. I do try to keep both parts of me honest. I guess I have the same problems relating to whites though. It was fun at Lausanne to just plunge in and talk with the Americans I met at the dinner table. It was rather fun and I was surprised at myself for enjoying it so much. In the place that is me, I have never felt that I am not 100 per cent a white American. There are lots of other layers, but inside, that is who I think I am.

I think it would be the ultimate lie to what I believe in for me to come home and do something "lucrative." I have come to feel that being poor has its good points. Maybe it will help my daughters to retain some of the ancient virtues. I am often reminded of Oliver Wendell Schenck's observations, that Schencks are too stubborn to ever get rich. I can't get rich anyway, having spent half my life here in Africa. I'll just have to live and die being content with living in a narrow place, having the faith that when I am up against it, some saint of God will offer me a loan.

October 24, 1974

These days I've been taking Stella Newswanger to Musoma in the morning and back in the evening on my motorcycle. She is holding down the bookshop for a few weeks while the manager is off on some meeting. There just aren't any working cars on the station, except the Bishop's Land-Rover. The road is terrible! It has had practically no repair done on it since last year's rains. Now it is the end of the dry season with the short rains over. So the disintegrating road has been piling up sand on its edges and as the road gets worse in the center the vehicles keep pushing the sand ridges farther and farther out into the fields. Stella agrees with me that riding this road on a motorcycle is an experience for which one should tighten one's bra straps!

This year, more than any other, I am having a positive spiritual encounter with the students. I think this is because we have the advantage of being the minority. The principal is increasingly coming through as a big tyrant.

The students are frightened of speaking to him. He has as a captain a fellow tribesman who is our poorest student, whose wife ran off from him and who has been going to the courts to try to get her ordered back. That in itself is quite a story. But this captain is also paranoid, terribly thin-skinned and much inclined to lecture his fellow students as if he were the principal. The students, of course, are intimidated and quite afraid to say anything which might get back to the principal. The captain controls all aspects of student life. So if the students complain about the food, then the captain reports who made the accusation to the principal and the principal in turn calls the culprit in and gives him a dressing down. There is sort of a gentleman's agreement between me and the students that we won't talk about these problems. So it means that when we talk about humility and servanthood and the tyranny of power we understand each other. The wonderful thing is that the students are coming through so positively and redemptively about the whole thing. They are being forced to make practical their Christian experience right here in the Bible school school! The principal controls all the money and the teaching assignments. But I really think this mix will make much better church leaders than the mix I presided over when principal. I tended to take the students seriously and they exploited every opportunity to palaver about bettering their condition. With this principal there is never any palaver and all discontent is looked upon as treachery. Once when they weren't getting enough food, the school very nearly got closed because the students voiced a complaint. And this is more in line with how the students will be treated once they are through their studies. The chap who survives this in a positive frame of mind must be a man of God. My students thought in terms of rebelling against the church, while any of these who think of rebellion would be shafted.

The principal's main obsession just now is to strengthen the fence he has had us build all around the school compound, separating it from the rest of the station. Every other *shamba* period we are all put onto cutting more thorn branches to stack against the barbed wire. So now, there is only ONE entrance to the Bible school. So now the domestic science women and the carpentry teacher who live down behind the school all have to walk around to come in between the big cement pillars that guard the entrance. Big iron gates are being welded so even that entrance can be locked, as occasion demands. We must have put over a thousand shillings into barbed wire, posts, cement pillars and iron gates, to say nothing of lots and lots of student and staff energy. Granted, there are fewer goats and kids stripping our trees, but I wish our principal wasn't so obsessed with the whole thing. Today he was punishing a student who he had spied jumping over the fence; the whole school and staff was then put onto cutting down more thorn trees to heighten the fence. I told him that he should punish me too as I had jumped over the fence without his seeing me, in full view of all the students. I loaned the student my *panga* so thus fellowshipped in his punishment. Today in class we got into a discussion as to whether drinking wine is a sin. I asked them if fence jumping was a sin! Thus the theology class goes on.

The children came home from Rosslyn (in Nairobi, Kenya). It was good to be with them again, especially Rosemary. Rosy has had a bit of a hard time adjusting to school life. She is thinner than ever with her big black eyes. I guess it is good we are planning to go home after '77, as it is getting harder to be separated from the kids as the years go on. Boy, things are really quiet though when they are away at school.

November 1, 1974

Do you want to hear about funerals? This woman has been looking for someone to take her to Shirati and had even sent someone to Bukiroba but had found no help. I was in a committee meeting at the time and hadn't heard about it. She really had an interesting story. She is the daughter-in-law of Dishon Bobo who is a church elder at Radyenya, Kenya. Bobo's son, her husband, is not a Christian. She is from Shirati and had asked her husband permission to go to Shirati to visit her parents. He gave this permission. But while at Shirati she learned that her brother's wife was operated on in Biharlamulo and at her parents' suggestion she went off with her little daughter to see her sister-in-law before going back to Kenya. At Biharlomulo her daughter got sick and was treated there. Then on her way home, the child got worse in Mwanza and was treated for several days in the hospital there. When she got better they began the trip home on a Mwanza-Tarime bus. But the baby got worse along the way and when the bus got to Musoma it broke down and the mother set off for the hospital for help while they fixed the bus. The baby died before it was admitted to the hospital. It was really a lovely little kid with no evidence of illness on her. So, she inquired after the Mennonites and someone took her to the hostel. The manager went off to get the pastor and to find a pick and someone to dig the grave. But in the meantime the woman got to thinking about how it will be when she gets home. She was very much in the wrong and the best she could hope to get was a sound beating. She could be divorced, and it is quite probable that she wouldn't even be able to get away from the derision of her fellow women. When she gets home and old hubby asks, "Where's the baby?" she will reply that the baby died. "So you buried it at Shirati without even telling me? You could at least have brought it home." "But the baby is buried in Musoma." "Musoma?" "I had gone to visit my sister." "Who gave you permission to go visiting your sister? I gave you permission to visit your parents at Shirati!" Silence, and at that point the blows begin to fall.

So, when this woman, who could speak practically no Swahili, found that no way was to be found to take her home, she committed it to the Lord in prayer and prepared to keep her lonely vigil in the church office, awaiting the postponed burial in the morning. I had a Luo student with me and he evidenced genuine distress at the plight of this poor woman. We prayed with her and came home. We talked to various people, including the Bishop. He observed that, "No matter what you do, she is in the wrong," implying that she would catch it, even if we drove her home. But when he heard that she was the daughter-in-law of old Bobo, he warmed to the idea of our helping her. So early the next morning, I set off with her and the student who is from her district. The idea was to take her to Shirati from where she could be taken into Kenya by bicycle. But when we got to Shirati we could find no one interested in helping her. "We all have work." I wondered what it was they thought we had back at Bukiroba. I was supposed to be in a committee meeting that day. And when I eventually got home the principal wondered what kind of school this was with the students running off all the time. The principal often doesn't sleep here, so he couldn't be informed of what I was up to and I guess the students were afraid to explain it all to him.

Finding no one at Shirati to help her, we decided to drive her to the home of a Kenya church elder who lives on the border. To our great joy we found him at home. He was supposed to be at Radyenya that very day, as all the district was getting together to plan the year's budget. He had not got off yet due to various interruptions. He welcomed us with great joy and listened with sympathy to the woman's story. He agreed to see that she was home by evening. Later we found out that he went to Banda and sent two brethren back with bicycles to bring her and the corpse. She had begun to walk. The elder then went on ahead to break the news. Of course, the husband threw a fit and refused to bury the child. But old Bobo calmed him down and he cooled off, went for a pick and began digging the grave, even before his wife arrived home. The last I heard, they were still at peace with each other.

The next day word came that the first-born daughter of the church elder at Bande had died. Her father is a relative of the Bishop. He was a student of mine in 1971. They were holding the funeral three days later, on a Saturday. So the Bishop asked me to take him, and I took Edith along with Becky. We took a tent for us three, and the Bishop and his wife slept in the church. This daughter had been sick a long time, for years in fact, but they had hoped she would outgrow it. She did seem at times to be making progress. She was fifteen or sixteen. The big deal for us was seeing how Becky fared on bush fare. She did very well, drinking tea like an adult! We went up Saturday morning and stayed for Sunday services. Early Sunday morning a man came from the congregation over near Migori, telling that the eldest daughter of the church leader there had been lost in the Migori River where she had gone to swim with her friend. They begged the Bishop to stop on his way home. So that afternoon we drove in to that church too and found that they had recovered the body, a ten-year-old, Dianne's age. They begged the Bishop to stay for the funeral the next morning. So we stayed.

The Migori River goes through the valley about a half-mile away. It is a lovely area, quiet and peaceful, with the faint murmur of the river. After setting up the Bishop's cots in the house, I set up our tent outside. That was a lovely night with bright stars overhead. Everyone was sitting around the campfire outside. We talked and talked. I like times like that because I get to understand and love the old man. There were none of the pressures that bother us at Bukiroba. The Bishop is really a grand chap, full of wisdom and warm fatherliness. He had a word that night and everyone listened. The dead child was first placed on a mat under the eaves of the thatched hut. After the coffin was made, that too, was put on a stand under the eaves. The Bishop asked if I knew why the coffin was outside. I, of course, didn't know, so he explained that it is the traditional belief that if someone dies in a river he is buried by the river. The wake is even performed by the river. This is to ensure that the river won't claim another victim from the same family. I then gave him my "phenomenology of religion" interpretation of what he said and because of his theological college training he understood me well, but remarked, "That is how you explain the underlying beliefs, but these people don't go under the skin of it." The funeral was early the next morning and we were back home in time for me to teach my afternoon classes. (I should add: since these were Christian people they brought the body up to the house from the river, but they still allowed the old beliefs to tinge their actions by not putting the body inside the house.)

November 4, 1974

I want to say a bit about the pastors' meeting. I was interested to see that the Bishop is pushing for the pastors' council to be the main authoritative body in the church. Conference is then to be just a rubber stamp body. As the constitution is now set up, conference is the ruling body. Conference appoints the committees. Conference is also pretty much the church secretary's baby and consequently he is the dominant voice on the committee. He convenes each committee the first time during the year. The pastors' council is supposed to be responsible for matters of faith, while conference is administrative. Now the Bishop wants the pastors' council to have authority to override the executive committee and to have the ultimate administrative authority in the church. Of course, when you tell all these old men that you want to give them more authority they welcome it gladly. They, however, are an unwieldy body with practically no executive or administrative resources. So practically, if the Bishop's proposal sticks, the result will be to give the Bishop even more power than he now has. In fact, there will be no effective check anymore.

It was interesting also to see that in one of the Bishop's speeches he pointed out how happy he will be to have another Bishop to help him, even three or four more bishops. He said then he could work through the agendas with them in advance so that he brings proposals to the pastors carrying more weight than he now has. "As it is now, I bring you a proposal and you all just reject it, so if we were several bishops you wouldn't reject what I bring before you." So he is thinking of a sort of bishops' executive committee. Of course all this is not in the constitution. So, we will see how all this develops. But what I see in the long run is a further collapse of our institutions. This is because the new power arrangement the Bishop is working for is designed to help suppress matters not to his liking. It certainly won't be a creative alignment. It was also interesting to me to see that in the meeting there was still complaining that we are not controlling Shirati. Indeed, Shirati is less controlled from Bukiroba than it ever was. I went back in my thoughts to the night the medical board was demolished and thought of all the torturous ways we have gone since, to where now Shirati Hospital just doesn't pay much attention to the church anymore.

We did a fun thing last evening. One of the Bible school students had been after me to go fishing with him. So I had nothing to do Sunday afternoon and so with yet another student we set out for the lake, collecting kids along the way. Three other students and a government driver saw us going and followed, so in the end, we must have been almost fifteen. I had a whole box of hooks and a whole bobbin of twine and a sharp knife. Everyone cut himself a pole and got strung up while several of us dug in the gunk for worms. We got a great many worms and then hiked over to the mountain, churned our way through the underbrush and came out on some rocks from which we could fish in the bay. The champion, a student, a man my age, caught 47. The station mechanic's son caught 31, and I got 30. The student who was after me to go fishing caught only a half dozen. He claims to be a great fisherman of long standing, but another student pointed out to me that this man's style and success mark him as a virgin fisherman. One little chap fell in the water, pulling his brother in with him. It was all great fun. (I forgot to mention: I got the biggest fish, one about nine inches long. The little chap got the smallest fish, one about the size of my pinky.)

1975

January 5, 1975

We decided this year to do the Christmas holiday by public transport and thus save money! It turned out to be an interesting vacation, but I doubt if we saved any money. We spent over $1,000 while in Nairobi during December! Granted, in that was over a thousand shillings of paying debts and some two thousand shillings for hospitalization for Rebecca. Still, it was an enormous amount of money to run through in so short a time. Every other day I would have to drop in to Standard Bank and withdraw another five hundred shillings. It is so different there in Nairobi from here in Bukiroba. There everything is humming, a real western-type rat race with everyone busy and all the shops full of goodies (at a price) while here, well you know how it is, just playing the Dr. Zhivago record over and over. It must be the difference between Alabama and New York.

This vacation the girls were often begging me for some story of when I was little and lived in Africa. So I told them how Mother announced her pregnancy to us. David had suspected it and clued me into his observations, but when we asked Mother, she was very noncommittal. At Christmas time Mother had primed Annie to tell us about a new family member who was on the way. After the presents were opened (I got a gilt-edged Bible) Mother announced that Annie had something special to tell us. Poor Annie was too embarrassed to say anything. So David and I began to shout that we knew what the announcement was. Mother tried to get Annie to speak up quickly before David got it out, but she was tongue-tied, hanging her head low and saying something so quietly no one could hear. So, finally, it was David who blurted out that there was a baby on the way. Mother still didn't accept this announcement until she got Annie to put her head up and say clearly that Mommy is to have a baby.

In Nakuru we attended a rendition of *The Messiah* in which Annetta (Miller) was the contralto soloist. We got there early and Annetta in blue jeans came back to greet us sitting in the back of the church. Her mother was NOT very pleased. Then to make matters worse, the bus which had brought the choir down from Nairobi went off, taking Annetta's little satchel along. So for a while poor Mother Miriam wasn't sure if Annetta would appear in her lavender floor-length gown or in her overalls. The rendition was late in beginning, with everyone waiting for the conductor and soloists to appear. Finally the vestry door opened, we all stood up, and in they came with Annetta appropriately clad. It wasn't a really excellent rendition, party due to the orchestra and choir being a stripped down version of what they performed in Nairobi. But it was good, especially the soloists. After it was all over Rebecca remarked from the back bench where she and I had retreated, "Daddy, long, long song." The next day she was singing the hallelujahs from that chorus which made me think she must have remembered something of it.

Several days after the older girls got out of school (and poor Rosy is thinner than ever with her huge black eyes; she just won't or can't eat) we got a night train to Mombasa. We couldn't get second class, so we traveled first. That meant that our six people were in three cabins, two of which were adjoining. It was very nice, but it cost more than hiring a Nairobi mission car. We started off for the train from the guest house—three big suitcases, assorted other grips, and six people standing down at the bus stop! It didn't take long until a big fat padre from Ireland drove up in his tiny Toyota, stopped, compassion having got hold of him. We and the baggage all managed to press in, and he took us right to the train station. That act of mercy cost us two hours of waiting in the station, but sooner that than carrying those great suitcases from the bus stand down to the train station, to say nothing of getting the mess onto and off the bus. We blessed him, for what it was worth to him, and he blessed us, quite taken in he was with all my "lovely girls!"

The next morning Edith and the two older girls went off to the dining car for breakfast, just for experience sake, while I and the two little girls, not needing such an experience, supped on left over supper from the Nairobi Guest House, and a great pot of coffee brought in by the porter. Thus fortified, we faced sweltering Mombasa. A taxi took us down town, and I hunted around for some place to put our stuff, finally getting a sympathetic Swahili ear from the deskman in a hotel. Then we shopped for groceries and walked a half-mile down to the market for a huge basket of fruit and vegetables. It was so delightful to browse around in that corpulent markets, that the basket just finally spilled over and we had to stop shopping. We got another taxi which took us across to Likoni and Shelly beach.

This year we found the place under younger management and all books were in order. We were there eleven nights. David and family came in two days after us. This year we went goggling out beyond the reef. We found a place where there was a large pool, maybe half a mile across, protected by an outlying coral bar, so we weren't really out in the deep ocean.

I've never seen anything so fantastic. All our former goggling paled in comparison. Fish were everywhere, of all sizes, shapes and colors, and the coral gardens were amazing in their variety of color, size and shape. I picked up a half dozen of the helmet conchs; they're those orange shells with bright red lips, six to eight inches across. I also got a lovely coral of delicate fingers, about eight by nine inches. I boiled the thing in soapy water and it turned out white as ivory. We must have gone goggling four or five times. Even Edith and Grace. Karen and Joyce are pretty good at it now. All these shells and stuff are on a display shelf in our living room. There's an easy chair just under the shelf, and one still picks up an occasional whiff of rot. It was a really nice time for relaxation. We didn't even get sun burned, thanks to some drug company which sent Shirati several huge cartons of Copper-tone.

Rebecca was the only cloud on our horizon. Normally she is the picture of perfectly robust health, but when she's down she's down *kweli*. Last Easter she had such terrible sores all over her mouth and throat. Then in August she had a terrible throat infection, so severe we thought she wouldn't be able to breathe. At that time she got quite a number of injections here at our local clinic for both malaria and penicillin. These chaps here have a poor sterile technique. And they have these huge blunt needles. Becky developed an abscess from these injections, a red spot on her buttock with a hard cyst inside about the size of an egg. On our first day in Mombasa she woke up with a fever of 102, so we took her to a doctor retired in Likoni. He said she must be hospitalized and made arrangements for us to be seen at the Katherine Bibby hospital in Mombasa. He even called the surgeon. In short order the thing was lanced and we went back to our camp before she was properly out of ether. Twice we took her to the doctor for inspection and dressing changes. The thing is still draining, today being three weeks since the lancing. Now yesterday a little kid was pushing Becky on Rosy's tricycle and she got her index toe in the sprocket, punching a hole in one side. But all of this she takes in stride. Well, to finish all this: I was a bit taken aback by the surgeon's bill. He was in the operating room only seven minutes, by Edith's watch, and for that we were charged Shs 1000/=. The anesthetist's charge was Shs 400/=;

the hospital charge Shs 350/=. The poor chap who diagnosed it got only Shs 40/=. Of course the mission board pays all this, but running it through my books helped me understand the surgeon's Jaguar!

While in Nairobi, I bought the following books: "The French Lieutenant's Woman," by John Fowles. "The God Beneath the Sea," by Garfield & Blishen, about the ancient Greek mythology, which I found very interesting as something popular on the phenomenology of religion. "The White Guard," by Mikhail Bulgakov, because I enjoy historical novels which give me an idea of how the world is put together. "An American Dream," by Mailer. "Birdless Summer," by Han Suyin, the second part to her trilogy which began with "The Crooked Tree"—deals with the war years between Japan and China, culminating with the communist takeover. "Onward Virgin Soldiers," by Leslie Thomas, some English bloke, a book full of nonsense. Reread "King Solomon's Mines," a book I bought for Joyce. "Wheels" by that guy who wrote "Airport." Just before vacation I finished "Jubilee," by Margaret Walker. "Evangelism in the Early Church," by Michael Green. His, a careful analysis of how he thinks the scriptures came into being. If I hadn't had that course at Temple on The Formation of the Gospels, where we studied Bultman, Kaseman, Diebelius, Form Criticism, and all that, I wouldn't have any idea what Greene is talking about, but now I find it very stimulating. He can be very witty with a deft turn of the language which makes the common come alive; deeply intellectual, and his knowledge of his subject is absolutely encyclopedic. Greene did a paper at Lausanne conference on the subject of his text, which I felt was the best in the lot. I wished then I could have him for a teacher; he's a Canon and principal of St. John's College in Nottingham, but after getting to his book I see that he was popularizing for us at Lausanne and I'm no more sure that I wouldn't be any other than a dud in his seminars. He packs three and four scholars into one sentence, the way Lauderette at NYU used to pack the missionaries in. (Certainly these profs would be driven mad by my spelling. But really, I write very little in English now).

January 14, 1975

We had our two-day meeting to ordain another bishop. I wondered during the proceedings how many hours I've heard our present Bishop Kisare preach. Finally, on the afternoon of the second day we got to the business at hand. The Bishop insisted on taking nominations from the floor. I didn't like that and felt a real chill because one is marked by whose name he mentions. Further, only three nominations were to be accepted. The first nomination was for Aristarko, and even so eminent a churchman as my father wondered if it hadn't been planned, although I very much doubt that. He's an excellent pastor but is semi-literate and in poor health. His churchmanship lies about ninety per cent in his hospitality. The second nomination was for Buteng'e with whom the Bishop has a sort of Saul-David relationship. Among the waving hands the Bishop then chose the one who would under any circumstances nominate the heir designate, Hezekia of Dar es Salaam. The nominee must get 75 percent, as the constitution requires.

Even with a second voting, no one had secured the 75 percent. The Bishop indicated that some were conducting a tribal campaign. "The rabbits were to quit standing on the elephant's rope!" There was even a suggestion that it was the "guests" among us who didn't know the score and were mucking up the business (there were five of us white missionaries eligible to vote). What hurt me was that after a long period of prayer and seeking the Lord's will, one less than half our number were being designated as hearing voices other than the Lord's. The Bishop then wanted to do a third vote, allow the bad boys to cross the floor, but the counsel went round and round the room until most had spoken and the overwhelming counsel was that we accept the Lord's answer: There is to be no second bishop just yet. Afterwards the pastors were reminding each other that it took nearly four years for the pastors to accept with 75 percent that Kisare be our first bishop.

Former missionary James Shank, on a visit, felt a bit cold-shouldered, not having been taken into consultation on anything. He was surprised at the way the Bishop helped to accentuate the lines of division. I must remind myself that this is how the Bishop views the world. He is threatened by the whites, so when the pressure is on they are the first to get pushed into a corner. Several days later the Bishop was his warm fatherly self again, but just then he was full of barbs and needles. Also, he tends to see the world as divided between his friends and his enemies. I don't think that he can appreciate that anyone who is voting for Buteng'e is not his mortal enemy. Put those two together and his gut sense is that the whites are voting for Buteng'e and further, he assumes that there are more of them than there are. That is how he is, was, and always will be.

When I told the Bishop about Becky's abscess, the Bishop said, "You know Velma Eshleman once tried to kill me with an injection. It was preparatory to my first trip to the States. My arm swelled up so that it stuck out straight and I had to eat with my left hand. Elam Stauffer wanted me to go to Ikoma to preach at the service for the ordination of Mahemba, so I went with my arm sticking out like that. I was in great pain and went for treatment at a clinic out there. On Sunday I pushed myself to preach. In fact, we left for the States and I still couldn't use my right arm. In the States I used the abundant hot water you have when bathing, and in a couple of days it came all right again. But until this day Velma never came to give me sympathy or to say she was sorry. She was even along with us to Ikoma and she never said a word. So all the time she is letting on that she is such a sister and that she is among the saved ones, but I still maintain to this day that she wanted to kill me." So the poison in his letter to the mission board was an expression of how much he didn't want her to return, didn't want her to find any fruitful ministry in Africa, or anywhere, for that matter.

A similar thing happened with Uncle Ivan, although not so bitter. When he was here the Bishop treated him coolly. Ivan was here over our annual conference, and I sat beside him as interpreter. He was asked to bring greetings, but it was sandwiched in and hurried along. Near the end of the conference I was asked by a department head to introduce the materials for teaching religion in the primary school; here again I was allowed almost no time, and the Bishop got up and went to the toilet while I was speaking. No questions were allowed from the pastors. I had asked also to use the Bishop's car to take Ivan to Serengeti the day following conference. But when I went to get the car the Bishop almost didn't allow me to have it. I thought it was because he wanted to go along and I had invited someone else. After conference Ivan wondered why the Bishop had been so very cold to him. I told him that I thought maybe it was his way of showing Ivan that Ivan's bishopric was nothing compared to his. And I assumed the coldness towards me was a reflection of my being Ivan's nephew.

The whole thing came into focus after the Bishop came back from the States the last time. I was sitting talking to him about his trip and he said, "You know, Joseph, every time I go to the States they ask me for my advice. What word of wisdom do I have for them, following my visit in the churches? The first time I went I told them that they are cold spiritually. Then your uncle, that man who visited here last year, stood up and asked me if all the money the members were contributing to mission could so easily be set at naught. That is how he challenged me."

So I understood why he was so negative to Uncle Ivan. What surprised me so much was that he would have remembered so well and so long. Fourteen years till the roosters meet again! Then during the pastors' meeting in October, when it was decided to choose another bishop soon, the Bishop said, "When I was in America this last time I told them that they are welcome to come to witness how we choose a bishop and when they come they are not to come as tourists. They're to come and participate in our meetings and visit our congregations and talk with our people. But every time when they come, they just run around like tourists and don't pay any regard to the church. So then that man who is Clyde Shenk's brother-in-law stood up and asked me, 'Was I, too, a tourist? Did I not pay any attention to your meetings?' And I answered him (here with a great sweep of the arm) "You were the greatest tourist of them all. Among the tourists you were the greatest."

So I said to myself that it is best not to cross Kisare, and I wondered what other postures he has reference his own people whom he cannot so easily expose. And I wondered whom he thinks I am to be so willing a recipient of his sour thoughts towards people of my own family. I do respect the Bishop deeply and honor him and love him, and this he knows and I suppose this means that he sees my personality as running parallel to his.

You who read this stuff may have found swelling in your breast an anti-Bishop feeling. So the Bishop who loves me, trusts me, and on occasion takes me into his confidence has through this relationship caused me to feel that he has done an injustice, that he has harbored in his heart what is less than the highest of Christian sentiments. But those sentiments are relatively harmless. They are in his spirit and they will pass away with him and certainly those whom he has felt badly toward have not unduly suffered because of it nor will history accord them any lesser marks. Yet, because of the power of the pen, this I have put in writing may live for a hundred years. Is not then the wrong I do him greater than any wrong he may do? This matter is becoming an ethical problem for me.

The other day Harold Miller asked me to consider how the black African must view himself at the end of 1974. The oil cartel is swinging the balance of the world's wealth away from the industrialized nations to the Arabs. The balance of world political power in the UN is swinging from the industrial world to the third world. In Africa itself the colonial powers are on the run, with Portugal getting out as fast as possible, and Smith teetering, and even Vorster in S. Africa feeling greatly threatened The trend toward socialism continues to be a major economic shift on the continent, especially now with Ethiopia working to abolish their centuries old feudalism. Are not the rich being sent away empty? Nyerere's recent analysis of the progress Tanzania has made in the past ten years said nothing about economics; rather, it was an analysis of how the country has succeeded in achieving its socialist goals. Do not the hungry thereby see themselves as being filled with good things?

Of course, Harold is a secularist and he sees all of what is going on in Africa somewhat as Harvey Cox viewed the secular city back in the mid-sixties.

But I am more of a traditionalist, religiously, and I ask what role becoming Christian actually plays in filling the hungry with good things. Does it mean that the Christians here in our *kijiji* are going to be last to starve? If so, then wouldn't that mean that the Christians are the rich who are to be sent empty away? You see, for example, I am certainly seen by all of this community as being categorized in the rich section, not the poor.

These days I have been tearing down the old tree house because the floorboards are rotting (and because I want the wood to make some laying nests for the chickens!) To my delight I found some historical markings: "KATRINA, DIANNE, JOYCE. The Best Tree House In the Whole World." Later, some non-believer stuck in the corner a little note: "Not true!" All of this dated the tree house as having been in existence at the beginning of the seventh decade of the twentieth century.

February 27, 1975

I got into print! The new international review *Missiology*, Vol I, No. 4, October 1973, pp. 505-515, "Missionary Identity and Servanthood," by Joseph C. Shenk. I am frightened to read it, as I am sure I won't like it now. Some four years after writing the article 49 copies of it arrived in the post. They sent 49 copies of the journal instead of money!

The word is out, all over the place, that Pastor Jona has married a second wife! I first got wind of this on the way home from the Nairobi consultation when the church secretary told me that one of the TMC's pastors has married a second wife. He was going to give me all the details but I told him I didn't want to know. But somehow I suspected that it was Jona. Of all our pastors he gets involved in the most scrapes and he has been sufficiently off the beaten track since he was moved out of Bumangi to make such a thing possible without its being noticed too quickly. Then a week ago the Bishop told me and asked that I drive him and a pastor to Mwanza to see Jona about it. The story is that Jona married this woman about three years ago and has already born two children to her. She now lives at a place owned by Jona with two of his daughters by Leah. He goes there from time to time to visit her.

Fortunately for me I had business around town to take care of so I dropped the Bishop and the pastor off at Jona's place around 4:30 and then went off about my other matters, getting back around 6:30 after all the discussion was over. So we three went off to town for supper and then back to the guesthouse for the night. It is part of the Jita and Ruri personality that sleep is preceded by extensive talk. I had hoped to read, but by 11:00 p.m., when talk finally died out, I had hardly read a page.

The Bishop called the pastor and me to his room to tell us what happened. It turns out that Jona's older brother has one wife who apparently is something of a battle-axe compared to her diminutive husband. They both drink, and when drunk, they sometimes fight, and when they fight, the wife wins. Jona felt very sorry about this sad state of affairs. Sooner or later his brother was bound to get hurt, maybe hurt badly, and by a woman at that. Furthermore, to have it noised about that one's wife beats one is just not the proper sort of thing for a Zanaki male to have to face. So Jona hit on the solution. Why not get a young maiden for his big brother, a woman who has the good sense not to beat up on her husband when he beats up on her and who would, in any case, be too small to do any real damage, were she inclined to get ugly. So Jona got for his brother a bright new young wife. The only problem was, his brother would have nothing to do with this new wife, so Jona was stuck with taking care of her. Thus, the general outline of what happened. Certain questions are still outstanding.

First is the question of whose wife this girl is according to tribal law. In some tribes, namely the Kuria and Kiroba, the rule of thumb is that the wife belongs to the person who has put up the bride price for her. Therefore, were I rich and wanted to get my younger brother a wife, I could pay the bride wealth for his wife and thereby he could get a wife, but according to tribal law the wife is really mine and she can leave my brother any time she wants to and come to me. The children who are born to that union also would belong to me. In fact, what has happened is that I have loaned my brother one of my wives until such time as he gets enough wealth to marry her. Neither the Bishop nor the pastor knew if this rule of thumb also applies to the Zanaki people. They asked Jona for clarification, but he wouldn't say. So this point is still to be investigated. But it appears that both Jona and the brother put cattle into the girl. These brothers have always had their herds together and some deal over cattle theft some years ago involving this herd had Jona in jail for some weeks here in Musoma. Another case involving this herd was being tried over the time Jona was here in school two years ago, and he was forever going off to the court, and thus missed a lot of his lessons. I even ran him around on my motorcycle on occasion in order to try to keep him in school. Anyway, the cattle for the girl were paid out of this herd. It is, therefore, possible that the Zanaki people account that herd to be Jona's and therefore they account the girl to be his wife, whether or not he has had relations with her. If this alone is the cause of the allegations, then they can be dismissed because the Christian law does not follow the tribal law.

A second matter is the parentage of the children. Jona points out that the girl already had a baby before the present transaction, making her part of Jona's family. The second child he says she bore to his brother. However, it has been alleged that Jona's brother never accepted this girl as his wife, and therefore possibly never had relations with her. Jona says he never had relations with her. But it must be investigated as to whether or not she did ever live with the brother. There is also the whole question of why she is living in Jona's country residence as sort of wife in charge if she is in fact someone else's wife.

So all of that will have to be worked out, but I am of the opinion that the Bishop will allow him to decide his own case. I tried to figure out why Jona got himself into a scrape like that. Part of it must be that he rationalized what he was doing and didn't pause to realize what he was getting into. It must have been something like that, given how defensive everyone here is about polygamy. It is very difficult for one of us to say anything about it, even in the classroom. So, with even such as the Bishop making defensive comments about it, it can be supposed that a pastor may rationalize himself into having a second wife discreetly on the side.

Pastor Jona was such a star in the early days of the mission and church. I asked him last year if the curse put on him by the Zanaki people still has power. He admitted that if he should leave the Lord it would still damn him. His protection then, as now, is in hiding within the greater power provided by Jesus. As soon as he leaves that shelter, they'll get him.

April 22, 1975

I'm here in Livingston College, Zambia. The Zambezi River is in flood stage. Edith and I are here for a TAP retreat (MCC's Teachers Abroad Program). The chap they'd lined up for presenter bowed out on short notice, so since Maynard Kurtz had just got our Christmas letter, he decided to beg us to fill the gap on short notice. I got the invitation by cable, and in due course the church secretary sent me written permission to come. We flew Nairobi, Lusaka, Livingston. Today is the second full retreat day, with three more to go. Edith and I get an hour every day for five days. This is really something else, being the core around which a retreat is built. I've been full of self-doubt, and likely will continue to be. I don't have a feel for what one does for all these days, and neither do I have ego necessary for acting the role, to say nothing of what I say being so far divorced from what these young people are thinking, that they don't know what I am talking about. We've been doing monograms: Daniel, David, John the Baptist, Jarius and the woman with the issue of blood, and servanthood—that thing which came out in *Missiology*. I give a half-hour in-put, and Edith introduces the discussion period.

But putting all that aside, we are enjoying so much being with white young people again; it is really fun. Edith especially is good at the socializing; I stay close to her and smile and stuff and behold, socializing isn't too terrible after all. Also, I am discovering that at least half the people are as afraid of socializing as I am.

May 27, 1975

I've suddenly got to writing to Daniel. I finally did what you suspected was in my blood long ago when you warned me not to be condescending to my kid brother. Well, after his circle letter contribution about what he was studying, I wrote asking who he was thumbing his nose at. I know it was a very presumptuous thing of me to write, but I sense that all his very sophisticated language to us simple folks seemed to indicate that he was trying to prove something. I went through his letter and did a sort of pop psychoanalysis of it. I guess it was pretty devastating. His reply didn't come right away, but when it did come, it made me feel pretty small. So, out of this has grown a correspondence with each of us explaining himself to the other. Also, out of that has come something of a candid exchange between Daniel and Daddy. When we were there the other week Daddy showed me Daniel's most recent letter about which he was very, very happy. I got to thinking that possibly through my little bomb we may get to know each other better.

September 8, 1975

Please forgive me for this very long silence. I've got some three letters from you, and two stories, without a peep from me. The reason is that I've got on to Daniel. You remember that family circle letter in which he wrote a longhaired thing about Sartre, etc., which was all a little incomprehensible? Well, I must have been flying high just then, and I sat down and did a pop analysis of why he would have written a letter like that. It must have really knocked him. In fact, I suspect he went down to Virginia to see his psychiatrist. Well, he finally answered my letter and our correspondence has been flying thick and fast ever since. I have had all my creative moods eaten up with writing to Daniel. He has opened up enormously, and I felt that if ever there was a time to give him some of my time it was now. So, all the goodies have been going his way.

I just finished reading Michener's "The Drifters." He is such a superficial writer that I suspect that he has researchers working for him, but his books do have a panorama. I read him for fun, but in the fun I learn a lot about the subject he is into. Irving Stone is a bit more stylistic. He also takes a historical sweep. The writer who most fascinates me just now is Han Suyin with her series of autobiographical accounts of Chinese history. It is so much more than history because she filters that history through the experience of a person living through the eras she writes about and amazingly she is able to give the experience of the colonial master in China as well as that of the Chinese who are struggling for liberation, and she picks up the vibrations of quite a number of strands of Chinese life. She is able to do this because she is herself half-European and half-Chinese. I am amazed at how she is able to picture so faithfully and so without bitterness a number of facets of the experience. Wouldn't it be possible to do that sort of thing with the mission field? You would have to take two generations of missionaries and two generations of Africans, showing all of the multifaceted interrelationships which occurred. It would have to have the historical sweep from the earliest missionary endeavor with its paternalistic overtones and its abhorrence for traditional African culture. You'd have to trace the development through to the time when the tables are turned and the missionary is the servant of the African church. It would need to be done in such a way that the reader would respond sympathetically to what is going on. There should be no villains, only understanding. Of course, what sort of pattern the missionary situation will take in another twenty years no one knows just now, and that will be another chapter for a later book.

I finished reading a biography on David Livingstone. But in spite of the author's attempt to paint him as humanly as possible, I found myself irresistibly drawn to him again. He was a real terror, much worse than our old headmaster. But when you consider the physiological and psychological equipment he had to work with you find him a truly towering and impressive figure. Often my mind returns to that great man.

This is now the evening of the day after tomorrow. I am still pretty sore from squatting on a hot tin roof all day. It was a hard job. The church over there across the bay, up the line from where we climbed the mountain, was abandoned during national villagization. So, after nearly two years, we went over one Saturday and took the roof off and moved it some three miles down the road to where the village now is. There a stick house is being made for a church leader. We put the rafters up on the stick house the first day, then on this last day we nailed the roofing on. The trouble was that George Smoker was not very careful about having his nailers on exactly straight, and then we had a hard time hitting the nailer anyway, so the tin sheets had the existing holes in places where it was very difficult to get them to match up with our nailers in such a way that we would make no new holes. But since we had about twice as many pieces of roofing as we needed we did manage in the end to sort things out so that only about two holes are not nailed shut. Now we must go back another day or two to finish making the doors and windows and then later to put a roof on the kitchen and toilet.

September 16, 1975

I am so often filled with hopelessness and my faith nearly peters out. I often wish for a fresh vision, and when that is lacking, I feel that I had better go home and get a job on a farm and work with the soil and thus await the day when I will lay down my life. Maybe I will mercifully die soon and thus not need to keep up the struggle all these many more years that are left to me. The whole business of futility. Another of my sins is that too often I am not sincere and I work too hard to keep up appearances and I want to be thought well of by everyone. I expressed to the Bishop some time ago fears that there is a movement underfoot to change the Bible School into a trade school. I knew the Bishop would be quite sympathetic to my fears. But neither have I gone to the principal to tell him that this is what I fear from him. In fact, I have helped him draw up plans for increasing the trade school aspects of the institution. But just yesterday, he told us in staff meeting that he was called in by the Bishop and given a dressing down for trying to change the nature of the school away from what it is as a leadership training center to a trade school. So there I sat knowing that I was responsible for at least some of the Bishop's attitude. And at the same time the principal thinks I am behind his program one hundred percent. I have many, many shortcomings. I seldom get done the tasks I should do. Most of my activity is just chaff. I don't properly prepare my lessons. I have work assignments on my desk going back more than a year, and some of it I know I will never get to. But I guess the worst is that I am confused. I used to be confused about wearing the plain Mennonite coat and that nature carries over to everything I do. I am quite confused even now about what I should be doing and what I should believe and what I should preach and whether there is even any sense in preaching anyway. People in church are there for other sociological reasons, not for what has been preached to them. And yet I don't want to be confused because I want my life to have counted for something. Increasingly I am tempted to copy the style of the great ones, being silly even in the thought to suppose that a Shenk missionary, the son of an obscure farmer Shenk missionary, could in any way play the game. So, instead of playing the game I sit on the sidelines and poke fun at the great ones, but my poking in no way either diminishes their greatness or increases mine. And all of this is very sinful. So what I hope is that I shall be able to survive somehow intact until the time when I can die and leave the struggle to someone else. I am awfully glad that each person somehow has a built-in desire to survive and make something meaningful of life because otherwise it would be quite a terrible thing I have done bearing four creatures like myself who in their turn must struggle along until one day they too can lay down the burden. That is who I think I am. If my fellow missionaries and other onlookers see me as being censorious toward them for somehow having not been adequate in their service, feeling that I cannot empathize with the problems they face then I feel that somehow I have been misread. At the same time it does hurt me deeply when our service has been self-seeking and when it is the cause for broken relationships, but why my expressing such a hurt should define me as being insensitive or self-righteous or exclusive is to not realize my own intense trauma. I also ask why I should be censured when I in turn put up with so much from other missionaries. I pulled out of a dominant role in the Fraternal workers administration just as soon as Victor Dorsch arrived. He even suggested to me that I might not be sensitive to missionary problems due to my being an MK. So I was delighted to have him take over the welfare of missionaries. It is true: I hadn't the interest or time to be sorting out the refrigerator problems, etc., of the missionary family, and I in no way begrudge Victor's role.

In addition to my having been supplanted as missionary rep, I have also been supplanted in the ministry I had at one time begun to have in the Bishop's shadow. I used to occasionally speak at conference, when I accompanied him. But now this role has also been taken over by Victor. My own personal analysis is that Victor's preaching is sufficiently abstract as to not absorb the thinking of the audience and therefore his message is no threat to the Bishop's. I find that when I preach I knock the Bishop off balance. He cannot regain the initiative. So I find my ministry with him to be counter-productive. He had a recurrence of his heart trouble when we were preaching together at Nassa about two months back. Since I was the only guest preacher besides him I was given a message in the second session. The Bishop went into a mild congestive heart failure that evening and couldn't preach at all the next morning, making it necessary for me to preach a second time. So the role I used to have with him has also been eroded. What I have learned is that one cannot remain static in the scope of his ministry. As foreigners here that scope may expand rapidly at first, but there comes a time where further expansion is a threat and therefore the ministry is contracted. So I am content to sit this one out. The only thing I worry about is that I shall continue to slip into eclipse and may never get a significant ministry either here or at home. But that isn't supposed to matter, and one of my besetting sins is that it does matter just a little to me.

I was asked by the Bishop to take over a district when that pastor left for further training at the Makumira Theological College in Arusha. This appointment has not yet been confirmed by the executive committee, but there is the possibility that I may continue in this job until furlough. Now, mind you, I wasn't relieved of any other responsibility, the point being made that this is a small district. Furthermore, I know the reason I was appointed rather than an African is that the Bishop knows he can handle me, or to put it more positively, he knows that I won't cross him. Ever since Kisare has been Bishop the pastorate here has had its problems because of its built in ambiguity as to who is the big rooster. The pastor usually sees himself as in charge of the congregation here at Bukiroba, which makes the bishop a guest. Other churches (Anglican, Lutheran, etc.) have the church at the Bishop's residence as the Bishop's cathedral. The Bishop is always in charge and he is given an assistant to take care of things when he is absent.

Seeing that there is this problem I went to the Bishop and told him that I envisioned myself as his assistant rather than as the pastor of the district. He was grateful that I saw it that way. But how to make that practical is more difficult. For example, he was here Sunday morning for the first since I have been given this assignment. I asked him a week earlier if he would be here with us and he said that he would. So I thanked him and told the man scheduled to preach that the Bishop would be with us and that he was to cool it. So Sunday morning at the beginning of worship the Bishop did not show up. I went up to his house to see what was going on. I found him dressed in his casual clothes and not planning to go to church at all. I told him that we had expected to have him with us and that he would bring the message. But he said that I hadn't asked him to speak. So there we were, run aground right off at the start. Actually he hadn't come because of spite but because he was tired from having been hunting all the day before and I hadn't seen him for final Sunday morning plans because we had a shipwreck the night before and had slept on the other side of the bay. So, in the end another man preached because he was scheduled. He is the local pastor's sidekick, but he is such poor stuff that after the service one of the church elders suggested to me that the pastor has so much other work to do that maybe it would be in order to relieve him of his preaching responsibilities!

About that boat wreck—actually it wasn't much of a wreck. We get together as a missionary community once a month and this round we were invited over to Komuge, the Catholic station, about four miles from Kinesi. There is a young Lutheran, David Ramsey, living there, and he invited us over. The plan was for us to cross over on the regular 3:30 p.m. boat and come back by chartered boat at 8:00 p.m. That big car-carrying ferry has sunk. In fact, we fished off it the other week when the girls were home. But there are some half dozen-passenger boats carrying about 50 people that go back and forth all the time. We were only 22 people, counting all the children. Our kids are back in school already, but we had Rebecca along. Everything went off as planned with an excellent worship service and a delicious supper. But at 8:00 when we prepared to come back a storm was blowing in from the Mara Valley. There was about a quarter moon, but that was well hidden behind angry clouds. There were so many of us that Ramsey had to take two carloads of us down to the boat. The first group was men who could get things stirring with the boat. As might have been expected the boat pilot was drunk and nowhere in sight. The boat clerk showed up out of the dark and he too seemed a bit unsteady. He told us that they were sure we had changed our minds. But we managed to persuade him to get the engine, thinking that he could run it. But he found the store locked, and he also disappeared looking for the key. In the meantime Ramsey came back with the rest of the party, and after a half-hour of doubtful debate, we decided to give it up and go back to Komuge for the night. Just then, the clerk showed up with two lads pushing wheelbarrows in which they had the outboard engine and the petrol tank. A third man turned out to be the operator. So, having flushed all that out, it seemed a bit of a poor show to back out now. Dale Ressler went off with them to help get the engine on the boat. The boat was some little way out in the water, and the engine had to be carried out in the dark and fastened onto the bobbing boat. Then the boat was brought over to the wharf. Doing that took some time, with the operator going round and round in circles, but he did finally manage to bring the boat alongside and a rope made it secure. It was bobbing round quite a bit, and it was then beginning to rain. A stiff wind ensured that the crossing would be quite choppy. But we all climbed aboard, each supposing that his better sense was really not sufficiently informed and that all was quite in order after all. We finally got aboard and seated. They untied us and we cast off into the choppy lake. Ramsey kept his pickup lights on us as we set out, supposing that that would help us to see. Actually, for us it was a lot of blinding light. Just the same, after one big circle, the operator steered out past the corner of the wharf and set course for Musoma. But just as we got well away from the wharf he swung back toward shore again, heading straight for Ramsey's lights, saying all the while, "Turn off your torch!" The outcome was that we ran smack into the wharf, knocking people all over the place. Everyone was pretty shook and the kids were screaming hysterically. The men in the boat jumped out and held fast and a missionary held on to the tiller to ensure that the operator would not back off into the storm again. In short order, we were all ashore again. The boat was badly damaged. Ramsey drove us back to the Catholics; we were all put up in the padres' residence. The padre there said that this was a first: women sleeping in their quarters. The next morning, the boat crew didn't remember anything of the incident! Were they all drunk?

About being separated from the children and whether we get used to it. That is a hard question because it is true that the house is very much quieter when they are gone, and we can get a good bit more work done. But we do miss them very much. In fact, we miss them more and more as the years go by. It must be that we realize more that they are growing away from us and soon they will be gone forever. I guess it is good we are pretty busy, because that way we don't think about their being away. But when you stop and think about it, it's pretty devastating. There is so very little time that we have with them. Almost all their raising and inculcating of values is done by strangers. How much that will affect our family we can't know until a few more years go by, but at the very least it means that we have been deprived of being part of the growing-up process our children are going through.

I did an eleven-page, single-space paper. Actually, once I got it going, I figured that I should try to make it a community effort, so I had the other missionaries here read it, and they got involved in making suggestions. It therefore is billed as a station effort and to a certain extent that is true. It is a paper dealing with the problems the missionary faces and how we feel that if the missionary would have a primary community relationship back in the States many of his problems would be helped towards solution.

En route home from Usimbiti the other week we happened upon a Dutch couple serving a medical tour at a hospital in Mwanza. A bus forced them off the road into a ditch. Both front wheel mountings were smashed. The *Roho* is front-wheel drive, and the car hit the ditch so hard that the one differential joint snapped apart, leaving the driveshaft on that side dangling. Thus began a three-day involvement with them. It took us about six hours to devise a way to drag their car into Musoma. Then it took hours of red tape to get the police reports and cost estimates and file insurance claims. I was with them the whole time. They stayed with us two nights. The woman and their infant son got a plane to return to Mwanza. (Victor and the principal were in Nairobi and left me with the school, so that was completely unattended for the duration.) I keep wondering why ever were they brought to our doorstep.

September 27, 1975

I'm writing from Mugango. Another weekend away from home, and this afternoon I'm feeling a bit pensive. I am in the tent alone. The others have gone to the lake to bathe. I don't feel like walking, nor do I feel like exposing my pink skin to the shore-side traffic, so I've stayed here. The tent is pitched under a huge fig tree that we played in when we were children here. The sun is slowly setting and the sounds coming in are those of people in conversation as they await their suppers and the night meeting with choirs and filmstrips. Last night we got rained out before the first film strip was finished. This evening there is a rumbling back inland and maybe that will develop into a party-buster, too. It's fantastic how terribly much these folks want that night meeting. Last night they kept on singing in the rain for quite a while. For their sakes I hope we can pull it off. This afternoon the Bishop preached for an hour and a half in the sweltering church while a back-up preacher slept! I did too!

This morning, just as the service was to begin Hershey Leaman drove in with the new E. Africa MEDA couple. Since they couldn't see the Bishop just then, they had to wait until after the service and consequently they had lunch with us. Then they saw the Bishop and took off again for Shirati. It just seemed to focus for me again the two worlds. The one is the world of the white Peugeot sedan that purrs powerfully over the roads and takes one to new places and new contacts to make new plans and new decisions. The other world is the one that walked 22 miles on Friday morning from Bukiroba to Mugango and that will walk back on Sunday afternoon—six hours one way of brisk walking, to attend a meeting of four sessions of three hours each, to sit on a cement pew listening to long sermons and two night sessions, hoping that the crowds haven't too many drunks in them to disturb the meeting. Yet, in both worlds the actors are the few and the observers the many. Hershey in his white Peugeot is a principle actor. We are here to validate his tripping around in the white Peugeot. Here at the meeting the Bishop and his four pastor assistants (Masese, Mato, Mabeba, Meso) are the actors, and all of us others are either props (food, light, amplifiers, water-haulers for bathing) or observers, those who authenticate or validate the posturing up front with all the long, shouted sermons. I guess that is how the world stacks up. Someone said all the world's a stage and each of us are actors, but I think, at least here at Mugango this weekend, that all the world's a stage and most of us need to be around to give the actors an audience. I think that is why I am pensive, sitting here alone in the tent this evening. Also, maybe it is that I drink so much strong coffee at home, so when I come out to the bush and the tea is barely colored water, I find my brain nearly flickering out. This evening Mama Kisare took pity on my predicament and asked for a handful of tea leaves to put in my cup, which brought it up to the standard that makes me feel a little glowing and that glowing made me think of writing. I had hoped that Edith and Rebecca would come this morning with Hershey, but he left too early for her, so that made me feel lonely too.

One of the sermons this morning really touched me. Years ago Mugango was the Bishop's residence for South Mara. At that time there was a girls' home and a boys' school here. So many of the S. Mara church leaders have roots here. Elisha Meso was preaching, recalling how revival started here in 1942 and how he was baptized here by Ray Wenger and how marvelously converted so many of his fellow students were. Then he remembered how few of those are still left and he remembered that at Bumangi he is the oldest of the Christians. All the older men here left the Christian way. (I remembered how when I was out at Bumangi with James Shank on a visit a few months ago, how Mama Meso got tea for us and how when we left she and Elisha stood side-by-side out on the path to save goodbye). And so when Elisha wept this morning as he preached, I sensed how it was and that too made me feel pensive this evening and made me want to write.

1976

January 13, 1976

How about a letter from Addis Ababa? Jacobs is into his new job as part-time overseas secretary. He called the Bishop to Addis for an Eastern Africa Mennonite consultation. I was brought along because I had my documents in order. Then on the way to the Nairobi airport I looked into my briefcase for my passport and it wasn't there! So we rushed back to the guesthouse, and I couldn't find it there either. So the rest left me. I figured it had got stolen. Then I had to admit that I couldn't remember putting it into the briefcase when I was at immigration the day before. So Norma Leaman rushed me over there. I dashed up to the counter, looked the clerk in the eye; she looked me in the eye and said, "You forgot your passport here yesterday." I said, "Yes." She said. "That is very bad." I said, "Yes." She gave it to me and I said, "Thank you." So I caught up with the others in the airport lounge.

The Bishop was asked to stay here for a few days on a fraternal visit along with me and Okello, David's new side-kick at the Nairobi Mennonite congregation. So we went down to Nazareth (Ethiopia) and spent a day with Dr. P. T. Yoder in the Awash Valley. It was a good experience. We visited three congregations in session and four out of session, that is, we met the evangelists and had a word of prayer in their churches.

But the shocker for me (and I've got a headache just now and don't know how to say it right) is that Edith and I have been chosen to do the Nairobi Mennonite Area Office, after Hershey leaves in June! The consultation formed an advisory committee to whom the Area Director is responsible and they then chose me to be their man. I was in sort of a daze for a few days. Now I'm not thinking about it, so I'm coming back to normal.

The main function of this area office is to act as an agent to facilitate fraternal interrelationships and understandings between the African churches, missions, and other church agencies—all Mennonite, of course.

January 15, 1976

Writing from Kigoto, Kenya. We're in the middle of a wide fertile valley sloping down from a backdrop of wooded mountains to a thicketed expanse of thorn scrub. The church is in the middle of the valley and the Christian community—immigrants for the most part from Magatini and Busawe. Villages lie on all sides. The church is made of cedar posts with corrugated iron siding and roof. The siding was painted silver inside and out by Mother. There are bright blue shutters and doors—as have all of the churches Daddy built through South and Central Nyanza (Kenya). This building is the community focal point. Last night there was a crowd of about a hundred gathered outside on church benches under a full moon for Bible pictures and singing. Every time I come to Kenya I see another of these churches. Daddy and Mother just now are on an eight-day circuit of churches for communion and baptisms. The Bishop has dropped in here overnight on his way home from Addis to dedicate the church. The elder lives here now, some fifty miles from Migori.

What I am seeing here is a microcosm of what is happening in mission work. Daddy has a vehicle and from somewhere the resources to help communities build these churches and to visit them periodically. But over the length and breadth of his 34-congregation parish there is no African pastor. The one African, trained, experienced, and dedicated to be able to partially shoulder this burden will never be ordained because he is of Tanzanian extraction. Even though he is of the same tribe and a long resident of this area, he is from the wrong side of the border. The most favored candidate can barely express himself in Swahili, knows no English, has a four-year elementary education, and one year of Bible training. So you have Daddy knowing that much of what he has been doing could collapse, yet the only way he could stay on here is to become the Bishop of the pastors who will be ordained. To do that would not be possible by any stretch of the imaginations. So, you have a missionary in his prime—languages, strength, skills, spiritual maturity, resources—who is going home because he has also become an anachronism.

I am developing a philosophy of nepotism. If you have a competent man who is systematically destroyed—the Bishop calls it restricting his area until he gets disgusted and quits— you are no further ahead than if you have a less competent person whose activities are encouraged by the hierarchy. In fact, you may be farther ahead. I have become so discouraged over this destruction of people—four hospital administrators, a couple of pastors, a couple of church officers, etc.—that I am ready to trade nepotism for peace.

I told my daughters that we'd all be together for their birthdays. I asked them to guess how that could be possible. They guessed that I would have a committee meeting in Nairobi. Finally Joyce said that there is only one reason that she can think of: "Mommie must be pregnant!" So finally I told them that we are moving to Nairobi. Joyce sat there and the tears just rolled down her cheeks and dropped off her chin. I had my hand over the back of the car seat (she was sitting in the back) and I held her hand. She rocked it back and forth, back and forth, and the tears silently rolled down. I think Dianne felt a bit guilty that now her freedom would be curtailed. Rosy seemed happy, but not deeply moved. I guess she is too young to feel deep emotion. She went off and got me a piece of candy before I had to drive off.

January 24, 1976

(I want you to have a copy of my confidential letter to the Salunga mission board secretary, even though much of it you'll find to be redundant).

"You gently asked whether it wouldn't be good to confront the Bishop on some of these matters that are mattering so much to us (fraternal missionaries).

This came just after Hershey also gently inquired as to whether it might not be a good thing to cultivate in the Bishop an appreciation for team-support rather than my one-person relationship. These reminded me of the day Jack Shellard of the Alliance Secondary School (my former headmaster) stormed into our living room here and demanded to know whether I was a rat or a man, on account of there being an issue to which he expected me to "get up and fight." I remember that my response was, "You are leaving Africa, but I am staying on." (Somehow on that one I managed to only mildly anger both him and the church officials, and therefore after the deed was able to re-establish a healthy relationship on both sides). But my answer to him has continued to be a quite strong thread in how I conduct myself here. When I leave, I don't want it to be because I had to.

"I went through quite a low couple of days. It came to me that maybe I should write out my testimony. Not that I ask others to follow my lead, but just so some of you who are vitally involved in the situation may understand me and how I have been putting the pieces together. Over the years I have been writing to Omar, detailing the specific situations and my travail over them. He has been affirmative and this in a large measure is why I have survived. I have felt too that if I wear my struggle on my coat sleeve here it only undermines morale and so I have usually put a good face on it with my fellow missionaries. Maybe this was the wrong thing to do. But again, I find that my way of thinking is often not understood. If I try to explain the church to the missionaries I find they think me preposterous, and if I try to explain the missionaries to the church they think it preposterous, and the rationale I am formulating to deal with the situation seems to be preposterous to both sides. But maybe if I try to glean from what I remember writing to Omar, it may not be preposterous after all. So let me emote.

"When we were in Addis, Jacobs pointed out again that our philosophy of mission is that the church is to inherit the mission to the point where workers are seconded to the church and the mission no longer has a say in programming. That is a good thing to say at a "removed" place, such as Addis was for me; it is good liberal philosophy and Christian, too. It assumes that all men are brothers. It negates racism. But it also assumes that men are equipped to be transcultural creatures. In fact, very few men are equipped to be that, and those who are have problems integrating themselves—being credible both to others and to themselves. I believe that the Jacobs' (and Orie O. Miller) philosophy will become unstuck if we cannot find ways to help this new kind of missionary survive, and not merely survive, but survive gloriously. When I was a teenager growing up in a strange culture away from my parents, I would occasionally write a bitter letter home. Never in the answers sent by my mother was there any show of the kind of sympathy which would accentuate my sense of bitterness. Rather, she would show how to survive and be positive while doing so. It set the tone of my thinking. 'Don't rebel and get bitter, but look for ways to hold on; make your situation live positively for you.'

"Before you can make the most of a situation you need to understand the nature of your situation. One fact about African society is that the rule is gerontocratic and autocratic. The African encyclopedia is a gray head, and that literally means that anyone older than you knows more than you. To advise, let alone rebuke, one older than you are is to despise wisdom. If I am to give advice, I must start with this presupposition. The advice must be given in private and it must be given by using the method of asking advice. Example: Bishop Ivan Leaman earned himself the eternal enmity of Bishop Kisare when many years ago Kisare made the observation that the Lancaster churches were not very spiritual. Ivan asked him in the presence of the assembled Lancaster bishops and mission board members if a large mission offering to support the world's Kisares didn't indicate some spirituality. Kisare remembered that comment for years, until one day at another board meeting Ivan asked if his own trip to Africa had also been just another tourist jaunt. Kisare pounced with a resounding, "You were a greater tourist than them all!" There is more nastiness back the line from when Ivan was here in Africa on a visit, but the point was that Ivan didn't know in that first encounter that an aged one's opinion is NEVER wrong. Had Ivan wanted to ask his question in an African way he would have invited Kisare for a meal and after he had suitably been honored with appropriate foods Ivan might have said, "Brother Bishop, I have a problem that has been bothering me." "Ah, my brother, tell me of your problem and I shall see if there is an answer, but of course with these gray hairs certainly there is an answer." "Well, my problem is that I had thought that my people were a bit spiritual and the reason I had thought this was that I see them giving so much money to mission, but now I see that they are not spiritual after all. Could you help me with how I should view this giving of theirs?" "My dear brother, this is a matter of a rich heritage of teaching which has made your people this way. My people are not yet aware of their responsibility to God to give. When I mentioned spirituality I meant that your people are not joyful in their worship and free while my people are. My people often publicly confess their sins while yours act as though they thought they had no sins." And so the two men would have parted brothers, and I in turn would have not had to endure such pain to hear Kisare recounting with great belly laughs how he had put old Ivan in his place over his being a WORSE tourist than them all.

"The Ivan thing hasn't just to do with gerontocracy. It involves authority too. In Africa, authority is autocratic and inherited. This sometimes upsets the gerontocracy as a young man may command authority over a much older man because of the position of his mother vis-a-vis the position of the older man's mother, their both being wives of one man. The African notion of authority gave rise to the chief system. Here we say "*Mtemi.*" The *Mtemi* is law. Right and wrong are defined in terms of the *Mtemi's* position on a given matter. The *Mtemi* is like God. He is never wrong. Wrong is any action or attitude which runs counter to the *Mtemi's* position. The one who has inherited authority can never do wrong. Wrong can only be done by those under him and then wrong is only that which runs counter to the *Mtemi's* position.

"Of course there is much liberal teaching going on in the universities and in the country as a whole, countering the gerontocracy bit and the *Mtemi* mystique, but it is still VERY much there. Maybe in future it will be muted, but for this generation it is very much with us. We delude ourselves when we think that Kisare alone plays this game and were he removed all would be sweetness and light. No way! Any man on the horizon to replace Kisare will be a worse *Mtemi* than he.

"Yes, Ivan Leaman is also a bishop and he also has gray hair, so why couldn't one gray beard be civil to another gray beard? But this society is tribal and by no means universal. In the tribal society only one's own clan and tribe count. If Kisare is the greatest here, that automatically means that he is the greatest everywhere. The only way for Ivan's word to have weight with him would be for Ivan to be born into his tribe and be part of the web of familial-political relationships whereby Kisare defines who he is and who everyone else is. So the outsider can never play the power game with a person who is built into the structure of the tribal society. The young people who come back from overseas training have come to believe the egalitarian rhetoric they hear in the West and they try to play an egalitarian role, and one by one they get slaughtered. But it is a mixed bag. Take for example the interesting role between Daniel Imori and Bishop Kisare. Imori will use his Western exposure to egalitarian ideas to rationalize his refusal to allow himself to live within Kisare's power structure, yet he runs his Bible school more autocratically than Kisare runs the church. He is either egalitarian or autocratic depending on which suits his purpose.

"Some months ago Imori asked Kisare to have a chapel meditation. Unfortunately, Kisare forgot, so Imori had to go for him. He was late getting to chapel. Imori told the students that Kisare was late because he had forgotten.

Mistake #1. The Bishop had got himself up in his most flashy threads. He was really a dandy with his brilliant blue jacket, multicolored shirt and iridescent tie. But Imori was every bit as well decked out in the most mod rags he possessed. Furthermore, Imori is a very much more imposing figure than Kisare. Mistake #2. Then after the Bishop's meditation Imori announced that the Christian Fellowship in Secondary Schools of Mara had asked our school to host a weekend seminar. The truth is that they had asked the church as well as the school. Kisare knew about it. But Imori went on at great length about what a great honor it was that they had been chosen as the venue and he went on to read the program, which featured everyone except the Bishop. That was because the Bishop would not be here that weekend, and he had declined an invitation to speak, but the students weren't told this. To them the Bishop was not part of the glorious upcoming weekend. Mistake #3. I expected an explosion, but Kisare held his peace until after we had all greeted him at the door and then he took Imori into the principal's office and chewed him out unmercifully, ending with a flat refusal for the meeting to take place on our grounds. This incident had a great lot to do with Victor's (Dorsch) disillusionment, but for me it seemed a natural consequence of Imori's playing at egalitarianism with the Bishop. Consciously he was saying, "The Bishop and I are equals, so I may say what I like when he is around." But unconsciously he was thinking very much as the Bishop did towards Ivan: "I am the big shot in this school. The Bishop has come under the shadow of my power structure, so while he is here I am the Mtemi and he must eat crow." Also, Imori's subconscious may have simply overlooked the Bishop, seeing that he is from another tribe and there are no tribal structures to attach Imori to Kisare (Peace was later restored and the meeting took place here).

"Another thing about Africans is that they are polygamists. It takes a certain kind of mentality both on the part of women and men to make polygamy work, let alone to revel in it. The man has to be dominant and the women subservient. It is further assumed that your worth depends upon who your mother was in relation to the other wives of your father and by worth I mean the amount of power you automatically inherit. Each wife in turn has her influence defined by her place relative to the other wives. Any overt challenge to one's position is ruthlessly suppressed, otherwise the village structure would unravel. So any challenge to one's assigned status has to be made through stealth and cunning. People get poisoned, as wives maneuver to change the mandated pecking order. Now any people who exalt polygamy must certainly revel in the kind of dynamics it produces so that one comes to enjoy destroying your rivals. At the very least it means that each person has a pretty definite set of ideas about who his enemies are and who his friends are. It is a whole psychological baggage that we in the West know very little about, particularly our women. The African loves women, but his woman is meek before him, never challenging his authority. A good woman holds her husband in such reverence that she won't even allow his name to cross her lips, sort of like the old Jewish scribes never writing the symbols for God. You read this in anthropology books, but we haven't taken seriously that this is actually how people in Africa view women. It causes considerable grief to the missionary woman. A career missionary like Velma Eshleman always rebelled at the subservient role the Bishop required her to play. She wouldn't go to his house every day to greet him, etc. She wasn't married so she had no Mtemi. Therefore, she came under the oversight of the village chief. As an orphan, so to speak, in the power structure, she became a ward of the Bishop. He delights in playing father to the single missionary women. But Velma would play no such game. Since she was acting out of character, Kisare came to think that she must have some kind of witchcraft brewing for him. Unfortunately, Velma gave him his injections for his first overseas trip, and unfortunately he had a very severe reactions to the shots, and unfortunately Velma didn't come wringing her hands over his condition, so he came to assume that she was trying to kill him. He believes that to this day. He wrote the mission board about their sending Velma to Somalia. His was a deep anger that anyone would consider a witch like Velma as missionary material.

"Missionary wives may have a harder time than single women. The woman is usually the one who came to Africa because her husband was called. In an alien culture she wants her husband to take her seriously and to modify his program so that she is taken into account. But the Missionary wives may have a harder time than single women. The wife is usually the one who came to Africa because her husband was called for a specific ministry. In an alien culture the wife wants her husband to take her seriously and to modify his program so that she is taken into account. But the African community in which her husband works puts very little emphasis on the nuclear family. "If she is at home caring for the children, whatever more could she want?" they think. The African wife is the ready servant of any of her husband's friends or colleagues who happen along. Like wise, it is expected, that the missionary wife should turn out a meal for any one who comes to see her husband on business. If guests arrive unexpectedly and the wife allows displeasure or distress to show on her face she is not considered a good wife by the African community. Some missionary wives who feel trampled upon can survive if their husbands help them, but just the same it is nearly an impossible role for an American woman to play. Also time is often arbitrarily demanded of a husband caught in the local power web; time which takes no account of his responsibilities to his wife and children. I remember the time when the Bishop very nearly had me take him away over Christmas. I felt at the time that he was doing it to help Edith to understand how she figured into things. The missionary husband has to be careful how he refuses demands made on his time by his superiors lest he become known as another westerner who is bullied by his wife. A missionary man was rated as being a very good man who gave himself to the African cause, but his wife demanded that they go home to the States because he didn't give enough time to her. The truth of it is that she saw herself being pushed into the role of a good African wife, and she wouldn't put up with it. Her husband didn't know how to keep both her and the African community satisfied; quite a balancing act!

"I think also that the African is more inclined to define good and bad in terms of his family than are people from the West. The Bishop trusts only Luos and in Luo country he trusts only those Luos from his clan. Imori trusts only Zanakies and other young men with overseas training. Bishop Moshi of the Chagga, I am told, gets cars only for pastors from his clan within the Chagga tribe. His son is the head of the Kilimanjaro Christian Medical Centre. I think this fear of outsiders is honest. The Bishop knows that anyone outside his tribal clan group will work for their clan's interest and not his. The Bishop tolerates people of other clans but if they ever show signs of wanting to erode his power he destroys them. He has destroyed four hospital administrators, three pastors, at least one church official, and a number of missionaries. By destroy I mean that he so eroded the person's base in the job he had that that person could no longer function in that capacity. In most cases, after the person left or was transferred to another more obscure post in the church, the person recovered but the hope for a fruitful relationship with the Bishop is seldom very bright. He cut me out for a while. He said that someone told him that I said the Bishop wants missionaries so they can be his slaves. After some six months it came out in a conversation. I looked real dumb and translated it to another missionary present in such an ambiguous manner that it looked silly, and I guess the Bishop figured maybe I wasn't dangerous after all. But the Africans say once he is against you there isn't much hope.

"But I didn't want to start down that road. The point is that here it is terribly important to know who is related to whom. Dr. Musser's trouble with the Bishop stems from his having chewed out the Bishop's brother who is a guard at the hospital. Manaen went to bat for Musser. I am sure that played no small part in the Bishop's decision to hound Manaen out of the hospital.

The Bishop will be relieved to have Musser out of there, but it makes him livid to think of Musser coming back to serve somewhere else in Tanzania. Now the Bishop's tribal grandson has been put in by the Bishop to administer the hospital. That man has a double dose of the Bishop's instincts, plus never darkening a church door for years, never having a church wedding, etc. But now he comes to church regularly and his marriage is being blessed by the church this weekend, but here in Musoma. I know that no longer will the Shirati folk complain about Bukiroba meddling in hospital affairs. The Bishop fought as a matter of principle with the four previous administrators. But he will NOT fight with his tribal grandson.

"Now back again to power structures. One of the problems we missionaries face is that of being too good at something, or maybe it is that we think we are good. For example, preaching. I happen to have a pretty good self-image reference my ability to hold an audience's attention. For some time now I have noticed that I cannot preach without putting the Bishop ill at ease. So it didn't surprise me that I was not often asked to preach anymore when we traveled together. For all the weekend meetings I went with him this past year I didn't preach once. Except one mini-conference where I was the only other pastor present, besides the local pastor. This way, it would have been awkward for me not to preach. I really played it low key, but this was the first I had preached in the Bishop's presence for about a year, and that night he went into congestive heart failure. It was mild, but he couldn't preach that Sunday morning because of it, so I had to preach again. I preached a very low-key sermon on an outline he had heard me use before and which he approved for that meeting. I used his life as my principle illustration and he loved me for it. But I knew I would never dare preach in his presence again. I don't know if he understood what happened or not, but I went to him the night we got home for a long talk. He was being medicated then, and he was up and around again in a week. But I realized that if I preach and the people listen to me more than to him then he has two options—either destroy me or destroy himself. It moved me tremendously to see that on that occasion he chose the latter. I have never again preached in his presence.

"Something of this happened with Victor, reference the Holy Spirit. The Bishop was introduced to the charismatic movement by Nelson Litwiller's visit. But he cut Nelson out of things when Nelson warned the Bishop not to keep too oppressive a hand on Shirati. The Bishop never mentioned Nelson or charismatics again. But in time, he met an Edmond John from Dar es Salaam who was praying for the sick. The Bishop accepted him and had him here for quite a dramatic series of meetings. Edmond prayed for the Bishop's heart problem, and the only recurrence he has had since was the weekend I mentioned above. This was, of course, something with which Victor is very familiar and it was new to the Bishop, so it sort of came about that Victor became the Bishop's teacher reference charismatics. This relationship hit its high watermark when the Bishop and Victor went together to the International Congress on Spiritual Renewal in Nairobi. It was after that conference that the Bishop suddenly realized that Victor is going to get ahead of him on things, if he doesn't watch out. Spiritual blessing has also social dynamics. It is the greater who blesses the lesser. It takes tremendous spiritual maturity to ask for the laying on of hands, especially so if those hands belong to your ecclesiastical inferior. I sense Victor struggling with this himself when he asked the Bishop and me to anoint Viola. With Victor it was just the missionary group that prayed for him. Well, for him to ask me, his junior in age and in the matters of the Holy Spirit, to pray for her is to put oneself into an inferior position. For a year or more the Bishop had been increasingly inviting Victor to accompany him on preaching missions, but when the Bishop realized that Victor was becoming his mentor he couldn't cope. The point is that especially in Africa, the elders are not equipped to handle the Saul-David relationship. It is to be expected that if you have a missionary David, the African elder will react like Saul did.

"Now all of this is what the missionary begins to see along about his third year on the field. It makes him bitter and then it is that bitterness which the African sees. The African is used to this environment so he doesn't realize the underlying reasons for the missionary's bitterness. So the African sees the missionary as a person bitter for no apparent reason. The missionary cannot explain himself, so he becomes angry and goes home with superficial explanations for what went wrong that places blame on the African. But if he is a spiritual person, he just goes home and tries to forget all about it.

"Okay? So that is the problem as I have come to figure it out. The more I see and hear the more I am confirmed in my opinion. So how do I cope?

"The biggest problem is to keep from prostituting myself. How do I stay true to Joseph C. Shenk and at the same time make peace with what I need to do to be a useful cog in the socio-political-power structure around me? An even harder question is how do I avoid doing violence to my family. When I am down, I dream my fears. Three times since 1969 I have dreamed that my youngest child was murdered by a church official, but never the Bishop. It is not that I fear murder in a physical sense, but I fear that I may betray my children by warping their personalities while they are still young. People assume, naturally enough, that since I am so well integrated into the local situation I must most certainly want my wife to be treated as other wives here and my children brought up as local children are brought up. Here people exchange children for long periods between brother families. People of several different tribes have so adopted me as to literally wish to keep my children for me, supposing that the children would be happier with them than with me. Just the other day Imori felt sorry for Rebecca's not having any siblings and felt the situation would be improved if he would take her home to live with his daughters. He was so serious that I was hard put as how to refuse without offending him.

"I had one such dream in Ethiopia after I was chosen to go to Nairobi. It followed on a conversation with an African widower in which he was telling me that he hoped to marry a missionary because whites don't care if they don't have any children and they are very interested in serving others. That way, he would get someone to care for his five children without her needing to complicate matters by having children of her own. My dream told me that all he wanted was a white slave to do his bidding. I guess my subconscious was asking me in my dreams what he must have thought I was to have told me that with a straight face. Or who do people think I am to tell me about Mother's displeasure at too many guests or to think I delight in hearing how my mother's sister's husband, and the birth-righted sister at that, was put in his place, to say nothing of his being my Millersville Bishop? There are many such windows the Africans have given me which put my people in bad light, and I always wonder to what extent I have prostituted myself to have allowed them to so intrude into my structures. When I talk like this Edith says we must leave Bukiroba. Maybe we should.

"But I must be honest and say that in these pages I have compressed eight years of Bukiroba experience, and it is the experience we have trouble with that I have put down. As you very well know there is a wealth of other experiences, too. I feel guilt writing like this, yet I must because it is this which is bugging us.

"I still haven't gotten to answering my question about how does one live creatively in such a situation. My answer in 1971 was "Servanthood" and I did that paper on that topic. I still hold to everything in that paper and so won't go over that again. But Victor asks me if becoming an "It" is really what Christ has called us to. To answer this question I wish that I had professional help. It is a question that needs to have answers if we are going to continue the kind of relationship defined for us by O. O. Miller & Jacobs. But lacking professional help, let me again emote my testimony.

"I start with the preconditions as one would in a geometry problem. 1: We are given a society like the one I have described. The people are Christian and this Christianity has softened the harshness or its difference from our Western society, but Christianity hasn't changed it in its subconscious, even as our Germaness hasn't been fundamentally changed by our becoming Christian. 2: We are given that our missionaries are to work in this society with such a relationship which makes us their servants. This relationship is such that confrontation is out of the question, if we are to maintain an ongoing relationship. 3: We are given that we are to be fruitful, happy, joyful children of our Lord and Savior Jesus Christ. Therefore, I must find a way. One method I employ is to try to see things through the eyes of the people here, say through the Bishop's eyes. I find that he is honest in his suspicion of the people he has problems with. In fact, one of the easiest ways to see him is through the Old Testament scriptures. I get great help from King David with the Bishop being David. I get a lot of help from the Samuel-Saul relationship with the Bishop being Samuel.

"Take Samuel first. He was so against Saul's being made king that he called down hail on the wheat harvest the day Israel was celebrating Saul's coronation. Samuel didn't want Saul because Samuel had put his rascal sons into judgeships and Israel was rebelling against those sons. Saul was of a different tribe from Samuel and Saul's ascendancy meant that Samuel's family would lose influence. Remember that Saul's first sin was to offer sacrifice after he had waited seven days for Samuel to come. Samuel was only some ten miles away, so why did he wait until all Saul's army had deserted him and then how was it that just as soon as Saul's sacrifice had been made Samuel showed up? Yet the most significant thing of all is that even though Samuel was being enormously obstructive of Saul's program, nevertheless God voted on Samuel's side. I am glad David didn't have a Samuel to put up with. It made things a lot easier for him.

"Take a look at David. He had a deprived childhood, being the son of a woman whom Jesse married late in life. This woman already had grown daughters by the time David was born. Possibly David was conceived in sin and his birth legitimatized through the marriage. In any case, Jesse didn't consider him one of his sons when Samuel came calling and he got nothing but dirt from his older brothers in the Goliath case. David had such an inferiority complex that when he gained power he was absolutely ruthless with whoever crossed his path. Remember that he was promised Saul's daughter Merab and then Saul gave her to another. Later Saul offered him Michal and demanded 100 foreskins. David brought 200 of the bloody things and then apparently never consummated the marriage, so after David was chased out into the bush Saul gave Michal to another man. When David became king he got Michal back and the scripture definitely says that she had no children because David didn't have intercourse with her. All of that just to spite Saul for not giving him Merab! Or how about when David was living in the Philistine country and raiding on the Philistines and during the raids killing everything that moved so that none would tell on him. Or how about when the Amlekites raided Ziklag and stoned David's wives and he killed every breathing member of the raiding party. Or how about when Nabal slighted him and David determined to slaughter everyone 'that pisseth against the wall' in revenge. How about when David slaughtered all the lame and blind as first order of business upon his taking of Jerusalem because he had been taunted that they could hold the city. Yet if anyone showed David kindness he was overwhelmed by it, Jonathan being the prime example. David recognized only one absolute in his life, and that was God. Hit him with anything else and he went up in smoke, but hit him with God and he melted every time. Further, the only people David trusted were his sister's sons: Joab, Amassa, and Ashahiel. Joab was the only one who ever got away with anything, and even David had him slaughtered by Solomon.

"So we have met these Africans before, in the Scripture, as great men of God, who they indeed were. I often think that the Bishop must envy David's easy way of being able to deal with insubordination.

"I get a lot of help too from history, realizing that the vast majority of mankind has always been oppressed. How did they live? If they could live joyfully then why can't I, too? Certainly their joy was derived from knowing their limitations as well as the areas in which they were not limited. Our problem here is wanting to be free where there is no freedom. If I have no freedom to preach at a conference, have I also been denied the right to preach in the bush? There are many creative areas that do not infringe on the power structures around us. I get great joy from my garden and from books and from fishing. Andrew Wyeth, the painter who did the Hans Herr House, points out that he has never lived outside of two localities, one where he winters in Pennsylvania, the other where he summers in Maine. He fears that were he to see more of the world he would become callused. The point for me was that there is abundant joy right here at Bukiroba, if I but look for it. If I cannot lay hands on the sick at a big meeting, I can move among them as they gather around the dispensary door on my way to and from class. If I cannot galvanize great crowds with my rhetoric I can deeply impress the lives of the students with whom I cultivate the school garden. If I cannot go to Ethiopia to attend a consultation I can have a cup of tea at Yusuf Adams and study the people as they come and go, and I can enjoy again the beauty of our hill and lake and canyon. It is all glorious whether in the dry dust of the rainless months or the fresh lushness of the monsoon. But always there are the people to greet, to know, to ache with and to joy with.

"My need to preach was first thwarted by Jack Shellard. I had been sent there as chaplain of the Musoma Alliance Secondary School; for that ministry I was ordained. Shellard allowed me only to recruit speakers but never to speak. So I rationalized that most preachers bored me to death and as I was very likely like most preachers it was a delusion to think that people liked to hear me preach. So if they didn't like to hear me preach why not let someone else bore them rather than me. I preached once in the first half year I was chaplain at Alliance Secondary. And for the three years I was there I am sure I didn't preach more than four sermons a year. But I determined that I wasn't going to get depressed about such a little thing.

"Just yesterday I got a big help from reading *Papillon* by Henri Charriere. He was an uneducated man yet he realized that if he were to survive with the Indians he would have to take pains not to in any way threaten their authority structure. I was enthralled to read how carefully he avoided in any way jeopardizing that structure. The Indians loved him dearly for it, and he was able to make genuine contributions to their society. Of course, we are Christians with a mandate to "turn the world upside down." But remember that we are not working with pagans. We are working with the church and our colleagues here are Christians. I have come to see that much as we hate the authority structures that confine us, we still aspire for power within that structure. So I ask, why do I want power? Then I would be as awful as the rest with the added disadvantage of being from an alien culture. So I ask, 'Why does the Bishop want to preach at all the big meetings?' 'To enhance his power.' 'So why do I want to preach at all the big meetings?' 'To bring the gospel to the heathen!' Now wait a bit. If it is to bring the gospel to the heathen, can't a person from the local situation do that better than a foreigner? Yes! Then maybe why I want to preach at all the big meetings is so that I will be known all over the church as a great preacher, i.e., so that I can enhance my power. Why then if I dislike someone else's power do I set about cultivating my own?

"But most of all I have been helped by Jesus. The thing which made the cross glorious for him was that he voluntarily embraced it. For me to be a missionary is to walk where Jesus walked. He considered that being God was nothing to grasp after but rather emptied himself. So why should I consider that my degrees or my eloquence or my insights are anything to be grasped after? Jesus embraced the cross with joy and in that way he became Victorious over it. It was God who raised him up. If God could raise Jesus and give him a name, why can't

He also do so for me? The point is that He can't until I indeed consider that that name is nothing to be grasped after so that the name is to God's glory and not mine. This is a lesson I have been trying to learn, to empty myself of the need to have a name so that Jesus could give me his name. It is like Moses in the wilderness, herding sheep and if you look later at the mess he had leading the Israelites you can see that he got nothing out of it. He needed to herd sheep so that he would be emptied of himself, so that his life could honestly become God at work through him to God's glory. I am afraid that as soon as I get to Nairobi I shall forget this lesson and begin to grasp after power again. It seems to me that this is how people generally react, but Jesus never, and this is the beauty of him. I have come to feel that being a missionary in our setting is one of the few places where we can learn what it means to follow Jesus.

"I am also helped by Jesus' attitude toward those who nailed him to the cross. He realized that they honestly did not know what they were doing. So, too, all of the conflicts we experience due to our cultural differences are something unwittingly imposed on us. The Bishop would be absolutely stunned were he to read the first part of this letter. He just has no idea that he pains me at times, and he couldn't understand why if I told him. If therefore he does not understand because of built-in cultural barriers, why should I hold it against him? All that he really has done is to help me understand Jesus better.

"Having lived here and having come to be loved by the people, by both the Zanaki and the Luo, as well as Jita and Kuria, to me brings a great sense of satisfaction. It is possible for a European to live joyfully in the kind of relationship spelled out for us by O. O. Miller & Jacobs. Jesus has proved it in my life, to his glory, because if it is to my glory then it all will evaporate again. Of course, I was born here, but most of the missionaries weren't. So my Victory is only partial, but theirs is complete—and always to the glory of God through Christ Jesus, as otherwise the Victory just becomes another story of conquest and human pride.

"So this is my testimony. Please treat it with the utmost discretion. Maybe if the names of people are edited out it can be shared around. I debated with myself whether I should speak of individual people and decided that only in that way could I convey the power of our experiences. But in no way should this be allowed to hurt anyone.

"So this is part of who I am and why I act the way I do.

"P.S.: It's way too long, but as I read it again I see that it is only an outline. I hope it's not so sketchy as not to convey the ten hours of intensity which I put into writing it."

February 1, 1976

The whole matter about whether or not I shall be able to do a desk job in Nairobi is precisely what frightens Edith too—and me! In Addis I told them that I am not an administrator, even before they voted the first time, and I re-emphasized it before the second vote. I said that even my wife declares that I am not suited for administration. When Hershey privately asked me as to whether I wasn't feeling a "call," I emphatically insisted that I didn't feel a call, but I admit now that for two days my pulse wasn't normal. I oscillated between knowing how delighted Edith would be and my own joy at being "free" in Nairobi, and the cold realization of just how difficult a job it was, given my aptitudes. For two days I was caught between terror and delight. So after they announced that I had been chosen and had made their speeches encouraging me, they asked for my response. I repeated that I did not see that I had the qualifications and that I had said that in the first place. But if they went ahead anyway and appointed me, then they would have to help me in my weakness and that I felt strongly enough about the validity of the call of the brotherhood that I was willing to "try." Hershey then pointed out that the new vision doesn't call so much for administration as it does gifts of being able to facilitate inter-church understanding and cooperation. Marian Buckwalter is the administrator in that office, and she will continue to carry much of the responsibility for what is going on with funding agencies, bookkeeping, reports, finances, etc. I would be completely incapacitated without her there.

I am afraid that I felt David was just a touch disappointed about his not being appointed to this, especially I felt that Grace would be happy to get out of those cramped quarters at Eastleigh. David has been wondering if it might not be possible for him to move out of the university classroom sometime soon. But his contract runs for another year or so. I am sorry for him, that the set-up is this way, and I'll try to be sensitive. In recent years David and I have managed to stay out of each other's hair.

I was sick for about two weeks after this Nairobi business was announced, a terrible heavy cold. It took a long time for my subconscious to catch up. Getting back to Bukiroba, everything just looked so preposterous that my mind played tricks on me, giving me to wonder if Addis wasn't some kind of cruel hoax. But now Edith and I have talked about it enough so that it's beginning to lose its aura of unreality.

February 2, 1976

Curiously no one has said anything about our next furlough. It seems that the first order of business is for us to get a hold of the Nairobi Area Office and then a furlough will be talked about.

Meanwhile, I am still a full-time teacher here in the Bible school. Victor is also full-time, but he is being appointed to supervise the construction of the Mugumu Hospital, and there isn't much likelihood that he will be teaching after Easter. Therefore, I'll be busier than ever. Further, just now I am the pastor for this district, as well as assistant secretary of the church, and chairman of the Shirati Medical Board, etc., etc. So I am pretty busy without the school. My pastor work focuses on the building of a church out at Nyankanga. That church is now finished except for the doors and the benches. The leader's house there also needs to be expanded and a kitchen-store building put up as well as a toilet. My dream is that Nyankanga can then become something of the center for the Bukiroba district, thereby helping to keep the district pastor out of the Bishop's hair. Bukiroba then becomes the Bishop's Seat rather than the district seat. This building is possible through the greatly increased giving on the part of the district, as well as the roofs of three churches that we had to abandon when the villagization scheme took effect here. This past year, for example, the congregation here gave over Shs 10,000/= in tithes and offerings.

You may have heard that Daddy had a bad fall. He was standing on top of the Toyota pickup hood and his right foot slipped. He hit the fender and slipped off that into the air. That threw him over backwards, landing him on the ground. This so knocked the wind out of him that he couldn't move himself for several days. He fell on Monday the 26th of January, and I made the *piki* trip up to see him on Friday morning. I found him at the dinner table for the first. He looked pretty gray and still could not walk without assistance. By Saturday he had his first bowel movement and the enormous bloating of his intestines had pretty well subsided, and he was eating again. He was also cheerful and able to sit for a while in a chair. The doctor expects him to be fairly active again, about two weeks from the fall. No broken bones, fortunately.

February 16, 1976

Dorsa Mishler (Elkhart mission board rep) was here. He was wanting to know how the missionary fares, and I shared my carbon copy of that long letter with him. He felt it shouldn't lie about in somebody's files. He urged me to send copies to additional people.

Victor and I were talking about that letter again. We concur that the paper maybe isn't powerful enough in showing the kinds of bind we get into here. The question is how do we work out a solution. If we were dealing with the world, then we would have no problem, but we are dealing with brothers in the church and of necessity one's inner commitment to a brother requires that he accept him into the circle. But how can you accept someone into the circle who appears to us to be so unlike a brother without prostituting our own integrity. We really need help on this one. If we don't get help we are not going to move into the next stage of missions.

I was rather schizoid for about two weeks after getting back from Addis, but I feel myself stabilizing again.

March 2, 1976

Myron Augsburger's planned East African Fellowship Tour has thrown us into mild panic. We heard that eight vans with forty people are coming. Musoma is off the tourist track and that many whites really creates a sensation, to say nothing of wherever to put up so many people. Musoma Hotels are sort of third class, for the most part, and most of them have permanent boarders due to housing shortages in the area. I did some scouting around and found that the old Musoma Hotel is being resurrected and operational by June. Hopefully about half of them can go there. Shirati has no hotels, making it impossible to have them spend a night there.

We're planning to put the group out into eight churches to minimize the impact of so many whites at any one place. We're asking each congregation to host their guests for the noon meal. What will happen most likely is that the elders at each place will be called together to share the meal with the visitors. A goat will need to be bought, for Shs 100/=, and rice, bananas, sugar, tea, flour, etc. all of which converts to about US$25. I want each van to pick up the tab for their fellowship meal. The psychology goes that every time a request is made from here in Africa for more money for a project, we are always told by the mission board that there is no money available in the U.S., except the annual budget, which hasn't changed for fifteen years. Now we get 40 Americans who come to Africa for a seminar and spend a lot of time in expensive hotels. This gives the observant African to feel that there is plenty of money in the U.S., but not for them. I want each vanload to make a sizable contribution to the work of the congregation that hosts them. Nothing less than US$100.

Bishop Kisare has requested that cameras be well under wraps, except for where permission is granted. I doubt that there will be a tour of the hospital. Forty visitors could easily grind the hospital to a halt for the day.

Africans are very hospitable people, and at no time have I picked up any feeling that the group is not welcome. All the flack came from us missionaries!

March 13, 1976

We're here at Shirati for the nurses' graduation. We came early because Salunga has precipitated a crisis for us by not being able to recruit any more doctors for Shirati. Salunga phoned Hershey in Nairobi; he phoned me and I talked to the Bishop, and then I phoned Hersh back and he phoned to the States. So the result was that Hersh came to Shirati to huddle with me and the Bishop as to why Salunga cannot get doctors anymore. After that we meet with the two doctors here (and their wives) for a discussion. This Shirati situation is just incredible!

Basically there are two factors. One is that the administrative set up (and now I am chair of the medical committee!) is such that no doctor is in the authority structure. The nurses aren't even responsible to the doctors. This problem could be improved by reinstating the old Medical Board with broad professional representation. Whether it will be possible for TMC to accept such a thing I don't know, but the Bishop seemed inclined to see it as a good thing. The second thing is the historical conflict between the Shirati pastor and the Bishop—a conflict so serious that it obscures all truth on either side. It is so bad—this blindness brought on by family rivalry—that last evening at the end of two hours of intense discussion—the African wife of one of the American doctors, sobbing and with tears streaming down her checks, begged the Bishop to get together with the Pastor to brother through their differences. The Bishop got quite upset over this and said that every time he calls the pastor to tell him what is wrong with him, the pastor tells his friends that the Bishop is unfairly accusing him, so matters are only made worse. Incredible, isn't it? Even so, the Bishop said, because of this woman's tears, he will "confront" the pastor again.

The Salunga board has been after Dan and Erma Wenger to come to Bukiroba to take our place at the Bible school. I am positively delighted and am going to very strongly urge the board to ordain Dan before he comes—if in fact he agrees to come.

March 18, 1976

I fear that some day one of my letters about TMC will get into the hands of the Bishop and give cause for my destruction. Also, it seems that everything is of a pattern. To tell you the goings on of any particular case is just to replay an old theme. I have been hoping that I will get a new breath, see things through different lenses and thereby be rescued from stagnation. But it is true too that I have been busy since being made pastor of this district. This is the story of a great deal of physical effort, moving roofs from old abandoned churches and putting up a new church at Nyankanga. I have even gone into debt personally, getting this place built. My dream is to provide a center for the Wakiroba other than here at Nyabange, which can flourish away from this campus. But there is still so much to be done there and so little time left before we move to Nairobi. Just now we are stuck for lack of cement to mend the old water tank and to lay the floors of two toilets and to cement in the doorframes to the church and do the floor of the kitchen and storeroom we built there. We have been having services in the new church for a month now, with attendance getting up close to the Bukiroba attendance. We want to have a supreme evangelistic effort out there at the time the church is dedicated. That must be in mid-June before Myron Augsburger's 40 come through and we move to Nairobi. So, you see, this thing has been absorbing me. (When I said we need cement, I meant that no cement has been available to non-government agencies in Musoma for some two months.)

We've had two big flare-ups very recently, about which I could write pages. But for reasons stated earlier, I really don't have much stomach for it. The one had to do with the selection of a pastor in the Migori area. This area of South Nyanza (Kenya) is really a political hot potato. For the first time in years when I was in Migori the other month I felt a chill towards me because I am a Mennonite. It reminded me of how it used to be at Alliance Secondary where people hated you because you represented something they were fighting against. There has been a political movement in that area ripening over the past few years, led by ex-Mennonites who are anxious that the Kenya church get independent of the Tanzania Mennonite Church. The Kenyans look on our bishop as something of a foreign colonialist. One faction of South Nyanza is insisting that they choose their pastor by vote of the members. But the Tanzania Mennonite Church constitution says that pastors are chosen by the ordained men's synod. We were given three names by the nominating committee, where the Bishop's voice was dominant. One needs 75 percent of vote to secure the position. But none could get that, the highest coming in at 60 percent. So after two attempts, the Bishop became angry. He kept telling us that S. Nyanza has their man, so why ever don't we follow the Lord's leading and accept him. The Bishop attempted to dismiss the meeting, but people would not leave. So I stood up and made a plea for this man, knowing the Bishop would work with this man. If we didn't get an ordained man in place, it would mean that when Daddy goes home (retiring), the district would be leaderless, and a split could develop among the churches in Kenya. So, after many words, the delegates voted again, and the man squeaked through with a 75 percent vote. Some days later I went up to see him. He poured out his irritation with Shirati. At the end I told him quietly, "*Mzee*, that is how we Germans are!" He seemed to have been hit by a bolt of lighting. Maybe on the basis of that revelation he is ready to forgive all of us.

The other matter has to do with the African administrator of the Shirati Hospital. The Bishop declared at a fellowship meeting, "They are full, full of lies, lies, lies about me." Many are stoking the fires of suspicion. At the Bishop's urging we are meeting here at Bukiroba four days a week (other than Sunday) to pray for revival. This gives me a very deep pain to write like this.

April 14, 1976

We have been getting rain! Possibly too late to raise much, but we've had the school in the *shambas* for two weeks and have put in a lot of beans and some cassava.

Hershey has found a car for us when we move to Nairobi. A 1972 404 Peugeot with 48,000 miles, for Shs 28,500/=. He says it looks as though it hadn't been out of the show room. Owned by a female staff person at the Swiss Embassy.

April 25, 1976

We're at a church dedication and ordination for Central Nyanza (Kenya). This is a lovely church—about the size of the Migori one, but even better built. This one has metal window frames and much bigger roof timbers. Yesterday was the dedication. They lugged four of the high praying-type benches down the hill from the Anglican Church. We men slept in the new church. One pastor had two of the large benches facing together, so he slept in a sort of high-walled box. The church has quite an adequate supply of Mennonite benches. Unfortunately, the church is located in a terrible place, way down in the river valley. The hills go up steeply on both sides of the river.

May 11, 1976

Now I'm in Arusha at the big Lutheran Centre, waiting for a response to tenders I've put out for building our Mennonite church in this town. The Bishop and I started out for here by bus a week ago. Why ever he needs to go banging around in buses to get bids on tenders, I'll never know. This time he hadn't slept well and got some medicine from our medic at Nyabasi before setting out on this grueling 400-mile trip. By the time the bus got to the Mugeta breakfast stop (45 miles), he was having fever and diarrhea. By the time we got to Fort Ikoma (90 miles) he could hardly sit up anymore. Fortunately a former church member lives there and we got taken in and they made up a bed for him. I was afraid that it was his heart again and was wondering what to do if he died. Fortunately there was a medic at the clinic and he administered some shots. In a few hours the Bishop was resting comfortably.

There was no traffic until after 2:00 p.m. I was into a sour milk dessert when I heard a lorry coming. I dashed out and waved both arms. They stopped. So I got a ride all the way back to within 20 miles of Bukiroba. Then I had to wait for another hour until a bus came along that had gone off the road the day before and was being pulled out of the ditch. The mechanics sent to put the bus on the road took pity on me and gave me a ride. They were so relieved that their bus had nothing mechanically wrong, except a sticky clutch, that they drove like maniacs, whooping and hollering all the way to Bukiroba. I got home just at dusk; it was quickly decided that Victor and the station medic go off that night for the Bishop and come back the next day. Poor Mama Kisare was sure the old one had died. She was sure that I wasn't telling the truth. It took all my persuasive powers, plus a little male authority, to prevent her from going along on the rescue operation.

May 12, 1976

Again in Arusha. It's nice to be alone in a town for a few days. You get all the doubts out of your system and you get a new vision. I've been reading *Teach Me to Dance* by Bruce Larson and Van der Post's *Heart of the Hunter* these days between meeting contractors. I am intrigued by his illumination of the Bushman's appreciation of animal characteristics to understand his own psyche. Larson's accounting for human nature in the salvation process is also helpful. I think all missionaries should have an in-depth course in the socio-psychic dynamics of human nature.

You've heard about Daddy having two serious falls. The first was over two months ago. He was standing on the hood of his Toyota truck, washing the cab roof when his foot slipped and he went down flat on his back. It took him four days to get out of bed on that one. Just as soon as he was well enough to be functioning again he drove down to Musoma for the selection of the Kenya pastors. (I wrote about all that). The Monday before the ordination of that pastor for Kenya, Daddy was putting up a corrugated iron shack for cooking at the new pastor's place. He was being helped by hired chaps he had taken along, not by local chaps. I deeply suspect that he had something of bitterness in his heart, seeing that he, the old man and senior pastor, was doing all the work while the pastor-designate sat around enjoying the fruits of the elder's labors. Daddy was standing on top of a three foot high box, reaching up to hold the first piece of roofing when a sudden gust of wind lifted it up, pushing him off the box. He fell onto his left hip, which was full of roofing nails. He told me later, "It was just as if a huge hand had reached out and flung me to the ground." Half way through the confession to me, he faltered, as though he felt that by saying the truth he would open the door to something he would rather have denied. In fact, he quickly closed that door in his mind by saying, "The wind just lifted it up."

He managed to drive home. The next day he simply could not walk without a cane to support all of his weight on that leg.

The Bishop said he had reconciled himself to not having Daddy at the ordination, but if we could bring him we should. When we showed up at Migori, Daddy said that he was reminded of the passage in Genesis, "Jacob's heart revived within him when he saw his sons."

So we took Daddy and Mother to the ordination. The Bishop had made out the order of service and the first lesson was printed with Daddy's name. But the Bishop told him that he had thought he wouldn't come. Twice the Bishop said, "If you cannot do it, your son David can." Twice Daddy replied, "I can do it." And the Bishop said, "But not the last verse." So when Daddy hobbled to the lectern to read, and had read all but the last verse, he said, "I have been told that the lesson ends here." On the way home, Daddy asked me why the Bishop hadn't allowed him to read the last verse in the Psalm. I told him, "Probably just to keep you in your place!"

Daddy still has plans for building a second house at Migori and finishing yet another church and taking the two new pastors around to all 33 of the little congregations he has been shepherding. Mother would like to get out of Migori by June; but Daddy wants to stay until October.

Nairobi

Church Road, Westlands

July 1976-July 1981

1976

August 12, 1976

Where shall I begin! Well, to start. It's a clear morning in Nairobi. I got up by moonlight and was downtown in the office reading letters by 6:30. The sun is now up, high enough to catch the tops of the buses on Haile Selassie Avenue, and the city skyscrapers are stark on their backsides with the sun lighting them golden towards the East. Every balcony and cement ornamentation shows this contrast of gold and dusk. Our porch thermometer registered 54 degrees this morning. We want to go up on the slopes of Mt. Kenya for two nights before school opens, and I expect it will be cold up there!

Yes, I get into my big white Peugeot every morning and drive alone down to the office. Then again at noon I get back into my big white Peugeot and drive over to the post office and then back to the family. Then again I get into my big white Peugeot and drive back to the office downtown. In the evening I join the crush of traffic and get home about five thirty. Actually I don't enjoy the Peugeot much except for when I must go out to the airport to meet someone. The city traffic is just terrible. These English have absolutely no notion of traffic flows. Their great sprawling roundabouts are an absolute hazard. I find myself getting really frightened of them. There are red lights now on all the roundabouts, so you go through after having accumulated a glut of cars which fills all four lanes going into the roundabout. This float of metal on wheels is then supposed to flow, some out of the roundabout to the left, some going round to the right, making a 90 degree turn onto the cross street, and the rest going out the opposite end from which they came in. Inevitably someone switches lanes in this process. And it is really complicated. For example, on the two biggest roundabouts you have in essence to switch lanes in order to be in the right lane. You go into the roundabout second lane from the right curb, and you come out against the right curb. Then again, if you are making a right turn and the light changes on you so that you have to stop within the roundabout, when the light goes green again the law of which lane is for what has changed because the traffic flow is now from another direction obeying different laws. Therefore, you are in the wrong lane for doing what you want to do, and an accident is almost inevitable. Of course, I made a lot of mistakes while learning the intricacies of the dumb things; even now I occasionally make a mistake. Marian, my assistant, suggests that I come and go via ways that avoid the roundabout or that I come and go late or early so that there isn't such a press.

How did you know that I sit at my desk, drumming my fingers at the edge of its broad expanse, swiveling around in my great executive chair (bigger chair, bigger desk than the secretaries) and wonder what to do? I even have a rug on the floor, so big the desk sits on it and it spills out on my side so I can't get my swivel chair properly up to the desk. The secretaries' have only a tiny throw rug in front of two visitors' chairs. I have four visitors' chairs. It is really impressive, all this status business!

The door to our two-room office opens onto the secretaries. They are face-to-face with whoever pushes the door open, and they must talk to that person and take care of his/her problems. My desk is behind a door so that even with the door open between the two rooms, the people coming in cannot see me and really don't know if I am in or not. If indeed they do want to see me, one of the secretaries comes and knocks and tells me with a smile that so-and-so would like to see me and I give the nod and in they come and sit down on the edge of a chair and act very impressed. The place is really set up to give you executive mystique. Of course there isn't all that much to do behind this big desk. The secretaries are the bods with work. I can dictate a letter in a few minutes that it takes Marian half an hour to do up right, you know, the correct number of carbons, the corrections going through all the layers of copies, the various envelopes with their addresses, etc. Then when it is all done properly the letters are neatly put on my desk for me to affix my thumbprint. Then back to the secretaries for folding, gumming, stamping, and driving over to the post office. I never open my post. Actually, I let Marian do it, even when I pick it up, so that she can see what is going on. The post is opened for me and laid neatly here on my desk. I am to come in just a bit later than the secretaries so they have already sharpened my pencils and put the post on my desk and got the Dictaphone outfitted with a new cartridge, etc. etc.!

There really isn't enough to do here. Sometimes I spend a whole day reading. And indeed there is an awful lot of stuff coming in that should be read. I find that I am quite ignorant of what all is going on in the Mennonite world, so I do spend a good bit of time catching up. In time, patterns will develop and I can become more selective in what I read. Then, too, to help fill the time I have begun writing. Marian says that Hershey never spent more than 20 hours per week in the office. What did he do? He left early to play tennis every evening. He took off one afternoon a week to play golf. He spent a lot of time running around town looking for auto spares. He was on a lot of committees that would take him away a day or two at a time. Marian seems to feel that when she had to work late at night to keep after and Hershey had spent the afternoon golfing that the difference between executive and secretary was getting to smack more of master and slave. But the truth of it is that most of the work is routine and Marian is more than able to keep things running. I get into it when there are letters or new procedures to write. We both think we need to get Marian another assistant. The present woman is pretty thick. If we had a better third member of the team, Marian wouldn't have to work so hard.

But back to my work. I believe fully 80 percent of my letters go to MCC—this office is basically MCC. I am then a brother to everyone else. I try to find out what Harold Miller is into and let him lecture to me. I smile and nod with Ron Moyer who runs Rosslyn Academy and needs no help at all from our office except to get their teachers' work permits. My brother David hasn't been in since I've come, but he too is entirely capable of taking care of everything he is into. He doesn't want me to bad mouth him to Bishop Kisare or to Salunga—so I'm to be positive about his activities! Of course Elizabeth Hostetter takes care of the Guest House with no more help from me than a fifteen minute once monthly prayer with her staff. Bertha Beachy takes care of Somalia. Charlie Bauman takes care of Sudan. Ethiopia corresponds only about the Eastern Africa Area Office Committee Meeting in October. Marian can see people off and on airplanes, as well as me. So, I am sort of enjoying myself, and I have just a little hunch that Hershey and Jacobs enjoyed themselves, too.

It is great to be with the family. The tremendous difference between here and Bukiroba is that no one intrudes. No one comes to our house to beg, borrow or steal. No one comes with great troubles that you must pronounce upon. And whenever we do things together it is just us. The other evening we were all sitting out on the lawn and no one was around to watch what we were doing. Of course, if I had a need to have people coming to me, that would probably make me feel doubtful about my self-image. But if people need to see me, they do it at the office. The great joy to me is that the family isn't intruded upon. At Bukiroba, even when the kids were home, people were demanding my attention. Now my attention isn't always pulled away. At Bukiroba, I would be sitting with the children, reading them a bedtime story when someone would "hodi." I would finish the story if the "*hodi*" wasn't urgent, but in any case, as soon as the story was over, I would need to give my undivided attention to whoever had come. Of course, there, whoever had come often hadn't come for any particular reason but just to talk. So Edith would pack the kids off to bed while I talked and listened. It would make Joyce sullen, and the younger kids would start roughhousing to create distraction.

Rebecca would forever try to talk to me when I had a guest, pulling my chin towards her, sticking a book between the guest and my face. I just thought yesterday—how nice it is not to be a missionary!

Last thing in Bukiroba before moving to Nairobi: Myron Augsburger and the EMC Alumni tour with Larry Nolt arrived. Augsburger quotes Bishop Kisare as saying this was the first group to come through there who wanted to be friends and not ask spying questions.

A day before their arrival I had gone over with a committee and the Bishop just what was to be done each step of the way. Then I got these instructions mimeographed. The Bishop greeted them when they got out of their vans, but he did not join them at the chapel where they ate. I passed out the schedule of events and made them familiar with it and then invited any questions they might have. Immediately Nolt began to ask the kind of questions that had been asked by that MCC Peace Section Elmer Neufeld tour. Bishop Kisare was frightened from the beginning that this was the sort of group that Augsburger was hosting. So I told Nolt not to ask such a question again, and told him why. At this point the Bishop came to the chapel door. I went out to greet him and invite him in. He was under such tension that his mouth was quivering. I could see that he was having a huge phobia: here were all these white people asking their spy questions, and I had taken them in and was filling them full of anti-TMC propaganda. That I was hiding from him what was going on by not having given him a schedule of events. So here I was running an anti-Kisare show and keeping him in the dark. He verbalized his distress by demanding to know where his copy of the program was. Implicit in how he asked it was his accusing me of completely ignoring and running the show as I liked. I again casually handed him several more copies of the program. He went off again without coming in to the chapel. As soon as I got the people packed off to their places, I went to find the Bishop and let him talk. I found him in his office, calm, and after fifteen minutes of chatting, his self-confidence was fully restored.

That is how high the tension runs when something like a Myron Augsburger group appears. So, when Kisare commended the group for their brotherhood, he was really confessing that he had thought otherwise, and he felt just a bit guilty for his earlier evil thoughts about them, and therefore really poured on the opposite sentiments. Of course, Kisare didn't know that the very questions he was afraid of were being talked about when he first came down to the chapel the day before.

Everything did pull off first rate. Everyone turned themselves inside out to show the Augsburger group a fine time. It is true, we would have been hard pressed to have taken any more than the four vans full that came. We did all in our power to help them to feel that TMC is a great place and they are doing the good Lord's will to keep supporting it with their contributions to Salunga. By their response I think we put our propaganda over pretty well.

Myron's concern was that Eastern Board should be giving EMC some direction on what sort of missionary is needed today. Myron would like EMC to be consulted in the recruitment of missionaries from among their students. Apparently Salunga recruits potential missionaries without getting a reading of the students from the college. Myron feels that Salunga has recruited some junk in recent years. He says Salunga says that they must take risks with people, but Myron thinks overseas isn't the place to take risks. He would sooner see the best come over here. I agree that Salunga could improve on its recruitment. I wondered if Myron would like to take Eastern Board under his wing!

One large brother with the group did not wash out his own shorts. He left them behind for the "natives." It would take a large "native" to fill them!

About our leaving Bukiroba for Nairobi. I don't know how much chicken and goat blood was shed, but it was a good bit, and blood, you know, is really the litmus test. We had chicken with the Bishop and Mama Kisare. And many times elsewhere. And fish and beef at Perusi's. The Bible school slaughtered a sheep for us and presented gifts of national cloth. The Bukiroba church district slaughtered a goat and made *ugali* out of ghee and presented gifts of basketry and an ivory-ebony cane. That ghee *ugali* is really a specialty. Only once before have I had it in all my years in Africa, and that was at a wedding. They stir the flour into heated ghee and sour milk, instead of water. It is really terribly rich, with a wonderfully delicate flavor. Then the night before we left, the central office with the executive committee slaughtered yet another goat, and offered prayers instead of gifts. Really, it had got to be too much. We were glad to slip away at dawn the next morning. Poor Mama Kisare was sobbing as we said good-byes at their house in the soft light of the early morning.

Another big thing for me was the opening of the church at Nyankanga just two weeks before we left Bukiroba. That filled my heart with joy. We visited almost every home in that district. Three or four times during the week I walked to Nyankanga because we didn't have enough transport or money to hire transport for everyone, so I felt that if I walk it will help others to walk too. We visited homes for four days. On Thursday night we had our first open-air meeting under a bright half moon. There was a great crowd and our loud speakers carried the message a half mile around. We showed pictures and had choirs sing. Then on Friday we had morning and afternoon meetings, with another large crowd that night. Saturday we repeated the morning and afternoon sessions. That night we left off the pictures, as people get drunk on Saturday and we ran the risk of trouble. But the people at Nyankanga had meetings in the church. The Bishop wasn't there. We had asked Nashon Nyamwino Nyambalya Mashaga (hope you recognize one of his names!) to chair the meetings for us. He is the evangelist who got the congregation going some 15 to 20 years ago. Now he is the pastor at Kisaka. So we had the evening service with lanterns in the church. He said it was packed out and a real revival broke out. (I heard about it all the next day.) On Sunday morning we had a really packed church, some 400 in all, with about half of those outside. Some 50 people stayed to be prayed for, which the Bishop did one at a time. That took something over an hour to do, but I felt the effort was important. I felt very good about that praying session. All of us ordained men put our hands on the head of each person while the Bishop prayed for his individual need. First the Bishop went around the room and asked each person to confess his sins and to say what his health problem was. Our house helper, Perusi, a gem of a woman, asked for her barrenness to be prayed for. She's been married six years. Dr. Weaver took out one ovary and tried unsuccessfully to put a probe through the other fallopian tube. Tears trickled down my nose as we prayed for her.

While we prayed inside the church, the whole crowd was eating. They had killed a cow and the local women brought *ugali*. After we got done praying there was a hot meat and *ugali* awaiting us. The leader told me that they gave meat away to the widows after everyone else had eaten.

I now must wear glasses! I thought I would wear them only for reading so got the cheapest frames. But now it seems easier to carry them on my face than to carry them in my pocket. I really don't like them. I keep feeling as though I am hiding behind a mask. I keep thinking that I must take them off when I talk to people.

I told you about our car? I'm sure I did. I left Hershey drive it the days we were together for my orientation to the new office. He drove it like a maniac. It certainly got robbed of its virginity. I found that I couldn't think well for up to an hour after I came to the office with him, something with the semicircular canals in the ears not being able to take all the spinning around the roundabouts.

I started a tomato garden, here in Nairobi!

September 1, 1976

Here's a copy of an article I am working on, entitle "Chocolate Brown."

It was in the Nairobi Airport, an Asian family with a European son. There among assorted other brown children was this white child. What caught my eye was his carrot-red hair. My fleeting eye jumped back for a second look. Whatever was going on here? Then it dawned on me that this Asian family had adopted the white boy; he will grow up to be a Patel or Singh or something foreign like that.

My response was one of anger. How dare the Asians adopt one of our children? They will teach him their language, their funny writing, their weird songs, their passion for shyster business, their religion. It was the religion idea that hit me the hardest—the kid will become a Hindu.

I nursed my anger and allowed it to guide my thoughts down that road to see where it would lead me. If I am angry with an Asian family adopting a white kid, how about all the children we middle class white Americans have been adopting all these years. Beautiful little children they are, those children we collect from Africa, Vietnam, Japan, China, Indonesia—the little brown kids with the dark hair and big solemn black eyes; we have been making them into Shenks and Leamans for quite a while now. What right have we to be doing that?

"We have rescued them," we say. Rescued them from poverty, a poverty whose fruits are hunger, nakedness, crime, ignorance, disease, and fear. They were abandoned, so we made them one of us; we are sharing with them our material blessings.

But haven't we missed something? On our last furlough we went to see and hear a rendition of the Martyrs' Mirror Oratorio. At the close of it I sat in my chair and wept, not for the pity of it, but for the glory. The mother who was burned at the stake, as interpreted by the actress that afternoon was, after she was burned, re-absorbed into the mass of witnesses surrounding the stake, so that her pain was lost to us as the living faithful absorbed and diffused it. Her children, too, became the children of the living faithful. There is a quality of experience and depth of understanding unique to the poor and oppressed. Our Anabaptist children, would we have wanted them taken from us and raised by the Catholics who were in government favor and who had all opportunity open to them? NO! Together we suffer and overcome.

On a Nairobi street I observed an old, tattered, dirty beggar lying propped against a wall, his begging bowl for the moment neglected. He had his little grandson with him, a plump little child of about eighteen months. This old man and this little child were laughing together. There was such joy in the old man's eyes as he held the little chap; life to life—old, poor, beggar's life sprung fresh in the form of the child with the joy, the bond between them. Should I take that child and make him a Shenk?

I think of the poor. They are the vast majority on this globe. I think of there being a grandeur and a wholesomeness in them. Life on our planet is a great cacophony of music—the poor along with the rich are part of the orchestra. It is we people, masses of us, each making the kind of music God has given us to put out. Much of it is pained and hungry, groaning and travailing, but orchestrated, many voices together, bound in common destiny. The poor have so little freedom; each is bound to his fellow in a web of life which determines his getting up and his going to bed and his doing. Swarms of people live within this web of poverty and circumstance and they make music, they know, they live.

The life of the middle-class white American also gives forth music of great joy and beauty. We have a global awareness. All knowledge is ours and we can through travel or books or film see and know all the beauty and wonder of the earth and beyond to other worlds. We are free to come and go as we wish; we glory in the joy of the open road with the wind in our faces. This, too, is music, a different section of the orchestra, to be sure, but part of the symphony of life.

But even as the life of the poor, in many ways, is a disgrace to us children of Adam and Eve, and those who have escaped from it would never wish to be poor again, even so the white middle class life is also, in many way, a disgrace to Him who breathed into us breath. The brown youth with black curly hair was sitting beside me on the back seat of a bus growling its ways across the vast Serengeti Plains filled with God's free cattle: wildebeest, zebra, ostrich, and everything. This lad told me, "It was easy for the white man to make up evolution because the white man lives in a make-believe world. All the places where the white man would touch life there is a bit of plastic. The white man's life is a cinema; it looks tremendous, but it is all fake." That is what he told me.

Nyabweki is plump and old and she has a glass eye that a missionary brought for her from Nairobi. She sells water from the public tap to the women in the *ujamaa* village at Bukiroba, Tanzania. She's a saint; you can tell by her beaming face. She's an elder in the Mennonite Church. I stop for a bit of banter as I go by her stool in the shade of the old garage from where she can keep her flesh eye on the goings on at the water tap. Nyabweki says, "Joseph, God will give you more children; you are still young and your wife is still young."

"But why would I want more children?" I ask.

"Joseph, you have no son; four daughters, but no son. God will give you a son."

"But my mother, our country is full. The people there judge me for having too many children already. Two, they say, is enough. They think I am greedy having four."

"Joseph, your country is sick. Your friend, my nephew, who drives the truck for the high school in town, tells me that in your country the students in your hospitals cannot learn how to birth babies because your women don't have babies anymore. Kishamuli, my nephew, tells me your hospitals abort more babies each year than are born in all of Tanzania. He tells me that in your country, the schoolrooms are no longer full because there are no more children. You tell me that your country is full of white people, but Kishamuli, your friend, tells me that your country isn't full with people; it is full with automobiles, but not full with people, not full with children.

"Joseph," she asks, "is it true what Kishamuli tells me, that in your country the women buy their children from the government instead of birthing them? Why do you white people who have medicine to keep you from birthing children, you who want us to use your medicine so we won't have children, why do you buy children from Vietnam?"

A prophet came to our home for super; he came with his wife and two children. "We don't have any more children," he tells me.

"I saw something unsettling in the airport," I said. I didn't want to tell him of my anger in seeing the Asian family with the adopted white boy. I was afraid he would point out how wrong I was to be angry. But he pried the story out of me.

"Joseph," he said, "you must look at the missionary tradition from which you have sprung. Take a careful appraisal and think through to their conclusions the beginnings you and your father have made." The prophet helped my thinking along.

Never in the history of the earth has an ideology been so successfully spread to the ends of the earth, as has the whole Western cultural, technological and religious package. As agents in doing this, Christian missions have been by far the most successful. The whole world now speaks the European languages, particularly English, French, and Spanish. European technology and commerce is by far the dominant theme in the world today. Even China has debts now to banks in the West. Millions of people around the globe have put their faith in Jesus Christ as part of this global wave of influence emanating from Western Europe.

Christian missionaries have so completely sold the concept of their superior culture and faith to the brown peoples of the earth that those peoples have offered their children to us for adoption. But this is only the beginning of mutual faith sharing between the races. The next step is for the brown races to adopt our white children. To resist this is to repudiate the process which Eastern Mennonite Board of Missions set in motion when they sent missionaries to Tanganyika decades ago.

The prophet jabbed his finger at me. "You may long for the comfortable compartmentalization of 'us' and 'them' but to cling to those forms is to deny your mission. It is to fail to become a part of the new age. It is to wither and die, clinging with nostalgia to something you destroyed. It is reactionary and will destroy the faith the brown races have put in you, for you to close off your life from their absorbing you as you did them. No, Joseph," he said, "you must embrace the new age and become part of it, for this is the kingdom."

September 27, 1976

We've had quite a shock here at the guest house. The part time receptionist committed suicide on Friday. It is quite a story, at least the parts we know about, and I am afraid that deep in the morass of circumstances we, too, are a contributing factor. Let me try to piece it together—at least what I know.

Evelyn Chunga has worked for us on a part-time basis for nearly two years. Before that, she worked at the Hilton. Why she left there, I don't know, but she was referred to us by a Mr. Okite, the editor of *Target* (a Christian magazine), a Luo from Rusinga Island with a lovely American wife. Evelyn was also from Rusinga, which forms the basis for her relationship to Okite. At the time Okite approached the guest house management about employment, Evelyn was already married to a Mr. Chunga who works for the attorney general. The Mennonites asked how Chunga felt about our taking Evelyn on as part-time hostess; he consented to our doing so.

Shortly thereafter, she bore a son and some months later ran away from her husband. He neither drinks nor smokes, so these were not contributory factors. It seems that it has to do with a second wife, or at least with his seeing other women. He seems to be something of a chauvinist who takes seriously the notion that wives are to stay at home and care for the children. But he, to his credit, did consent to her part-time employment, so as to keep up her exposure to the outside world and to give her some personal spending money. So she ran away, leaving the baby son at home. In due course, she was reconciled to her husband again and returned to live with him. Apparently their house is one of the good modern ones, not like anything in the slums.

Then some two or three weeks ago she ran away again, this time with the son and a maid. She went to Okite who found her room with another young woman who is working for *Target-Lengo* in company housing. This second woman got mad at Okite for imposing three more people into her cramped quarters. The next day Evelyn came to the office to ask us to take her on fulltime at the guest house. Because her Shs 500/= per month was not enough to support her, her son and a maid. She had told Elizabeth (manager of the guest house) that her husband had chased her away from home at knifepoint. So I acted on the assumption that he had thrown her out. She also wondered if we could provide housing for her. I told her that I would do what I could. She was a very attractive young woman, dangling golden earrings, skirt just mini enough to not be improper, hair neatly done, eyes shining and attractive—you know, a nice kid that you'd like to do something for.

Right after she left Okite called me to ask for the same two things: fulltime employment and a place to stay. That is how I found out that he was in hot water over having put her into this other woman's flat. I assured him that I would do what I could.

I went home to see Elizabeth about it. She felt that Evelyn didn't have the capacity to develop to the place where she could take over the management of the guest house. In any case, to take her on fulltime would really mean her replacing Elizabeth, and no one is suggesting at this point that Elizabeth retires. Of course we have no housing for her. When Evelyn came to the office I asked her if she would seek employment elsewhere if we could not take her on fulltime.

At this point I went on safari; when I got back I didn't make it a point to see Evelyn right away. Before I got to her with the news about no fulltime employment, her husband called me at the office. He wanted to know how it was that we had promised his wife fulltime employment provided she run away from him. He had also heard that we were making arrangements for her to go to Canada on a scholarship. He said that she had simply disappeared the other day and for five days he didn't know where she was. Then he found her at the *Target* house and thereupon got her father, who lives here in Nairobi (a man with three wives) and they brought her to her father's house. So I explained to him what I have written above and this seemed to mollify him somewhat. Then the next day he came to the office. Marian was out, so I spoke to him in the presence of Agnes, a secretary, because a Catholic priest was in my office going over some information concerning a couple we want to place at Komuge. The husband's word in the office was that he wanted us to fire her immediately from her job at the guest house. He felt that this job was giving her a means to escape from him. He said that she has been buying kitchen and household things with her money and putting these at friends' houses in preparation for the day she will run away to begin life anew. I told him that if she doesn't come for work, we will consider that she has broken contract and that will be the end of it. But he pointed out that she will not break contract on her own, and lawfully he cannot force her to quit. He pointed out Hershey had asked Chunga's consent before employing her, and he now is withdrawing his consent, and on that basis he insists that we terminate her employment. In fact, he wrote a letter to that effect which I got two days later in the post. But I told him that our agreement was that either party must give one month's notice. So we agreed that I would ask her to terminate her employment at the guest house as of 22nd October. I told him that what we really have here is a conflict of the modern and the traditional societies. In the traditional society he has full authority over his wife's activities, but the western way gives the wife full autonomy. I told him that I am a westerner but was born in Africa, so I think I understand the conflict. They were married in the traditional way with an exchange of bride wealth—no church or government wedding. He is Catholic; she Adventist.

After he left and I had finished with the priest, I put a letter on the belt, terminating our contract with Evelyn. When Marian roughed out the letter the next day, she felt she could have no part with such high handedness. So we were at an impasse and in casting about for help decided to call in a Mrs. Opio who is taking over the NCCK's literature department, and she was just down the hall that day, so I went down to see if she'd drop over. She came in about a half-hour later. She is really a cracking good woman, many years a headmistress of various girls' schools, etc. She is also Luo, as is Chungu. There was a good hour of exchange. She pointed out that the matter has to be solved by the relatives on both sides. Seeing that the girl is in her father's house is a good thing. She urged us as employers to call both the husband and wife to our office to talk over what we should do. I understood this to mean that solving the quarrel is not our place as employers, but rather to discuss together the husband's request that we terminate Evelyn's employment. Mrs. Opio was afraid Evelyn would not consent to come and suggested that we might try to surprise her into meeting Chungu. It turned out that that wasn't necessary; that same afternoon we got them together here in the office. I thought it a good omen that they both came so willingly, so almost eagerly.

I was really stumped as to how to go about this interview. We prayed first, and then I just monologued, spelling out my problem. I talked mostly to Evelyn, telling her what her husband was asking us to do and why. I have never seen an African blush as she did. But as we continued talking, her flush died away and it seemed like the initial angry response on both sides eased off. Marian was the only one who didn't say anything. The item Evelyn got the most heated about was her going overseas. She insisted that Chunga knew about it and that it was still in the works, to which he said, "So, there is something to it after all?" I have the impression also that on the various levels of communication she was saying that he threw her out and he was saying maybe he did in a moment of anger, as a sort of corrective measure, never expecting her to take him that seriously. But quickly he pointed out that they have no business telling us about their quarrel. That is a matter for the families. Then they crossed swords again over whether or not Okite was welcomed to the family palaver that had taken place a few days earlier, and if he was, why he didn't come. Obviously all along Chunga has been terribly angry with Okite. I guess I am naïve to suppose that twenty minutes of soft talk can resolve any of these deep angers. But at the time both calmed down and I really felt that we were maybe on the right track. Evelyn said that if Chunga wanted her to stop working she was ready to do that. We talked again about the modern-traditional conflict. Then Marian got the draft I had prepared and both of them read it and agreed that it was okay. So we parted with good feelings. Evelyn particularly said good-bye to both of us very warmly, and Chunga affirmed that he would take care of her and see her home.

That was on Tuesday afternoon. Thursday I left for Arusha by car to meet with the folks building the Arusha church. We had a good two days, and by the time I left, the plot of land already bore our footprints in the form of a partly constructed shed and a laid out church foundation. I got back to Nairobi. The next morning Elizabeth called me to ask that I come over before I did anything else. That was Saturday morning. I went over and found that Chunga had come at 7:30 to collect Evelyn's pay to be used towards funeral expenses. Elizabeth had him come back at 11:00, at which time I was there and talked with him.

It seems that on Thursday, Evelyn had a good day at the guest house. No deep strain was evidence. But on that day she picked up her notification of termination of employment, effective one month later. That night she had a violent quarrel with her father, or at least so it has been reported. It seems that her father was insisting that she go back to her husband. The husband had apparently initiated repayment of dowry, although this, I believe, had begun some time before. Possibly it was that the father was not able to repay the dowry and was therefore pressuring her to go back to Chunga, likewise insisting that if he has not given back the dowry she must return. I really don't know, but it does seem fairly certain that the quarrel had to do with her going back to her husband. So Friday she went to town and bought quite a supply of anti-malaria medicine. At noon she prepared food for the small children in the home, one of who was her son, and then drank a glass of milk. On the way into the house she had joked with the neighbors that today she is going to die. They just laughed with her over the comment. Then, after drinking the milk she locked herself into a room. This was around noon. At three some boys came home from school and asked where Evelyn was. Upon hearing that she had locked herself in a room, they became alarmed and broke the lock. She was already dead.

Right after this discussion with Chunga, Okite called me. From him I learned that he had been arranging a scholarship for Evelyn to go somewhere in Missouri for a short-term trainee course. He is arranging for four girls to go, one of whom is his sister, and one of whom is the girl in the *Target* house who had been assigned to take Evelyn in the first time. Okite speaks very softly on the phone and the phone has a buzz in it, making him terribly difficult to understand. He was saying something about one of the four being married according to Luo custom and that this could jeopardize her going, as the girls were supposed to be unmarried. He got loud, in explaining that Chunga had approved that his wife be sought for a scholarship to go overseas and that Chunga is lying in that he now claims to know nothing about it. He pointed out several times that he had taken Evelyn's name off the list at the point when Chunga rescinded his consent for her going. Okite pointed out that Evelyn was not completely innocent in the quarrel with her husband, that she is unstable and that although on the surface she seems happy and free, she becomes terribly angry at times. I told Okite that earlier it had seemed that Chunga was not very happy with him and that is why I had not consulted him at the time we called in Mrs. Opio. I was happy to assure him that in Evelyn's purse were letters to her parents accusing particularly her father of an unsympathetic attitude, which drove her to suicide. Also, there was a letter to Evelyn from her brother, urging her to run away from Chunga. Chunga had latched onto this letter as evidence of who it was who was mucking up his family. On Saturday morning he seemed no longer to be blaming us or Okite, but the brother. Of course, he let out that her whole family is accusing him, and he is scrambling to protect himself. "She ran away to her father and she DIED in HIS house!" I can still hear him saying it. The poor chap was in something of a dither.

So, I have had to repent. I think the best advice came from Boaz, the head of the guest house staff. He said that in a matter like this nothing should be hurried. Had I only had such good sense a few days earlier and told Chunga to cool it for a month. But I was anxious to have the problem over with and worked through the procedures in record time. Chunga said Evelyn will be buried at Rusinga as soon as the police release the body. He assured me that a memorial service would be held somewhere in the city, but maybe given the circumstances of the death, their Adventist-Catholic twist, he might not find any place to hold such a service.

November 3, 1976

I want you to read several paragraphs of a long letter I wrote Hershey and Jacobs at Salunga:

"The notion of using foreigners to prevent the emergence of an indigenous opposition party is not a new one. Nebuchadnezzar used it. The sultans of Turkey used it. As did Idi Amin in Uganda. Our bishop in Tanzania also uses foreigners to keep legitimate political opposition from emerging in the church. It happened first to me when we graduated our second batch of theological college students. Toward graduation day it became clear that there was no intention of taking those students seriously. After graduation they were to go home—period. It fell to me to impose that decision on the students. They told me they wished for an African principal because then never would that principal accept so meekly the decision of the church's executive committee.

"Now to the Kenya Church. The Bishop allowed Daddy to be relatively free in the Kenya church for these past five years. But the price he exacted from him was that Daddy not allow to emerge a responsible administrative structure there. Every time the church would get all fired up about something, they would bring it to Daddy, and he would take it to the Bishop, and then the Bishop would chew him out like he was a stupid little boy. This happened often. Once the Bishop chewed out Daddy for an hour out on the porch until Daddy was so weak that he simply said nothing.

"It is possible to ordain people who do not have administrative aptitude provided you have a missionary between him and the people. It is significant, for example, that when the Bishop asked for a small advance to cover expenses until you get the budget worked out, that all he asked for was wages for three people. He didn't mention the telephone, the electricity, the post office box, church work transport, etc. It is also significant that he did not know what arrangement had been used to pay those three men up to now. He can get away without knowing those things because there are missionaries between him and the people who do that stuff.

"Now David (my brother) has been allowing the Nairobi Church Council's voice to be heard by the Bishop. He has done it in a "safe" way because he does not act as their messenger. He sets up the situation so the African speaks to African. The Bishop knows he cannot use David because David will never allow himself to get between. So, of course, the Bishop makes all the nice sounds when he is with the Nairobi Church Council. But that is a safe one because he doesn't need to take them very seriously. None of them are ordained. The real power lies in Migori. Arwa is to be the guardian of the Bishop's authority in Kenya. Of course he lacks the acumen to succeed in that, so it will be necessary to have a missionary to prop him up. That missionary is very obviously Joseph C. Shenk. It was an excellent thing that Joseph got moved to Nairobi just at the time when it was necessary to find a replacement for Clyde Shenk. A month ago Nashon Adera told me that it is the Bishop's plan for Joseph to handle the money from the States (for Kenya). We are to receive the money from Salunga and pay the monthly checks to South and Central Nyanza. In effect, they want our office to act as their clerk for disbursements of money. That way, Nashon never needs to even know how the balances stand. All he needs to do is make his requests, and he will get money as I have it to give. I will, in effect, run that church very much as my dad has done. The price I will pay for that kind of influence is to keep the people there from getting at Nashon or the Bishop.

"I can hear Hershey saying, 'But Joe. Refuse!! Don't just sit there on your cotton-picking ass and say "Yes, yes" to that Bishop!!' It isn't that simple. I don't believe a person can change his approach to an issue without losing his credibility. In order to survive at Bukiroba, I adopted a certain way of going at problems. I have a certain special relationship with the Bishop, cultivated over those twelve years of relating to him. You cannot be serious when you ask me to suddenly change my approach to him. It is tricky enough moving to Nairobi without its going to my head, without my consciously setting about altering a relationship forged over many years through the absorption of much pain, a relationship which now allows me to speak more intimately with the Bishop than can most.

"What I must do, if I am to survive in Nairobi, is to establish such structures in which to work which will shield me from being misused. I had got pretty good at playing this game, even at Bukiroba. I, as do all good Africans, always accept an assignment but allow circumstances to intrude in such a way as to prevent my getting emasculated by that assignment. The danger in doing this is to appear to be "tricky," a condition which I detest.

"This is why I pled with you to set up a structure that will protect me. The structures set up between Fraternal workers and the Tanzania Mennonite Church are such that the missionary has little room for playing the game any differently than my dad has been forced to play it. For years I have been helping my fellow missionaries to live creatively within those perimeters, or at least I have considered it my duty to try to help them to do so. Whether or not I have succeeded I have no way of knowing. But it means that when Daddy and Mother come complaining to me, I have always had to put such an interpretation on it as to help them cope with the situation. One dare not allow the missionary to look at his condition in its stark reality. As soon as he does so, he leaves. Witness the doctors at Shirati, which makes my heart cry; my responsibilities to them was to try to help them live creatively within the perimeters of the situation, and my responsibility to approach them on that level prevented them from seeing how painful my own struggle had been or how sympathetic I was to their impossible situation.

"I had forged a creative way for me and my wife and family to survive at Bukiroba. I managed that one, and I am truthful in saying that we as a family enjoyed Bukiroba. But it is one thing to guide your family into that kind of discipline and quite another to bring all the Mennonites in Nairobi into that kind of discipline. I have sensed that this place was pretty apprehensive about my coming here. I imagine people wondered how much I was going to impose Tanzania Mennonite Church on them.

"Marian and I spent half a day talking about Bishop Kisare's wish that I handle the Kenya Mennonite Church budget. I suppose Salunga will sell me down the river. They'll say: 'Who can help the Kenya church to emerge if you don't? You have been brought to the palace for such a time as this. You know Andera cannot administer this budget. You had better help them over the hump.' If I refuse, they'll tell Kisare that Joseph refuses to administer the money and Kisare will come to Nairobi and ask me, 'What in the world is the matter with you? Has Nairobi gone to your head? Don't you know who put you in Nairobi? Now why have you got so stubborn and refused to do what we ask of you?' I told Marian that then I will be finished and that the only way to maintain credibility with that church will be to accept. After accepting such an arrangement I am afraid that my home will become a meeting place like Daddy and Mother's house was at Migori. At any time someone will show up needing to be fed and lodged. Every time there is some issue about money, Andera will show up in Nairobi. The Bishop, too, will be here more and more often. Since I am administering his money for him he will always be my guest. I told Marian, 'If they sell me out, I will insist that two rooms be kept permanently vacant in the guest house for such emergencies.'

"But you brethren at Salunga seemed to see my problem right away and had it minuted that I am not to do anything for any one church on behalf of the Area Office without the express approval of the Council. I was so happy I walked on air.

"Now you tell me that $600 is to pass through my hands; I got frightened. I felt cornered because I saw no way to undo that precedent. Like a frightened animal I felt cornered. I asked you to go back to Kisare and say, 'Sorry, Joe won't do that after all; we must make another arrangement.' Kisare will know that it is because I have refused and my prescience will be right on target. If I go tell him myself that I will not do that, I remain in the same position, only a better one because I will state my case in such a way as to allow me room for maneuver. In the end, I chose the lesser of two evils and accepted to tell him myself.

"So, Bishop Kisare is at the gates, more so than he was when you turned the Nairobi Office over to me. It is a precarious assignment. We can go at it in something of two ways. We can fight a Jack Shellard sort of retrenchment which will build up such a dam of resentment that it will all be swept away, or we can creatively interact and help to emerge something of a mutually respectful community. To do the latter is going to take delicate diplomacy, and only by God's grace can it be pulled off.

"Weren't you anxious to have me in Nairobi because you felt I was sufficiently half-caste to be able to help happen peacefully what eventually must happen? But if you want me to pick up after you, to bring full circle the office you started, then isn't it necessary that I must be part of the decision-making process? You will say, 'But Joe, Bishop Kisare, Nashon, and we all decided together . . . . ' Yes, you decided something fundamental about this office without consulting me. You know, you have made me feel guilty at times about how I have needed to encourage the TMC missionaries to accept the servant stance. You say it is demeaning to make people be servants, and in a way you are right, yet that is the relationship you just handed to me.

"So I am sure it will not surprise you for me to confess that in the quietness of our night at Amboseli, I concluded that my position here is really not tenable. The position of a half-caste standing between two races is really not a tenable one because each race makes automatic assumptions about him which are not valid for the game he has been called on to play. It would be much better to have a Tanzanian pastor or a Salunga bureaucrat to be here because then we could carry on the war in the traditional manner and nobody would have any misconceptions."

November 26, 1976

I was quite stunned some months ago when I got a phone call from a woman completely unknown to me, and me to her, asking if I as a Mennonite would do the Thanksgiving message for the Nairobi American community. She was trying to get a cross section of the American personality in the city, and it struck her that a Mennonite might be something unique to listen to. I am afraid I was a bit selfish, in not passing that morsel on to some other gifted Mennonite in the city. I just accepted to do it myself. So enclosed please find my poor effort. So far I got only one bad reaction to it, this from a dear English woman who chided me afterwards for making so much of the horrid London merchants. I begged pardon, pointing out that I could have used any frame of reference, but chose that one as it was so far back in history. So we both had a laugh. The best I got was the wife of the leader of the U.S. delegation to the current UNESCO conference going on in Nairobi. She wanted a copy to show her husband, as he was busy and couldn't come. So I gave it to her, and she got it photocopied and returned it with a nice note.

Life has been a bit rough for me these months, particularly in light of such matters as the suicide, the dismissing of the current secretary, the row with Salunga. Anyway, I am beginning to come out of the cloud.

Thanksgiving Sermon
(Nairobi Baptist Church, 25 November, 1976)

My fellow Americans, we have met here today to give thanks to God for His many blessings to us. We certainly have plenty for which to give thanks. We tire of the litany of superlatives—most powerful economy on earth, the mightiest war machine that ever existed, and so on. Our soil is among the most productive in the world. Our farmers are increasingly called upon to make up food shortages around the globe. We are the most traveled people ever to have existed—5,000 of us in Kenya alone. As a people, we are scattered across the earth, influencing in many ways what is going on. Our wealth has given us unparalleled educational opportunities, even our physically deformed and mentally retarded have many opportunities for dealing creatively with their disabilities. We are full and lack nothing. Our poverty is the rest of the world's wealth. Some of the bounty even gets a bit ridiculous with dozens of varieties of breakfast cereals on our supermarket shelves, scented plastic bags for our garbage, and diet food for our overly-fat dogs.

With all this blessing and largesse, and we struggled to achieve it, I don't deny that, mind you; it would be indecent of us not to give thanks. Appropriately, we have institutionalized a special day to remind us to be thankful. An uninformed anthropologist looking on might conclude that we are anxious to appease the gods of bounty so they continue to keep us rich and well fed. We give the gods a day to show them we are not arrogant about the largesse we enjoy. And yet, I am sure that you, my fellow Americans, know that there is more to what we celebrate today than a eulogy to our wealth and success. The day we celebrate was born through tragedy, a tragedy of human experience which taught those Pilgrim ancestors of our that when peoples reach across to help each other without ulterior motives, that this is a happening so precious that when we witness it we need to pause and give thanks.

The other day I went to the United States Information Library on Government Road, Nairobi, to search again for what had happened to bring about that first Thanksgiving celebrated by the Pilgrims. I think Nairobi not a bad place from which to look back through the centuries to that thin, precariously situated little colony on the New England shore. We, too, today are foreigners in a strange land, as were they. Looking at history requires a certain detachment from the soil of our childhood, from the things we assumed were the natural construct of human existence. In our own "expatriateness" we can maybe understand a bit better how it was 355 years ago.

These refugees landed on a foreign shore—a winter landing with only the cold, blustering hospitality of the forests to welcome them. There were 24 families that had crowded onto the tiny Mayflower, plus numbers of others who had been pressed upon the Pilgrims by the moneylenders in London who had financed the voyage. These "strangers" cared nothing for the cohesive social structure that bound the Pilgrims into a community of interdependent faith—they were a cancer of dissension in their midst. The voyage had gotten off to a late start because of the unseaworthiness of the ships the London merchants had sold them. After a false start, one of the two ships, the Speedwell, had to be abandoned and everyone packed together into the remaining one. This delay insured that they would land in the New World at the beginning of winter. It was a November landing, and 'ere long the settlers began to sicken and die. By spring, of the 24 women, 20 were dead, leaving only four. Of the 24 men, 13 were dead, leaving only 11. Only a few able-bodied men and boys were left to plant the crops.

Have you ever planted crops? These few surviving Pilgrims knew nothing about the business. All of them were from the working class, town laborers, people who knew how to work, but who knew nothing of the soil. The *Ujamaa* village in Tanzania where I lived for the past number of years required that every person has his own *shamba*. Now I am from rural American stock, and I have worked many summers as a farm laborer. But farming with a hoe in a foreign land is not the same as farming with a tractor at home. Every year in Tanzania I worked mightily with my hoe, turning up the hard soil, planting corn, beans, tomatoes, spinach—but it never amounted to much, never more than a few weeks of eating for my family. These Pilgrims who had no agricultural background were faced with the task of growing enough food to last a year. They would have failed had it not been for two natives of the New World who came to their aid.

Two Indians came out of the forest to help the dying settlement, to cup the flickering flame of life with their protective knowledge before it could be completely blown out by some new adversity or ignorance. The astonishing thing for the Pilgrims was that these Indians, Samoset and Squanto, spoke English. It is like finding people on Mars who speak American! If we probe that one, how it was that Indians coming out of the forest could speak English, we get to the secret of the meaning of the Thanksgiving we celebrate today. Those two Indians had been captured by British soldiers and made slaves on their war ship. How they escaped, the history books do not tell us. What we know is that there on that inhospitable shore two strands of humankind met, both of whom had been much defrauded and taken advantage of. These two peoples, the dying group of refugee Pilgrims and the escaped slaves, must have recognized in each other brothers in the same human family, a recognition born through their common experience of tragedy and misfortune. Here were the weak and poor and downtrodden of the earth (weren't those refugees known as pilgrims?), these dispossessed reaching out to each other and helping each other. It is out of this symbiosis that survival springs and from such a relationship a thankful heart is born. Something in our subconscious tells us that those Indians and Pilgrims were onto something. This is why we have preserved the myth. Remember how the story gripped you when you were a child in school? There is something in what happened on that rocky shore that tells us how we might survive today. There is something there that points the way for us in 1976.

Our American culture is so success-oriented that we look at everything through that prism. I got the feeling when I was a child that with this Thanksgiving celebration the Pilgrims had insured their continued prosperity. Our natural American inclination on hearing how the Indians and Pilgrims met each other and did the decent, human thing towards each other is to assume that the next chapter will be a big success story in the great American tradition. But what of those Indians? Did Providence smile on them and bring their people to glory and power and wealth? We all know the subsequent history of the American Indian. And what of the Pilgrims? Under the leadership of their new leader, William Bradford (the first, Brewster, was among the dead of the first winter), they took on themselves the responsibility to repay the entire debt contracted to the London merchants who had financed the voyage. Over half of the shareholders were dead, and the "strangers" put onto the Mayflower by the moneylenders had absconded, but those remaining agreed to pay the whole debt. Thereupon the London merchants proceeded to alter the records so that in the end the survivors paid back far more than the original debt. In fact, these Pilgrims never did survive in what we call the American tradition. They continued poor. Everywhere new more prosperous settlements sprang up around them, their more powerful, aggressive and successful neighbors.

So, you see, the celebration in the first place wasn't about prosperity. It was a thankfulness that God had kept their settlement from extinction through the gift of the Indians, a gift of knowledge and friendship. As a child I used to wonder if the Pilgrims in all their puritanical clothing were embarrassed sitting at table with the Indians. (Remember how the pictures used to show the Indians in loincloths and the Pilgrims in those high hats with silver buckles on their shoes?) How could they have been embarrassed? For they realized that survival meant interdependence, each for the other and neither for selfish advantage. This is what they were being thankful about, their survival through that symbiosis expressed physically in their sitting at table together.

Did you know that it was President Abraham Lincoln who first decreed that Thanksgiving should be an annual American holiday, that it was first so celebrated in 1863, a few days after Lincoln delivered the Gettysburg address? Isn't there something of the same truth here with Lincoln and the slave blacks that we glimpsed between the Pilgrims and the slave Indians? How was it that a man had done so right a thing in reaching out to the oppressed and to have instituted as a symbol of reconciliation "a day of thanksgiving and praise to our beneficent Father," that this good man should have so shortly afterwards been shot dead? The myth of Lincoln persists in our tradition as a powerful emotional magnet. There is something in our subconscious that tells us he was pointing the way for our survival.

To be a success has been the American dream. We think this is the American hope, to be a success is to be most completely fulfilled as a human being. Yet the single-minded pursuit of this dream makes us beasts. Increasingly, success, individual success, in our world today means someone's failure. If I am taller than everyone else, it is most likely because I am standing on somebody and in so doing I demean both myself and the chap I am standing on. Success we have in America, but what is happening to our communities? What is happening to our homes? What is happening to our children? Our social fabric is unraveling in the midst of all the bounty.

The London merchants were successful and prosperous, but in part, that success came through selling the Pilgrims rotten ships and multiplying their debts. We wish the London merchants had been more just, but in spite of that, a beautiful Thanksgiving took place over there in New England. However, what is happening today is that the Pilgrims of the world have been learning how to stop being Pilgrims and start being London merchants too. People the world around have learned the lesson that in order to succeed and be prosperous, they must be London merchants. We don't have many Pilgrims left, poor we have, true enough, but not Pilgrims. They are poor learning how to be London merchants. And this is the tragedy of our world today. It is the despair of our development agencies and of our international bodies. Prince Philip, as reported in the *Daily Nation* last week, puts it that the whole world is headed for violence, a violence, I would add, which the success motif has taught us.

Just a few days ago Jimmy Carter's home church in Plains, Georgia, debated in closed session whether or not to accept blacks into membership. It was raining during the debate. Standing outside in the churchyard in the rain waited the Rev. Clennon King for the verdict. What was said in that meeting the world will never know. But during three hours of debate it was decided to no longer exclude people from membership because they are black. When Jimmy Carter and his wife came out onto the steps of the church following the decision, Rosalyn was crying softly. This is that Lincoln and the Pilgrims were all about. The man standing quietly in the rain, the woman softly weeping. Anywhere in our world today when we see people coming together, reaching out to each other across the fissures that fracture our earth, meeting in that spirit of mutual concern without ulterior motive for selfish advantage, let us then give thanks and praise to our beneficent Father, for it is in this spirit alone that our world can long endure.

December 23, 1976

I'm writing from Khartoum. I've just had a long walk alone down at the Nile. On the way back had a cup of coffee at a sidewalk café a block from our hotel. It is morning and there is a cool wind coming off the river. This bank has a high stone wall containing the river with a highway running along the top of the embankment. Rows of huge fig trees line both sides of the highway, so enormous that they join at the top, making a canopy over the road. The coffee is really unique. The coffee sellers have great round trays with double rows of coffee pitchers (in the shape of an erect phallus) all around the edge of the tray, nestled among charcoal bits, which keep the coffee on a constant boil. In the middle of the tray is a tin can full of sugar and a stack of tiny porcelain cups. The vendor fills the cups half full of sugar and hands that along with a coffee pitcher to you. There is enough coffee to fill the cup twice and amazingly the sugar dissolves into it without stirring. You really get a high off the stuff. I think two of those pitchers could give you a heart attack! I bought one of the phallic-shaped pitchers to take back to Nairobi.

Last night we heard there were traditional dances over in Omdurman, so we went. The national theatre is unroofed, so we had Venus and Jupiter overhead. It turned out to be a school competition with a 17-point program, having lots of items as fillers between the 17. One continuous round of lengthy skits, readings, dances, jazz bands, etc. etc. After five hours of sitting, we finally went home to bed.

The first day we were here we went over to Omdurman to walk around in the bazaar. Rows of each kind of thing clustered in one place: gold, silver, ivory, hides, cloth, spices. The alleyways were putrid with the odor of rotting urine and clogged with honking horns, scabby horses pulling huge over-loaded carts, and scrubby donkeys jittering along under their solemn owners sitting cross-legged on top. It was there that I bought the coffee container. None were among the heaps of tin ware. So I tried to buy it from the vender himself. Soon a great crowd of white-clad, white-turbaned men crowded around, trying to figure out what this white man wanted.

December 30, 1976

Greetings from the old place—Bukiroba. We spent two nights camping at Seronera on our way here for the annual general church conference. Never had I had so much trouble with flat tires as on that trip—and I had no pump or patches. First, a half-worn out Michelin tire on the back went low and before I noticed it, I hit one of the thousands of rocks scattered all over the road, and shredded the tire. We put on the spare and drove the few remaining miles to Keekorok. But they had no tires or tubes, so we went on. About five miles further, the other back tire was going flat. Fortunately we met a chap with a pump, so we pumped it up and rushed back to Keekorok. It turned out there that the steel-belted radial tire was worn in such a manner as to have the tiny hair wires coming through on the inside and chewing tiny holes all over the tube. So we took an old tube, slit it and used it to cover the inside of the tube. We then put four patches on holes on the tube for Shs 45/=, more than the price of a new tube! That contraption got us to the Serengeti gate and Klein's Camp. By the time we got through the red tape there (four vans full of tourists were being processed) the same tire was flat again. One van gave me a lift to Lobo Lodge where I found that three of the four patches had come off. They had van tubes there, so I bought one for Shs 40/= and stretched it over the rim. Then the tourist driver who had brought me to Lobo took me back to Klein's Camp for Shs 150/=, unreceipted! So by 5:30 we were set up again. Off we dashed for Seronera. Just at dark, somewhere between Lobo and Banagi we came on a desperate party of Asians in an old Land-Rover with a dry radiator. All their drinking water too had been put in the leaky radiator. We had a big plastic jerry tin full of water, so we filled up everything for them and off we dashed again for Seronera and then for Lobo. We got into the camping area at 7:30 and used the headlights to set up the tent. When we got out of the car we found that the spare tire we'd put on now going flat. Within ten minutes it had no air at all. We breathed a prayer of thanks that we hadn't had to sleep in the car. The next morning I borrowed another pump and got into the workshops and got fixed up. Since then we had no more trouble.

On the way out of Serengeti we followed the western corridor and came upon a huge herd of wildebeest. There had been lots of rain and the grass was still young and bright green. And by the side of the road was a whole family of bat-eared foxes—nine of them, soaking up the first rays of the morning sun.

When we got near the black cotton flats we met a truck and two cars coming the other way which stopped us and declared the road impassable. So we turned around to go back and came out the Ikizu way. But it was three in the afternoon and after a few miles we stopped and looked at each other. We had a tent and plenty of food and water, and we had a hoe and *panga* and we have some know how, so we turned around again. Then we met a Land-Rover with four young Europeans in it who declared the sun hot and the mud deep and the road impassable. But even they failed to turn us back again. Once we got down to the mud flats we found the day's sun had dried things off pretty well. About four miles in we found a 504 Peugeot station wagon with a man and a woman stuck in shallow water at a place they had tried to go around a mud hole in the road. He was trying to pull up grasses with his bare hands to put under the wheels! Soon a VW with four American men showed up—also going to Seronera. So we pushed the stuck Peugeot out and then watched the rest of us careening through the water. We got home to Bukiroba without further trouble.

1977

January 31, 1977

Sorry I used a letterhead in my last letter. Being here has not gone to my head! I am not General Director at all. I am something of a coordinator. But the letterheads have been printed, so I use them, and furthermore, my committee hasn't told me yet just what they do want me to be called. It is interesting to me that even the missionary community here in Nairobi can't seem to see that my role has altered considerably from that of the previous director. He was Mr. Eastern Mennonite Mission Board. I am the chap designated to carry out what the committee, also as yet without a name, of Eastern African churchmen plus the mission board wants me to do. For the most part that means taking care of the missionary and MCC personnel. It also means having a sort of chairman role reference the Eastleigh Fellowship Centre, the Bible Correspondence course, and the Somali literacy project. But brother David executes these three, and he is happy to have me play something of an observer role. So, as "General Director of Mennonites in East Africa" I am very harmless, I assure you.

March 3, 1977

Thanks so much for sending that biography of T.E. Lawrence (of Arabia), particularly his twenty-seven points on how to deal with Arabs. The Bantu and Luo are not nearly so volatile as Arabs. But I found Lawrence's analysis excellent for putting form to my Musoma and Bukiroba experiences. I think he has done a document on how a highly-trained expatriate might function anywhere. Much of what he says has universal application. I went through, marking the points which I could especially respond to. Just for feedback, let me point out a few that I felt were especially good.

Point 3: Deal only with the top. I often told the people at Shirati that they should deal with the man who has the power and not go around shouting at the small fry. When the doctors finally did go to the Bishop with their concerns, they broke Point 4: Strengthen the leader's prestige at your own expense. Point 5: Keep in touch with your leader; know when to be around and when to get lost. I was amazed the other day to hear that a new missionary hasn't yet had a cup of tea with the Bishop! Point 10: Call the leader by a special name is hard for some to do. It means calling the Bishop "Baba Askofu," and doing it naturally. Point 11: On sandy foundations: terribly true, even for me who was born here. You let them say that you should take out citizenship, etc., but you always act as though you understand your place perfectly, that of a guest and stranger. "If you succeed you will have hundreds of miles of country and thousands of men under your orders, and for this it is worth bartering the outward show." Point 15: They will admire your good craftsmanship, but you will never become a part of their community that way. In time, return a gift with interest, Point 16: Good, and his advice not to let them ask you for things. In Point 18: Lawrence makes a remarkably insightful statement when he says, "Complete success, which is when the Arabs forget your strangeness and speak naturally before you, counting you one of themselves, is perhaps only attainable in character: while half success (all that most of us will strive for—the other costs too much) is easier to win in British things, and you yourself will last longer, physically and mentally." Point 23 is excellent, more so for Somalis than Bantu and Luo. "The open reason that Bedu (Arabs) give you for action or inaction may be true, but always there will be better reasons left for you to divine . . . . Experience of them and knowledge of their prejudices will enable you to foresee their attitude and possible course of action in nearly every case."

Reading this bit of wisdom by T.E. Lawrence helps to put into structured form for me the reason that I was so emotionally distressed over the time we moved to Nairobi and the previous administrators made the decision about routing Migori (Kenya) money through me. Can you imagine Lawrence suddenly being put by the British at an executive desk to handle their relationships to the Arabs in traditional style? Lawrence's credibility with the Sheiks and Sheriffs would have been completely shattered, and possibly he would not have cared because after all, he was something of a fifth columnist. But my relationship to Bishop Kisare and company was honest, and I like to think that Lawrence's was too, that he was distressed when the British double-crossed the Arabs at the end of the war. I despair of ever having Salunga come to an understanding of how it works. I doubt if any of Lawrence's generals ever understood what was going on between him and the Arabs. When I got mad at Salunga they assumed that I see KMT as a bad thing, something I am sick and tired of and want to have nothing to do with and so they complied and cut me out of the relationship. So I find that at this point Salunga uses this office not at all in its relationship to the churches here. And I suppose that is quite understandable. If you are going to use Lawrence in an executive office in Damascus, you must use him for matters that don't relate to Arabs. But I would still think that with the definition of this office not being one with administrative authority in the churches might leave room for using it in the Lawrence style. But if you haven't understood what Lawrence was doing, then of course, you have no need for an office in his mold, and you had best just bypass it.

Through this reflective correspondence we've been carrying on for these past nine years I have been able to come to understand myself and my role, perhaps not anywhere near a full understanding, but at least an outline. But I have not had any of this sort of thing with the home mission board. Should I even try to work on dialogue with them?

We climbed Mt. Kenya. Eighteen of us went out to the river lodge at Naro Moru and then only thirteen had a go at the mountain. Five got to the top. That mountain is more beautiful than Kilimanjaro. It has a whole mass of peaks; the center one is quite easy to climb. The altitude and miles walked are much less than Kilimanjaro, making it not so great an exercise. This time it got terribly cold at night, about ten degrees at the tent, and zero on the mountain peak. Joyce and Dianne slept with me in my tent. I got them hot chocolate in bed the next morning before setting out on the mountain.

I'm sure you want a word on Luwum. From quite reliable sources we have it that Amin (dictator of Uganda) determined on his execution following the writing of an open letter to the president by the Ugandan Bishops. We are circulating that letter, and it has a real Anabaptist flavor about it. It seems that two cabinet ministers refused to countenance his executions, so they too were marked for killing. The three were taken to the place of execution and the soldiers ordered to shoot them, shot only the cabinet ministers. Thereupon Amin personally shot the Archbishop in the mouth and chest, three bullets. He then shot the soldiers as well, those who refused to execute the Archbishop. Amin then ordered the three bodies mangled by a vehicle, but again the soldiers refused to mangle the Archbishop's body. All were secretly buried.

The Tanzania border with Kenya remains closed, with severe implications for our building the hospital at Mugumu.

March 11, 1977

These years I've been philosophizing on what it means to be a missionary. I was always looking at what was happening and trying to understand it for my own therapy. That T. E. Lawrence article was helpful. He was able to analyze what was happening to him in Arabia and hang it on to a philosophical framework which gave meaning to the whole of it. It is the sort of exercise I wish I could do reference our missionary involvement in Africa today. Studying Lawrence helps things to fall together for me.

In his preamble, Lawrence qualifies his observations considerably. But I think most of what he says applies to any highly trained person in a primary society. The shading is different but the gut business is the same.

If we are to serve as Lawrence did, it must spring from an honest commitment to live that way for the sake of the Kingdom. If one serves as Lawrence did, in order to eventually control things and to get things to go one's own way, then one is deceptive and acting out of character for a Christian. But if you serve as he did (for us out of commitment to the church) and your role as a resource, if what you do springs from a bedrock of truth, if you really do respect the decisions of the African structures and you are genuine in your self-effacement, then that approach is valid and Christian and worthy of a missionary.

We have a feeling that churchmen in the younger (African) churches take themselves far too seriously and that they need to be knocked down occasionally, so they don't get bigheaded. This is a false approach because firstly, the missionary is an outsider and as such is able to see much more clearly the petty devices employed for status maintenance in the society to which he is alien than he can in the society he came from. Secondly, the most fundamentally, it is wrong to feel it necessary to knock authorities down a couple of pegs, because God alone can speak to a man's heart and show him his need. When we knock people, the whole colonial heritage (not to mention simply human nature) rises up to completely obscure the issue, and the situation becomes worse instead of better.

Thirdly, missionaries feel that if they are to be resource people they should influence the decision-making process. When wrong decisions are made they feel they must speak up. But I have always felt that mature, responsible, decision-making machinery will never emerge if the missionary overtly influences the process. Many examples could be given. Of course a good missionary does influence, but not in an overt way. As Lawrence points out in No. 4: "The less apparent your interference the more you influence."

I've seen enough of what it costs to be a good missionary that frequently when I encourage someone to be one, I have a nightmare. Recently I wrote to the Elzingas, asking them why they don't come back to Garissa. That night I dreamed they were executed. One loses something, especially a Westerner, when you subject yourself to discipline, but you gain something, too. I felt deeply affirmed when Bishop Kisare said of me at a farewell party at Nyabange: "From among the missionaries, Joseph has always taken me seriously." (*Hakukosa kuniheshimu na kuthamini maneno yangu.*)

March 28, 1977

I'm writing from Wajir. (Recently I had to fly down to Dar es Salaam. Saw Castro in the back seat of President Nyerere's Mercedes on my way into town!) Two days later I left with Bertha Beachy and two Somali men, to do a swing through North Eastern Province. We shot up past the western flank of Mt. Kenya, dripping down on to the plains at Isiolo. From there we cut across 120 kms of barren land by dirt road to Garba Tula, where we spent a night with the Risslers. That school is the craziest thing you ever saw! Garba Tula is a depression in an ancient riverbed that always holds surface water—fresh water. There must be a big lake underground there and some years back a little town grew up with a Methodist boarding school for primary grades. The Somali *shifta* (bandits) depopulated the place and destroyed the emerging infrastructure. Then the Germans came along with their money through the Kenya Christian Council and put up an ultra-modern primary and secondary boarding school beside this water pan. Each day from ten to two, great herds of goats, sheep, cows, and camels congregate at the pan for water and rest in the shade of big thorn trees. They then disappear again—completely—into the thorn scrub. And here is this modern school complete with gas cookers and European style flush toilets. The two which I saw were choked with human waste and cardboard, so that all around the school bush is littered with sun-parched bits of human excrement. Petrol is 120 kms to the west or 90 kms to the east! The local shop sells beans, rice, and sugar. To make matters worse, this pan is about three miles off the main road. Everything, including the kids, must be trucked in. It is in a Borana area, but well over half the kids are from up on Mt. Meru—Kikuyu and Embu people. This makes the locals livid because they consider the schools theirs, yet they cannot supply enough students. The place is co-ed with a single stream throughout. An Olympic size enclosed swimming pool is in the plans. The Headmaster is an American. Recently his assistant was nearly killed in a local tribal brawl.

But the fantastic thing about our trip is that it rained last night! People here in Wajir say that they hadn't seen such rain for five years. It started after the morning prayer call blared from two minarets (one beautiful mosque was built by Saudi Arabia from its petro-dollars). Then all hell broke loose with terrible lightning and thundering and torrents of rain. From time-to-time you could smell the ozone in our bedroom. In the first light of dawn the whole town showed up under inches of water. A river rushes past the corner of our bedroom.

What we are doing is reading the Somali literacy materials Bertha has helped to develop. Ten people around a long table jabber in Somali. The thought struck me that maybe you'd like to get into this program. Three years at Garissa, working a Land-Rover all over the northeastern province, setting up adult literacy schools within the existing government primary school infrastructure. We've been beating the bushes for a year for a person to do this. All Salunga has come up with is old "Aunt Beth" of *Words of Cheer* vintage!

I wrote to Lancaster Mennonite High, asking if they'd take me on their staff beginning 1978. Someone needs to do a lot of thinking about this Nairobi Mennonite office, but my present inclination is to feel that the mission board got off the track when it created this office.

March 29, 1977

I'm now writing from Garissa. On the way south yesterday we had wet only half the way to this town. For the first 160 kms, the road was still under water in many places. In one low place we drove several miles through foot-deep water, and during that stretch we came upon a huge herd of camels. First we came on the women and girls with babies up on top of their load-bearing camels. Bertha thought there were six babies on one camel. The road was terribly slick and only because it had been graveled did it allow us to pass unstuck. It was funny seeing the camels with their huge feet slipping around on the mud like cows on ice. We asked, but they would give us no permission for pictures.

We stopped for lunch where a low place collected moisture, causing huge trees to grow. We scared two deer off and made it ours for an hour. There must have been 30 species of birds in the area. Later we passed an old man with two daughters following a great herd of black-headed sheep. He held up a teapot, but in my western ignorance I thought he wanted a ride and drove on. The Somali with us said with pained incredulity, "He wanted water." So we slid to a stop and went back. They must have drunk a quart of water each. I'll never forget those beautiful white teeth, the white turban, and the new pink long-sleeved western shirt, as the man squatted there, putting his aged face to the purple teapot and grinned up at us between great draughts of clear Nairobi water. He had one hundred miles to go, back to where the camels were slipping in the mud. The girls had a wooden water cask with a big round plug in the top. We filled their hollowed-out urn with water from our tins.

I have a beard again these days. I started it on the way up Mt. Kenya and it is just the right size now. It's a full one, with the neck and cheeks shaved to give my face some length. I had a terrible head of hair and started combing it back, giving me baldness on top with masses of fur on the sides and back. I found that people didn't recognize me anymore. Edith likes the beard for kissing!

June 3, 1977

A Brethren-in-Christ chap came through here. I'm supposed to orient him to the personnel needs of Kenya, so I took him out to Garissa, along with Aden, the Somali chap. We left Nairobi at 3:45 and at 7:30 we were within 100 miles of Garissa when I hit a loose rock which punched a hole in the sump and all the oil ran out. There we were on a deserted stretch of road with nothing but thorn scrub. We had water and four bananas. In due course, a lorry came by which took Aden back to a town where he got two gallons of engine oil. He came back by bus, so by 1:30 we were on our way again. He also brought some much needed Coke and bread. So we got to Garissa at 3:30 instead of 10:00 as planned.

Tonight Aden took us downtown for a spaghetti supper, topped off with papaya and tea with camel's milk. Then we visited his sister's home and got an invitation for lunch tomorrow before we leave for Nairobi again.

At lunch, she wondered if we would eat Somali style or European style. I said I preferred the Somali methods, so she put the meat in a bowl in the center of the big circular tray with *chapatis* all around it. We then dipped in the common bowl, which Sofia declared would bring us a blessing. We got home to Nairobi without further incident.

July 14, 1977

My fingers are stiff from the cold of an early morning snorkeling expedition with Joyce. We're at Diani Beach, Mombasa. I think we're going to have a storm because the whole horizon is a dull gray and the wind has been high.

I determined to read the Burkholder, Redekop book *Kingdom Cross and Community*. So I put it first on my reading agenda for this vacation. I've never taken this Mennonite business very seriously. My last exposure was in high school, studying some Kauffman's doctrines. I had a course in Mennonite History and Thought at EMC, but got a "D" and can't remember anything about it. Harold Miller, on the other hand, has been an avid amateur scholar on the subject ever since his Pax days in Germany. So my reading this book has helped me to get things in perspective and see how the "think" has moved since the 1950s. One of the things that impressed me was that the Eastern Mennonites are completely missing in this anthology. John Lapp is the only contributor from the East and he is now embedded in Goshen. I must get Harold to illuminate for me on how insignificant a role Lancaster, Franconia, Virginia Mennonites have played in the development of Mennonite thought and practice. Even Hesston plays a much stronger role than EMC. In fact, I detected no role at all for EMC. I remember how Phoebe Yoder used to remark on her having schooled with the significant Mennonites of the past quarter century when she was at Hesston College. There was, of course, an occasional reference to Orie Miller.

Why the sudden interest in things Mennonite? The personal inner urge comes through an attempt to understand why I get so dreadfully depressed every time one of the great ones from the mission board office shows up in Nairobi . . . . I told them that when I got to Nairobi I found a secretary who was putting in ten to twelve hour days at the office and who was terribly uptight about executives who piled on the work and then went off doing fun things. I told them it wasn't my style to develop relationships with Nairobi's beautiful people. That I hadn't the talent or interest in becoming important on this or that NCCK (National Christian Council of Kenya) committee, and that I did find Salunga and MCC's and the tourist's demands quite enough to keep me busy most of the time, but that I saw no reason why I personally was crucial to such an operation.

What to do? If we stay on here in Nairobi it means that our kids will have been without effective U.S. involvement for eight years. How about Joyce going into the U.S. world when she is ready for college, and not having the opportunity to learn the job market and make a few hundred as a down payment towards schooling? If the family had the assurance that Nairobi needs US and that the brethren in the USA knew what sort of problem that is going to make for our daughters and would be prepared in some way to stand with us through those problems, then I think we could ask Joyce and Dianne to bear with us, and I have the confidence in them to believe that they would do that and that they would survive. But lacking those sort of mandates, and I think I am completely unrealistic and exceedingly covetous to desire such mandates for myself, I cannot see that staying on here is warranted. If the office were moving rapidly into something of Africanization and an old salt were needed to steady the helm for a few years, I might feel constrained to stay on, even without the other affirmations. Or we could go home next year!

I admit that I enjoy being where things are going on. Both at Musoma and here I have met so many people. And it isn't only the meeting of people; it is the unpredictability of life. At Bukiroba you never knew in the morning what the day would bring forth. It was a bit precarious for Edith sometimes. But I really enjoyed being a part of all that was going on, particularly being mixed up with the people. I loved riding down Musoma streets on the cycle and in every block seeing someone I knew, loved sitting in the tea shops sipping spiced tea and letting the clatter and shouting of eating feel a part of me. I exulted in riding the buses—the roar of the motor, the grit of the dust, the banging and shoving, the shouting and sweating, the debate and quarrel, the humanness of close community in travel. I loved knowing what was going on in TMC and the knowledge that I alone knew, that I could throw light on most issues for most of my fellow missionaries. In Nairobi I've lost all of that which I loved, but I still walk through the people to the post office every day, know what is going on in the white Mennonite world of East Africa, which at some point flows across my desk. It is fun. Still, I wrote to the mission board that if there is one irrevocable decision I have made it is that I want no job connected with them when I get home.

About teaching at LMS. Would I really be able to hack the confinement of that world? I would be back to where I was in 1960, teaching at a Mennonite high school. The salary and job doesn't frighten me so much. I know that I will die threadbare, but it is the dropping out from significant involvement that frightens me. I am ordained. That should help a bit. But given Lancaster's pastoral notions, I'd probably end up pastoring a place like Rohrerstown; I can't imagine anything duller!

On reading *Kingdom Cross and Community* I find everywhere affirmed is the mandate that leadership springs out of the community, that the imposition of decisions onto the people from above is an anti-Anabaptist outgrowth of the disillusionment that set in following World War I. As we came to define salvation in narrow categories there developed a machinery to dictate these categories. Amazingly, I find Harold Miller and Bertha Beachy the most fiercely sensitive to this Mennonite hierarchical structuring of authority of all the Nairobi Mennonites. Both speak to the issue out of the Amish tradition, which never lost its original Anabaptist understandings of authority. The Amish have never defined salvation in the individual terms, in terms of a code of ethics. Salvation for them has been finding one's accepted place within the community. Both Bertha and Harold have scars from their encounters with Mennonite Church authority structures.

I am sending you a copy of my piece "Two Women." This is all a true story and I got the consent of the principals to write it into an article. But after writing it and passing it around for them to comment on and make changes, they got to quarreling together. I guess it wasn't quarreling. It was that each one somehow felt that she had a corner on truth and each set out to convert the other. It was really touch and go for awhile as to whether we would be able to contain the conflict. It even came around at one point that I was trafficking in others' souls for my own ends. I had to spend a lot of time trying to explain why I was exploiting a pastoral situation into an attempt at inter-Mennonite exposure of myself through publication. The matter is still very touchy and I have resolved not to publish it or to circulate it. But I do think it is a good article and maybe says something that needs being said. I do admit that for the sake of contrast and good reading I did present the positions as something of opposites and tried to distill one strand from each personality. This was for the sake of clarifying the issues. I am sending it along to you, confidentially. Don't in any way assume that the caricatures presented here are in any way definitive of any living person.

"A Tale of Two Women"

"Well, how did it go?" Dorothy asked me as we maneuvered through the evening Nairobi commuter traffic. I had spent the afternoon in conference with an attractive English woman, some years my senior, on the impossible refugee situation. "You know," I said, "in her youth Rosemary must have been a particularly striking girl." Dorothy exploded. She must have been thinking about the subject of men and women because she spun out quite a line in which she freely expressed her own struggle for recognition in a man's world. It went something like this:

"You annoy me. In fact, you make me angry! I ask you about what you discussed and what you decided on refugees and here you dismiss what Rosemary had to say on these two counts of beauty and age! It is so typical of men. They feel they have the right to evaluate women on that basis. By neatly dropping her in a box, you refuse to take this intelligent, caring woman seriously as a person. You make me so angry because you Mennonite men are doing this all the time to us women, especially to single women. You only measure a woman by whether or not she has attracted a man and married him. I know that my singleness puts my femininity into question in Mennonite circles. You cope with a woman who is unmarried and pursuing a career categorizing her as a 'woman's libber,' your perfect put down, implying by it that she is not really feminine, but some battle axe.

"Yet, I know that at a very deep level I am a woman. All my responses in every situation are in those terms, even my anger. I know that love, caring and involvement with people's inner heart throbs are feminine qualities, and I believe that when I have a worthwhile contribution to make to a particular discussion it is because I have been dialoguing and caring and sharing, not because I'm fighting some sort of war.

"I enjoy children, having my own home, and doing creative things with my hands. The easiest thing I can do, as well as the greatest joy to me, is cooking and entertaining guests. It feels good to have these gifts recognized. The same is true of nice clothing. All of these are feminine qualities. But please don't evaluate me only in these terms. I see these qualities only as a means of freeing me as a woman to truly be the person that I am.

"I feel threatened when I am not taken seriously as a *person*. Frequently men and women stereotype me because my interests range far beyond those traditionally assigned to our sex; you stereotype me and then dismiss me. You men, above me in the hierarchy, don't take me seriously when it comes to using the money in my own program budget. On paper I am responsible for the development program, but you keep me worried and off balance by using my budget without consulting me. You fix it by not listening so that I have no one with whom I can candidly discuss problems related to my work. You talk down to me because I am a woman. A woman seldom rates supporting staff in carrying out programs. You men all have secretaries, but I do my own typing. You define my place as fitting meekly into the structures your sex sets up. I get hurt and then I get angry and bitter because I am hurt. I hurt when you don't see me as a *person*. 'She must have been good looking in her youth,' you say, and *phitt*, into the box goes Rosemary, safely disposed of in your masculine world.

"But even my anger can be a creative force for helping me to bring change. I want to be vulnerable, open, to continue talking and working at these problems. The Mennonites are making a little progress, and I believe it is my anger and the anger of women like me, which is helping to bring change so that our sex may relate to yours as normal wholesome *persons*. But please see that I don't get angry because I hate; my anger springs from a very deep sense of caring for people. It is a sort of love from which my fire springs. Can't you see that?"

That night there was a potluck supper at our place to bid farewell to Jim who was going back home after three years of voluntary service. There was ice cream and pie for dessert. In the course of the evening I found myself sitting near Judith. She's single and she's a teacher at the International School. We were small-talking our way through the recent burglary at her school and the difference between psychological fear and intellectual fear, when someone passing us remarked on my growing beard.

"Yes, it's nice," I said, feeling it. "It's sort of spongy."

"You mean like when a woman gets her hair cut?" Judith asked.

"You know, Judith," I said, "I noticed right away that you had gotten your hair cut and set and I like it very much. I think it is attractive; it suits you nicely. But I was afraid to say anything because Dorothy just told me that this is what is wrong with us Mennonite men—we just notice how women look and not what is in their minds."

A couple of days later I got a letter. It was from Judith. I had really hurt her and made her angry at the party for putting on the intellectual talk bit without bothering to compliment her as a beautiful, tastefully dressed, pleasant and lovable woman. She admitted that if it was "mind" I was after then she would tell me what was on her mind. She wrote:

"To me, much more important than for a man to notice my intellectual and mental ability is to be trust-worthy and entrusted with his concerns, to be caring and allowed to care about his feelings, to be sensitive and able to communicate my *guts* or to understand his, to be lovable and appreciable and enjoyable. Of course, this takes some intellectual facility. But it also makes an unmarried woman much more vulnerable to express these values and needs than to ask for recognition of thought. A man makes himself much more vulnerable in giving affirmation (to any woman other than his wife) in these areas, than in affirming a woman's mind.

"Recognition of a woman's mind (in my mind) requires a lot less involvement and commitment than recognition of her ability and willingness to trust and care and understand and share. That is rare! It's even more rare for a single woman to find affirmation from the opposite sex for her womanhood —affirmation which can accept her love and express recognition of her love, and still respect her as a safe, trustworthy *person*. True, many women have abused their own dignity. Many women are not trustworthy. But I believe the main reason this respect is so difficult to find, even among brothers and sisters in our Mennonite society, is that we have truly believed in the past that it was dangerous or abnormal for an unmarried woman to recognize and enjoy her own womanhood. It was immoral for her to be lovable, enjoyable, and appreciable. That makes the recognition I refer to indeed a rare gem.

"Thanks for the compliment the other evening."

I showed the letter to Dorothy over coffee at the office.

"You liked her response better than mine, didn't you?" she asked. "Judith responded the way you men expect a woman to respond. You understand that."

"You know, Dorothy," I answered, feeling for words. "When I relate to you on your terms, and I do try, you are helping me; when I relate to you, it doesn't threaten me. I am not vulnerable because it doesn't infringe on my relationship to my wife Edith. But with Judith, I become vulnerable, as she says, because how do I handle that and keep things open and healthy with my wife. I went on a ten-day trip with you, visiting your projects, and I felt perfectly comfortable because you didn't elicit from me the sort of response Judith would have. To have gone on a trip like that with Judith, I would have found a bit precarious. But what do you think about Judith's letter?" I threw the ball back into her court.

"Judith and I are two different people. I think Judith's particular needs are the ones that men usually recognize. You can understand her, but, as she says, for you to respond affirmatively toward her makes you vulnerable. The usual way that men, and their wives, cope with this vulnerability is to cut women like Judith completely out of their orbit, ignore them, have nothing to do with them, let them go their lonely way. Often a man's wife makes it easier for him to relate to single women like Judith. If a wife is free with her husband, if they both share openly with each other, no secrets between them, then this sets you both free to relate meaningfully and with integrity to single men and women outside your home.

"And with me, men—most men—are very vulnerable, too, but in a different way. My job and responsibilities put me into a man's world and many men just cannot cope with a woman who is heading a program. Forgive me, Joseph, if I say that I see men as needing to play a dominant role when relating to women and it just threatens them terribly to have a woman relating to them as an equal. What you do, often unconsciously, is to give us the put down. You make knowing jokes about our abilities when you are out golfing. You freely tamper with our budgets and become all surprised and hurt when we don't meekly go along. When we do speak up, you give us the ultimate put down by categorizing us as heartless, militant, abnormal women."

Coffee hour was about over. As she swung out the door with her cheery smile, Dorothy paused a moment to emphasize, "I think we should keep on talking about these things. It helps us to recognize each other's needs and to relate more meaningfully, realistically, creatively, and affirmatively. See you, Joe."

November 21, 1977

It is dark, a three-quarters moon occasionally covered by scudding clouds. Frogs are croaking all around me. Far off in the distance I hear a lion roaring. There is a frog right here beside me with a sort of more croaky throat than the rest. Some sound like a hen clucking, others like little tinker bells, and all through the background it sounds like an orchestra of crickets.

Today I did a lot of listening. The northern wing of the Serengeti is practically empty of people. The closer you get to the Tanzania-Kenya border, coming in from the Mara Masai side, the smaller and less traveled the road. (Another lion from a different quarter is now roaring.) After crossing the border, one finds the Tanzania side to be almost completely desolate, with the road now badly eroded in places. Some ten miles into Tanzania you come on the entrance gate to Balongonja and from there on the road gets progressively better.

It really gives you a strange feeling being completely alone in this no-man's land. (Wow, another two lions roaring now, and quite distinct!) I just stopped from time to time, shut off the motor, got out of the pickup and listened: Flappet larks burrrP burrrP burrrP burrrPing their way high into the sky, guinea fowl clucking and flying on whirring wings at about head-level dodging through the thickets, barking zebras waWAwa waWAwa waWAwaing distant by the kopjes, meadow larks, plovers, mourning doves, all with their familiar cries, the grunting gnu worried by my having stopped so as to divide their herd. Remember the little barbet which sits on a twig, winding himself up? Even now in the moonlit night the doves and plovers are crying to each other, and far away the crowned crane sings his n'gowang n'gowang.

But even more than all the nostalgic sound of the wild was the silence—bright, green, short grass covering the pastures, rocky outcrops scattered across the meadows, blue black rain sky beyond the range of low mountains, sunshine bright and clean sweeping across the vast veldt and everything just absolutely silent, as silent as the single enormous giraffe standing stolidly beside his tree brilliant checkered black on gold in a burst of pure evening light shot east across the savanna under the darkening rain clouds. So many lizards on the road—they must have been cold and come out onto the road for a touch of evening sun, those geckos with red heads and blue stubby tails. The busy dung beetles—why do they have to get their balls of manure across the road?

The fireflies are silent but startling nonetheless. One winking his yellow green light at me gave me a start, causing me to think for a moment that someone had happened along my resting-place.

There were eland today, a herd of eleven—young ones in their prime, cantering along single file a couple of lengths in to my right. Their leader seemed to fancy crossing the road so I slowed down to encourage him and then when it seemed he had the edge on me I accelerated as if to cut him off, but I over did it and they broke from canter, dew laps flapping in unison, to a gallop and then the leader doubled back on his tracks and everything bunched up in confusion before they set off abreast this time away from me over the rise of ground above the road, twenty-two spiraling horns swaying uniformly, majestic against the evening sky. The second herd was older, with a lot of gray-brown among the younger reddish-ocher. And buffalo, rumbling roll of hurried hooves stampeding down the hillside across the road, joining their fellows in the valley beyond, huge backsides, quivering fatness, put to unaccustomed strain, churning to distance themselves from me.

I haven't been so happy or refreshed in many months. I had forgotten how stimulating it is to be alone on the road. It is a ton of disassembled door and window frames that I am trucking in a little Peugeot 404 pickup, but today felt like the old motorcycle days again. Now I am hopelessly stuck about 20 miles from the Mugumu hospital building site. It is a place around a bridge—a really long stretch of black mud, water and tree branches. I got fourth-fifths of the way through before the pickup sank to its axles. It was dark then already and I waded out in my boots, carrying my shoes, determined to walk all night to Mugumu rather than sit in this mud hole.

Once I got out onto the road on the other side of the bridge, I hid my boots behind a bush, put on my safari shoes and started off up the road. But in about ten minutes reason prevailed and now with the lions roaring and the hyenas howling, I am glad I did return to the pickup. The boots are now parked outside the truck door. Fortunately there was a great lot of rain recently; this flushed out the mosquitoes. I have the truck window open, with the light on inside to write in longhand, and all it attracts are a few bugs. From up on the road I could see the lights of Fort Ikoma Lodge, now an army post again 60 years after the English shelled it out of commission in World War I with the Germans here.

Later: Later in the night I crawled into the back of the tarp-covered pickup and stretched out on the ceiling board that was loaded on top of the door frames. I had a very good night and was awakened in the morning by three chaps on the bridge-building crew asking loudly whether anyone was in the car. They, and four others, helped me unload, carry the stuff to the road, and then pushed the pickup out of the mud. I got to the hospital site about nine that morning.

December 4, 1977

Edith and I have been invited to the MCC Retreat in Malawi, December 22-31. By stretching our ticket we can take the whole family. Tonight Edith took the girls to see a movie, and I chose to stay at home to write letters.

What has the major flow of correspondence between Salunga's Africa desk and me been about? (1) The Eastern Africa Area Office and my role in it. The committee is to meet January 19 & 20 for the first time since October 1976. At that meeting something should be decided. I've got Salunga to the place where they no longer care what happens just so long as I shut up and stop bothering them. I've applied to Lancaster Mennonite High School to teach Bible. But deep in my spirit I think that 1980 will find us still right here in Nairobi. (2) We have written a lot about Uganda refugees. The NCCK so far has been adamantly opposed to Festo Kivengere's return, so Salunga has called a halt in their involvement.

Annetta had her picture in the Sunday *Nation* with an article on the work she is doing at Kestral Manor, teaching music. She is really exceptional. We hope to have Rebecca begin there in January.

The past several weeks I went through the wringer emotionally. Joyce stopped having her periods. She told us it was late the last time she was home. Then she didn't have the second one, and Edith wrote saying she was to see the school nurse. Joyce wrote back saying the nurse is sending her to see the doctor. At that point it suddenly dawned on me that the girl is pregnant. Kijabe School isn't far away, but press of work and appointments just kept us from getting out there to see her. I was in agony. Then I began to see what it would be like to have your daughter in Canada living with an unchristian, divorced black, as in the case with one missionary daughter I know. Well, eventually Joyce came home, three days ago, and she isn't pregnant although she still hasn't had a period, having already missed two or three. But she is her normal, jolly, open self. I really did a lot of thinking in the past few weeks. It was a leveling sort of thinking. I have always had it in the back of my mind that no matter how my colleagues and superiors may think of me; at least the proof of my being genuine will come out in my children. Now suddenly to be faced with a fifteen-year-old pregnant daughter, possibly with a mulatto child who cannot be hidden in the crowd, this lays me open to derision by everyone. I had to think of ten of our African Mennonite pastors with illegitimate grandchildren. I even wondered if this happening to me would make me a brother to them. And then I thought about three older missionary children already divorced, and I began to see that I am joining my fellows. I seriously considered that we should come home and move back to Michigan and I'd take up painting houses with my father-in-law. Even if I never have an illegitimate grandchild, I hope I don't forget these feelings.

Just before Geneva Rufenacht left, she, Marian, Jane Myers and Edith went by over-night train to Mombasa. They were gone four nights. Dianne really managed the house wonderfully in Edie's absence.

December 7, 1977

There's an executive committee meeting of the NCCK meeting here in Limuru. Frankly, I feel just a little awkward here. There are four Europeans here this morning. This afternoon and all day tomorrow there's to be a meeting of heads of churches to discuss certain problems, namely church splits, etc. At the beginning of this session it was announced that the Europeans, Tanzanians and Ugandans, although not excluded from the meeting, would NOT be welcome to make any comments. Joshua Okello is here this morning for the first time as representative of the Kenya Mennonite Church. The funny thing is why the Mennonite mission board should continue on the NCCK. If we are a national body, then the Kenya Mennonite Church takes our place. If we are a multinational, then we shouldn't even have been a member on a national organization. Once again, what we are up against is a Mennonite institution set up to allow a particular Mennonite to do his thing. Anyway, when we meet in January, I believe this matter will be discussed.

About our furlough: this office cannot go without a person for a year, and if you'd like to replace me, then replace me forever! Again, for us to go home for a year means that Joyce switches schools, once for every year of her high school training! So for these two reasons I cannot see us coming home for a year. Either we come home for two months this summer, or come home "forever."

December 25, 1977

Merry Christmas! Along with our good wishes comes some family news.

Joe & Edie: leaving on December 23 for an MCC retreat in Malawi. All the girls are going along and we'll start our "going-home" tickets from Lilongwe, the capitol. That way we can afford it and not be a burden on MCC. Return is to be January 1, 1978. On January 2, the Kenya, Tanzania, Sudan Ethiopia MCC retreat begins. We start a New Year fully "retreated"!

Joe: These days he's trying to repeat his stick-in-the-mud lion experience. He left yesterday morning with a pickup load of ceiling board for Mugumu Hospital. Let's hope the bridge was fixed. There's a medical board meeting to attend at Shirati. Then home again on Sunday.

Edie: She is trying to make and bake Christmas gifts this year—plates full of cookies, candies, and Christmas breads. We had an enjoyable Shenk-Miller-Wenger Christmas dinner. Twenty-two present!

Joyce: Successfully finished a term at Rift Valley Academy with all As and Bs but is glad for a four-week break. Roomed across the hall from her cousin Karen Shenk, who was a big help to her. Likes to help in the kitchen. Would like to finish high school in the States.

Dianne: At thirteen, enjoys life, has lots of friends who are more important than lessons and piano practice. Heidi Wenger is one of those friends.

Rosy: A new bookworm who finds school interesting—and challenging. Has lots of interest: making candy, tanning rabbit skins, drawing, raising guppies, making money, having pen pals, making more money!

Becky: Can hardly wait for a plane ride. Is looking forward to her first glimpse of America next summer. But will first attend two terms of school at Kestral Manor.

December 26, 1977

We are now on our way to the MCC retreat for Malawi and Zambia personnel. On the way we spent two nights at the Robert Blake Secondary School in Dowa, Malawi. It really brings back all the memories. The Headmaster of the school is a second generation missionary from South

Africa. It is a really lush setting on a hill with high trees all over the place, and beyond the school campus everything cultivated in maize. It's been a wet November and December. I hope it doesn't mean we will have a rainy retreat. The school is in vacation but the political atmosphere one senses is right back there in the mid-1960s at Musoma Alliance, with the Europeans obviously in control, maintaining a high professional academic standard for the local people.

When Edith and I were asked to do the Bible studies for this retreat, we decided to try to get permission to cross the Kenya-Tanzania border in our car and drive down here. But as retreat dates here were twice pushed forward we soon saw that we couldn't do that and get back in time for our own retreat in January. We then decided to bring the whole family by air, we picking up the cost for our girls.

Peace.

1978

April 3, 1978

Last night we sat down as a family and got to sorting out where we'll be and when, this summer. Yesterday we got a letter from Uncle Ivan saying that there will be an ordination service for a new pastor at Millersville on July 23. Seeing that I am a member of the district bench, he would like for us to be present at that service. Joyce's school leaves out on July 21 and both Rosslyn and Kijabe open September 4. We plan to take Joyce out two weeks early and put them all back in school one week late. As far as I know these are the only markings around which we need to frame our time in the USA this summer. Tentatively, leave Nairobi July 7 for five days in Israel; Lancaster, Indiana, Kansas (for Mennonite World Conference), Michigan via Montana, Indiana, Lancaster, Virginia, Lancaster, return to Nairobi by September 11.

April 6, 1978

This is a thatched hut in which I sit this late afternoon, in a big arm chair before a large round table with one very tiny cockroach trying to find a place to crawl under my paper. In the adjacent hut there is the rattle of cups in preparation for afternoon tea. A child is crying in self-pity on the path past a third hut leading to the clearing where I have my tent. A rooster crows, another answers, crickets buzz, a high-bosomed girl comes in for a folding chair, a bird twitters, far away the shouting sounds of another village's life. In the kitchen hut the sounds of blowing pipe and crackling fire give promise of an early tea.

I am at Pastor Musa Adongo's place. There's a four-day seminar for bush church leaders, and I am one of the seminar teachers. Tomorrow I'll be out while the rest wind things up. I'll be going with the Anglican bishop of Kisumu to Rusinga Island in Lake Victoria, for a board meeting there. Whether or not I will go back to Nairobi tomorrow night depends on what time we get back from Rusinga and on how dry is my tent. We have had heavy rain these first two nights and a good downpour this afternoon. Frogs croaking in the gravel pits down by the road continually remind us that it is a very wet year.

A $30,000 station is being built by EMBMC across the way from this quiet village. It is almost finished already, but feels so big and strange, compared to the comfortableness here. Someone forgot that Mama Moses cooks with a wood fire when the house was designed. So Father Moses says they must build another house out back for a kitchen so that Mama Moses won't blacken everything.

I had a terrible fright the other day in Nairobi. I had parked my car in the morning and when I went for it later, it wasn't there. I had parked it over a yellow line in the middle of a wide stretch of road, so figured that just possibly the police had towed it off. I asked a bank guard which police station dealt with that area. So I went back to the office and called Edith who came in about a half-hour. The police at the station asked me why my eyes were so wide open. I told him it is because I am filled with uncertainty because my car is missing. He wanted to know where I had parked it and after I told him, he castigated me soundly for a whole list of wrongs done by me. I told him that I have nothing to say to all these accusations because it is true that all these wrongs I have done. So he asked me the car number and looked it up in his enormous book and informed me that they have my car. Whereupon I smote my breast, rolled my eyes heavenward and declared, "Gracious, better you to have taken it than the thieves!" So everyone standing around laughed and the officer, with a twinkle in his eye, pounded the table and ordered me to be back in the morning with Shs 80/= in my hand. Which I did and I got the car back with no damage other than a cracked taillight cover. The car is just outside the door here and whenever I sit back in my big chair to stretch my back and to think of what next to write about, I look at it admiringly. It's a nice car. It's worth $3,500. It has 99,000 kilometers on it. It gets 8 kilometers per liter of petrol. That's only 22 miles per imperial gallon. I think I should get rid of it.

There's a new MCCer going to Tanzania to work with President Nyerere's Friesian cows. He's a 22-year-old Quaker whose father works with the Ministry of Agriculture in Dar es Salaam. Interestingly, last month, there was a misunderstanding between the Cubans operating the artificial insemination plant at Butiama where Dan Maxwell is to be placed and the Tanzania government. So Dan's dad was sent to Musoma to mediate the dispute. The Maxwells are Americans. Anyway, Dan came through Nairobi on his way to Musoma, so I could brief him, and we bought an MCC Honda XL175 for him. Since the papers for transfer are not yet ready, Dan went on without his cycle. So I have a spanking new cycle to ride around on! It is still too new, so I cannot drive fast, but it is really fun to be on one again.

It seems that since we moved to Nairobi I haven't kept you briefed anymore on things. So the gap between who we are and who you know us to be is widening. I've been doing an awful lot of writing, but most to the mission board Africa desk, in an attempt to get their vibrations into sync with mine. It is the sort of stuff I used to write about only now it's in-house administrative stuff that goes into the files in offices, and isn't so interesting. But still we work at understanding the same theme.

Well, it's 4:15 and no tea yet, so I'm going to wander over to the church to see if it's time for me to say my bit—lecturing on tithing.

April 20, 1978

What we'll be able to do this summer depends a good bit on what sort of transport Salunga can get together for us. They sound awfully strapped for cash these days. About Millersville, I've given Uncle Ivan a pretty dim view of how I would be able to respond. But that aside, Millersville is my ONLY point of Lancaster Conference reference anymore. Yet I cannot afford to not pay attention to them.

April 24, 1978

I had a really beautiful experience the other day. We have been having a lot of rain—out of a field of 77 in the Safari Rally only 12 finished, mud and more mud. Ed Rissler called me one morning to say their road was cut and he couldn't make it in the small car we had left for them. Going for them was fun. I took the little Land-Rover we had used for Bertha's safari. Two TAP teachers went along to help push, if necessary. We got off about 3:15 a.m., which put us up on the flank of Mt. Kenya at dawn. I had expected the mountain to be clouded over, but along about 5:30, a sliver of moon appeared over in that direction, followed shortly by Venus, and then the stark, black outline of the mountain. The road we took passed up the west flank cutting across to the north before dropping down into the desert. By the time we got around to the north the first rays of the morning sun were catching the peaks. We stopped. I had a pee and some coffee; the teachers took pictures. The area is wheat, gently rolling fields. The larks were getting awake and the still, cold morning air was filled with their trilling. A lot of snow was on the mountain peaks. They are reddish in color. A rain-swollen brook over across the first wheat field burbled its music, a theme note around which the larks built their song.

Some 20 kilometers beyond Isiolo, on the dirt road now, we came on an old Land-Rover with people sleeping around it. They were "khat" merchants coming back from a tough eight-day trip to Mandera. At 2:00 a.m. that night they were barreling along, hoping to pick up a fresh cargo at Meru and get back to their deprived customers when a contingent of game police flagged them down. They paid no heed and got their rear tires shot out. The impressive thing for me was the lanky, brown-toothed, blue-eyed, hippy Yank who was in charge of the outfit. They needed a tire pump, so I pumped up two mended tires for them. But they leaked as fast as I could pump, so after a half-hour of that I gave up and we left them. They were gone by the time of our return trip.

The desert was green. All the dry twiggy bushes were in bountiful leaf. A little white lily blanketed some of the lava-rock strewn valleys.

On a whim I wrote to the principal of Lancaster Mennonite High. He responded with a warm invitation for me to apply for a position as Bible teacher for the 1978-79 school year. What should we do? Being in Nairobi only two years isn't enough time to leave any tracks. I am finding Salunga not very helpful in moving towards the handing over of this office to the East African Area Office committee. Salunga now talks about turning this Nairobi office over to the Kenya Mennonite Church! Having the Tanzania border sealed tight doesn't help the situation.

April 26, 1978

I've been having malaria. For several days I was running a fever of 100 degrees, but kept going. Finally, last night, I threw in the towel and went to bed. This afternoon I broke into a terrific sweat and my temperature returned to normal.

I was reading the EMC bulletin piece on EMC and the seminary. It is really a foreign psychology to me: you have there all this good Christian struggle and sacrifice, but all of it yielding ever greater laurels of success, position, prestige, etc., to the participants. I guess if you look at what I am into here, it is pretty big and exciting too, yet at the bottom line, it is the same as Bukiroba—letting the thing down as gently as possible, keeping the Hershey-Jacobs machine functioning, a system doomed to disintegrate sooner or later, either because it is an expatriate organization or because of the infighting when it does get turned over to Africans. I think, too, part of my problem lies in the fact that no one in authority is interested in my pilgrimage and what insights I may have gathered that are applicable here. It looks like a lost cause I was into. These two years in Nairobi have been most helpful in helping me to sort that one out. What I fear most is becoming incurably bitter, so that I end up a bitter, old ex-missionary.

Going home frightens me—I wish we didn't have to go home, except for seeing the family. I don't want to sit in Salunga administrators' offices or at their dinner tables and get stroked about nothings, like the ugly American got to bring him back into the mainstream of things, being slowly seduced.

Forgive my crying, but then I am free again to be full of life and joy and good will to everyone around. Incidentally, sick eight days, the doctor now thinks it was not malaria, but tick fever.

May 10, 1978

Today is my eighth day in Ethiopia. I am on the ALERT campus where a Dr. Lee Yoder and Ph.D. Gerald Stoner work. ALERT is a leprosy control and research center, one of three or four in the world, the others being in India and Brazil. It is a beautiful campus, a little enclave of mowed and watered lawns with well-tended flowerbeds in this socialist city. I'm not feeling too swift again, but this city is so high, maybe it is just the altitude that leaves me feverish and giddy.

Out of these eight days, three were spent at a retreat. The Sudan Interior Mission has a lodge on the banks of a central lake. It is just a small lake, about half a mile across, with most of its walls almost perpendicular to the lake. On one side the Catholics have their retreat center with the SIM on the opposite. My work was over with a Sunday afternoon communion service. So to celebrate I got the canoe paddle and went for a ride in their over-sized aluminum canoe. There was an occasional stiff breeze which just caught the canoe and pivoted it around. My seat was in the stern so that I was facing the opposite of where I wanted to go. Later I learned that in a wind the rower sitting in the bow controls a one-manned canoe. By myself I had discovered that I could just manage the thing if I sat in the middle. I managed to get across the lake to some gigantic fig trees where the water was calm because of the steep walls of rock. The water was crystal clear and the birds in the reeds and trees abundant.

Surprisingly my being here five unstructured days seems to have been a strange phenomenon for these people. I don't know how often I was asked what my plans are. I had been told that I was to meet the church executive committee—agenda-less—but some churches got closed down in the Awash Valley, and some church leaders beaten up and imprisoned. So I do some reading and writing, lending a hand. Made a box for shipping one of the nurse's stuff home to the States, helped on an autopsy of a Swiss goat that died, dissembled a VW engine, and tucked in the cracks, a fair amount of listening and brothering. It is funny how a revolution works. Many things seem the same, as always, but there is the midnight raid by security men on the school dormitories, the locking up and beating of some forty students who didn't say the raised clenched fist anti-imperialist oath at the weekly village youth rally, the periodic assassination of government officials by the anti-government "white terror" and the occasional spread about of dozens of mutilated corpses, which one finds in the morning, the work of the government counteractive "red terror," the drying up of supplies, the tanks practice shooting against the hill behind the Bible Academy, the frisking by armed guards at many places, yet the school fields are again being plowed by oxen which pull the ancient Ethiopian wooden plow with its steel spike, the school teachers are still running all over the place on their motorcycles. And I saw an English woman on an Addis street got up in all the traditional foxhunt attire out riding her horse. At a Chinese restaurant, the staple was Uncle Ben's rice! The missionaries keep asking me what I think about what is going on. I say that I seem to have heard it all before: Tanzania and Somalia.

I just phoned the Kenya Airways and found, to my great delight, that their scheduled flight to Nairobi is indeed on this evening.

We had communion and feet washing at the mini-retreat. The chairman of Meserete Kristos Church was with us throughout—an ex-Muslim who gave some lectures on Islam. His name is Shemsudin. A petite fellow about my age who works for the Lutheran church, and would be happy to see the MKC absorbed by the Lutherans, a good idea I think, seeing that the MKC has never been able to get registered with the Ethiopian government, and that the MKC is so terribly congregational in its government that their central office is almost peripheral to their exercise. Their guest house is empty these days, except for staff lounging about the place. One evening Shemsudin mentioned that he was going to the Ministry of Health for a meeting. The ministry has declared that it will replace all the American doctors at the Nazareth Hospital with Cubans. Salunga was hoping the ministry would take over the hospital but keep the American staff: two doctors and three nurses. I had started to tell about Shemsudin—a man with a beautiful Christian spirit. When it came to feet-washing, he brought a basin of water to where I sat and said that he would show me how they wash feet in Ethiopia. He removed my shoes and socks, and then washed my feet, first my left, than the right. With his thumbs he cleaned the hollow behind the ankle bone, and with his fingers he cleaned between each of my toes until the skin squeaked between his fingers. Then he wiped the water from each foot with a long movement of the palm of his hand, flicking the water drops from his fingertips into the basin. He finished by wrapping the foot in his towel and messaging it dry. I then washed his tiny feet, and we embraced as we do in Tanzania. Lastly he gave the basin to another Ethiopian, a teacher at the academy who was with us, told him to pour out the water and get fresh. I was too tired to weep, so I sat with my head in my hand and gave thanks for this gift of love, and then the rest were finished washing, and we were singing and the moment passed.

May 13, 1978

We're having a mess at Rosslyn with the principal just not being able to get his show together. I am the board chairman, so the noise keeps coming to me. When I take it to the board, they don't see it as so serious because they haven't been getting the noise. So I must somehow work with the board in such a way as to help them see how serious the situation is without their interpreting the effort as my personal vendetta with the first Baptist principal the school has ever had.

Did I tell you that Richard Detweiler wrote asking me to join him at the Souderton congregation? His letter came about two weeks after Uncle Ivan's letter about the ordination at Millersville. It isn't my being in the lot that makes me wish to heed Ivan's request that we be there for the ordination. It is just that with my being away so long I simply do not have a point of orientation in the U.S. any more. It is like that poem, home is the place that when you've got to go there they've got to take you in. I am not able to appraise the place; there simply are no pegs onto which I would hang anything. Nairobi was the same way. I never paid any attention to Nairobi or what it was about until I got moved here. Now I have quite a Nairobi facility and I can take anyone who asks through the dynamics, backwards and forwards. I really feel very lost when it comes to the USA.

So I told both Uncle Ivan and Richard Detweiler that I simply cannot get away from Africa for two more years. So if I get put into the lot and get "hit" they'll just have to wait for me until 1980. I also told Uncle Ivan that I could not consider such an assignment as permanent but would hope that after the children are on their own we might get involved in the mission of the church overseas again.

June 1, 1978

This is one of those Kenya days that are just too bright and clear to be true. The sky is blue with scattered cottony clouds, bright sun with just a trace of nip in the air under the trees. This afternoon Edith took the children down to the Westlands swimming pool while I finished up some sorting of papers in preparation for packing to come home. Later I walked down to the pool only to discover the car was full, having David's kids also. So I walked home, stopping in Westlands for a double ice cream cone. On the way back I was thinking about you; I was wondering if there is any place to walk now that you're down in Mississippi. Walking is better for companionship than motorcycling. And I wondered what we would talk about. Our lives during these six years have certainly gone their own separate ways. Complaining about Salunga and EMC is not of much value. Really, I don't find it interesting to talk about administrative business. It is just a mad scramble day after day, and you have to be careful that people stay happy. I don't think I do a very good job of that. You can tell me about Faulkner.

I'll be forty in just a few days, and I really intend to sit down about then and do a think about it. When we filled out our forms when leaving Salunga the last time, the last question asked if the candidate had anything particular he/she would like to say. I wrote, "Yes, on my next furlough I will be forty." And indeed our departure from here will be just 13 days after my 40th birthday. So, with that sort of build up, I would suppose that I should have some thoughts for the occasion.

Yesterday the vice chairman of Rosslyn Academy school board and I had the thankless task of going over to the school and informing the principal that he is fired. Earlier we had spent several days interviewing all the teachers, the principal, and parents. We found a unanimous feeling among the staff that the principal is a pretty incompetent administrator and that he is arrogant in addition. We'll pay for his way home and we will pay his salary through October. He fought it as a fish fights the hook. Finally after an hour of fighting he became silent and we said we were sorry and departed. That was really something. I was trembling all over. Fortunately, my companion was the chief spokesman. But I wrote the dismissal letter.

How I wish we could get back to the good old days when people assumed when they went overseas that they were doing it for a career. Wouldn't it be just positively wonderful if we could get a good administrator who would stick with that school for ten years! Wow, that is just something never heard of, let alone thought of these days.

June 14, 1978

This letter comes during a ten-day trip to Tanzania. It comes due to taking part in a three-day district spiritual life conference at Bukiroba, which was kicked off by an ordination for a deacon for the district. A constitution committee meeting for Shirati Hospital, and a Medical Board meeting, then a site meeting at the Mugumu hospital.

We left Nairobi at 3:45 a.m. last Thursday, caught up with the truck which had slept at Narok, at the Mara Masai gate, and then came with the truck the rest of the way, getting to Mugumu at 1:00 p.m. We had a Tanzanian police letter allowing us to drive in and out—with one passenger.

I have never seen such a conference at Bukiroba as we had that weekend. There were some ten choirs from as far away as Nassa and Kisaka. The best choir was from Nyankanga, the place where I built a church just before coming to Nairobi. They had no choir then. On the last morning there were over 500 people present and that morning's offering was Shs 2,300/=. The preaching was the same old business with the Bishop preaching three times, Simeon Hurst twice, and Aristarko Masese twice. But just to see so many people come together and to see how the district managed to feed them all was wonderful. Another joyful thing was that about half the choirs used a little drum for rhythm and there was a lot of nodding and tapping of the foot, which was something new. The drum business will now sweep the church and take the place of clacking sticks and Fanta bottles. The deacon ordained was the leader at Nyankanga which is no doubt at this point the most vibrant congregation in the district.

The lack of drugs for Shirati Hospital is becoming critical. Very, very few are available. Dr. Glenn told me yesterday that as the drug supply becomes more critical one must learn to doctor by helping people to "think positively." But I suspect that Dr. Godshall would sooner doctor with "*dawa*" than with "think." It is like fighting a war without soldiers or ammunition. These vacuums will no doubt eventually be filled with Cubans. The USA is abandoning Africa to the Cubans and it is because our psychology is one of disengagement.

The Bishop called me aside just before I left Bukiroba for Shirati. We sat out back of his house enveloped by the smoke from his daughter's supper fires, night breezes rustling the trees in the black hill behind us. He wondered why I am so somber and don't laugh anymore. I told him I don't go for hypocritical laughing, but also that I didn't realize how firing the principal at Rosslyn had affected me. But I told him, too, that I am sad to see how isolated he is with a church secretary who is never present. But, as an aside to you, certainly no one has taken the Bishop's interests to heart, as did Joe Shenk!

August 19, 1978

I'm writing from Oden, Michigan. Home from Kansas, Mennonite World Conference, I felt like a most blessed father when I got off my fourth plane for the day in the Pellston (Michigan) airport and walked into the arms of four laughing, shouting, hugging, kissing daughters, with a radiant wife standing in the background awaiting her turn. We sort of clogged up the traffic flow in the lobby for a few seconds. I am sure my fellow passengers figured I had just been released from a North Vietnamese POW camp and was meeting my family for the first time in four years. Wow! With a family like mine, I think I could even survive moving to the USA to live.

September 9, 1978

We're sitting in this jam-packed KLM 747 at 1:45 a.m. We have just finished supper while sitting here on the plane. Some computer is bust, so there is a slow down and our plane which was to leave at 10:10 yesterday evening is only now getting towed out of its berth. In addition to this, we were to have left two (or three, if you count this as Saturday) days ago. Uncle Bob and Daddy and Mother drove us, or started to drive us to New York in a Salunga Ford van. We got to the last Howard Johnson's on the PA turnpike and stopped for a rest stop and we couldn't get the dumb thing started. First we thought it was vapor locked and tried all the tricks for that, like my blowing in the gas tank until I had stretch lines up and down my ballooning cheeks and a black ring around my mouth. Lots of people gathered around offering other bits of classic advice, like holding the throttle to the floor and wrapping the carburetor in wet, cold rags. Soon the battery was flat—meaning it hadn't any more juice, and someone brought jumper cables while someone else brought his car around so we could use his extra battery. Eventually everyone realized that we were hopeless and went away, leaving us to ourselves as we had been in the beginning. Daddy and I then pushed the van over to the petrol tanks so we could fill up and thus force, through greater petrol pressure, some gas into the carb. We then pushed the van to a neutral place, borrowed two spanners and a pliers from the attendant and took off the big plastic bubble that covers the engine in these vans that have the engine somewhere between the driver and his other front seat traveler. We could then get at the carb and discovered lots of gas, so we decided it was battery and pushed the van over to the workshop, which didn't have a mechanic in residence, and hooked up to a battery charger. In about three-fourths of an hour it became clear that the battery was fully charged and we still didn't have any encouraging results from our grinding on the starter, an activity all the males in the party had taken turns at doing. (It's now 2:00 a.m., September 9, and we're taxiing out to take off, so I'll close later. Crumbs, the captain just announced that we'll be taxiing for twenty minutes! So, I'll continue). At the point this dawned on us, I went and called the Turnpike wrecker service for them to send a mechanic. It took over a half-hour for him to get there and when he did he pronounced our timing chain to have slipped a cog and offered to tow the van to a garage for repairs. I phoned Salunga to ask them to have someone collect our four escorts and sought their advice about whether we should go for broke, to make our flight. They thought we should, but I couldn't get any limousine service to take any party of six with three hundred pounds of luggage to J.F.K. in one and a half hours from the time I was calling, to allow the two hour required checking in. (Today I found that we were actually still some three hours from J.F.K., to say nothing of any limousine service having to locate us first.) So when Salunga arrived at 9:00 p.m., they took the whole shooting match back to Lancaster. Then sent someone to tow the kaput van back to Lancaster the next day. The night before, Rosy vomited some dozen times, and Dianne some quarter dozen times, and at the Howard Johnson's Joyce barfed as well, and the whole way home Daddy nearly barfed. (It was the flu, we think). So, we were rather happy to get home. On Thursday I waxed the Ford we had been driving during this furlough, in preparation for re-selling it, and trimmed all the dead wood out of one of Mother Miriam's gigantic pine trees. The trimming put me into a terrible sweat. So, now, here we are again, brought by the same people in a rescue van, and everyone is feeling just great and it is 2:15 and we are taxiing again!

I got a fresh brainstorm on what to do after we get home in two years. (Good grief! Other planes just keep going past us on the right and as they take off their blast rattles our over-head racks.) Why not spend our furlough year building a house? EMBMC will give us one year to get retooled for re-entry to the American rat race!

September 29, 1978

Just a bit ago I was asked by an elderly Somali here in Garissa (Northeastern Kenya) if I was going to prayers. He was deeply disappointed to hear that I worship God through Issa (the Arabic/Islamic name for Jesus). I am staying in a hotel in downtown Garissa. It's a Somali hotel and the quieter part of it is under a small mosque with steps leading up to a sort of boarded up rooftop. I was here last week with three others, but this weekend I'm alone. On both occasions I've been helping our new irrigation MCC couple to get housing. It is dark now and prayers are over and I am chatting with you, waiting for it to be time to walk over to Velma Eshleman Nzesi's home for supper. I wish you were here, as it is the right sort of atmosphere for talk. We've been seeing birds: doves, hundreds of ring-necked doves, carmine bee-eaters, Buffalo weavers, horn bills, plovers, marabou storks, vulture guinea howl, black-bellied bustards, etc.—lots of dik-dik and a number of gerenuk.

October 22, 1978

Edith and I are in Botswana for a meeting of all the African country representatives of MCC. Surprisingly, we all arrived in time. We flew over from Jan Smutts in J'burg in a DC-3. It was terribly rough, but I managed to keep things together.

The office situation in Nairobi hasn't settled down properly since our getting back. I don't have it well analyzed but some of what I read is that my assistant was very happy with running the place while I was away in the States! For one thing, she could slip into her comfortable Swiss-German efficiency and attitudes without my constant pressure to be realistic. But she also got pretty tired, and this fatigue helped to rob her of the resilience she needed to work through the implications of my return. She has finally focused the problem on our African secretary's being an inefficient dolt, so she won't give her any work to do because it takes more time to have Rose do it than it would were the secretary to do it herself. What to do!

November 3, 1978

It's been two weeks today since we left home for Botswana. Some of us had transit visas for South Africa. So I have been in the forbidden country (Transvaal) and have slept in the forbidden city (Holiday Inn). The coffee was just as wonderful this time as it was the last time I had coffee in a Holiday Inn, that time with Edith on our honeymoon. The next day we flew from Blantyre to Dar es Salaam, then on to Mwanza and Musoma, arriving at Bukiroba for lunch and on to Mugumu for a late supper. On Monday morning I drove the MCC contingent in Victor's Mercedes Benz to Buhemba for lunch. On the way we went via Fort Ikoma to see the animals, which just now are outside the park in great numbers. We drove off the road at several places where the grass was coming up fresh, emerald green—great sweeping meadows covered with gnu, zebra, *topi* and giraffe. We visited one of the dairy projects Maxwell is involved with.

The MCC group left by MAF on Tuesday, on the same plane that brought Peter Batchelor. Two nights before the Tanzanian air force was doing a practice run up the lake from their Mwanza base. Three MiGs came over Musoma where one was shot down. A second went down at Butiama, although whether from running out of fuel or from being shot down, we don't know. So when the MAF plane, arriving early, buzzed Bukiroba, we didn't know whether it might also be mistaken for a Ugandan craft and be shot down. No problem, fortunately. Peter Batchelor is a development consultant working out of London, but responsible to a committee based in Nigeria. MCC contributes to his budget.

I am staying here at Nyabasi (Tanzania) for their annual spiritual life conference. MAF is to bring a load of baby chicks to Musoma and pick me up to fly back to Nairobi. Last night the Tanzanian broadcast aired President Nyerere's declaration of war against Uganda, and already we hear that petrol is not being sold in Musoma, and Air Tanzania scheduled flights are being canceled. Maybe I'll be in Tanzania for a long time. For my part, I am getting to the place where I need my wife!

November 30, 1978

Funny place I am. It is on a stretch of road between Bigo Nata and Mugumu where no one lives. It is like being in a game reserve. I've been here for an hour already, and all that I've seen in the line of Homo sapiens is a bus that just roared past going towards Musoma. I am here with Dan Wenger's motorcycle and a torn drive chain. This morning I got up at Bukiroba at 3:00 a.m., got a glass of coffee, tied the loads onto the cycle and set out for Mugumu. The idea was that the truck waits for me at Mugumu until up to 9:00 a.m. I was to go with them to Narok or Kijabe—whichever seemed to work out best for getting a *matatu* to Nairobi, as the truck's business is to pick up furniture at Kijabe. So, just a few minute after the sun slipped up across the eastern horizon, the cycle engine jammed and something let loose with the rear wheel, allowing the cycle to free wheel. This is the classic torn chain symptom, because the loose chain wraps up on the front sprocket and jams the engine while at the same time having pulled off the rear sprocket. So I took the chain cover off and found the above to be so and un-jammed things, etc. But with no extra chain-link there is just absolutely nothing to do but sit here with the birds and tsetse flies. The bus was going the wrong way. I am about twenty miles from Mugumu and right in the middle of about a twelve-mile stretch that has no village. I expect to eventually hear something coming from Musoma to Mugumu and can hopefully send a message for someone to come collect me. But by then the hopes of getting a lift further will be dashed. The idea was that I get back to Nairobi today, hit the office tomorrow.

I bought 20 mangoes to take along back to Nairobi, so after getting the cycle all put back together again and ready for putting on a pick-up, should such happen along, I wiped my greasy hands off on my hankie and dug a mango out of one of my three bags and peeled it with my teeth. That was an enjoyable thing to do! I am here under a bush by the side of the road and I am going to try to get a little sleep—in spite of a few testy tsetse flies. It is after 10:00 now. I was wakened with a start about half an hour after falling asleep by a hurrying young man on a bicycle sliding to a halt beside me. Immediately a swarm of tsetse flies settled on his back. These flies are programmed to follow anything that moves, so as long as he is cycling, he stays ahead, but when he stops, the flies settle down on him. He took a note for me to Mugumu and just after him a Lutheran missionary in a Land-Rover came along going to Musoma, so I asked him to tell the folks there. Then a petrol truck came, going to Mugumu, so I sent word with him too. Then I ate another mango and took three long hikes into the wooded forest on either side of the road, scaring up eleven duikers and two vervet monkeys, along with attracting swarms of tsetse flies which I tried to keep away with waving a small tree branch. The woodland here is mostly single trees standing twenty to fifty feet apart, with fresh short green meadow grass between them. Scattered here and there through the grass are little red flowers. It is really most delightful, except for the tsetse flies. Since the petrol truck, no further traffic of any kind has passed. Sitting here now in the shade, I hear something coming. It is our truck. (I got home at 12:15 a.m. the next morning!)

1979

March 2, 1979

It is such a beautiful day, the morning dawning blue-clear and cool. All day it has been thus, with just enough of smog around the bottom of things to keep us from seeing Kilimanjaro from the window here in Church House. The last two years have been wet, with grass and thickets growing profusely. I've finally discovered that bananas do well around the house, so have pretty much given up on my horticulturing and in my spare time dig holes for putting rabbit manure, grass, earth and bananas in. I now have seven stands of bananas with three of these having one bunch of fruit apiece ripening. I've a really healthy papaya tree, but it turned out male and bears nothing. Two smaller ones are too young to know whether or not they'll fruit. My six citrus trees do nothing but collect smut and aphids. The five mulberry bushes have had so much wet that they much prefer bushy riotous growth to fruiting and I need continually to prune them back to keep them in hand. I've got a fig, which is so strangled by mulberries that it just grows straight up. My delight is our 1976 Christmas tree planted right in the middle of the lawn. A year ago it developed a cancer in its terminal shoot which I had to rig up a ladder for reaching to cut out, tying instead an offshoot upward which has now become the terminal shoot and is once more reaching for the sky. It is a joy to sit on the porch in the early morning with a waking cup of coffee or in the evening with the *Time* magazine and just admire its vitality as it establishes itself in the earth.

There was suddenly a silence in the usually hectic roundabout below our office window. In due course, the presidential limousine with its attendant fleet of motorcycles and police vehicles came slowly into sight. President Moi was standing up through the open top of his expanded Mercedes and as he moved past the crowds broke into hearty roars of "*Nyayo, Nyayo!*" This has become the new Kenya slogan. Translated it is "footprint" or "track." Moi calls on the nation to follow in his "*nyayo*" even as he is following in the "*nyayo*" of the Mzee, Kenyatta. "*Nyayo*" has come to mean all that is straight and just. Now again the 5:30 p.m. roar of traffic.

I don't know where to begin telling you about myself. I go to Tanzania, from time to time. I have a sore shoulder, so that writing with a pen is difficult for me. It has something to do with the nerves from the neck going down my right arm. It comes and goes. Mostly it means that as I truck around, I don't write—very much anymore and that is why you haven't been getting bits and pieces from me as you used to. I was in Tanzania some two weeks ago and need to go again next week for another ten days. It is lengthy going and coming. Just now it is MAF (Missionary Aviation Fellowship) to Kilimanjaro and then either commercial or overland to Mwanza and Musoma. No longer do buses run between Arusha and Musoma. Further, since the Iranian mess, Kenya has run out of fuel for small aircraft, so that soon the MAF will fly no more. One used to be able to cross the border on foot, getting permission in Musoma, but now all such permissions must be gotten in Dar es Salaam.

After two and one-half year, Salunga has suddenly come across with plans to hand this Nairobi office over to the African churches. Hershey sounds as though this is what he had been striving toward all the time while I was reading him as being the one who was obstructing that development. In any case, the picture is now suddenly different, and everyone is making noises about our staying on for awhile.

August 26, 1979

Where are you, brother? Grief, what has happened to our letter writing? I'm here at Nyabasi/Nyarero. Nurse Elva Landis' chickens have just set up an infernal racket due to a little weasel ducking around in the woodpile. I'm in her guestroom looking out across a deep valley to the patchwork of *shambas* on the far hills. It is so completely silent here—except for the chickens, and a pair of sunbirds chasing themselves around in the flowering bushes outside the window, and now and then a fly goes by—but otherwise, just complete silence. This is Sunday afternoon, 4:00 p.m.

I left Nairobi on Wednesday morning by the architects' plane to Mugumu Hospital for a site meeting. On Friday I got a bus to Shirati, arriving there in time for a late afternoon bowl of millet "*uji*" at Bishop Kisare's home—sitting around in the evening shadow at the back door. Saturday morning I bummed a cycle from the Brubaker brothers—an old wreck that I'm amazed didn't let me down—and cycled out here to Nyabasi. I met the TMC church treasurer to tour the old Mara Hills School complex with him. It was recently vacated by the Tanzanian army, and the church is anxious to do something with it quickly, before the government requisitions it again for something else. Surprising the army left without notifying anyone. The locals moved in immediately and helped themselves to electrical fixtures and doors. Fortunately only some $2,000 worth of stuff walked off before the church got wind of it and posted a guard on the place.

Today was communion for four congregations, so the church was full—normally only some 50 worship. I preached on the resurrection in the light of needing to look to the Lord to revive our church and community following the war which was naturally enough socially disruptive and which has left the country economically prostrate with very little fuel, for one example—therefore, few buses and no vehicle for me to get about in.

Why am I here? The surface reason is that the church is split in two and Hershey's willing to come out from Salunga and help put Humpty-Dumpty back together again. I am to find out if he is needed and wanted and in what capacity, when and for how long. I find both Bishops, Kisare at Shirati and Sarya in Dar es Salaam quite disillusioned with their executive secretary at the central office. So much so, that I'm not even going to see him, although constitutionally he is now head of the church and the only person I should see. Kisare is old, and like me, tired of an "understudy" in the office not playing ball. Sarya is full of starry-eyed visions of laying kingly claim to all the manifold riches in the West and the East, and to all the wealth stored up in the church's local institutions. I think I must have the wrong view of the church because everywhere the more I look at the church the more it gives me a splitting headache. I wished so much this morning that I could really believe the resurrection miracle whereof I was preaching, bursting golden across these Nyarero hills. But rural Tanzania is increasingly a backwater.

Under the official reason for my coming down to Tanzania is the need to again eat *ugali* with these people, to drive their dusty roads, to claw my way again on to a packed bus—fighting to get in before every seat is filled, to hear again the noisy chatter of the familiar Luo and Kuriya tongues (I don't know what they say, but it sounds like home!), and to once more feel the dust in my eyes, cycling over the open road—in short to escape again briefly from the hectic days of a busy Nairobi office that strives mightily to maintain its Western level of efficiency and accountability. —The eyes of those two frightened new Shirati doctors' wives I met on the path, telling me that there is no Afrigas and they must cook with wood, and it takes all their working hours to keep food on the table, and what food? Well not wheat, rice or Irish potatoes, and no kerosene for their refrigerators. And two more frightened wives coming next July.

November 19, 1979

It's been quite a while since I've updated you on stuff. Aren't you terribly curious? The problem is that I'm writing to Hershey at Salunga all the time, only my letters make him sweat instead of happy. So after I've explained everything to Hershey I don't have the interest in having to go at it another time.

Recently Jacobs (who passed through Nairobi) commented to me that I should do a compilation of my feature articles published in the *Missionary Messenger*. I was excited enough to comment on the process of writing, but he saw another bird to identify, so I figured that he too possibly is just working to keep me happy and useful.

You would be horrified to see a photo of me now. I comb my thinning hair straight back over the scalp, which makes me look very bald, sort of like Jerry Ford. Then I have this great black beard that I leave my second shirt button open so as to accommodate it between the lapels of my shirt. I began it on March 15 and have only trimmed the sides since; it gives me a rather long-faced look. People who see it for the first time declare it patriarchal. Others say all I need is a big cross on my chest to look monkish. The worst was at the retreat in Tanzania last when a little two-year-old boy blurted out, "Hi, Jesus!" as soon as he saw me.

Are all these slick smoothness, spit and polish stuff simply props? I'm always tempted to start insulating myself from my fellows by becoming proper and dignified, cultivating mystique, keeping the riff-raff at bay. But what's the point? If I can't be with anybody and by my come-on say, "Hey, buddy, I'm a guy, like you; I don't have anything over you, so you needn't figure the angles with me"—why then what does our faith amount to? Granted, like the last time I went to Bukiroba and I got up early morning, got my own cup of coffee, carried my suitcase up to the bus stop on the hill and sat there for nearly two hours waiting for the bus to Tarime, I do sometimes ask myself if it wouldn't be wise to start acting more impressive. Once I went by truck from Mugumu back to Nairobi. I let a woman have my seat in the cab. I stood in the back in a Tee shirt with a hankie around my head, dusty, bleary-eyed, completely ordinary. When we got to the Balagonja Gate, there near to Keekerok, the Customs Official had seen me from afar and was loaded for bear when I jumped down and went in to be processed. He was sure I was a tourist and was ready to lock me up. Even my papers being all in order failed to mollify him. He nearly stripped me of all my money and in the end went through my few personal things with a vengeance. Later I almost wished I had been wearing a suit and riding properly on the front seat. Another time

I was riding a bus between Mugumu and Musoma, before I was properly checked into the country, having come down by the architect's plane and there being no immigration people in Mugumu. It was during the war and there were a lot of roadblocks where each and every person and parcel on the bus was searched. Again I began to feel that I was foolish to not have insisted that one of the missionaries give me a vehicle to drive into Musoma. How could I prove in my most ordinary duds that I was the link across which the twelve million shillings have flowed into Mugumu for that hospital project! The obvious question would be, "If you handle twelve million, what are you doing on a bus with the peasants?" Fortunately that day my cable stating boldly on the top, "State House, Dar es Salaam" got me by without even any search of my bag.

Am I being silly about all this? Should I really get all coiffured, hold a pencil and look meditative when my picture is taken, looking like stateside heavyweights? Anyway, if I don't play the part, at least I won't look silly if my work turns out to be a dud!

I am so glad you wrote recently. Something happened back in 1972 that began our drift apart. It wasn't specific, just a turn in the road, a turn I made and I'm sorry for that, but it's having happened I haven't known how the paths might converge again. Now during the past two years the distance has seemed almost farther than our reach. I'm not so traumatized now as I was in '69 and '70.

Do you remember the time we cycled across the bay, had a picnic which you photographed with your time-delayed camera, and then we climbed the mountain and later had a cup of tea at that dirty little ramshackle hut on the banks of the Kirumi? Some two months ago I was cycling up past that mountain on an old Yamaha I'd borrowed. It had something wrong with it and wouldn't go much over thirty. It was so dry, with fire having burnt off the grass so that every stone and boulder now stood out starkly, right up to the top of the mountain. Suddenly I heard a shout, "Huyo, huyoo, huyooo!" Stopping the cycle I looked back and here comes a lean and tattered man followed by a boy, running parallel to the road, a hound dog out ahead running hell bent for leather. "Must be a hunt," I thought, and there she was, a duiker, just keeping her own in distance from the dog. Soon she was on the rocks, up and up and up, with the dog hard on her heels but soon losing distance, unable to maintain the pace. On and on she went until she topped the sky ridge and disappeared from sight. The dog, only half way, still pushing, but very obviously chasing now only a fading scent, the man and boy slowed now to a panting walk. They called the dog and went back to beating the bushes, and I to my slow cycle wending my way on to Shirati. I was glad for the duiker on that mountain to be free and to escape and to laugh at her pursuers.

So what is happening at Salunga mission board? I find it very interesting that our brother David writes that he is "submitting himself to the process of being brothered by the Salunga community." The notion of submitting oneself to the council of the brotherhood being so very much a revival fellowship motif so dear to David's heart, coupled with the annoying fact that he is sitting right on Salunga's doorstep all day, every day, a man without a job, a man academically supremely qualified, a man with all the experience credentials and pedigreed ancestry for twice the position at stake, a man even now churning out relevant texts and making appropriate speeches and appearances, a man turning Herhsey's hair gray and Jacob's visions to shimmering mirage, such a man submitting himself humbly to the scrutiny and judgments of Salunga. I sound truly awful? Yeah, I do sound even cynical. But my spirit is not so bad off as words would suggest. David wrote recently that there are to be seminars, theological ones, held around Salunga during the winter months. Then in the spring, a theological decision will be made about who is to take Jacob's place. Whatever that means, I do not know, except that Hershey is trained in hospital administration and in rural development, not theology. It's very true that Hershey's a good administrator who knows his way around in an efficient manner.

I told David that I'm doubtful of his ability to rally a staff around him. Very unfortunately, through his missionary experience, having Grace at his side has helped to insulate him from his fellow American, so he has not needed to develop those administrative graces which make for good team work. Further, most of his involvement these six years he was in Nairobi were with either African organizations or with non-Mennonite ones. In this light it would have been far better for him to have been in my shoes over the past three years, having to hassle plans with my administrative assistant, rather than through his wife. Still, another factor is that David is an almost right-wing evangelical, which will alienate many workers. I think he would tend to polarize his constituency. Further, one finds that David runs a very tight ship. On issues he understands well he finds it difficult to compromise. Now maybe that is the way one has to lead here in Africa. Certainly that is how all the Bishops I know have run their ships, and that is how Jack Shellard ran his secondary school at Musoma. The way it is now I know that I can get really mad at Hershey or write a terrible letter to Jacobs, and for the most part, it will be received with grace and effort will be made to accommodate to Joseph's ravings. But with David, I have very much more the impression that he will read me the riot act if I don't fall in line. Maybe that is what leadership is all about.

I've finally decided that I know the basic difference between Harold Miller and me. He likes it here in Nairobi, and I don't. I do like it here, some, but I have always felt under the skin that I would like it better in the States than here in Nairobi. I see my being here as something of a sacrifice on my part. I am probably wrong, but I know that I enjoyed the two years teaching maths at Christopher Dock. But I also have the notion that I am useful here, being now as I am the senior Mennonite male in East Africa, in terms of years served. I've the advantage of having grown up here, which adds another twenty years to the perspective. So, I have kept thinking that if Salunga sees my perspective as useful, and acts that way, then I'm prepared to stay on for the sake of the whole.

And now we have the Advisory Committee in place. At least there is now a vehicle which gives rationale on why I should be here instead of just any other North American administrator. And most of my creative energy during the first two and a half years I was here went into fighting Salunga on this issue of making this office part of the churches.

As I was saying, I now see reason for staying on in East Africa. So the matter has had to go to the family for sorting out. We decided that Edith should go home the summer of '80 to put Joyce into college. Then in '82 we all come home for a one-year furlough and get reassigned either to something in the States or to something else in Africa, different from the Nairobi office.

I'm getting tired. I've slipped a disc. I've quit wearing the neck brace, except for on car trips. I should wear it though, and that is why I haven't gone recently back to the doctor, as I know he will sentence me to another three months in the neck brace. And I find the brace gives me arthritis in the neck. Further, I can manage without it, in that I don't have a lot of pain. But my coordination in the right arm is not what it used to be; typing a lot is one of the things that bugs it. Maybe I'll have to go and make a real sob story to the doctor and get him to send me home next summer for tests and an operation. Then we'll see what happens to this office!

This brings me to the other great matter of creative effort over the past three years. It is this whole bit of how do you run an office given who I am and given that the stronger administrator in the office is a woman all bound up with being a quiet little Mennonite girl who has at the same time fantasies about what she would be were she a man which gets translated into complexes about being exploited. In the end, it has sorted out to be a bit like the old

Bishop Kisare relationship, a sort of balancing act, only in this case there is a great deal of time spent in talking, which I find emotionally exhausting, but sometimes instructive and fruitful.

On the Bishops Kisare-Sarya squabble. The short of it is that on the morning of the big meeting, Kisare motored down from Shirati to Musoma. Hershey and Jacobs motored in from Bukiroba. Sarya and his men had spent the night in Musoma. When we arrived we were served breakfast at the Mennonite Centre Hostel, but before we got to eating breakfast people asked where was Sarya. They were told he was at the airport waiting for the plane! It turned out that the night before he had gotten word that his daughter had died in the asylum at Dodoma. She has been mentally ill for years and was a woman in her twenties. The plane was to arrive at 11:00, but Sarya was over waiting for it by 8:00! So Jacobs and Hershey got Kisare, and the three of them went out to the airport to greet Sarya. This was the first that the two bishops have met since Sarya was ordained in February! During the airport meeting Sarya told those of his men present that they were to go ahead with the meeting even though he would not be present. But when it came time for the meeting Sarya's men refused to meet. So after considerable discussion it was decided that the officers of the old executive committee should meet. But this, too, Sarya's men refused to hear to. So Jacobs then met with each of Sarya's men individually and sort of chewed them out for allowing the church's unity to disintegrate.

I am into too much stuff just now. I'm pastor of the Nairobi District, executive secretary of the Kenya Mennonite Church, MCC country rep for Kenya, Tanzania, and Uganda, chairman of the Shirati Medical Board, chair of the Mennonite Islamic Ministries Council, chair of the Rosslyn Academy School board, General Director of Mennonite Mission board in Eastern Africa, co-ordinator for the Eastern African Area Office, secretary for the Advisory Committee of the Mennonite Board of East Africa, chair of the Fraternal workers (Kenya) Administrative committee, responsible for the finances reference the building of the Mugumu Hospital project and the Eastleigh (Nairobi) Fellowship Centre, husband of one wife and father of four daughters. I am responsible for the maintenance of five or six vehicles, five properties of the mission board in E. Africa, and one motorcycle left here by a former MCC chap. I find I do not spend much time in the office. But worse than that is that many of the committees I am on meet either at night or over the weekend. (MEDA asked me to be their representative in Kenya, but this one I refused.) Oh, wow, it makes me tired.

December 21, 1979

I'm writing from Brackenhurst Baptist Assembly grounds at Limuru. Yesterday we climbed the Elephant of the Aberdare Mountains. It was very good with some 49 people along. This was the third time I've climbed it, and for the first time we didn't get wet. It was terribly windy with sheets of fog whipping across the top—but for all that, it was great fun, and from the top we could see across to Lake Naivasha, it being an extraordinarily clear day.

This year for the first time at our Mennonite retreat we had an African doing the Bible studies. Bishop Silungwe from Brethren-in-Christ, Zambia. He had excellent written studies, but they lasted only about five minutes, for something scheduled to last an hour! Also present was Paul N. Kraybill, now executive secretary for Mennonite World Conference.

I asked Kraybill to come sometime to help sort out what is happening administratively in Nairobi. He took one look at our organizational chart and with horror pronounced it "General Motors." "Cut it up," he ordered. So I did, producing seven organizational charts to picture what I had on the first one. This, too, he couldn't see much value in, asking rather I detail the office activity by nature under the categories of "Services Performed for Missionaries," "Properties Owned for Missionaries," "Liaison Activities," and "Mutuality Involvements." Naturally enough, my several pages showed that most of what we do is missionary stuff. So he declared it foolish to pretend that the Nairobi office is multinational when obviously its functions are Salunga's responsibilities. So, at the East Africa Area Office committee meeting, it was ordered that the office be given back to Salunga. Then EAAO was scuttled. The group of Eastern African churchmen who meet from time-to-time are now called the Council of Eastern Africa Mennonite Churchmen, or some such thing. So, I am now Salunga's appointee, period! After that session I told Hershey that I have resigned and am ready to move out just as soon as he can find a replacement for me. I put it that if he can replace me before June 1980 then we'll all go home next summer. If it is later than that, then I would like to have an alternate assignment until June 1982. In discussing this with Bishop Kisare I said that I am anxious to cause as little disruption as possible, and therefore will not pull out precipitously.

Why must I resign? Must I have a reason? I'm not sure myself that I know why. Most likely it is because Bishop Kisare found me very useful to him in sorting out his relationships to the church and to the missionaries. I absorbed and deflected a lot of the tension there. I like to think the church in Tanzania would be less split today had I stayed on there. Now I am being used by Salunga on the opposite side of the fence, to help them manage their people and programs—to deflect, so to speak, Africa's knocking on Salunga's door. But where I could do this for Kisare and for the Area Office, I cannot see my doing it for Salunga. That's one aspect.

Another related aspect is that I find almost consistently I come out on an issue on opposite sides from where Hershey and Marian come out. I simply come out on the African side—not that there are African and American sides, but an African stacks up the evidence one way and an American another way, and I find I simply get worn out trying to keep these two tensions from getting out of hand. I am simply tired of fighting this war. Since I win so little it seems that others' perceptions are still not well enough developed—else they would see what I see. (Of course, if what I see isn't there, then my resignation is even more overdue.)

Yet another aspect is that up to now in my life I've been stop-gapping for others, and I think I should get off for a bit to see who I really am. That's silly, isn't it? Because once one gets off, can he ever really get back on again? Also, if I would discover myself, what assurance do I have that anyone would foot the bill for me to do that thing? But my problem, in working at the idea of identity, is that I increasingly see myself as coming out a Willy Loman, always ready to be of service and thus never with an identity. I did during the past three years fight hard for African involvement in what we are doing, but I don't see that any of that attempt at identity has been in any way helpful. I don't see anyone as having moved toward an understanding or appreciation of the way of looking at things which I've been pushing. Somehow I've a feeling I've said all this once before in a previous incarnation—say the Musoma one—and my repeating it only reinforces that I am a sort of treadmill kind of guy and should accept that. I come back to telling myself that my gift is in stop-gapping, being everyone's servant—so why not accept that I am a Willy Loman. Probably I would if I could somehow get really affirmative about Salunga. It's that devil in me that doesn't want to prop up their show, and I think I'd feel the same way no matter who was running this place.

So, I've resigned, and Salunga has accepted it—period!

This is now tomorrow. My attitude bothers me. So, let me just say that I think someone else should do this administration. I don't like administration. If its for Africans, then I'll try to do it, but white people have enough good administrators, so let one of them do it if it is for white people. There, does that take the poison out? I hope so.

We had a delightful Christmas dinner with Marian, Mary Oyer and Harold and Annetta Miller. We had rabbit and chicken from our flocks and *sukuma wiki* from Harold's garden.

God bless us all in this New Year!

1980

January 6, 1980

It's one of those hot, hot tropical afternoons with the sun blistering the sidewalks. I've just been out for my daily walk up to the post office and am back now and got the urge to update things with you. I missed lunch because the Uchumi Coffee Shop was closed by the time I got there. So I got some yogurt and with a mug of office coffee I've managed not too badly.

It seems that over the years I write when I need some sympathetic ear to grouse to. My assistant is away this week, so that gives me a breather for doing some personal things. Like writing letters on office time—naughty, naughty!

This office is being closed. I guess I over-played my hand last year when Hershey was here. I am sure I've written that story how Paul Kraybill declared it preposterous to think that this office be in anyway responsible to the local African churches. I said nothing. In fact, I pushed their line that the office should revert to Salunga. I knew that it would be very difficult to do this with another administrator coming in, and I figured that I would just sit behind some bush and mirthfully watch what goes on after August 1981. But Salunga did a fast one: several months after that meeting, they decided to close the office down!

On Salunga's official memo of what happened there is some sort of blurb that there is too much politics and expense, etc., so that it is not possible for the African churches to participate in the running of the office. So, it has had to be reluctantly closed. What is most interesting is that MCC has picked up on the effort and their blue print for setting up an office here is very nearly what Salunga's idea had been back then in 1976 when we were tapped on the head. To me what it boils down to is that MCC is taking the initiative and I think they will do very well.

It is a sociological dynamic that one influences the direction of an organization least when one becomes an integral part of that organization. An agitator on the outside does more toward influencing a change of direction than does the chairman of the outfit.

About the future: David wrote a year ago saying that Daddy had loaned him money to buy a house and that I could borrow the same money after he had paid it back to build my house and that he expected I would continue on the mission field until such time as the money could be recycled! So that is where he would like for us to be anyway.

The Kenya Mennonite Church has asked us to come back "to help us in our church work." When informed of this Salunga wanted to know what sort of job description that was. The point is, of course, that a church like this simply cannot do a job description. However would it be possible for them to know what opening they would have for us in mid-1982? They can't. Never in all my experience in Africa has a church given me a job description. If my mission board came to me with a specific proposal and requested that Edith and I give serious consideration to such a proposal, then I would do just that. But in the absence of a proposal articulated by the mission board, I really do not see much future in bumming around here anymore.

It is significant to me that the mantle has slipped from the shoulders of the clergy. Where it is at with Eastern Board is no longer with the church. It is at the development end of things that interest and program is evolving. Harold Miller makes that observation clear when he points out that Mennonites have never naturally gravitated towards church planting and evangelism. "Look at the income differentials," he says. "Whenever there is an appeal for relief or development you get strong, gut-level Mennonite giving." But on the church issues you get mere tokenism. Of course development people are discovering that they can't do development outside of people's faith-concepts, so the development people need to study belief systems as much as they study development dogma. So what you have is the development people dabbling in belief systems in much the same way the evangelists used to dabble in pseudo development.

Again, thinking about what I'll do when I come home. I must just go in one of two directions, either accept that I've got muddled, something that is a new experience for me, and take up a bread-earning job when we get home and settle down to last the stretch to when my body decides to give up the effort, or find some quiet place where I can do some thinking and sorting out and get out of the muddle and then join something and carry on crusading for something or other.

The Norfolk Hotel blew up on New Year's Eve. There was one hairy great KABOOM about 8:45 that evening. Our family was having a quiet dinner when this low boom rattled the windows. And Elizabeth Hostetter's dog took off with a frightened whimper for her hide-away in the Guest House public shower. We went outside but could hear no more. We decided it had been a sonic boom from some low-flying fighter jet. Some Mennonites were in the city and went to have a look. The bomb blew most of the face off the hotel. As it turned out it was a twenty-pound gelatin bomb planted in a room over the main lounge. The culprit was apparently Maltese, and it must have been a gesture against the Israelis who own the hotel. By today the death toll has risen to 15. Only two of those were Kenyan.

January 11, 1980

I'm writing this from the Jomo Kenyatta Airport. It's after midnight, and I'm waiting for Mary Oyer's Lufthansa from Jo'burg.

I don't like navel-gazing, but I am drawn to it like a moth to flame. I have by now written my official letter of resignation. I've written to Daddy explaining it as well. You know I feel like I've destroyed my career, even my future.

Why did I resign? I mean, why now, three weeks later after all the anger has ebbed away? I am sure it is because my colleagues now have me by the tail. I'm tired of being pestered all the time about how I do my job. I'm tired of explaining my position all the time. I'm tired of my administrative assistant trying to make me feel guilty for how much work she has to do. I'm just tired of trying to explain to Salunga that an office in Kenya needs to listen locally, as well as to the home mission board. I'm tired of Salunga having so much power. I'm tired also of being poor in a post, which my predecessors exploited to make themselves comfortable. Before, I could use the fact that I've been placed here by the churches to fight off the mob. But now I am naked and alone and if I don't get out they will destroy my soul.

But where am I to go? True, there is so much to do. But if Salunga saw what there is to do then why send these last two couples who lack any vision. If there is reconciliation to be done in Tanzania then why does Salunga put the damper on my involvement? If the Kenya Mennonite Church desperately needs an executive secretary then why is Salunga so cautious against getting too involved?

Am I rambling? That's the way I am these days. Career? What's my career? Crumbs, math teacher to theology teacher to Bible teacher to airport runner. I do a lot of laughing these days, but it covers a somber despair.

March 10, 1980

In brief then:

1. Salunga is in charge of this Nairobi office, but I do not believe this can long endure because of the presence of the Kenya Mennonite Church.

2. I do not see value in convening the East Africa Mennonite Advisory Committee because this committee has no constituency and in any case they have no power of the office. I had used the Advisory Committee as an African counter-balance to Salunga's overwhelming power, but I cannot use it as such any more. To convene it only makes it look as though we are interested in African input, whereas in fact, we aren't. With the loss of the Advisory Committee I have lost my ability to lead.

3. There is enormous need in Eastern Africa in the area of theological education, but I do not believe the way to go about helping the situation is to create another supra-agency floating around doing it. Further, what the Kenya church wants me to do is to become their assistant bishop for something like ten years and this would be a good base for operations. But I cannot do that because the Kenya Mennonite Church would use me to fight the mission board, and I am not interested in being used that way, even thought I agree with their premises.

4. I am sorry to be leaving Africa just now, but the situation has become untenable for us.

5. This whole matter is full of pain for me. I am sure I must get away from it as soon as possible. But to what? Every way I look my maze seems blocked. The problem for me is that in spite of the very considerable difficulties in working with the young churches in East Africa, I do know the situation possibly better than other missionaries. I have felt that for the most part my contribution has been affirmed by them. But in my movement over the last four years (here in Nairobi) away from the churches, my spirit has lost its freedom. So, although all these things I can do well, my spirit is not now free. It is a foolish thing, I take it, to walk out like this. It will be on my record that there was a problem with me in Kenya. It would be better for me to just shut up and go along with whatever it is that Salunga works me into. But if

I did that just now I would lose myself. Better to lose a future than to lose myself.

6. Don't fret about me, brother. I'll find something to do and, who knows, in a few years I might heal inside and be ready for some more of Africa.

1981

March 16, 1981

We're applying for that job of student pastor at EMC, which we saw advertised in the *Gospel Herald*.

Earlier I was speaking with Bishop David Thomas, who was traveling through Africa, about what we should be interested in for the next block of time. He told me that the possibility of pastoring at Mellingers has blown apart. But he said he'd see about getting me involved in Lancaster Conference's leadership training program. He also promised to see if it might be possible to find a congregation to which we might relate. I urged him not to locate anything for me in the Manor District.

After Bishop Thomas left, I noticed this ad in the *Gospel Herald*, and after some meditation and discussion, I applied. I tried to sound in my applying, both appropriately self-confident as well as fully aware that an application is an application and that most are turned down!

I am concerned that I put distance between myself and the mission board office. I don't think that is just sour grapes. My view is that the missionary—African church—mission board triangle is in a mess. One example: in Salunga's last visit with the churches here ended in little more than their being called to respond to a long shopping list of the African churches. The missionary situation is in a mess. Everybody is new, yet there are a lot of missionaries. This office had been in the potential situation to be a stabilizing influence, and I know my saying that is suspect because I'm the general director. But that game is now up. The next several years will be a shakedown where things will sort out and new shapes emerge. It is a period where the potential for people getting hurt is fairly high—like being in El Salvador just now.

March 17, 1981

I haven't done any writing for *The Missionary Messenger* in three years. They've printed everything in my file. I've just lost interest, a sort of confusion about what I had been writing about.

MCC is doing considerable creative thinking. They are streets ahead of Salunga. I find here in East Africa that increasingly the MCCers are better chosen and they are better placed. They identify well with their organization, have a lot of pride in it. But among the missionaries there is a lot of confusion. They are good people, but the glow is with MCC.

Back to MCC and EMBMC. I really do want to be at a distance from those organizations. I do not understand anymore how the system is to work. I thought when we came to Nairobi that I knew what that was for, but all the noise over the past years has just slowly petered out to a great silence. It is quite a lonely sort of business. I feel now like the Masai that Dr. Shaeffer of Flying Doctor tells of: He grew up in a missionary home in Masai land. He tells of when his father would be bushwhacking in a Land-Rover with a Masai guide. At times the guide would get disoriented and lost. He then would ask Father Shaeffer to stop the vehicle, and the Masai would walk some hundred yards away to be well clear of the vehicle, and then he'd stand in meditation. After a bit he would come back and off they'd go, lost no more. I feel that I understand the African church, but it is obvious I do not understand the American church. I think a stretch of listening at some distance from Lancaster is what I need just now. Not that I have any illusions about my own leadership, only that I want to get over feeling lost. Is there any better place to listen than from the vantage point of student pastor? What does a student pastor do!

April 3, 1981

Were you trying to scare me by your litany of drudgery at EMC? It seemed you were saying life is a drag there and that you were sorry to have me join the drag. Life here, too, is a drag. I leave the house sharply at 7:30 every morning, and leave the office at 5:30 every evening. Once this week it took an hour to drive the distance between office and home due to traffic jams. But usually I am home by about 6:00. I do get around some with traveling but much of that is by bus, which is terribly tiring, especially in that I travel by night. My slipped disc then acts up when I am on these bumpy roads. Then again, the work in the church, so much of it is sitting in endless committee meetings where the tiniest details are wrangled over for hours. I do not find life awfully exciting here either.

The story has it that back in December '79 when Paul Kraybill persuaded Salunga that including the African churches in running this office is a bad idea, that then I resigned. And that was no scare tactic. I really believed Salunga wanted to run the office as they always had, and I do not blame them for that, but I will not be a part of it. So I resigned. But it has taken these eighteen months to get that resignation effective.

In February I was at Shirati with Bishop Thomas. Bishop Kisare asked me one day, "Joseph, what is the reason for Salunga wanting to close their Nairobi office?" I told him, "I had better not answer that question as I might not give the right answers. You should ask Salunga." He grinned and said, "I'll do that." But he never did.

Last summer Jacobs told me that I could of course join MCC and be their administrator in Nairobi. I told him that I am a Lancaster person and would never join MCC. Not that I have any quarrel with MCC. They are really terrific, streets ahead of Salunga in terms of relevance in their line of service. But I am a churchman with a different point of reference.

Salunga is trying very hard (or at least trying very hard to make it look so) to get me back to work in some sort of capacity with the African churches. I am saying, "No thanks." The reason is that from the time Salunga opened this office, traditional missionary roles were considered low class. An example is: they'd never let missionaries attend the MCC retreats. There was a feeling that the church is really dumb and those missionaries working for it get sort of bent out of shape. Interesting people, those missionaries, and to be commended now and then, but essentially they're a backwater.

The real reason for closing this area office is because we could not survive without being swallowed one way or another by the Kenya Mennonite Church. So, in order to prevent that, you give the office to MCC. It will just build a wall around itself, shutting the local church out. Of course you cannot have an international office if the local church dominates it, so you must prevent yourself from being swallowed. Salunga scotched that development by handing the problem off to MCC.

What will now happen is that the church and office will drift apart. One Salunga man recently said that he doesn't hear anyone being enthusiastic about the Mennonite church in Kenya. That is precisely why one needs to have this office and church linked, so that the church's dumbness is agonized over. Or if you want to do as they did in India and cut the ties, then you need to cut all the ties. But to ask me to come back to work with the Kenya church while some 30 other MCCers and missionaries in Kenya go their merry way is to ensure that even as the Kenya church is already not understood and unloved, so will be the missionary struggling to be relevant to that church. To accept their proposal insures that I slip into a backwater and come out of it at 65 like my Dad today.

Don't worry about me. The Lord has always been good up to now, why shouldn't he continue to be?

(Note: In August 1981, Joe and his family moved to Harrisonburg, Virginia. He became Campus Pastor at Eastern Mennonite College/University that month.)

Mennonite Theological College of East Africa

Nyabange/Bukiroba III

January 2003-July 2005

January 2003-July 2005

We are now in the era of e-mails. Curiously, few passed between Joe and me during these recent years, on his return to the theological college. Most of his were addressed to multiple readers, thus were not personal in nature. Curiously, I saved none of them. I do not know what the 65-year-old Joe Shenk was thinking about during those years, again at Bukiroba. While I have some ideas, I have no right to commit those to paper. Even the silence must be honored.

Coda

1

Joe's Stories

For a year I heard Joe tell stories about teaching math at Musoma Alliance Secondary School. He was in grad studies at New York University and New York Biblical Seminary. I was teaching frosh comp at Eastern Mennonite College in Virginia. Although we were three hundred miles apart, we saw each other frequently. Being brothers-in-law we pitched up at the same Shenk tribal gatherings in Lancaster (PA) that year of Joe's furlough from Tanzania, summer-to-summer, 1965-1966.

I remember stories about food riots—boys boycotting meals, boys throwing vegetables, boys attempting to break into the commissary. Not all three hundred boys, of course. But maybe a hundred—enough to over-power the unlucky school prefects, those darlings of the Headmaster appointed as student monitors of every aspect of a boarding school boy's life.

I remember stories about supervising boys on detention after class hours, boys smacked there by their huffy teachers, chiefly for classroom disturbances. The delinquents would be assigned to *panga* grass, scrape walkways, or work at other menial labor for an hour. The teacher on duty for the week supervised the reprobates made sour by sinning against their masters.

I remember stories about Headmaster Shellard marching school boys around the football (soccer) field in an attempt to drill post-colonial discipline into the "the slouching laggards!" And then the whole school trotting off to Musoma for a *Saba-Saba* (Independence) Day celebration. Some four miles later the boys arrived sweaty, dusty, and in an unChrist-like mood.

I remember, too, stories about taking classes on overnight camping expeditions on the Serengeti Plains, stories about missionary family cookouts on a crocodile-free beach of Lake Victoria, stories of visits with Africans teachers and African cooks.

Joe was a masterful storyteller as a missionary on furlough. He spared us listeners none of the abrasion between teachers and students. Nor of the authoritarian rule of the Headmaster. But he also told of radiant sunsets over the lake, of village African goat stew, of zebra and gnu herds thundering the Serengeti. Musoma Alliance sounded like a swell place. I was enamored.

Reading hundreds of lethargic Anabaptist-Mennonite frosh comps and living near a little college campus nestled among the safe Virginia hills paled beside Joe's ventures in the Musoma classroom and on its playing fields, in the motorcycle dust of Mara Region's unpaved roads and the raucous Sunday markets.

The rough scrubbings for a season had produced a lovely patina to Joe's spiritual demeanor. I coveted his sufferings' glow. Covetousness morphed into hunger, hunger into wanting a call. I needed to burn off the suburban fat from my soul. I welcomed again the discipline of being a missionary teacher in Africa.

And then Paul N. Kraybill, executive secretary for the Lancaster Mennonites' mission board, EMBMC, said, "Come." He said, "Go." He said, "Go to Musoma."

Six years after Somalia, I returned to Africa, taking home Anna Kathryn, my African-born wife, Joe's sister, and our first child, Katrina. Tanzania was not my beloved Somalia—but that, too, would be part of the suffering borne with magnanimity.

So I arrived late August 1966 at Musoma, smothered in the protective warmth of my evangelical call, trusting the Christ behind Kraybill who said, "Go." Later, I would learn that Joe possessed a tougher psychic metal than mine; his, even though anvil-tempered, remained malleable and sweet. His Swahili language wizardry, his birth and boyhood spent among these peoples, made Joe culturally adept. He understood intuitively the throes of schoolboys, cooks, and subordinate staff, scuffling it up with the white headmaster and his administration.

Joe had moved through his own country, made his own climate while at Musoma. Though I now shared the life of Joe's old school with his fine stories, his was a land I could never enter. I was glad when early they said unto me, "Go home to MCC, Akron."

Omar Eby
October 2006

2

Joe Shenk, An Outsider for a Crossroads

"All the students look alike," the new Campus Pastor mused in 1981. That might be expected of a man out of Africa. Born, reared, and 20 years employed in Africa as teacher and preacher, Joseph C. Shenk (C 60, S 96) could read African faces effortlessly. It would take years for him to distinguish American college women and to stop calling every college male Mike.

A man of two continents on opposite sides of the equator, Joe felt the deep rift in his psyche; he often described himself as an "outsider." He did outsider things. Walking a mile to campus he rescued earthworms stranded on the tarmac, washed there by a thunderstorm. From a concocted recipe he brewed his own runny yogurt. Biking, he looked as if he had ridden out of the 19th century: he wore not a stitch of fancy pants spandex; the Bike's reversed handlebars made him a matador taking a bull by the horns; he sat as if nailed to a straight-back chair. To better know students, for weeks Joe donned a chef's hat and latex gloves to hand out sloppy Joes in the cafeteria line. All was fine, until a visit by the big mama from food services. The only thing she knew to do with this outsider was to throw him out.

The outsider worked hard to weave his ministry into the fabric of student lives. He preached memorable short sermons aimed at mainline Mennonite children. Jesus' presence at a Galilee wedding became, "When Jesus comes to your party." Still, inevitably, Joe attracted the marginal. International students found him a soft touch, when they needed money. Homesick or angry at damn Yanquis, they found a warm man in this outsider they mistook for an insider. Joe pored over the Myers-Briggs personality test until he became something of an expert—inflicted it on anyone who expressed mild curiosity. He found in it an entrée to understanding certain types of students—and faculty, the malleable and the precious. He was, after all, Campus Pastor, not just spiritual father to students. All found in Pastor Joe a "warm, generous, spiritual man," as his colleagues and assistants in Student Life remember him. He prayed for everyone as he ran, two miles before breakfast, then twice weekly on a ten-mile block of rural roads around the university, and later, eight marathons. "Joe had a great set of legs," his running and biking mates exclaimed.

Joe arrived on campus with a new president, Richard Detweiler. His was an era of transitions. Not only were on-campus student dances permitted, the compulsory thrice-weekly chapel attendance became optional. The on-campus Sunday morning worship service arranged by the pastor's office passed to Shalom, a congregation meeting in Strite Hall. Although Joe took change in stride, after seven years, he felt that the college, now a university; needed a sophisticated insider for a Campus Pastor.

Joe discovered there was life after EMU—even a good life. In 1986 he became lead pastor—an outsider at an old southern congregation-at Weavers Mennonite Church, a position he held until his retirement in 2002. Whereupon, with his wife Edith, Joe went home to Africa as principal of the Mennonite Theological College of East Africa, Musoma, Tanzania. There among the Tanzania Mennonites, as among the Virginia Mennonites, and the EMU bureaucrats, Joe never let the political background static distract him from his unfailing trust in the mission of Christ's church.

Then, a lorry loaded with charcoal struck Joe, out for his morning jog near his African home. He died July 21, 2005 in a Nairobi, Kenya hospital.

Omar Eby (C 57)

(Note: A shorter version of this article first appeared in Crossroads, Fall, 2005, the alumni magazine of Eastern Mennonite University, Harrisonburg, VA).

3

The Weavers' Joe

Elsewhere I wrote of my grieving over the death of Joe Shenk. Now I write of other things about Joe.

I want to assure the people of Weavers Mennonite Church that your sins—gross, mean-spirited, or petty—if you got around to confessing them to Joe-are safe in the grave. As they always were with Joe. Some people assumed that because Joe was my very close friend he shared with me the lives of Weavers' congregants, that I heard the gossip—and the truth. But Joe never, never, never talked about his parishioners, not about any of the dynasties: Heatwole, Brunk, Blosser, Martin. Not only because he was professional, but also because of his deep sense of loyalty to you individually. He knew well enough that, like any old salt, I would enjoy hearing gossip!

Not that we didn't talk about the economy of human relationships, but not about his parishioners. Not that we didn't swap tales (perhaps not of "hot sex" as Gil Reed claims), but also tried "talking ourselves into existence," as Frederick Buechner puts it.

I had to remind Joe that Anna Kathryn and I were members of Weavers before he came on the stage to play his pastoral role. That we had paid our dues to be worthy of committee assignments. Still, Joe was uncomfortable with us being on committees with him. He thought it looked too suspiciously like a power block. "Get over it!"—advice given to Joe by elder church statesman Wayne North—didn't always work for Joe. He wanted nothing tribal, as he saw its ugly head rise from time to time in the Tanzanian Mennonite Church.

Joe always thought he was an outsider, not a true Virginian. (Grace Showalter, former librarian at EMU, declared that "your parents had to be in the Valley before the Civil War" to qualify as being southern. So much for us damn Yankee Mennonites among you!) Additionally, Joe was so deeply African in his psychic instincts, that occasionally both Edith and I told him he was paranoid. But that blunt, cheap psychoanalysis rarely made a dent.

When my Park View and EMU dandies asked me why I attended Weavers, I always said it was to hear Joe's inimitable preaching: telling stories, biblical and contemporary, never fictive. He trusted the power of narrative as a method for conveying wisdom. His rhetorical mode appealed to me, also addicted to stories, even if chiefly written. When my old EMU friends wonder why I continue at Weavers, with Joe's escape to Africa, I tell them that their question reveals their ignorance about the vitality of this old southern Mennonite congregation. I don't need their country clubs for spiritual nurture.

About that boulder Joe carried down off Mole Hill—like some reenactment of Moses, even if nothing was fire-fingered into his slab. He insisted on lugging down this boulder about the size of Goliath's head. I think this 500,000,000-year-old igneous basalt rock of the Paleozoic Era (just before Jurassic Park residents trundled into the movies) spoke to something deep in Joe's soul. It conjured holy stones of the Old Testament, appealed to his sense of a place of remembrance: Jacob's altar after an all-night mano a mano with an angel; the twelve boulders set in the Jordan River as the tribes passed into the Promised Land settled with pagans who would need routing.

But to me, seeing Joe carrying that boulder brought memories of an image in Frost's poem, "Mending Wall." Frost and his farmer neighbor meet in spring to mend the stone wall, the "upper boulders spilled by the frozen-ground swell."

> I see him there,
> Bringing a stone grasped firmly by the top
> In each hand, like an old-stone savage armed.

About Joe's running. You'll also remember that he ran marathons (26 miles 385 yards!) At least twice I was his "designated driver" for the Richmond marathons, when he was too drunk with fatigue to drive himself home. He did fine for his age group, 50 to 70-year-olds. At least the street cleaners who drove vans behind the runners never had to scoop him up off the pavement. We rode home in silence for a good many miles: Was he reliving the thrill of ascending a particularly stiff hill? Was he reliving the sting of being passed by a woman older than himself? When he gained strength to talk, I'd ask, rather rudely: "Why do you run? Are you running away from something? Or towards something?"

"No, I'm just running."

I'd enshroud my laziness with, "When I became a man, I put away childish things." Joe would rejoin with verses about running "not as one who beateth the air," or something about "not running in vain . . . ."

I miss Joe. But I have let go. Let him now run the streets paved with pure gold—if you like or need that imagery (I find it a bit gaudy for my taste). Let him sit on a grassy hill beside the new Sea of Galilee and listen to the best Story Teller employ in parables the eternal mysteries of the divine scheme—chiefly about a God who through his Son loved us, loved Joe.

Omar Eby
"The Weaver" August 2006
Weavers Mennonite Church news/magazine

4

Joseph Shenk is Dead

Joseph Shenk is dead. I remember Job's bitter lament on the finality of death: "He who goes down to the grave does not return. He will never come to his house again; his place will know him no more" (7:9,10).

Joseph Shenk is dead. His place knows him no more. Not his place as a grandfather for Reuben's four boys. Not his place as Dad to his daughter Rose. Not to any of his family: wife, daughter, grandchild, in-law. Nor as brother. Not as Principal of the Mennonite Theological College. Not as the *Mzungu* pastor fluent even in colloquial Swahili for the old Tanzanian peasant woman. Not as that strange white man the Africans saw running every morning at the side of the road. Not eventually as an old quiet sage in this Weavers congregation.

Joseph Shenk is dead. Joe and I often joked about that passage in Exodus (1:8) which reads, "Now there arose in Egypt a Pharaoh who knew not Joseph." A Jew boy Prime Minister of Egypt who inaugurated a federal program for emergency food storage and distribution during a seven-year drought that saved the national populace—and nobody remembers him? How many, or how few years later—was it already the next generation who had forgotten? And how stupid a Pharaoh is this who doesn't even know his own national history? But Joseph Shenk would grin and declare: that's the way it is in life.

Joseph Shenk is dead. Gone is the uncommon grace with which he filled our days and nights—and my life. Our hearts are wrung by the death; we try to make some sense of it. But his rendezvous with death which began on a rural Tanzanian road and ended in an ICU bed in Nairobi, Kenya, is inexplicable, final, a man-made accident—or perhaps even God-wrought? The heart cries out in protest, in anger, in remorse: there's been some dreadful mistake. Joseph Shenk will be back soon.

But Joseph Shenk is dead. And we ask: Who's managing this universe, anyway? Our complaints are as bitter-edged as Job's. We remember again Job's lament and hear only the silence, silence from the grave, silence from the Heavens. And at the Joseph Shenk places which will know him no more—there is silence.

But at least we have this assurance, about our bitter complaints against God. It is written of Job (1:10): "In all this Job did not sin in what he said." And that old Hebrew who said, "I demand to speak to the Almighty and to argue my case with Him" (13:3), ends with these exultant words, familiar to all believers: "Oh, that my words were engraved in a rock forever: I know that my Redeemer lives. I know that in the end He will stand upon the earth. I know that I myself will see Him with my own eyes-"

So, in the end, Joseph Shenk is not dead?

Omar Eby
(Funeral Service Bulletin Insert)

5

Obituary

The Rev. Joseph C. Shenk, 67, died Thursday, July 21, 2005, in Nairobi, Kenya, from injuries he suffered in an accident in Tanzania.

Joseph was born June 23, 1938, at Bukiroba, Tanzania, the son of the late J. Clyde and Alta Rebecca Barge Shenk.

He was a graduate of Eastern Mennonite University and Seminary, Harrisonburg, Virginia, and of New York University, New York City.

He served in Africa for 20 years. He served as minister of Weavers Mennonite Church for 15 years and worked with the Virginia Conference Board of Missions, and Eastern Mennonite University. He was the principal of the Mennonite Theological College of Eastern Africa, Bukiroba, Tanzania.

Survivors include his wife, Edith Newswanger Shenk, whom he married June 18, 1960: four daughters and sons-in-law, Joyce Yvonne and Daniel Maxwell; Dianne Louise and Kenton Zehr; Rosemary Jo Stoltzfus; Rebecca Sue and Ryan Roberts; three brothers: David Shenk and John Shenk of Lancaster, PA, and Daniel Shenk of New York City; and one sister, Anna Kathryn Eby of Harrisonburg; and 12 grandchildren.

Joseph was preceded in death by his son-in-law, Rueben Stoltzfus, husband of his daughter, Rosemary Jo. Stoltzfus was killed July 12, 2005, in a car accident in Charlottesville, VA.

A funeral service will be held 3:00 p.m. Sunday, July 31, 2005, at the Weavers MennoniteChurch, 2501 Rawley Pike, Harrisonburg, with the Rev. Jeff Kauffman officiating. Burial will follow at Weavers Church Cemetery.

The family will receive friends from 6 to 8 p.m. Saturday at Shady Oak, Weavers Mennonite Church, and at 2:00 p.m. Sunday, before the service.

Memorial contributions may be made to the Mennonite Central Committee, 21 S. 12th St., Akron, PA 17501.

(*Daily News Record*, Harrisonburg, Virginia, July 29, 2005)

Index

L

M

T

U

V

W

Y

Z

Printed in the United States
99099LV00003B/169-207/A